D1590140

The Physical
and Psychological
Effects of Meditation

The Physical and Psychological Effects of Meditation

*A Review of Contemporary Research
with a Comprehensive Bibliography
1931–1996*

by Michael Murphy and Steven Donovan
2nd Edition

Edited and with an Introduction by
Eugene Taylor, PhD

Institute of Noetic Sciences
Sausalito, California
©1997

The Physical and Psychological Effects of Meditation
by Michael Murphy and Steven Donovan, 2nd Edition,
Edited and with an Introduction by Eugene Taylor, PhD

For information address:

The Institute of Noetic Sciences
475 Gate Five Road, Suite 300
Sausalito, California 94965   2/99

Library of Congress Number: Cataloging–in–Publication Data

Murphy, Michael, 1930 Sept. 3–
    The physical and psychological effects of meditation: a review of contemporary
research with a comprehensive bibliography, 1931—1996 /
by Michael Murphy and Steven Donovan. -- 2nd ed. / edited and with an introduction by
Eugene Taylor.
        p.   cm.
    Includes bibliographical references.
    ISBN: 0-943951-36-4
    I. Meditation.   I. Donovan, Steven.   II. Taylor, Eugene.
III. Title.
BL627.M886 1996
291.4'35--dc21

                                                        96–46701
                                                        CIP

Table of Contents

Preface ix

Introduction
by Eugene Taylor 1
Some Definitions 1
The Americanization of Meditation 3
Meditation as a Scientific Study 9
The First Edition 10
The Present Update 12
TM and the TM-Sidhi Project 13
Herbert Benson: The Mind-Body Medical Institute 15
Jon Kabat-Zinn at the University of Massachusetts Medical Center 17
Cognitive-Behavioral Approaches in Psychology 19
Health Psychology and Complementary Medicine 22
The Qi Gong Database 24
Yoga Research in India 25
The International Meditation Bibliography, 1950-1982 26
The Historic Significance of Murphy and Donovan's Text 26
Psychologists Debate the Issues 27
Governmental Research and Medical Science 30

Chapter 1:
Scientific Studies of Contemplative Experience: An Overview
by Michael Murphy 33
Studies of Zen Buddhist Monks 40
Difficulties of Research with Religious Adepts 41
Contemporary Meditation Research 42

Chapter 2: Physiological Effects
by Michael Murphy and Steven Donovan 45
The Cardiovascular System 45
    Heart Rate 45
    Redistribution of Blood Flow 48
    Blood Pressure and Hypertension 50
    Other Cardiovascular Changes 57

The Cortical System 57
    EEG: Alpha Activity 58
    EEG: Theta Activity 58
    EEG: Beta Activity 59
    EEG: Hemispheric Synchonization 59
    EEG: Dehabituation 59
    Specific Cortical Control 60
    Other Cortical Changes 61
Blood Chemistry 63
    Adrenal Hormones 63
    Thyroid Hormones 66
    Total Protein 66
    Amino Acids and Phenylalanine 66
    Plasma Prolactin and Growth Hormone 67
    Lactate 68
    White Blood Cells 68
    Red Blood Cell Metabolism 68
    Cholesterol 69
The Metabolic and Respiratory Systems 69
Muscle Tension 72
Skin Resistance and Spontaneous GSR 73
Other Physiological Effects 74
    Brain Metabolism 74
    Salivary Changes 74
    Effectiveness in the Treatment of Disease 75
    Treatment of Cancer 76
    Changes in Body Temperature 77
    Alleviation of Pain 77
    Exceptional Body Control 79

Chapter 3: Behavioral Effects
by Michael Murphy and Steven Donovan 81
Perceptual and Cognitive Abilities 81
    Perceptual Ability 82
    Reaction Time and Perceptual Motor Skill 84
    Deautomatization 85
    Field Independence 86
    Concentration and Attention 87
    Memory and Intelligence 88

The Physical and Psychological Effects of Meditation

Rorschach Shifts 89
Empathy 90
Regression in the Service of the Ego 92
Creativity and Self-Actualization 92
    Creativity 93
    Self-Actualization 94
Hypnotic Suggestibility 101
Anxiety 102
Psychotherapy and Addiction 115
    Psychiatry and Psychotherapy 116
    Addiction and Chemical Dependency 124
Sleep 130
Sex-Role Identification 134

Chapter 4: Subjective Reports
by Michael Murphy and Steven Donovan

by Michael Murphy and Steven Donovan 135
Equanimity 135
Detachment 135
Ineffability 137
Bliss 138
Energy and Excitement 138
Altered Body Image and Ego Boundaries 139
Hallucinations and Illusions 140
Dreams 141
Synesthesia 142
Extrasensory Experiences 142
Clearer Perception 142
Negative Experiences 143

Endnotes 147

Bibliography of Meditation Research
by Michael Murphy, Steven Donovan, and Eugene Taylor

by Michael Murphy, Steven Donovan, and Eugene Taylor 153

About the Authors 279
About Esalen 281
About the Institute of Noetic Sciences 281

The Physical and Psychological Effects of Meditation

Preface

The present volume was published in its first edition in 1988 by Esalen Institute under the direction of Michael Murphy and Steven Donovan as part of Esalen's then newly founded Institute for Exceptional Functioning. The second edition has been produced in collaboration with Esalen Institute, Marius Robinson, and the Institute of Noetic Sciences. It adds almost four hundred new entries to the original alphabetized bibliography, which now extends into the first months of 1996. The original essays by Murphy and Donovan were lightly edited and augmented to preserve the historical nature of the text, while the early matter of the first edition has been completely replaced with a new introduction by the present editor and an entirely new and more extensive overview of scientific studies of contemplative experience by Michael Murphy, taken from sections 23.1 and 23.2 in *The Future of the Body*, by permission of Jeremy P. Tarcher, Inc. Acknowledgements are gratefully extended to Michael Murphy and Steven Donovan for the opportunity to collaborate with them on their text; to Tom Hurley and Marilyn Schlitz for approaching me with the project in the first place; to the staff at the Institute of Noetic Sciences for numerous courtesies; and to Saybrook Institute and Graduate Research Center for essential faculty support. Margaret Livingston assembled many of the entries from 1988 to 1994 and put them into presentable form; LeAnna DeAngelo and Michael Nagel, graduate students at Saybrook Institute, assisted in collating updated material from 1994 to the present; Sue Beer at Saybrook and the Reference Department at Treadwell Library at Massachusetts General Hospital conducted literature searches; William Mikulas, Herbert Benson, Charles Alexander, Jon Kabat-Zinn, Ann Massion, Jonathan Smith, and Deane Shapiro granted their valuable time and energy to be interviewed, while Michael Murphy, Charles Tart, and Michael Maliszewski read over and commented on the prepublication draft. At the Institute of Noetic Sciences, Carol Guion, Liz Kalloch, Annette Leeland, and Rebecca Madrone have been instrumental in bringing the manuscript into its final form prior to publication.

Eugene Taylor, PhD
Cambridge, Massachusetts
June 1, 1996

The Physical and Psychological Effects of Meditation

INTRODUCTION
by Eugene Taylor

Some Definitions

Meditation—that great and mysterious subject which in the past has always conjured up the image of the solitary Asian ascetic sitting in deep trance—is fast appearing in unexpected places throughout modern American culture. Secretaries are doing it as part of their daily noon yoga classes. Preadolescent teenagers dropped off at the YMCA by their mothers on a Saturday morning are learning it as part of their karate training. Truck drivers and housewives in the Stress Reduction Program at the University of Massachusetts Medical Center are practicing a combination of Hindu yoga and Buddhist insight meditation to control hypertension. Star athletes prepare themselves for a demanding basketball game with centering techniques they learned in Zen.[1]

Dhyana is the generic Sanskrit term for meditation, which in the *Yoga Sutras* refers to both the act of inward contemplation in the broadest sense and more technically to the intermediate state between mere attention to an object (*dharana*) and complete absorption in it (*samadhi*).[2] The earliest known reference to such practice on the Indian subcontinent occurs on one of the seals, a figure seated in the lotus posture, found in the ruins of the pre-Aryan civilizations at Harappa and Mohenjodaro which existed prior to 1500 BCE. Most of the orthodox Hindu schools of philosophy derive their meditation techniques from yoga, but superimpose their own theoretical understanding of consciousness onto the results of the practice.[3]

Meditation is also referred to as a spiritual practice in China. Chinese forms of meditation have their origins in the early roots of popular Taoism which existed long before the codification of Taoism as a formal philosophy during the seventh century BCE. However, there is no concrete evidence to prove that meditation first arose in Hindu culture and then spread elsewhere. Thus, for the time being the original meditative traditions in China and India should be considered as separate and indigenous. To further complicate the issue, analogies between meditative states and trance consciousness suggest that even earlier precursors to the Asian meditative arts can be found in shamanic cultures such as those in Siberia and Africa.[4]

As for modern developments, in trying to formulate a definition of meditation, a useful rule of thumb is to consider all meditative techniques to be culturally embedded. This means that any specific technique cannot be understood unless it is considered in the context of some particular spiritual tradition, situated in a specific historical time period, or codified in a specific text according to the philosophy of some particular individual.[5] Thus, to refer to Hindu meditation or Buddhist meditation is not enough, since the cultural traditions from which a particular kind of meditation comes are quite different and even within a single tradition differ in complex ways. The specific name of a school of thought or a teacher or the title of a specific text is often quite important for identifying a particular type of meditation. Vipassana, or insight meditation, for instance, as practiced in the United States is derived from the Theravada tradition of Buddhism, and is usually associated with the teachings of the Burmese monk Mahasi Sayadaw; Transcendental Meditation is associated exclusively with the teachings of Maharishi Mahesh Yogi, whose tradition is Vedantic Hinduism; and so on.

The attempt to abstract out the primary characteristics of meditation from a grab bag of traditions in order to come to some purified essence or generic definition is a uniquely Western and relatively recent phenomenon. This tendency should be considered, however powerful and convincing its claim as an objective, universal, and value-free method, to be an artifact of one culture attempting to comprehend another that is completely different.[6]

At the same time, however, Western styles of meditation have long existed in the form of contemplative prayer, and contemporary interest in Asian practices has kindled a resurgence of interest in Western parallels. *Orison*, the repetitive and devotional meditation on Christ, repetition of the Holy Names, the spiritual teachings of St. Ignatius, and the Eastern Orthodox practice of the *philokalia* are examples from the Western contemplative tradition that come nearest to meditation as it has been cultivated in Asian countries. Indeed there is an unbroken tradition of mysticism which can be said to embody forms of meditative practice in the West—from the NeoPlatonists such as Plotinus, through the medieval mystics both early and late—Johannes Erigena, St. Bonaventure, John of the Cross, St. Teresa, St. Bernard of Clairvaux—followed by such personalities as Robert Parsons, Margaret Mary Alacoque, and Emanuel Swedenborg, to modern Christian contemplatives such as Pierre Teilhard de Chardin and

Thomas Merton, and now Schlomo Carlbach, Bede Griffiths, and David Steindl-Rast.[7]

But for purposes of carrying on a coherent discussion about the subject, while mystical awakening can be found in some form in all cultures, meditation per se should be taken as a uniquely Asian phenomenon which, wholesale, has only recently come to the attention of the West. In its new Western context, particularly in the United States, however, it has undergone a significant reformulation. In the US it has become indigenized, so that now one can say that Asian forms of meditation have become thoroughly American.[8]

The Americanization of Meditation

Ideas about Eastern meditative traditions began seeping into American popular culture even before the American Revolution through the various sects of European occult Christianity that transplanted themselves to such new settlements as Germantown and Ephrata in William Penn's "Holy Experiment," which he named Pennsylvania. Early framers of the Declaration of Independence and the Constitution were influenced by teachings from mystical Sufism and the Jewish Kaballah through their membership in secret fraternities such as the Rosicrucians.

Asian ideas then came pouring in during the era of the transcendentalists, especially between the 1840s and the 1880s, largely influencing the American traditions of spiritualism, theosophy, and mental healing. The Hindu conception of *Brahman* was reformulated by Ralph Waldo Emerson into the New England vision of God as the Oversoul, while Henry David Thoreau's ideas on civil disobedience arose out of his reading of Hindu scriptures on meditation, yoga, and non-violence. At the same time, spiritualists—those who believed that science had established communication with the dead through the medium of the group seance—also dabbled in Asian ideas. Helena Blavatsky, co-founder of the International Theosophical Society, is usually credited with introducing Hindu conceptions of discarnate entities into American spiritualist circles. In this context, the Theosophists also translated Hindu texts on meditation and for the first time made them available in popular form to English-speaking audiences. Similarly, New Thought practitioners—followers of the healer Phineas P. Quimby—also included meditation techniques such as guided visualizations and the mantra into their healing regimes.

In general, by the late nineteenth century Americans appropriated Asian ideas to fit their own optimistic, pragmatic, and eclectic understanding of inner experience. This usually meant adapting ideas such as reincarnation and *karma* into a very liberal and heavily Christianized, but nevertheless secular, psychology of character development that was closer to the philosophy of transcendentalism than to doctrines in any of the Christian denominations. (Today, the same standard for interpreting Asian ideas persists but in the form of a neo-transcendentalist, Jungian, and counter-cultural definition of higher consciousness.)

The World Parliament of Religions, held in Chicago in 1893, was the landmark event that increased Western awareness of meditation. This was the first time that Western audiences on American soil received Asian spiritual teachings from Asians themselves. Thereafter, Swami Vivekananda taught meditation to the spiritualists and New Thought practitioners in New Hampshire and went on to found various Vedanta ashrams around the country in his wake. Anagarika Dharmapala lectured at Harvard on Theravada Buddhist meditation in 1904; Abdul Baha followed with a 235-day tour of the US teaching the Islamic principles of Bahai, and Soyen Shaku toured in 1907 teaching Zen and the principles of Mahayana Buddhism.

By then, the idea of comparative religions had caught on as an academic field of inquiry in the universities. Following the Sacred Books of the East Series, edited by F. Max Mueller, and major translations of the Theravada scriptures by the Pali Text Society in England, the Harvard Oriental Series appeared after 1900 under the editorship of Charles Rockwell Lanman. Meanwhile, the Cambridge Conferences on Comparative Religions, carried on by Mrs. Ole Bull in her Brattle Street home near Harvard University, and the Greenacre School of Comparative Religions, operated by Sarah Farmer in Portsmouth, New Hampshire, had been bringing ideas about meditation to interested New Englanders since the late 1890s.

During the 1920s, American popular culture was introduced to the meditative practices of the Hindu yogi Paramahansa Yogananda. Gurdjieff, the Georgian mystic who had toured the US in 1924, was spreading the gospel of meditation in action to American expatriates in Paris by the 1930s. A young Hindu trained in theosophy named Jidhu Krishnamurti had been touring the US around that same time. Settling in Southern California in the 1940s, Krishnamurti would soon be joined by English émigrés fleeing the European war, such as Christopher Isherwood, Gerald Heard, and Aldous Huxley, who were themselves writers and practitioners of the meditative arts.

During World War Two, Huxley, Heard, and others became disciples of the meditation teacher Swami Prabhavananda, head of the Vedanta Society of Southern California. Together, they produced such influential books as *Vedanta for the West* and assisted in the popular dissemination of texts such the Hindu *Upanishads* and the *Yoga Sutras*. Meanwhile, on the east coast of the United States, Swami Akhilananda of Boston frequently met with leading university intellectuals in psychology, philosophy, and religion, including Gordon Allport, Peter Bertocci, William Ernest Hocking, and George H. Williams. One product of this liaison was Akhilananda's *Hindu Psychology* (1946), with an introduction by Gordon Allport, a text on the philosophy and psychology of Vedantic meditation.

Another momentous event introducing Asian ideas to the West was the arrival in 1941 of Heinrich Zimmer, Indologist and Sanskrit scholar, who had been a friend and confidant of C. G. Jung. Zimmer brought the young Joseph Campbell, comparative mythologist and folklorist, to the attention of the newly formed Bollingen Foundation. Subsequently, the Foundation produced the English translation of Jung's collected works, as well as numerous books by Zimmer, which Campbell edited, among other titles. Perhaps the most influential product of this endeavor was the Bollingen edition of the *I Ching*, or Chinese Book of Changes. The *I Ching* was a Taoist oracle book revered in Chinese religious history as one of the four great Confucian classics. Translated by Richard Wilhelm with a preface by Jung, the work has continued to enjoy immense popularity since its first publication in 1947.

The 1950s represented a major expansion of interest in both meditation and Asian philosophy. Frederic Speigelberg, a professor of comparative religions at Stanford, opened the California Institute of Asian Studies in 1951, which highlighted the work of the modern Hindu mystic and social reformer Sri Aurobindo Ghose. Alan Watts, a student of Zen and former Episcopalian minister, soon joined the faculty and within a few years produced such best-selling books as *Psychotherapy East and West* and *The Meaning of Zen*.

It was also during this time that Michael Murphy first came under the influence of Speigelberg, was introduced to the teachings of Sri Aurobindo, and began the practice of meditation. With the assistance of Abraham Maslow, Alan Watts, Willis Harman, Aldous Huxley, George Leonard, and others, Murphy would soon collaborate with Richard Price to launch Esalen Institute, which quickly became the world's premier growth center for human potential.

During the same period of the early 1950s, with the help of Watts, D. T. Suzuki came from Japan to California and introduced Zen to a new generation of Americans. Suzuki settled in New York, where he accepted a visiting professorship at Columbia. His seminars were open to the public and subsequently had a wide influence. Thomas Merton visited him. The neo-Freudians such as Karen Horney and Erich Fromm were his students. Suzuki even took Horney on a three-month tour of the religious shrines in Japan. John Cage heard him, as did J.D. Salinger. Soon, Suzuki was profiled in *The New York Times*, and many of his previous works on the history and philosophy of Zen, published in relative obscurity, were translated and reprinted for American audiences. Zen, embraced by the beat generation, had suddenly come to the West.

What occurred next opened an entirely new era of popular interest in meditation. This was the confluence of three major cultural events in the 1960s: the psychedelic revolution, the Communist invasion of Asia, and the rise of the American counter-culture, especially in terms of widespread opposition to the Vietnam War.

By the early 1960s, mind-expanding drugs were being taken by a significant segment of the post-war baby boom, a generation which numbered some 40 million people born between 1945 and 1955 who came of age in the late 1960s and early 1970s. This led young people in their teens and twenties to collectively open the doors of inward perception, experiment with alternative lifestyles, and question established cultural norms in Western society. An entire generation soon established their own alternative institutions which began to operate in defiance of traditional cultural forms still dominated by the ideology of their parents' generation. Subsequently, this was to have important political, economic, religious, and social consequences in the West, especially in the United States, as enduring but alternative cultural norms began to take root in the younger generation of the American middle class.

At the same time, the increased Soviet influence in India, the Cultural Revolution in China, the Communist Chinese takeover of Tibet and

Mongolia, and the increased political influence of Chinese Communism in Korea and Southeast Asia were key forces that collectively set the stage for an influx of Asian spiritual teachers to the West. An entirely new generation of them appeared on the American scene and they found a willing audience of devotees within the American counter-culture. Swami A.C. Bhaktivedanta, Swami Satchitananda, Guru Maharaji, Kerpal Singh, Nayanaponika Thera, Swami Rama, Thich Nhat Hanh, Chogyam Trungpa, Maharishi Mahesh Yogi, Swami Muktananda, Sri Bagwan Rajneesh, Pir Viliyat Kahn, and the Karmapa were but a few of the names that found followers in the United States. While there remain numerous contemporary voices, such as Guru Mai, Thich Nhat Hanh, the Maharishi, and Sogyal Rinpoche, there can be little doubt, historically, that the most well known and influential figure in this pantheon today remains Tenzin Gyatso, the four-teenth Dalai Lama of Tibet, winner of the Nobel Peace Prize in 1989.

As a result of such personalities, there has been a tremendous growth in meditation as a spiritual practice in the United States from the 1960s to the present. This phenomenon remains largely underestimated by the pundits of American high culture who see themselves as the main spokes-persons for the European rationalist tradition in the New World. In the first place, from a socio-cultural standpoint, it is clear that from the 1920s to the 1960s Freudian psychoanalysis was the primary socially acceptable avenue through which artists, writers, and aficionados of modernism gained access to their own interior unconscious processes.

For a new and younger generation of visionaries, however, psycho-analysis was soon replaced by psychedelic drugs as the primary vehicle for opening the internal doors of perception. This occurred as a result of experiments undertaken in military and university laboratories associated with the US Central Intelligence Agency (CIA). The CIA was interested in developing mind-control drugs for potential use in psychological warfare. At the same time that the CIA began testing substances such as LSD on unsuspecting populations of soldiers, businessmen, and college students, some of these chemicals came into the hands of the scientific and medical community. Researchers themselves began ingesting mescaline and LSD. Soon, by the late 1950s and early 1960s, from the psychiatrists' couches in Hollywood to the hallowed halls of Harvard University, the youthful and educated elite of the American middle class began to experiment with psychedelics in ever-increasing numbers.

The counter-culture movement that followed was considered a revolution in consciousness, driven by mind-expanding drugs, as well as defined by spiritual teachings from Asian cultures, each creating the conditions for expansion of the other. As the psychedelic revolution of the 1960s subsided for the post-war baby boomers maturing into the 1970s, meditation, and all that it implied, then became fixed as an enduring ethic of that generation. The belief was that meditative practices not only cleansed the consciousness of psychedelics, and confirmed the commitment to pursuing alternative lifestyles, but they also informed the socio-cultural direction that the lives of many young people would soon take in establishing new and permanent forms of lifetime spiritual practice. Now, after thirty years, these developments have produced advanced Western practitioners, who themselves are qualified senseis, roshis, swamis, and tulkus. We know them as Ram Dass, Sivananda Radha, Jiyu Kennet Roshi, Maureen Friedgood, Jack Kornfield, Robert Frager, Richard Baker Roshi, and others. They have begun to teach these Asian traditions to Western audiences. In so doing, they are also participating in their modification by forming new lineages of meditation practice that, while informed by Asian influences, turn out to be uniquely Western. Such teachings are already being transmitted to a second and third generation of younger people in the United States and in Europe as well, altering irrevocably the shape and direction of spiritual life in contemporary Western culture.

Not the least of these influences has been renewed interest in the Western contemplative traditions. Examination of Western mystics has increased dramatically since the 1960s. Witness, for instance, establishment of the Classics of Western Spirituality Series, published by the Paulist Press, or the appearance of the newly formed Mysticism Study Group within the American Academy of Religion. At the same time, popular books on Christian meditation are clearly linked to the spiritual awakening that has occurred in the counter-culture. Avery Brooke's *Learning and Teaching Christian Meditation* (1975), Joan Cooper's *Guided Meditation and the Teachings of Jesus* (1982), and Swami Rama's *Meditation in Christianity* (1983) are but a few of the titles that have enjoyed continuous printings since they first came out. There is also a case to be made for the idea that the fundamentalist revival in the Christian right has been a direct reaction to the larger upsurge of spirituality that has occurred in the American counter-culture.

Perhaps the most significant opportunity to arise out of the new stream of Western meditation practitioners has been heightened awareness of Asian cultures, especially in terms of their unique integrity and outlook. While the Judeo-Christian, Greco-Roman, Western European, and Anglo-American tradition continues to export its beliefs and values into other cultures on a grand scale, the Asian worldview is also fast asserting itself as a competing economic, political, and social force. But is a clash of world epistemologies inevitable? Perhaps. Meanwhile, Westerners within a new and younger generation have appeared who are fast becoming skilled interpreters of these non-Western traditions as legitimate worldviews in their own right. Their vehicle, the practice of meditation, could, instead of the predicted clash of cultures, potentially set the stage for an exchange of ideas between East and West that may yet turn out to be unprecedented in the history of Western thought.

Meditation as a Scientific Study

Within this context scientific interest in meditation has grown significantly over the past quarter of a century. This has occurred partly on the justification that science might be able to show us objectively what meditation is and what its effects are, but also because the scientific method represents one of the few ways in which our culture can peer into the depths of another culture so radically different from our own. To objectively study meditative practices, however, requires that they be taken out of their subjective context. One quarter claims that science produces objective truth independent of cultures, while another maintains that the scientific attitude has its own implied philosophical context, so all we are really doing is taking the subject out of its original frame of reference and putting it into one we can more easily understand. The methods and theory surrounding the practice of meditation techniques thereby undergo a radical change.

According to this second view, no more quintessential example exists of the Westernization of an Asian idea than the scientific study of meditation. Science, the product of Aristotelian thinking and the European rationalist enlightenment, now turns its attention to the intuitive transformation of personality through awakened consciousness (and other such Asian meanings of the term *enlightenment*). This means that the faculties of logic and sense perception, hallmarks of the scientific method, are now being trained on the personality correlates of intuition and insight, hallmarks of the traditional inward sciences of the East.

To grasp what meditation is has proven to be no easy task. The underlying and usually hidden philosophical assumptions of traditional rationalist science do not value the intuitive. They do not acknowledge the reality of the transcendent or subscribe to the concept of higher states of consciousness, let alone, in the strictest sense, even admit to the possible existence of unconscious forces active in cognitive acts of perception. Meditation, therefore, is a topic that characteristically would not be taken up by mainstream scientists. One would expect that research funding would be scarce, peer review difficult, and publication channels limited. The evidence shows that, at least until recently, this has been exactly the case.

The essential difficulty here is not just the reformulation of meditation techniques to fit the dictates of the scientific method, but rather what might be called a deeper, more subtle, and potentially more transformative clash of world epistemologies. It is not simply that meditation techniques have been difficult to measure but rather that, in the past, meditation has largely been an implicitly forbidden subject of scientific research. Now, however, major changes are currently underway within basic science that presage not only further evolution of the scientific method but also changes in the way science is viewed in modern culture. An unprecedented new era of interdisciplinary communication within the subfields of the natural sciences, a fundamental shift from physics to biology, and the cognitive neuroscience revolution have liberalized attitudes toward the study of meditation and related subjects. Meanwhile, the popular revolution in modern culture grounded in spirituality and consciousness is having a growing impact on traditional institutions such as medicine, religion, mental health, corporate management strategies, concepts of marriage, child rearing, and the family, and more. Increasingly, educated people want to know much more about meditation, while our traditional institutions of high culture remain unprepared as adequate interpreters.

The First Edition

As a result, when it first appeared, predictably, *The Physical and Psychological Effects of Meditation* drew wide attention within the meditation community and eventually sold out. Its authors, Michael Murphy and Steven Donovan, leaders in the American growth center movement and themselves seasoned meditators, presented their bibliography as a project of the Center for Exceptional Functioning, a newly founded program within Esalen Institute. Esalen, which Murphy had co-founded with Richard

Price in 1961, was, for many, the premier growth center for personal development in the United States.

Interest in meditation actually began out of the earliest programs at Esalen. Alan Watts, the well-known interpreter of Zen to the West, and Al Huang, a Chinese Tai Chi master of movement meditation, both taught meditation-related workshops when Esalen first opened. Throughout the years, figures such as Suzuki Roshi, Baker Roshi, Maharishi Mahesh Yogi, Lama Anagarika Govinda, and various Tibetan Buddhist tulkus introduced different forms of meditation into the growth center environment and helped to shape the basic theme of the Esalen program. This theme Murphy conceived as nothing less than the transformation of personality.

The immediate impulse that launched the bibliographic project, however, was publication of Murphy's speculative fiction *Jacob Atabet* (1977). This was a tale, set in modern San Francisco, about a writer, Darwin Fall, who had been investigating various miraculous events for the Catholic Church in Rome and doing research into all kinds of transformative phenomena. Fall meets and begins to chronicle the story of Jacob Atabet, who is actually in the process of transforming every cell of his body into the higher spiritual light. Atabet, for his part, finds in Fall someone who at last understands what he is going through. In the course of the novel, Atabet needs to be instructed in the contents of the massive text summarizing Fall's not yet complete research. The monumental tome, given to Atabet in outline form as a work in progress in that fictional account, later actually became Michael Murphy's voluminous *Future of the Body* (1992).

Meanwhile, scientific publications and other material collected in the course of putting together *The Future of the Body* became the basis for the first edition of the annotated bibliography in meditation research, which appeared in 1988. Before the advent of the revolution in personal computers, before managed care took over the health care industry, and before the full impact of rapid developments in the cognitive neurosciences were felt, Murphy and Donovan had collected a database of some 10,000 articles on various aspects of human potential and higher consciousness. Out of this cache they extracted 1253 scientific and literary studies on meditation which formed the core of the first edition. They introduced their bibliography with a series of essays to make a statement on the physiological, psychological, and behavioral effects of meditative practice as it was understood in the Western literature. To this analysis they brought a meditator's reading of both the Eastern and Western contemplative traditions, which provided insightful comparisons to the slow but steadily growing study of meditation according to the methods of Western science.

The first edition clearly indicated that the scientific study of meditation was fast becoming a growth industry. In the wake of its publication, Esalen, in cooperation with the Institute of Noetic Sciences, and with financial assistance from Marius Robinson, launched an annual series of invitation-only conferences on advances in meditation research. These conferences, held annually at Esalen from 1988 to 1996, brought practitioners of meditation together with scholars in comparative religions and scientists interested in experimental and clinical investigation in order to generate cross-disciplinary dialogue about the experience and the effect of meditative practice. One fruit of those conferences has been this second edition of the Murphy and Donovan bibliography.

The Present Update

In the eight years since the first publication of their work, basic experimental studies on the subject of meditation have steadily increased, while outcome research in clinical settings has grown at an even faster rate. At the same time, when compared to what had gone on in the field in the fifty years preceding 1988, the total rate of increase between 1988 and 1996 in articles in scholarly and scientific journals as well as trade books has been nothing short of spectacular.

The second edition, in keeping with the first, chronicles mainly scientific and scholarly works, revealing several key trends and changes. Since 1988, not only has government sponsored research increased, but meditation is now a category on the National Library of Medicine's list of computer search subjects. There also has been an increase in the number of studies reported by researchers outside the US, especially from Asian countries. While more studies are being undertaken overall, the majority of research programs appear to be conducted by practitioners of meditation who are also skilled in the techniques of modern experimental methods. Finally, and perhaps most important from the standpoint of basic science, investigation has moved from the level of gross physiology to more detailed points of biochemistry and the voluntary control of internal states. From a philosophical standpoint, these studies have also raised a number of issues about the role of spiritual experiences in both psychology and medicine.

TM and the TM-Sidhi Project

As Murphy and Donovan pointed out in their first edition, and as the present update of their work has confirmed, the most prolific research on meditation in the United States in sheer numbers of published studies has been and continues to be on Transcendental Meditation. Transcendental Meditation is the specific introductory program taught by Maharishi Mahesh Yogi, a Vedantic meditation teacher originally from Madhyapradesh, India, to thousands of disciples, most of whom are in the West. Meanwhile, the TM-Sidhi program (an anglicized version of the Sanskrit *siddhi*, meaning supernormal powers) represents more advanced training in the Vedantic interpretation of the *Yoga Sutras* of Patanjali. This experimental research program into the effects of TM is carried on largely at Maharishi Mahesh International University (MIU) in Fairfield, Iowa (now called the Maharishi International School of Management), but there are other centers and individuals engaged in TM research as well.

Over the past two decades, David Orme-Johnson, one of the key investigators at MIU, and his colleagues have compiled and edited 508 studies on TM in five volumes under the title *Scientific Research on Maharishi's Transcendental Meditation and TM-Sidhi Program: Collected Papers* (Orme-Johnson and Farrow, 1977; Chalmers, Clements, Schenkluhn, and Weinless, 1989a, 1989b, 1989c; Wallace, Orme-Johnson and Dillbeck, 1990). These studies are arranged approximately in chronological order in each volume under the headings of physiology, psychology, sociology, and then either theoretical or review oriented papers. Experimental studies reported are about evenly divided between articles in refereed journals and those from TM conferences and in-house TM publications.

The content of the collected papers indicates that, historically, TM researchers began by positing the existence of a fourth state of consciousness—a hypometabolic waking state which their physiological measures suggested was distinctly different from either normal waking consciousness, the state of sleep with dreams, or the state of deep sleep without dreams. Studies then began to show effects when TM was applied to medical conditions such as asthma, angina, and high blood pressure.   Personality variables also became a focus of research. These included measures of intellectual problem-solving ability, thinking and recall, creativity, field independence, sense of self-esteem, and self-actualization. Researchers then moved into applied social situations, looking at the effects of teaching TM to the police, the military, and such populations as juvenile offenders, incarcerated adults, high school students, and athletes, as well as managers in the corporate environment. Meanwhile, more subtle biochemical measures of blood chemistry were also undertaken. These included endocrine levels, effects on neurotransmitters such as dopamine, noradrenaline, and serotonin, and the measurement of altered cell metabolism. TM was also examined in the context of various psychiatric disorders.

By the late 1970s studies began to appear testing the abilities of advanced meditators in the TM-Sidhi program on numerous variables during deep meditation and during what they described as yogic-flying. Along with individual studies, TM researchers also began reporting evidence for an inverse correlation between the amount of meditation going on and sociological variables such as the local and national crime rate for a given period. This has been labeled the Maharishi Effect. Finally, there are numerous papers on TM and world peace.

After almost a quarter of a century of scientific investigation, TM researchers now describe their findings in theoretical terms referring to "Vedic psychology" and "Vedic science." Their system clearly acknowledges the reality of the transcendent and subserves materialist methods of Western scientific investigation under the larger domain of spiritual experience within the philosophical and religious context of Hindu monism. Their expertise with certain aspects of Western science has become quite sophisticated, however, creating an altogether new avenue of investigation at the interface between science and spirituality. In the new and more open scientific climate toward research on the subject of meditation, TM researchers have successfully been able to master the blind peer review process and were recently awarded some $2,500,000 in research grants from the National Institutes of Health. Their studies will look at the large scale application of TM in the treatment of alcohol and drug abuse and in such conditions as hypertension.[9]

Their preliminary research has shown that, with regard to drug dependence, the traditional single-cause-for-a-single-illness model is unworkable. Instead, addiction is viewed as a progressive behavior pattern involving a complex of physiological, psychological, and socio-cultural variables that can be successfully influenced by meditative practice at key points. In the case of hypertension, they have shown that psycho-pharma-cology is still the preferred medical intervention but remains complicated because of toxic side effects, issues of patient non-compliance, and the fact that drugs work well on preventing stroke but not coronary heart disease. Their previous studies have confirmed that meditation works better than drug placebos, but is slower acting than pharmacologic agents, leading them to confirm the current recommendation that TM is most effective when used in combination with other therapies.

Herbert Benson: The Mind-Body Medical Institute

Another of the most visible research projects into the effects of meditation originally reported in the first edition of the Murphy and Donovan bibliography has been going on under the direction of Herbert Benson, cardiologist at Harvard Medical School. In the late 1960s, Benson began studying Transcendental Meditation practitioners. He has since expanded his work by looking at Tibetan Buddhist meditators, and generic forms of relaxation capable of being elicited by the general population.

His first major work, a trade book entitled *The Relaxation Response*, appeared in 1975. In it, he described procedures he believed were generic to the onset of meditation and other contemplative practices. The conditions necessary to evoke the relaxation response involve a quiet environment, repetition of a sound or phrase, a passive attitude, and relaxed watchful breathing. Meanwhile, in the medical literature he identified the relaxation response as a natural reflex mechanism which, when practiced twenty minutes a day, reduced stress and physiologically had the opposite effect of the fight-flight reflex.

Beyond the Relaxation Response appeared in 1984, and combined Benson's research into both the relaxation response and the placebo effect. This text emphasized the role that harnessing physiology can play in improving quality of life and character. Benson followed in 1987 with *Your Maximum Mind*, a text that clearly associates the positive physiological effects of the relaxation response with the hopefulness of the patient's own religious beliefs and values.

Since publication of *Your Maximum Mind*, Benson has launched the Mind-Body Medical Institute, a for-profit research and training initiative in behavioral medicine, in conjunction with the Deaconess Hospital in Boston and the Harvard Medical School. Two major streams of Benson's work on meditation are carried on at this Institute. One involves ongoing programs in scientific research, while the other is dedicated to community education.

Since 1967 Benson has been working on identifying the physiological and neurochemical underpinnings of the relaxation response, which he defines as a hypometabolic state of parasympathetic activation, that is, a state of deep rest. His early work showed the effect of the relaxation response on lowering conditions such as essential hypertension, headache, and alcohol consumption. Studies then moved to show the effect of the relaxation response on various forms of heart disease, serum levels in the blood, and on psychiatric disorders such as anxiety. Other studies compared the relaxation response with other forms of relaxation such as hypnosis.

The next major phase was to assess the effects of the relaxation response in a variety of clinical situations. Women experiencing moderate forms of PMS were found to benefit from the technique. Patients at a major health maintenance organization were found to utilize the facilities less and to report less illness over time when taught Benson's method. Recently, the Institute has inaugurated a successful relaxation curriculum for high school students.

At the same time, Benson has also been investigating advanced meditators. While he began with practitioners of TM, as work on the relaxation response became more sophisticated, Benson turned his attention to measuring the physiological changes in advanced Tibetan Buddhist meditators, using monks who follow the Dalai Lama. These were on-site investigations at monasteries in Nepal in the Himalayas. Most recently, Benson and his colleagues have been testing out the physiological effects of different forms of practice, as well as assessing metabolic and electrophysiologic changes in advanced meditators.

On the educational side, the Mind-Body Medical Institute offers regular one-week training programs for health care practitioners in all aspects of the relaxation response. The Institute franchises out its model to hospitals and other health care facilities and periodically launches educational programs for the public.

In December 1995, for instance, the Institute sponsored a major conference on "Spirituality and Healing in Medicine." The three-day program was aimed at clinical practitioners, including physicians, psychologists, nurses, clergy, social workers, allied health professionals, and health care administrators. Perhaps for the first time, scientists and Western health care practitioners joined with scholars in comparative religions to assess the relationship between spirituality and health. Here presentations on scientific evidence as well as historical and thematic scholarship attempted to interpret the life-world of radically different epistemological frames of reference from those of the laboratory scientist. It also meant taking seriously the claims of faith traditions in the West such as Pentacostalism, the Charismatic Catholic movement, and Seventh Day Adventism which the scientific outlook normally rejects. As well, Islamic, Hindu, and Buddhist scholars took up the more difficult task of interpreting the spiritual traditions of non-western cultures as significant sources of healing. Throughout the conference, the practice of meditation played a central role in these discussions.

More recently, Benson has released *Timeless Healing:The Power and Biology of Belief* (Benson and Stark, 1996). In this text he renames the placebo effect "remembered wellness." By using this new term he takes the idea of the placebo, which carries a negative connotation in science as something "not real," and reexamines it as a new psychological tool in medicine. In the term "remembered wellness" he here redefines the old term "placebo" as the person's natural desire for health and the person's right to choose the kind of healing to achieve it. To pharmaceuticals and surgery, Western medicine must now add the patient's own capacity for self-healing. Expectations, beliefs, values, and the practice of meditation, Benson maintains, are among the new forces we must now harness for health and growth.

Jon Kabat Zinn
at the University of Massachusetts Medical Center

Another major program of research on meditation continues under the direction of Jon Kabat-Zinn in the Department of Medicine, Division of Preventative and Behavioral Medicine at the University of Massachusetts Medical Center in Worcester, Massachusetts. Kabat-Zinn's program, primarily for patients with medical disorders, combines elements of Vipassana, a Theravada form of Buddhist meditation from Burma, and Zen practices from Japanese Buddhism with Hatha yoga, a tradition from the Indian subcontinent, in a training regime identified as Mindfulness-Based Stress Reduction (MBSR). The Stress Reduction Clinic takes referrals from all services throughout the hospital and elsewhere and deals with a wide range of referred conditions, including hypertension, heart disease, cancer, chronic pain, irritable bowel syndrome, headaches, HIV and AIDS, as well as disorders of stress and anxiety.

Each patient is interviewed individually prior to enrollment in the program. The course includes eight weeks of classes, two two-and-a-half hour classes per week. Each class contains between twenty-five and forty members. Home study is required as well. Six days per week, with the help of audiotapes, patients practice meditation and yoga for forty-five minutes on their own. At week six, they attend an all-day seven-hour silent meditation. All participants in the six to eight concurrently running classes (approximately 240 people) participate in this silent weekend meditation retreat together. Following the program, each patient meets individually with the instructor. Three eight-week cycles of the course are held each year.

Patients are taught a basic regime of stretching and relaxation, plus different forms of seated meditation that they can continue to practice at home. They are also taught a method of body scanning, which entails following the path of the breath through different parts of the body as a guided visualization. In groups, they also discuss issues of formal meditation practice and ways to integrate what they learn there into their daily lives.

The program has enjoyed considerable success and notoriety. Kabat-Zinn has summarized his work in two popular trade books, *Full Catastrophe Living* (1990) and *Wherever You Go, There You Are* (1994). In 1993, the work of the clinic was prominently featured in the PBS series *Healing and the Mind with Bill Moyers*. In addition, over 100 centers in the US and abroad started by colleagues trained by Kabat-Zinn now conduct research as well as deliver clinical services. Beyond this network, in Massachusetts alone, MBSR training is presently offered bilingually, in Spanish and English, in neighborhood health centers and taught to both inmates and staff as part of an ongoing prison project. Also, training programs are offered for first and second year medical students, corporate executives, and staff at local HMOs.

While Kabat-Zinn and his colleagues have undertaken extensive outcome studies of their program on meditation, recently they have moved into more basic research that tries to refine the identification of specific biological markers that show the effects of meditation on the body.[10] Currently, the key variable of their investigation has been melato-

The Physical and Psychological Effects of Meditation

nin, a hormone which is produced in the pineal gland and thought to be a scavenger against cancer cells, acting to inhibit cancer growth at certain intermediate stages of cell proliferation. Melatonin is known to be photo-sensitive and is produced in greatest quantities in the body at night. Kabat-Zinn and his colleagues suggest that it is also psychosensitive, in other words, that psychosocial interventions can also increase its production. In a recent study employing graduates from their program, for instance, Massion, Teas, Hebert, Wertheimer, and Kabat-Zinn (1995) demonstrated a significant increase in melatonin levels among meditators. Because the oncology literature provides support for the concept of psychophysiologi-cal interactions in survival among cancer patients, the Worcester group suggested not only that melatonin might be a marker for other types of psychosocial interventions, but that meditation might be relevant in the treatment of certain types of cancer, especially of the breast and prostate.

Kabat-Zinn and his colleagues have several research projects currently underway that are in their preliminary stages and have not yet been published. One is the effect of guided visualization on psoriasis. Another, funded by the US Army, will look at the effects of behavioral interventions such as nutrition and meditation in patients suffering from early-stage breast cancer. In another experiment, just completed and not yet pub-lished, Kabat-Zinn joined colleagues A.O. Massion, J. Teas. J.R. Hebert, and M.D. Wertheimer replicating their original findings and once again found a positive relationship between intensive meditation practice and increased melatonin levels.

Cognitive-Behavioral Approaches in Psychology

In an important new development, academic psychologists in the tradition of cognitive behaviorism have launched experimental research programs in meditation. William Mikulas (1981) at the University of West Florida has pointed out that, when analyzed in detail, meditation practices can be broken down and understood in terms of traditional constructs in experimental psychology, such as vigilance, attention, and concentration. As well, the new trend in cognitive therapy applying principles of classical and operant conditioning in order to inhibit or facilitate both mental images and thought processes has brought experimental psychologists a step closer to the type of instruction typical of various Eastern meditative practices. The continuing obstacle is, according to Mikulas, that cognitive psychologists have overemphasized a mechanistic model of the mind as a computer instead of expanding their definition of behavior.

To rectify this situation, Mikulas has outlined a program to study what he called "Behaviors of the Mind" (mind, a decidedly unbehavioristic term, he defines as the subjective center or agent of mental activity).[11] Three such behavioral variables relevant to the study of meditation that he has studied are concentration, the ability to focus attention on an object for varying periods; mindfulness, a generalized state of alertness where the mind remains unfocused but is prepared to attend to any potential stimulus; and clinging, the tendency of the mind to attach to and to dwell on specific thoughts or objects.

Such constructs, Mikulas believes, can be operationalized as a way to understand meditation from a cognitive-behavioral perspective. Moreover, this addresses what is actually going on at a mental level in a much more sophisticated way than just studying physiological measures or a single experimental variable.[12]

Another cognitive-behaviorist, Jonathan C. Smith, at Roosevelt University in Chicago, has developed an extensive research program on meditation as part of his Stress Institute (J.C. Smith, 1975a, 1975,b,1975c,1978, 1984a,1984b, 1985, 1986a, 1986b, 1987, 1988, 1990, 1991,1993). Thinking along lines similar to Mikulas, Smith had already begun his own research by conceiving meditation as just a special form of relaxation. Psychologists have numerous relaxation strategies available to them, including progressive muscle relaxation, yogic stretching, guided mental imagery, contemplation, a focus on the gross aspects of the body, and a more refined focus on subtle body functions. Yet another is meditation, which can be either focused, as in Transcendental Meditation or Benson's relaxation response, or open and unfocused, as in Zen practice or Buddhist mindfulness.

His empirical research, relying heavily on factor theory, has more recently caused Smith to revise his thinking about theories of relaxation. In a complete reversal, he now considers relaxation a subset of meditation (J.C. Smith et al., 1996). In the old Benson model (one that still largely prevails), relaxation was confined to measurements of reduced physiological arousal. Another explanation that has been most popular among traditional stress researchers, such as Davidson and Schwartz (1984, 1976), defines relaxation in terms of cognitive-somatic specificity, i.e. there are two kinds of relaxation, physical and mental, which require two different sets of techniques, physiological and psychological. Then there was Smith's approach which saw all types of relaxation as the refinement of cognitive skills involving passivity, receptivity, and focusing. As more research results came in, Smith then came to believe that, in addition to just cognitive skills, relaxation was most successful when it included supportive cognitive structures, such as those found in personal philosophies of life.

Now, his research has further indicated that relaxation is composed of four separate effects: 1) the initial evocation of the relaxation response, which is purely physiological (which accounts for only 5% of the variance of relaxation); 2) tension release, the combination of physiological relaxation plus positive thoughts and feelings (as when one describes oneself as limp, melted, soothed, peaceful, calm); 3) disengagement, which is an attentional effect, creating the sensation of being distant, detached, forgetful, and becoming less aware of the world; and 4) engagement, opening up to and becoming more aware of the world, but in a passive way.

He has further operationally refined engagement by defining it as an advanced level of relaxation, having four subcategories. The first is engaged awareness, feeling aware, clear, focused, strengthened, and energized. This can be attained through yoga and breathing. The second is engaged prayerfulness, being open not just to the world, but to a greater world, in the sense of feeling reverent, spiritual, or selfless. Meditation is the key to attainment here. Third is engaged joyfulness, meaning a rainbow of feelings (feeling simultaneously loving, thankful, inspired, warm, healed, and infinite). (He suggests that joyfulness accounts for 40% of the variance of relaxation, and further, that while progressive relaxation does not evoke it, yoga, breathing, and meditation do). Finally, the final subcategory he defines as mystery, the experience of mystical feelings. He claims that initially he did not have enough subjects to measure this variable, that it was identified only by a small statistical effect, and that more study will be needed in the future to confirm it.

In addition to his empirical research, Smith has also developed an applied program. Here, he demystifies meditation, takes it out of its Asian context, and packages it as a training course that covers all the generic forms one can find in both Eastern and Western contemplative traditions, making meditation accessible to the common reader.

The significance of work by such researchers should not be underestimated. Programs such as these, the new cognitive-behaviorists believe, have greater potential for connecting traditional systems of Asian psychology with basic science than the more experiential approaches of humanistic or transpersonal psychotherapy. At the same time, interest in the subject by cognitive-behaviorists indicates the extent to which meditation has penetrated into the mainstream of American academic psychology as a respectable research subject.

Health Psychology and Complementary Medicine

Another important development in the field of meditation research has been alternative or complementary medicine. The historical evolution of the alternative medicine movement in the United States is long and too detailed to go into here. However, the main point can still be made that beginning in the 1960s and '70s, with the emergence of humanistic and transpersonal psychology as major forces in the human potential movement, the clinical practice of psychology and medicine began to fuse with a more sophisticated understanding of spiritual growth affecting certain key areas of modern culture. Now, after more than thirty years of personal and scientific experimentation with encounter groups, sensitivity training, psychedelics, somatic body work, parapsychology, guided imagery, yoga and meditation, biofeedback, hypnosis, and the like, alternative, or what is now being called complementary, medicine has emerged as an important challenge to Western reductionistic approaches to healing. Western medical science radically separates mind and body; complementary medicine unites them. Western medical science focuses on the physical symptom; complementary medicine looks at the symptom in the context of the whole person. Western medical science presumes that it is science that heals the sick; complementary medicine presumes that it is our manipulations that harness the patient's own resources for self-healing.

Complementary medicine, first of all, is now being defined by a new generation of scientist-practitioners. Those who before were but the mere students of their subject matter have now become both advanced meditators and recognized scientists capable of carrying off sophisticated research. We remember the pioneering work of Arthur Deikman and Charles Tart done twenty-five years ago Then we listened to Herbert Benson and Robert Keith Wallace. Then, in the 1970s and 1980s we heard from Dan Goleman, Daniel Brown, Jack Engler, Roger Walsh, Deane

Shapiro, Elmer Green, Alyce Green, Michael Maliszewski, and Michael West. Today, we read Charles Alexander, Robert Orme-Johnson, Richard Friedman, Mark Epstein, and James Spira.[13] The trend began as a study of meditation as an isolated practice, whereas it is now viewed in the much larger context of complementary medicine and one's overall sense of health and well-being.

Complementary medicine is complementary because it interfaces with scientific and medical reductionism. It not only advocates a combined approach to healing, but also points to the importance of holistic change. One does not merely take a pill and then return to the same lifestyle that contributed to the creation of the problem in the first place. The practice of meditation, as well as the pursuit of other forms of complementary medicine, means an alteration of basic attitudes, dramatic and positive lifestyle changes, and perhaps even radical overthrow of old, habitual ways of perceiving on the part of the person being healed.

Complementary medicine also reflects the major social revolution now going on at the interface between popular middle-class culture and the delivery of clinical services in the health care professions. A recent issue of the *Sharper Image Catalog,* for instance, advertises tapes, videos, and books by physician Dean Ornish of the University of California at San Francisco, who has pioneered in the treatment of heart disease using diet, meditation, and lifestyle change.[14] *The Wall Street Journal* and *Forbes* have carried articles on the therapeutic application of meditation in corporate management for stress reduction, new product development, and team building, while the November 1994 issue of *Psychology Today* indicated that meditation practice is at the heart of a contemporary spiritual awakening affecting not only pastoral counseling within traditional Christianity but also a large segment of the psychotherapeutic counter-culture.

In addition, there is clear evidence of the rising influence of complementary medicine within traditional institutions of modern culture. One sign has been the recent founding of the Office of Alternative Medicine within the National Institutes of Health. The OAM, working on a small budget, has commissioned individual investigators to run clinical trials on alternative therapies such as meditation that can be used in conjunction with traditional scientific medical practice. They have also recently established a network of research centers throughout the United States targeting specific experimental problems in complementary medicine.[15] Another sign has been the launching of several new journals, the most successful of which has been *Alternative Therapies in Health and Medicine.*[16] Edited by Larry Dossey and Jeanne Achterberg, and sponsored by the American Association of Critical Care Nurses, *Alternative Therapies* regularly reports on advances in meditation research in the context of other approaches such as homeopathy, vitamin therapy, hypnosis, biofeedback, and psychoneuroimmunology.

The Qi Gong Database

In addition to the inclusion of meditation in complementary forms of medicine in the United States, research on various forms of meditation is also occurring in other parts of the world. The Qi Gong database, a report on one aspect of meditative practice in China, is made available through the East-West Center for the Healing Arts in California and was assembled by a team of researchers led by Kenneth M. Sancier.[17] It contains some one thousand abstracts of unpublished papers delivered at a series of international conferences on Qi Gong and traditional Chinese medicine held since the late 1980s in China. Paradoxically, the Chinese Communist government wants to promote traditional Chinese medicine to the world at the same time that it severely restricts the ability of Chinese researchers to communicate freely with other investigators. The bibliography is therefore valuable as one of the only large scale sources of information available on the practice of Chinese meditation techniques related to Qi Gong; at the same time it suffers from a certain lack of oxygen because the material is presented in a contextual vacuum which presumes that traditional Chinese medicine is automatically testable by Western scientific methods.

Qi Gong is the traditional Chinese practice of meditation upon the *chi*, or life force, which is believed to continuously circulate throughout the body and which regulates the daily and seasonal functioning of the person in dynamic relation to the environment over the entire life cycle. The internal form of Qi Gong can be practiced as a seated meditation, while its external aspect may take the form of different movement disciplines. Qi Gong is the mother of tai chi, for instance, the most familiar style of Chinese health movement known to the West.

The database clearly indicates that there is a continuously growing body of information on the positive clinical application of Qi Gong therapy.[18] However, to really appreciate the information presented requires a detailed knowledge of the Taoist philosophy of yin and yang and the five elements, a knowledge of acupuncture, acquaintance with the philosophy behind the important Chinese works such as the *Book of Songs* and the *Book of Changes*, and a knowledge of the major classics in traditional Chinese medicine. Western scientific medical practitioners will therefore find it difficult to assess the clinical significance of unpublished studies presented only as abstracts and based on an epistemological system so radically different from the Western analytic tradition that the very frame of reference used in many of the discussions will to them remain incomprehensible. For the knowledgeable researcher, however, the hermetically sealed quality of the research at least gives an internal consistency to the one type of meditation studied.

Yoga Research in India

Scientific research on yoga and meditation appears to be going on all over India, but only a fraction of this work makes its way into the Western scientific and medical literature. An effort has recently been made by the Yoga Biomedical Trust, a non-profit research organization in Cambridge, England, founded in 1983 to collate more of this normally unavailable information on yoga and meditation.[19] Principally, their bibliographic references have come from yoga centers, private collections, specialist publishers, and researchers themselves, in addition to scientific conferences held periodically in India, the Indian social science literature, and the international medical research literature, which includes references normally unavailable to Western investigators.

In the Trust's primary publication, the *Yoga Research Bibliography: Scientific Studies on Yoga and Meditation* (1989), Monro, Ghosh, and Kalish present over 1000 citations ranging from essay-commentaries to clinical applications and pure empirical research. Again, however, as with the Qi Gong database, the *Yoga Research Bibliography* will be appreciated most by individuals trained in scientific research who also have an extensive knowledge of the classical texts in yoga and the philosophy behind the techniques, as well as a detailed experiential knowledge of specific yogic practices and their Sanskrit names. Again, the trend is clearly toward a mounting body of evidence showing the efficacious use of yoga techniques and Hindu meditation practice in specific disorders such as hypertension, diabetes, cancer, cholesterol regulation, alcoholism, anxiety disorders, asthma, pain control, and obesity. As compared to studies in the Chinese database, the level of scientific expertise in various experimental studies on yoga and meditation is quite sophisticated by Western standards. There is a much more subtle empirical demonstration of the relation of brain states to mental states in this yoga literature by Indian researchers than has yet to be demonstrated by non-Indian researchers.

The International Meditation Bibliography, 1950-1982

The only work comparable to the present text is the *International Meditation Bibliography, 1950-1982*, authored by Howard Jarrell and commissioned by the American Theological Library Association.[20] Its linguistic breadth is somewhat larger, in that it contains articles in English, books in English and German, with some titles in French, Spanish, and Portuguese, and dissertations in both English and German. The total number of entries (just over 2,200) is also somewhat larger. There are 937 journal and magazine articles, all of which are briefly annotated, over 1000 books, 200 doctoral dissertations and master's theses, titles from 32 motion pictures and 93 recordings and a list of 32 societies and associations. In addition there is a title index, an author index, and a subject index.

The Transcendental Meditation people seem to have had more than a passing hand in creating it, as there is a eulogistic preface extolling the benefits of TM, although the editors may have been simply trying to reflect the fact that the majority of experimental studies reported up to 1983 involved TM techniques. The work also does not discriminate between trade literature and more scholarly, academic or scientific publications, but rather presents them all as part of the greater bibliography. The impression that gets reinforced, quite accurate in my historical opinion, is that in the United States, at least, the majority of interest in meditation has come from popular culture rather than from the universities or the scientific establishment, which have remained largely reactive.[21]

The Historic Significance of Murphy and Donovan's Text

Murphy and Donovan have done the field of meditation research a valuable service on several fronts. Perhaps the most important of these has been to highlight the epistemological differences between those who meditate and those who do not as a crucial determinant of how and under what circumstances scientific research into this new subject can be conducted. They have also raised the issue of what a new science that takes meditation seriously might look like in the future. This issue is the same we raised earlier: namely, how can the methods of science be applied to a subject whose full understanding may transform the very foundation upon which reductionistic science is based? Murphy and Donovan produced their first edition during a time when there was fast-growing and widespread cultural interest in the subject, but great resistance from the basic science community. They not only collated a vast wealth of information on scientific research when the subject of meditation was less acceptable than it is today, they also emphasized the importance of meditation for understanding the larger issues of how we actualize our human potential. Now there has been a significant change in outlook and such issues are being taken more seriously by a younger generation of thoughtful leaders in modern culture. From an analysis of recent history, the Murphy and Donovan bibliography in its first edition contributed significantly toward advancing this discussion because it was a milestone that marked the current cultural revolution focusing on spirituality and higher consciousness. Two historical examples suggest this conclusion; the first was an episode that took place within the profession of psychology, while the second has occurred within the wider area of government-sponsored research in the medical sciences.

Psychologists Debate the Issues

Twenty years ago, the American Psychiatric Association recognized the need for controlled experimental research when it called for an in-depth study of different types of meditation and their positive effects on health (mentioning also that we should be investigating their potential "dangers").[22] Then, just before the first edition of the Murphy and Donovan bibliography appeared in 1988, a significant exchange on the experimental evidence underlying certain claims about meditation took place in the pages of the *American Psychologist*, main organ of the American Psychological Association.

The controversy began in 1984 when David S. Holmes, a staunch behaviorist in the tradition of Pavlov, Watson, and Skinner, who was from the University of Kansas and who had studied a few Transcendental Meditation practitioners, challenged a large mass of previously published experimental literature by claiming that there was no evidence that meditation reduced somatic arousal (Holmes, 1984). Holmes came to this conclusion through a few studies of his own and a review of the research literature. From this literature, however, he excluded consideration of all studies that were merely case reports and all those that involved subjects who had first acted as their own controls (within subjects designs) on the assumption that such research represented bad science. This left only studies which had used separate experimental and control groups. He then evaluated these remaining few and concluded that none showed meditation as producing a significant lowering of arousal different from simply resting.

A year and a half later, the editors of the *American Psychologist* devoted an entire section of their June 1985 issue to criticisms of Holmes' article, including responses from Holmes.

John Suler from Rider College maintained that on purely method-ological grounds Holmes had invoked a fairy tale definition of psychology as an exact science in order to discount studies on meditation, and that Holmes had limited himself to studies on TM which were not generalizable to other types of meditation (Suler, 1985).

Michael West, from the University of Sheffield, England, a researcher, practitioner, and author of a well-known text on meditation, believed that Holmes did not look carefully enough at the research literature so that his conclusions were overgeneralized and unwarranted (West, 1985). Needed instead, West maintained, was a more complex discussion of evidence and more double-blind, randomly assigned experiments controlling for expectation and group differences. He believed that someone also needed to undertake longitudinal studies of meditators and a big picture needed to be constructed that included case reports and within subject designs.

Deane Shapiro, clinical psychologist, meditation practitioner, and researcher at the University of California, Irvine, who has been one of the key pioneers in the field, waded in and concluded that Holmes had not looked at all the literature, that what he had looked at he had completely misinterpreted, and that conclusions drawn from Holmes' experiments using laboratory subjects were not automatically generalizable to clinical populations anyway.

Ignoring Suler and West, Holmes replied only to Shapiro, since in all likelihood he saw him as the more formidable opponent (Holmes, 1985a). He asserted on grounds of scientific rigor that Shapiro's own review of the meditation literature, which Holmes himself had originally ignored, contained numerous errors. Further, he clearly stated that Shapiro did not know how to conduct or analyze scientific research.

Harvard cardiologist Herbert Benson and SUNY psychologist Robert Friedman, practitioners, teachers, and researchers of the relaxation response then joined the chorus of voices. Benson and Friedman's point was that the relaxation response was common to all forms of relaxation, including rest and meditation, so that Holmes' distinction of meditation from rest was purely artificial (Benson and Friedman, 1985). Further, the trophotropic response as a complex of opposite physiological reactions to the fight-flight reflex had been established in physiology since the time of Hess (et al., 1947; Hess, 1953)—for which Hess had received the Nobel Prize—and the relaxation response had been experimentally established in the medical literature as an extension of Hess' work. Benson and Fried-man then pointed out other numerous errors in Holmes' work, suggesting not only that Holmes did not know his basic physiology, but also that he did not know how to conduct and interpret a scientific experiment.

Holmes (1985b) responded by implying in his opening paragraph that Benson and his colleagues did not know anything about meditation, physiology, or science, and then proceeded with an essay of some 3,000 words to deliver a barrage of rhetoric about what constitutes legitimate data in reductionistic science and what were the criteria for legitimate designs of various experiments in psychology, meanwhile having nothing much to say about meditation per se.

The final word was given in another issue of the *American Psychologist* a year later. This last comment that the editors permitted on Holmes was delivered by Jonathan C. Smith, cognitive-behaviorist and meditation and stress researcher from Roosevelt University (J.C. Smith, 1986a). Smith, theoretically in a reductionistic camp closer to Holmes than anyone else who had responded, maintained that the recent studies by Holmes on meditation and Roberts on biofeedback (see Roberts, 1985) that claimed no evidence for a reduction of somatic arousal were based on outdated assumptions concerning the nature of relaxation. Psychology had actually progressed from a 1950s definition of overt observable behavior as simply stimulus-response connections to a more sophisticated picture demon-strating control of mental and physiological operations. According to Smith's own model, both stress and relaxation were complex cognitive and interactive responses. Simply comparing meditation, biofeedback, and other relaxation techniques to each other is not sufficient; one must get at the extent to which each technique enhances the subject's skill at deploy-ing attention in a focused, passive, and receptive way. Even so, Smith suspected we would then find that genuine relaxation is not necessarily always associated with changes in arousal.[23]

This exchange tells us that within psychology as an academic experimental discipline there has been significant movement from reductionistic modeling that does not even acknowledge the reality of consciousness—the position of the radical behaviorists who controlled much of the methodological dialogue in the discipline since J.B. Watson's infamous proclamation of 1913—to at least a consideration of those aspects of meditation that can be operationalized. It further suggests that scientists who are also practitioners are not only more active in cross-disciplinary research, but by the 1980s were ready to engage in discussions with their more reductionistic colleagues on issues of method and interpretation. Subsequently, history has shown that the discussion has not only moved out into the wider field of medical science, but continues to develop in the direction set not by the reductionists but by the scientist-practitioners of meditation.

Governmental Research and Medical Science

More recently, an assessment of meditation has emerged in several statements made by investigating agencies of the United States government. Between 1988 and 1991, the National Research Council, in a project commissioned by the Army Research Institute, issued a series of findings on the assessment of techniques believed to enhance human performance.[24] These included, among numerous other topics, such approaches as self-help groups, subliminal tapes, and meditation. The overall conclusion of the investigators regarding the effect of meditation was widely disseminated in the public press as the official position of the NRC. Their assessment of the available scientific research led them to the conclusion that meditation seems to be no more effective than established relaxation techniques; and it was therefore unwarranted to attribute any special effects to meditation alone.

More than this, however, the overall tone of the entire research endeavor was negative and skeptical to begin with. Numerous criticisms emerged afterward of misinterpretation of data and false conclusions even from established experimentalists. As well, the analysis of the experimental literature on meditation was undertaken by two psychologists who had no expertise in the area of meditation research, although, somewhat ludicrously, they attempted to launch a definition and explanation of what

The Physical and Psychological Effects of Meditation

they considered to be the different types of meditation. They compared a few specific studies that had no basis for factual comparison according to the experimental standards they themselves had set, and they based their overall analysis of all experimental studies undertaken on meditation by reading a single outdated summary that had been commissioned some years earlier from a single researcher. To underscore the fact that their conclusions were based on a philosophical bias rather than basic research, they even included an epistemological coda admitting that to be the case.[25]

In October 1995, a more positive and forceful recommendation was made in a joint statement issued by agencies within the National Institutes of Health. The recommendation was based on the outcome of a major technology assessment conference that attempted to integrate behavioral and relaxation approaches into the treatment of chronic pain and insomnia.[26] One of the major interventions considered was that of meditation. The sponsoring agencies for this conference included The Office of Medical Applications of Research and the newly founded Office of Alternative Medicine. These groups were then backed by co-sponsoring agencies that included the National Institute of Mental Health, the National Institute of Dental Research, the National Heart, Lung, and Blood Institute, the National Institute on Aging, the National Cancer Institute, the National Institute of Nursing Research, the National Institute of Neurological Disorders and Stroke, and the National Institute of Arthritis and Musculoskeletal and Skin Diseases. Combining meditation under the same heading as autogenic training and progressive muscle relaxation, and determining that these were deep rather then merely brief methods of standard relaxation therapy, the conference members concluded that "the evidence is strong for the effectiveness of this class of techniques in reducing chronic pain in a variety of medical conditions."[27] They recommended the commitment of funds to research trials that tested these combined forms of therapy and the integration of alternative medicine with traditional scientific medical practice.

Here again we have the classic differentiation between the attitudes of laboratory versus clinical researchers. Basic researchers believe that they are doing the real science and only what comes out of the laboratory should be applied in clinical situations. Clinicians, on the other hand, faced with the real live complexity of human problems, maintain that most of what comes out of basic science is done to prove some theory, while what they say they really need is data on concrete, workable interventions for immediate life situations. While there is a revolution now going on in the neurosciences affecting how basic scientists communicate with one another, a completely different revolution is going on at the level of clinical services, one that has deep roots in values and attitudes, lifestyle choices the patient alone can make, alternative forms of healing, and an appeal to the spiritual dimension of human experience. Consequently, the National Research Council has had its say on the scientific validity of studying meditation, which has now been superseded by the more recent conclusions of the National Institutes of Health.

As this brief overview indicates, in their first edition Murphy and Donovan gave us a summary of meditation research that anticipated, among other trends, the rising influence of psychology in general medicine, the increasingly important role of beliefs and values in the healing process, the possibility of a new dialogue emerging between science and religion framed in terms of spiritual experience, and the potential impact that different models of consciousness might have on our understanding of character development. Presciently, as the current update suggests, these still seem to be rising trends for the future.

CHAPTER 1

Scientific Studies of Contemplative Experience: An Overview
by Michael Murphy

Scientific studies of meditation and other forms of contemplative experience have only recently become a subject of scientific interest within the last half century. In 1931 Kovoor Behanan, an Indian graduate student in psychology at Yale, was awarded a Sterling Fellowship to undertake what has since been recognized as the first empirical study of yoga and meditation. Supported in this research by Walter Miles, an eminent professor of psychology, Behanan wrote a book about yoga that described quantitative studies of his own yogic breathing. During 72 days of experiments at Yale, he found that one breathing exercise, or *pranayama*, increased his oxygen consumption by 24.5%, a second by 18.5%, and a third by 12% (Behanan, 1937; Miles, 1964). This study helped stimulate interest in meditation research by showing that the physiological effects of yoga could be examined in the laboratory (Behanan, 1937). Unlike many tales by travelers to the East, Behanan's straightforward, well-observed account of his laboratory research was free of exaggeration and mystification.

Behanan also studied Indian yogis. He was guided in this work by Swami Kuvalayananda, who promoted yoga research at a center for meditation practice he founded in the 1920s at Lonavla, a hill station near Bombay. Kuvalayananda developed a system of physical culture that included asanas and pranayamas, and he established a yogic therapy for many afflictions. His work was supported by several Indian states, two provincial governments of British India, Indian health agencies, and American foundations. For many years, the results of his laboratory research were published in a quarterly journal, *Yoga Mimamsa*, which also provided instruction on postures, breathing exercises, and other disciplines. Many people interested in yoga research visited Lonavla, among them psychologists Basu Bagchi of the University of Michigan Medical Center and M. A. Wenger of UCLA, who gave new impetus to meditation studies in the 1950s. From the 1920s into the 1960s, Swami Kuvalayananda did much to promote the scientific study of yoga.

In 1935 a French cardiologist, Therese Brosse, took an electrocardiograph to India and studied yogis who said they could stop their heart.

According to Brosse's published report, readings produced by a single EKG lead and pulse recordings indicated that the heart potentials and pulse of one of her subjects decreased almost to zero, where they stayed for several seconds (Brosse, 1946). Her finding was criticized, though, by Wenger, Bagchi, and B.K. Anand in their later, more thorough studies of yogic adepts (see below). Brosse also studied a yogi who was buried for ten hours, and described other examples of self-control she had witnessed. Like Behanan and Swami Kuvalayananda, she helped promote the idea that yogic feats could be studied with scientific instruments.

The instrumented study of yogic functioning was expanded by Bagchi, Wenger, and Anand. Anand was then chairman of the Department of Physiology at the All-India Institute of Medical Sciences in Delhi. Their landmark studies during the late 1950s were reported in American scientific journals. Along with studies of Zen masters by Akira Kasamatsu and Tomio Hirai in Japan (see below) the Indian studies gave new momentum to meditation research. For five months in 1957, Bagchi and Wenger traveled through India with an eight-channel electro-encephalograph and accessory instruments to record respiration, skin temperature, skin conductance, and finger blood-volume changes. During their trip they established experiments in Calcutta, Madras, Lonavla, and New Delhi, and conducted further tests in homes and a mountain retreat (Bagchi and Wenger 1957; Wenger and Bagchi, 1961; Wenger et al., 1961; Bagchi, 1969). Among the subjects they examined, one could perspire from his forehead upon command in his freezing Himalayan retreat; a second could regurgitate at will to cleanse himself (Wenger and Bagchi, 1961). Three others altered their heartbeats so that they could not be heard with a stethoscope, though EKG and plethysmographic records showed that their hearts were active and their pulses had not disappeared.[28] In tests to compare relaxation in a supine position with seated meditation, Bagchi and Wenger found that four yoga students had faster heart rates, lower finger temperatures, greater palmar sweating, and higher blood pressure during meditation, though their respiration rates were reduced. Five yogis given similar tests exhibited even faster heart rates, lower finger temperatures, greater palmar conductance, and higher blood pressures during meditation than the students, though their breathing was slower. Such differences suggested that for these yogis meditation was an active rather than a passive process (Wenger and Bagchi, 1961).

Bagchi and Wenger also studied the effects of breathing exercises and found that some of their subjects, especially experienced ones, could produce bidirectional changes in every autonomic variable that the experimenters measured. Though the two psychologists found that their subjects exhibited some dramatic physiological changes, they were cautious in drawing conclusions about yogic claims in general. "Direct voluntary control of autonomic functions is probably rare among yogis," they wrote. "When such control is claimed, intervening voluntary mechanisms are usually employed." They made this qualification, however: "We have met many dedicated yogis who described experiences to us that few Western scientists have heard of and none has investigated. It is possible that the mere presence of a foreigner precludes optimum results"(Wenger and Bagchi, 1961).

Other researchers have confirmed the discovery by Bagchi and Wenger that some subjects exhibit more than one pattern of physiological activity during their yogic practices. N.N. Das and H. Gastaut studied seven Indian yogis, who registered no muscular electrical activity during periods of complete immobility though their heart rates accelerated in almost perfect parallel with accelerations of their brain waves during moments of ecstasy. The most accomplished among these seven subjects, moreover, exhibited "progressive and very spectacular modifications" in their EEG records during their deepest meditations, including recurrent beta rhythms of 18-20 cycles per second in the Rolandic area of the brain, a generalized fast activity of small amplitude as high as 40-45 cycles per second with occasional amplitudes reaching 30 to 50 microvolts, and the reappearance of slower alpha waves after *samadhi*, or ecstasy, ended. In summarizing their study, Das and Gastaut concluded that:

> The modifications [we] recorded during very deep meditation are much more dramatic than those known up till now, which leads us to suppose that western subjects are far from being able to attain the yogi state of mental concentration.

> It is probable that this supreme concentration of attention ... is responsible for the perfect insensibility of the yogi during samadhi; this insensibility, accompanied by immobility and pallor, often led people to describe this state as sleep, lethargy, anesthesia, or coma. The electro-encephalographic evidence here described contradicts such opinions and suggests that a state of

intense generalized cortical stimulation is sufficient to explain
such states without having to invoke associated processes of
diffuse or local inhibition (Das and Gastaut, 1955).

Das and Gastaut's conclusion does not contradict the widespread
findings of subsequent meditation studies that many or most meditators
experience the trophotropic or relaxation response described by E.
Gellhorn, W. Kiely, Herbert Benson, and other researchers (Gellhorn and
Kiely, 1972; and Benson, 1975). Most subjects in meditation studies do not
experience yogic ecstasy and so do not exhibit the cortical excitement
that Das and Gastaut observed. Furthermore, different kinds of religious
practice produce different types of experience accompanied by different
types of physiological change. Kasamatsu and Hirai's Zen masters, for
example, exhibited high-amplitude alpha and theta waves, not beta waves,
during their deepest meditations (see below).

Further evidence that contemplative practice produces different
physiological profiles was provided by B.K. Anand, G.S. Chhina, and Baldev
Singh, who found that four yogis exhibited persistent alpha activity with
increased amplitude during trance. These four yogis exhibited no alpha-
wave blocking when they were bombarded with loud banging, strong lights,
and other sensory stimuli, and two of them showed persistent alpha
activity while holding their hands in ice-cold water for forty-five to fifty-
five minutes(Anand, Chhina, and Singh, 1961a). The yogis in this experiment
exhibited physiological differences during meditation from at least two
other groups of accomplished meditators. They did not exhibit alpha
blocking in response to strong stimuli, in contrast to the Zen masters
studied by Kasamatsu and Hirai (see below). Nor did they exhibit the beta
waves that appeared on the EEGs of Das and Gastaut's subjects. The
difference from the Zen masters probably resulted from a basic difference
in focus between the two groups, the yogis having withdrawn their
attention from external stimuli, whereas the Zen masters remained aware
of their external environment. Their difference from Das and Gastaut's
yogis, on the other hand, might have been due to differences between
their styles of meditation, the conditions of the experiments, or the
qualities of their experience. The strong stimuli Anand gave his subjects, for
example, may well have prevented the more ecstatic absorptions experienced by Das and Gastaut's yogis. The published reports of the Das-
Gastaut and Anand-Chhina-Singh experiments do not provide enough
detail to fully explain their different results, but they remind us that there

are different kinds of contemplative experience. Roland Fischer, Julian Davidson, and other researchers have proposed some ways in which internal states might be correlated with different physiological profiles (Fischer, 1971; and Davidson, 1976).

In a study published in 1958, the Indian researchers G.G. Satyanarayanamurthi and B.P. Shastry described a yogi whose heart kept beating for thirty seconds even though his radial pulse could not be felt and his heart could not be heard with a stethoscope. This yogi's EKG showed no abnormalities, moreover, and finger plethysmography showed that his pulse was present though greatly reduced. The two researchers claimed that fluoroscopy conducted while the yogi was lying down showed that for several 30-second periods the beating of his heart was just a "flicker along the left border below the pulmonary conus and in the apical segment of the left ventrical." They concluded that he achieved this control through the Valsalva maneuver.[29]

Elmer Green and Alyce Green, with their colleagues at the Menninger Foundation in Topeka, Kansas, also observed exhibitions of yogic heart control. Their subject, Swami Rama, while sitting perfectly still, produced an atrial flutter of 306 beats per minute that lasted for sixteen seconds. During a fibrillation of this kind, a section of the heart oscillates rapidly while its chambers do not fill and its valves do not work properly, but Swami Rama gave no sign that the maneuver caused him any pain or heart damage. The swami also produced an 11F difference between the left and right sides of his right palm. While he did this, the left side of his palm turned pink and the right side gray (Green and Green, 1977).

Yogis frequently use abdominal contractions to slow their heart rate rather than intervening more directly through the central nervous system. Curiously, though, an earlier study had examined a man with no yogic training at all who could stop his heart without such maneuvers, simply by relaxing and "allowing everything to stop." By this procedure, he could induce a gradual slowing of his pulse until he started to faint, at which point he would take a deep breath. When EKG tests showed that his heartbeat did indeed disappear, the doctor who examined him concluded that the man's cardiac arrest was induced through some mechanism which, although under voluntary control, is not known to the patient himself. Careful observation did not reveal any breath-holding or Valsalva maneuver. Apparently the patient simply abolished all sympathetic tone by complete mental and physical relaxation (McClure, 1959).

Like heart stopping, the live burial of yogis has excited the interest of several researchers. A physician, Rustom Jal Vakil, published an account in the British journal *Lancet* of such a confinement that was witnessed by some 10,000 people near Bombay in February 1950. According to Vakil, an emaciated sadhu named Ramdasji sat cross-legged in a subterranean 216-cubic-foot cubicle and remained there for sixty-two hours. His pulse remained steady at eighty beats per minute; his blood pressure was 112/78; and his respiratory rate fluctuated from eight to ten breaths per minute. Though he had some scratches and cuts, Vakil wrote, Ramdasji appeared "none the worse for his grueling experience" (Vakil, 1950).

In June 1956, a more closely observed study of yogic confinement was conducted under the auspices of the All-India Institute of Mental Health in Bangalore with a Hatha yogi, Krishna Iyengar. Hoenig, a psychiatrist from the University of Manchester, witnessed the experiment and described it in a review of yoga research published in 1968 (Hoenig, 1968). According to Hoenig's report, a pit some two by three by four feet was dug on the institute's grounds and covered with wire meshing, a rubber sheet, and cotton carpet. An electrode junction box connected to an EEG and an EKG was placed in the pit along with instruments to measure temperature and concentration of gas. The yogi was confined for nine hours. When he was released he immediately walked about the grounds, according to Hoenig's firsthand account, and demonstrated athletic feats including a headstand with his legs in the lotus position. The percentage of carbon dioxide in the air in his enclosure, which was 1.34% at the beginning of the experiment, was only 3.8% at the end, lower than would normally be expected. Iyengar's heart rate gradually slowed from 100 to 40 beats a minute in recurring twenty- to twenty-five-minute cycles, but his EKG record did not register any other abnormality and the cycles did not coincide with his breathing or brain-wave patterns. The yogi's EEG showed a normal waking record for the full nine hours, characterized by a stable alpha rhythm of 50 microvolts with no evidence of sleep or interference caused by physical movement. From these records, the experimenters concluded that their subject lay motionless and wide awake, without the active cognition that would have reduced or eliminated his alpha rhythm. Iyengar said he had maintained the shavasana, or corpse pose, using ujjaya breathing while remembering the names of God. He was surprised that his heart had speeded and slowed, and could not explain why it had done so. It beat normally, however, after the experiment.

Because the earthen pits used in most yogic confinements leak oxygen and carbon dioxide, Anand, Chhina, and Singh tested a yogi named Ramanand in an airtight glass and metal box, once for eight hours and again for ten hours. The yogi's average oxygen use during the first experiment decreased from the basal rate of 19.5 liters per hour to 12.2, and during the second experiment to 13.3 liters per hour. His carbon dioxide output went down during both experiments. Ramanand, moreover, did not exhibit any rapid breathing or speeded heart rate as the oxygen in his box diminished and carbon dioxide increased. "Sri Ramanand Yogi could reduce his oxygen intake and carbon dioxide output to levels significantly lower than his requirements under basal conditions," Anand and his colleagues wrote. "It appears from this study that [he] could voluntarily reduce his basal metabolic rate on both occasions he went into the box."[30]

During a remarkable experiment reported by L.K. Kothari and associates, a yogi was buried for eight days in an earthen pit and connected by leads to an EKG in a nearby laboratory. After the pit was boarded up, the subject's heart rate sometimes went as high as fifty beats per minute, until a straight line appeared on the EKG tracing when the yogi had been in the pit for twenty-nine hours. There had been no slowing of his heart immediately before the straight line appeared, nor any sign of electrical disturbance, but the experimenters proceeded with certainty that their subject had not died. Suspecting that their EKG leads had been deliberately or accidentally disconnected, they checked their machine and continued to monitor its tracings. To their astonishment, it started to register electrical activity some seven days later, about a half hour before the yogi's scheduled disinterment. "After some initial disturbance," they wrote, "a normal configuration appeared. The [speeded heart rate] was again there but there was no other abnormality." When the pit was opened, the yogi was found sitting in the same posture he had started in, but in a stuporous condition. In accounting for his remarkable EKG record, the experimenters argued that a disconnection of the EKG lead would have produced obvious markings on the tracings in their laboratory, as they found when they tried to simulate ways in which the yogi might have tinkered with it.

Furthermore, the yogi was ignorant about such machines, and the pit was completely dark. If the machine had malfunctioned in some way they could not ascertain, it seemed an extraordinary coincidence that it started again just a half hour before their subject's scheduled release. Apparently, the yogi was operating with some kind of internal clock that did not depend upon the daily cycles of light and darkness, for the most likely cause of the straight line on his EKG tracing was a dramatic decrease in the activity of his heart. Kothari and his colleagues finally could not account for this remarkable cardiac record (Kothari et al., 1973).

Studies of Zen Buddhist Monks

In a study that attracted much attention among meditation and biofeedback researchers during the 1960s, Akira Kasamatsu and Tomio Hirai, physicians at the University of Tokyo, studied the EEG changes exhibited during meditation by Zen teachers and their disciples (forty-eight in all) from Soto and Rinzai centers in Japan. For experimental control, they studied the EEGs of twenty-two subjects with no experience at meditation. They made EEG recordings; recorded their subjects' pulse rates, respiration, and galvanic skin response; and tested their responses to sensory stimuli during meditation. The recordings on the Zen monks were made during a weeklong retreat, or *sesshin*, at a Zendo, except for a few tests at the experimenters' laboratory. The Zen teachers and their most experienced students exhibited a typical progression of brain-wave activity during meditation, which Kasamatsu and Hirai divided into four stages:

> Stage 1: Characterized by the appearance of alpha waves in spite of opened eyes.
> Stage 2: Characterized by an increase in amplitude of persistent alpha waves.
> Stage 3: Characterized by a decrease in alpha frequency.
> Stage 4: Characterized by the appearance of rhythmical theta trains (Kasamatsu and Hirai, 1966).

Not all four stages were evident in every Zen practitioner, nor in any of the controls, but a strong correlation existed between the number of stages a given student exhibited and that student's length of time in Zen training. This correlation was supported by a Zen teacher's evaluation of each student's proficiency. The teacher ranked the students in three levels, without seeing their EEG records, and his rankings correlated well with Kasamatsu and Hirai's assessment of their EEGs.

The Kasamatsu-Hirai study also revealed significant differences between four Zen masters and four control subjects in their response to repetitive click stimuli. Like the Zen masters, the controls exhibited a blocking of alpha when a click sound first occurred, but they gradually became habituated to such stimuli so that their brain-wave activity no longer responded when a click was made. The Zen masters, however, did not become habituated, but continued to exhibit blocking as long as the stimuli continued. This finding indicates that Zen practice promotes a serene, alert awareness that is consistently responsive to both external and internal stimuli (Kasamatsu et al., 1957; Hirai, 1960; and Kasamatsu and Hirai, 1963).

Difficulties of Research with Religious Adepts

Though people testified under oath before the Congregation of Rites that they had seen Saint Teresa of Avila or Saint Joseph of Cupertino defy gravity, no scientific studies have recorded instances of levitation. There are at least three possible reasons for this lack of evidence. First, of course, it might be that levitation has never happened. Second, the contemplative traditions might have lost their power to evoke the phenomenon. Third, levitation might only occur during rare and spontaneous ecstasies that cannot be programmed to meet the requirements of a scientific experiment. Superordinary lifting from the ground, if it in fact occurs, would require an improbable set of circumstances which a scientist would be lucky to witness. Levitation, like other holy powers, would have to be caught "in the wild." In a laboratory, with wires attached to his head and a thermometer up his rectum, a yogi or lama is unlikely to exhibit a capacity that is rare in any case. In studies of extraordinary functioning there is a trade-off between robust results and scientific precision. Uninhibited by recording machines and safety rules, for example, the Maharaja Runjeet Singh could bury Haridas for forty days. More recent studies of yogic confinement, however, have been constrained by procedural controls and humane considerations.

Furthermore, there is often a disjunction between a scientist's attitude toward exceptional powers and an adept's ideas about them. Elmer Green, for example, described differences he had with the healer Jack Schwarz in interpreting Schwarz's intuitive diagnosis of illness. According to Schwarz, the question was:

> Are the auras one sees always radiatory patterns of energy from
> the human body ... or are they automatic mental projections of
> one kind or another that are used psychologically to interpret a

"knowing"? Sometimes when we "know" something in this way we tend to "see" it in the same way that we see a memory (Green and Green, 1977, p. 240).

Green was sympathetic to Schwarz, however, realizing that a scientist's constant doubt can inhibit or destroy a psychic's intuitions. This fundamental difference between scientists and psychics, Green wrote:

Need not cause problems if each takes time to understand the framework in which the other necessarily operates. If the psychic tries to pull apart every perception in order to find out if it is incorrect, so as to better determine the "truth," what is most likely to be pulled apart is the faculty of "seeing." The talent for perceiving might well fade away. On the other hand, if scientists stopped trying to find alternate explanations for the facts, they might get lost in a maze of [incoherent] ideas. For both scientists and mystics, however, the area of facts rather than interpretations is common ground. Excluding the opinions of fanatics, most of the arguments that we are aware of between the two camps have revolved around interpretations. Because psychics almost always have idiosyncratic factors in their frames of reference, scientists often do not understand them. And psychics do not understand what seems to them to be a destructive attitude on the part of scientists (Green and Green, 1977, p. 242).

Sympathy between scientists and adepts was evident in Swami Kuvalayananda's projects noted above, and in other experimenter-subject teams described in the preceding pages. Even the stern mutual challenge between Haridas and Maharaja Runjeet Singh exhibited an exemplary, if somewhat perverse, cooperation. Productive study of extraordinary functioning requires understanding between accomplished subjects and imaginative experimenters.

Contemporary Meditation Research

Meditation research increased dramatically during the 1970s and 1980s, particularly in the United States. This burgeoning effort was stimulated in part by the studies of yogis and Zen masters noted in the previous section, and in part by the publication of landmark studies by Herbert Benson and Keith Wallace in *Science*, the *American Journal of Physiology*, and *Scientific American* between 1970 and 1972 (R. Wallace, 1970;

Wallace et al., 1971b; Wallace and Benson, 1972). The Transcendental Meditation Society supported much of this work, though its enthusiastic claims and advertising efforts caused doubts among some researchers about the highly favorable outcomes in studies it sponsored (Shapiro, 1982). These doubts led to further research, which has either contradicted, tempered, or confirmed the TM-sponsored claims. Since the early 1970s, more than a thousand studies of meditation have been reported in English-language journals, books, and graduate theses. The range of outcomes included in this research has grown considerably since the studies of yogis and Zen masters by Bagchi, Wenger, Kasamatsu, and Hirai. Cardiovascular, cortical, hormonal, and metabolic changes, several behavioral effects, and alterations of consciousness resulting from meditation have been explored in recent years. The medical instrumentation, psychological tests, and methods of analysis used in such experiments have been improved, and the range of subject populations has been enlarged to include different kinds of subject groups. This growth in sophistication of method is gradually improving our scientific understanding of meditation in ways that complement the insights contained in the traditional contemplative literature. However, the overall picture of results on the subject of meditation produced by modern research remains uneven. Some effects have appeared consistently, but others have not.

The apparent inconsistencies defining the effects of meditation can be accounted for in various ways. Some physiological processes, perhaps, are unaffected by meditation, no matter how proficient or experienced the meditator might be; or perhaps they are affected to an insignificant degree. For some changes, such as amino acid concentrations in the blood, there has not been enough research to establish a consistent picture, partly because there has not been as much interest in these variables as in the effect of meditation on blood pressure, heart rate, and other indices that have an obvious bearing on health. Taking blood samples during meditation, moreover, is harder to accomplish than recording blood pressure or skin responses.

Individual differences also present a special problem for understanding the results of meditation studies, because subject populations have included people of both sexes, all ages, various levels of education, and different kinds of social background. Many subjects have been college students with no previous experience at meditating; others have been recent converts to religious groups; but only a few have been highly skilled in spiritual practice. The incentives to concentrate during experimental sessions have also varied. Some subjects have wanted success for religious or other reasons, while others seem not to have been well motivated. And differences between meditation styles also complicate the results of such research. Though most studies have used some type of quiet concentration, some have used active methods such as rapid breathing. Julian Davidson, Roland Fischer, and others have distinguished between two classes of meditation, those that relax and those that excite, associating their effects with the trophotropic and ergotropic conditions of the central nervous system modeled by Gellhorn and Kiely (Davidson, 1976; Fischer, 1971, 1976; Gellhorn and Kiely, 1972).

The results of scientific research on the subject of meditation are accumulating now, forming a publicly accessible body of empirical data that can serve generations to come. Unfortunately, however, these data are derived mainly from beginning practitioners of meditation, and taken as a whole do not reflect the richness of experience described in traditional contemplative teachings. They are also limited by the conventional scientific insistence that results be repeatable. Certain important experiences occur only rarely in meditation, and a science that disregards them loses important empirical results. For these reasons, contemporary research does not illumine the full range of experience described in the contemplative scriptures and the oral traditions from which they come. Modern studies give us only a first picture of the foothills, with a few glimpses of the peaks. Still, what they give us corresponds in several ways with traditional accounts.

CHAPTER 2

Physiological Effects
by Michael Murphy and Steven Donovan

*[While meditation can be considered as a cognitive strategy by which
consciousness gains control over normally non-conscious states of
awareness, including involuntary bodily processes, the physiology of
meditation has received more attention than any other subject from
Western scientists quite out of proportion to all other dimensions of
meditative experience.*

*Historically, this is largely because, for three hundred years, the dualism
of Descartes has required an absolute separation of mind and body,
while its handmaiden and more recent dictum of research, scientific
positivism, asserts mechanistically that what is immediately physical
and material constitutes all there is to reality. Hence, the most visible
and palpable form of a phenomenon is the only proper object of
scientific scrutiny.*

*Modern researchers, by virtue of the fact that they are engaged in
applying the methods of reductionistic science, even as they apply such
methods to seemingly disreputable topics, cannot avoid these con-
straints. Thus the physiology of meditation has been the starting point
and remains at the center of most research efforts. Ed.]*

The Cardiovascular System

Heart Rate

Many contemporary studies have indicated that the heart rate usually
slows in quiet meditation and quickens during active disciplines or moments of ecstasy, as we would expect from contemplative writings that
describe the calming effect of silent meditation[31] and the stimulation of
exercises such as Tantric visualization or devotional chanting.[32]

Most studies of Transcendental Meditation (TM), Zen Buddhist sitting,
Herbert Benson's "relaxation response," and other calming forms of
meditation indicate that meditating subjects generally experience a
lowering of the heart rate. The results of such studies vary to some
degree, since they depend on different kinds of subject groups and various
experimental procedures, with some showing an average decline of seven

beats or more per minute among their subjects and some showing two or three beats per minute among some of their subjects. Bagga and Gandhi (1983) found an average decline as high as fifteen beats per minute among some of their subjects. Some studies indicate that meditation lowers the heart rate more than biofeedback, progressive relaxation, other therapies, or simple sitting, while other studies indicate that these various activities have an equivalent effect on the heart rate. Once again, such differences in outcome can be accounted for by differences among subjects and experimental designs.

A decline in heart rate is more pronounced among experienced meditators, according to a few studies, though here too the evidence is not unanimous. The only generalization we can make safely now is that some subject groups demonstrate an average lowering of heart rate during meditation, and that some experienced individuals may achieve a permanent lowering of the heart rate with continued practice.

In studies involving active methods such as rapid breathing, though, the heart rate has risen. Such studies suggest that patterns of physiological activity are specific to particular practices.

Julian Davidson (1976), Roland Fischer (1971, 1976), and other researchers have distinguished excitatory from relaxing forms of meditation, associating their effects with the ergotropic and trophotropic conditions of the central nervous system modeled by Gelhorn and Keily (1972). Fischer (1971) has said that the extreme trophotropic state of samadhi sometimes triggers an extreme ergotropic reaction, which may be ecstatic, so that the physiological effects of contemplative activity show wide variability.

The following studies show a decrease in heart rate during meditation. Bono (1984) found that the reduction of heart rate during TM was greater than the reduction resulting from sitting quietly with eyes closed. Delmonte (1984f) found that heart rates were slightly lower during meditation than rest for fifty-two subjects. Holmes et al. (1983), however, found that while meditators had lower heart rates while practicing TM, they did not experience lower arousal than control subjects who were simply resting. See follow-up discussion, particularly Dillbeck and Orme-Johnson (1987), Morrell (1986), and Holmes (1984).

Bagga and Gandhi (1983) compared groups of six TM practitioners and six Shavasana practitioners (relaxing while lying on one's back) with six controls, and found significantly reduced heart rates for both experimental groups versus the control group. Cummings (1984) observed reduced heart rates for those practicing a combination of meditation and exercise. Throll (1982) found that a Transcendental Meditation group displayed a more significant decrease in heart rate than a group using Jacobson's progressive relaxation.

Pollard and Ashton (1982) divided sixty subjects into six groups in a comparison of heart rate decrease obtained by visual feedback, auditory feedback, combined visual and auditory feedback, instructions to decrease heart rate without biofeedback, sitting quietly, and abbreviated relaxation training. A comparison group of meditators with a minimum of six years of experience was also studied. The results indicated that there was no advantage of a heart rate decrease task for subjects receiving visual, auditory, or combined biofeedback, though all groups showed evidence of a decline in heart rate over the testing session. The meditation group showed the greatest overall decline, with a decrease in heart rate of approximately seven beats per minute, versus three beats per minute for the groups using biofeedback techniques.

Cuthbert et al. (1981) had results demonstrating clear superiority for meditators using Benson's relaxation response versus heart rate biofeedback, especially when the subject experimenter relationship was supportive. Lang et al. (1979) placed the heart rate decrease for advanced TM meditators with more than four years of practice at 9%. Bauhofer (1978) found that the heart rates of experienced TM meditators were lowered by TM more than those of less experienced TM meditators. Corey (1977) and Routt (1977) reported that Transcendental Meditation appeared to decrease heart rate under nonstress conditions. Glueck and Stroebel (1975), Wallace and Benson (1972), Wallace et al. (1971c), and Wallace (1971) found that the heart rate decreased from three to five beats per minute during Transcendental Meditation. Reports of reduced heart rates during meditation extend back to Paul (1969), Karambelkar et al. (1968), Anand and Chhina (1961), Wenger and Bagchi (1961), Anand and Chhina (1961), Bagchi and Wenger (1957), and Das and Gastaut (1955).

Kothari et al. (1973) reported the case of a yogi who was confined to a small underground pit for eight days and continuously monitored with an EKG. From the second day until the eighth, EKG activity was below a recordable level, indicating that the yogi had either stopped his heart or greatly decreased its electrical activity. The authors believe that the yogi could not have tampered with the EKG leads without creating an obvious electrical disturbance.

Some studies indicate that heart rates increase under certain circumstances, such as deeply absorbed trance (samadhi) [see Lehrer et al. (1980), Parulker et al. (1974), Wenger and Bagchi (1961), and Das and Gastaut (1955)]. Other research shows no consistent changes in heart rate with the practice of Ananda Marga Yoga or progressive relaxation [see Gash and Karliner (1978), Elson et al. (1977), Travis et al. (1976), Wenger et al. (1961), and Bagchi and Wenger (1957)].

We could not find accounts in the traditional literature describing the number of heartbeats one should expect during meditation, with which we could compare the numbers in modern studies. Contemplative masters did not share the scientific passion for quantitative analysis and generally appreciated the differences in physiology and temperament among their followers. They also did not have the means to measure bodily changes precisely, and generally wouldn't have used them if they had.

Redistribution of Blood Flow

Blood flow is directly or indirectly manipulated for mental clarity, health, increased energy, or the promotion of religious emotion through hatha yoga postures, breathing exercises, prostrations, tai chi movements, dervish dancing, and other activities associated with the contemplative traditions. Traditional teachers could not measure blood flow with scientific exactness, of course, but some of them could skillfully guide their students' practice through empathy, intuition, and kinesthetic feel, and in doing so they sometimes looked for bodily signs related to blood circulation, such as flushing of the face and chest and changes in skin tone and complexion.[33] The picture of meditation's effect on blood flow provided by modern studies is quite preliminary, though. Most of it comes from TM-sponsored research.

Delmonte (1984f) tested fifty-two subjects and found that meditators showed a significantly greater increase in digital blood volume during meditation than rest. Jevning, Wilson, and O'Halloran (1982) studied muscle and skin blood flow and metabolism during states of decreased activation in TM. They concluded that acute decline of forearm oxygen consumption has been observed during an acute, wakeful behaviorally induced rest/relaxation state. This change of tissue respiration was not associated with variation of rate of forelimb lactate generation. Since forearm blood flow did not change significantly during this behavior, the decline of oxygen consumption by forearm was due almost solely to decreased rate of oxygen extraction. Decreased muscle metabolism was a likely contributor to these observations. The occurrence of sleep was not related to the metabolic change. The lack of coupling between the metabolic and blood flow changes during this state of decreased activation suggests limitation of the hypothesis of obligatory coupling between systemic and/or regional cardiovascular and metabolic function.

Earlier, Jevning and Wilson (1978) reported that TM increased cardiac output among twenty-seven subjects by an average of 16% (ml/min measured by dye dilution methods), decreased hepatic blood flow by an average of 34% (ml/min measured by clearance methods), and decreased renal blood flow by an average of 29% (ml/min measured by clearance methods), suggesting an increase of approximately 44% in the nonrenal, nonhepatic component of blood flow (versus an increase of approximately 12% for an eyes-closed rest-relaxation control group). Increased cerebral or skin blood flow may account for part of this redistribution.

Jevning et al. (1976) found an average 15% increase in cardiac output, an average 20% decline in liver blood flow, and an average 20% decrease in renal blood flow among a group of six meditators practicing TM. A control group of six showed no change in cardiac output and liver blood flow, and a significant decline in renal blood flow. The authors believe that decreased skin and muscle blood flow was suggested by other, indirect data, and that since cardiac output increases and all measured organ blood flows decrease, it is possible that cerebral perfusion increases markedly during TM. Jevning et al.'s findings were a surprise because earlier studies had indicated a decrease in cardiac output of 25% during TM (versus a decrease of about 20% in deep stage-four sleep) [see Wallace (1970)].

Wallace et al. (1971a) speculated that the fall in blood lactate during meditation might be due to increased skeletal muscle blood flow with consequent increased aerobic metabolism. These researchers referred to Riechert (1976), who recorded forearm blood flow increases of 30% with unchanged finger blood flow (using a plethysmograph). Jevning and Wilson (1978) found that frontal cerebral blood flow increased an average of 65% during TM for ten teachers of the technique (five to eight years of regular practice), and remained elevated afterwards, with brief increases up to 100-200% (measured by quadripolar rheoencephalography). Levander et al. (1972) measured forearm blood flow (using a water plethysmograph) in five subjects 180 times and reported that the pretest period mean blood flow of 1.41 ml/100ml tissue volume/min increased to 1.86 ml/100ml tissue volume/min during TM, and returned to pretest values during post-testing. Wallace and Benson (1972) found an increase in forearm blood flow of 32% for their TM subjects.

Blood Pressure and Hypertension

There is strong evidence that meditation helps lower blood pressure in people who are normal or moderately hypertensive. This finding has been replicated by more than nineteen studies, some of which have shown systolic reductions among their subjects of 25 mmHg or more. In some studies a combination of meditation with biofeedback or other relaxation techniques proved to be more effective than meditation alone for some subjects. Several studies, however, have shown that relief from high blood pressure diminishes or disappears entirely if meditation is discontinued, and few people with acute hypertension have experienced lower blood pressure in experiments of this kind.

At the time of this writing, speculation regarding the mechanisms mediating meditation's beneficial effects on high blood pressure appears to be inconclusive. Meditation often helps relax the large muscle groups pressing on the circulatory system in various parts of the body. It might also help relax the small muscles that control the blood vessels themselves; when that happens, the resulting elasticity of blood vessel walls would help reduce the pressure inside them. Other mechanisms may be involved, which further research will reveal. The following studies explored meditation's effect on blood pressure and hypertension:

Cort (1988a) It was hypothesized that the large variability of results in different studies on the effect of meditation on hypertension may be due to differences in compliance to the meditation regimens. This study of fifty-one black adults supports the claim that greater compliance to a meditation program leads to greater decreases in blood pressure.

Delmonte (1984f) Forty nonmeditators and twelve experienced Transcendental Meditators were randomly assigned to four experimental cells devised to control for order and expectation effects. All fifty-two (female) subjects were continuously monitored in seven physiological measures during both meditation and rest. Each subject was her own control in an experiment comparing meditation to rest. Analysis of variance on change scores calculated from both initial and running (intertrial) baselines revealed small but significant condition effects for all variables except diastolic BP. With respect to systolic BP, the nonmeditators showed a significantly larger drop from initial baseline during meditation than during rest. With respect to running baseline, the meditators demonstrated a significantly smaller increase in systolic blood pressure with the complete trial data and a greater decrease with the end-of-trial data during meditation than during rest.

Wallace et al. (1983b) This study measured systolic blood pressure using a standard mercury sphygmomanometer on 112 Transcendental Meditators. The subjects had a mean systolic blood pressure 13.7 to 24.5 less than the population mean. The analysis also showed that meditators with more than five years of experience had a mean systolic blood pressure 7.5 lower than meditators with less than five years of experience.

Bagga and Gandhi (1983) The authors studied a group of eighteen people who were equally divided into a TM, Shavasana (relaxing while lying on one's back), or control group. After twelve weeks of practicing, the TM and Shavasana groups showed significant declines in systolic blood pressure as high as 10 mmHg, whereas the control group demonstrated no decline.

Hafner (1982) Twenty-one hypertension patients who had been randomly assigned to eight one-hour sessions of either meditation training, meditation plus biofeedback-aided relaxation, or a nontreatment control group were studied. Statistically significant falls in systolic and diastolic blood pressure occurred after both training programs, although overall reductions in blood pressure were not significantly greater in either program than in the control group. Meditation plus biofeedback-aided relaxation produced falls in diastolic blood pressure earlier in the training program than did meditation alone. All patients practiced meditation regularly between training sessions, but the amount of practice did not correlate with the amount of blood pressure reduction after training.

Seer and Raeburn (1980) Forty-one unmedicated hypertensives were randomly assigned to three groups: TM training, placebo control (TM training without a mantra), and no-treatment control. The results showed modest reductions in blood pressure in both treatment groups, compared with no treatment, with diastolic percentage reductions reaching significance. There was considerable subject variation in response, with an overall mean decline in diastolic blood pressure of 8-10% on a three-month follow-up.

Surwit et al. (1978) This study compared the separate effects of three procedures for the reduction of high blood pressure in three treatment groups of eight patients, each with medically verified borderline hypertension. The three treatment groups used the following procedures: (a) biofeedback for simultaneous reductions in systolic blood pressure and heart rate; (b) biofeedback for reductions in integrated forearm and frontalis muscle electromyographic activity; and (c) meditation relaxation based on the relaxation response procedure developed by Herbert Benson. Each patient was studied in two baseline sessions, eight training sessions, and a six-week follow-up. Half of the sample returned for a one-year follow-up. Analysis of variance of the three treatment groups over eight training sessions, with twenty trials per session, revealed significant effects for trials within sessions. However, there were no significant main effects or interactions related to differences between the treatment conditions or to changes in blood pressure over the course of training sessions. Although all groups showed moderate reductions in blood pressure as compared to initial values, no technique could be seen to produce a reduction in pressure greater than that observed in the baseline sessions. Blood pressures of patients reporting for the one-year follow-up were not different from pretreatment baseline levels.

Pollack et al. (1977) Twenty hypertensive patients, nine of whom were on stable dosages of hypotensive medication, were taught TM. Blood pressure reductions were 10 mmHg systolic/2 mmHg diastolic after three months and 6 mmHg systolic/2 mmHg diastolic after six months. The only statistically significant reduction in blood pressure occurred after three months. Meditation plus biofeedback produced decreases in diastolic blood pressure earlier in the training program than meditation alone.

Simon et al. (1977) Five borderline hypertensives were taught TM. After they learned the technique and practiced it for an average of thirty-two weeks, their mean blood pressure decreased from 153/101 mmHg to 138/92 mmHg.

Blackwell et al. (1976) Seven subjects on stable dosages of hypotensive medication were taught TM over a nine-twelve week period. They recorded a mean blood pressure reduction of 4 mmHg systolic/2 mmHg diastolic, and 3 mmHg systolic/4 mmHg diastolic during a follow-up six months later, but there were changes in drug treatment during the follow-up period.

Stone and DeLeo (1976) Fourteen hypertensives were taught a "Buddhist" meditation that involved counting breaths in five twenty-minute training sessions over six months. Five hypertensives were used as controls. While supine, the treatment group had mean blood pressure reductions of 9 mmHg systolic/8 mmHg diastolic. While upright, the treatment group had mean blood pressure reductions of 15 mmHg systolic/10 mmHg diastolic. While supine, the control group had mean blood pressure reductions of 1 mmHg systolic/2 mmHg diastolic. While upright, the control group had mean blood pressure reductions of 2 mmHg systolic/0 mmHg diastolic.

Patel and North (1975) Thirty-four hypertensive patients were assigned at random either to six weeks of treatment by yoga relaxation methods with biofeedback or to placebo therapy (general relaxation). Both groups showed a reduction in blood pressure (from 168/100 to 141/84 mmHg in the treated group and from 169/101 to 160/96 mmHg in the control group). The difference was highly significant. The control group was then trained in yoga relaxation, and the blood pressure fell to that of the other group (now used as controls).

Patel (1975a) Thirty-two patients—twenty-one females and eleven males—between the ages of thirty-four and seventy-five years with essential hypertension of known duration from six months to thirteen years were randomly divided into a treatment group and a control group. Fourteen patients in the treatment group and fifteen in the control group were receiving antihypertensive drugs. Baseline blood pressure was first obtained after a twenty-minute rest in the supine position. The patients were given two stress tests: an exercise test (climbing a nine-inch step twenty-five times) and a cold pressor test (immersing the left hand in cold water after alerting the patient sixty seconds in advance) at the beginning and again after six weeks. Blood pressure was taken during the alert, at the end of each test, and every five minutes until it returned to the original value or up to a maximum of forty minutes. In the six weeks between test periods, all patients attended a twice-weekly clinic. The treatment group was given training in relaxation and meditation based on yogic principles, which was reinforced with biofeedback instruments, and group members were asked to practice relaxation and meditation at home twice daily for twenty minutes. In the treatment group there was a significant reduction in the pressure rises as well as in recovery time. Mere repetition of the tests did not influence these indications of stress. When the differences between the groups were compared, all measurements except the systolic pressure rise after exercise showed significant improvement in the treated group.

Patel (1975b) Twenty hypertension patients, nineteen of whom were using hypotensive drugs, were taught yoga, breath meditation, muscle relaxation, and meditation concentration. Their average blood pressure was reduced from 159.1/100.1 mmHg to 138.7/85.9 mmHg. The average blood pressures of twenty control subjects, eighteen of whom were using hypotensive drugs, who rested on a couch for the same number of sessions and were given no relaxation training, was reduced from 163.1/99.1 mmHg to 162.6/97.0 mmHg.

Patel (1975c) Twenty hypertensive patients treated by psychophysical relaxation exercises were followed up monthly for twelve

The Physical and Psychological Effects of Meditation

months. Age- and sex-matched hypertensive controls were similarly followed up for nine months. Statistically significant reductions in blood pressure (BP) and antihypertensive drug requirements were satisfactorily maintained in the treatment group. Mere repetition of BP measurements and increased medical attention did not in themselves reduce BP significantly in control patients.

Benson et al. (1974d) Twenty-two borderline hypertensives not using drugs were taught TM, and their mean blood pressure decreased from 146.5/94.6 mmHg during the premeditation control period, lasting 5.7 weeks, to 139.6/90.8 mmHg during the postmeditation experimental period, lasting an average of twenty-five weeks. They were tested throughout the premeditation and postmeditation periods.

Benson et al. (1974f) Fourteen hypertension patients on drugs were taught the relaxation response. During a control period of 5.6 weeks, blood pressure did not change significantly from day to day, and averaged 145.6/91.9 mmHg. During an experimental period of twenty weeks, blood pressure decreased to 135.0/87.0 mmHg.

Patel (1973) Twenty hypertension patients using hypotensive drugs were taught yoga, breath meditation, muscle relaxation, and meditation concentration. Their average blood pressure was reduced from 159.1/100.1 mmHg to 138.7/85.9 mmHg. The average blood pressure of twenty control subjects, who rested on a couch for the same number of sessions and who were given no relaxation training, was reduced from 163.1/99.1 mmHg to 162.6/97.0 mmHg.

Deabler et al. (1973) In this study three groups of hypertensive patients were tested. Six subjects, who were taught progressive relaxation and hypnosis in eight to nine sessions over four to five days, had average blood pressure reductions of 17 mmHg systolic/ 19 mmHg diastolic during their experimental sessions. Nine subjects taking hypotensive medication, who were taught progressive relaxation and hypnosis in eight to nine sessions over four to five days, experienced BP reductions of 16 mmHg systolic/14 mmHg diastolic during their experimental sessions. A control group of six subjects showed no significant blood pressure changes.

Benson and Wallace (1972a) Twenty-two hypertensives with no meditation experience were given the standard TM training. Their mean blood pressure before meditation was 150/94 mmHg. After four to sixty-three weeks of meditation practice their mean blood pressure was reduced to 141/87 mmHg.

Datey et al. (1969) Forty-seven hypertension patients practiced "Shavasana," a yogic breathing concentration and muscle relaxation technique, thirty minutes daily for approximately thirty weeks. Of these forty-seven subjects, ten who did not use antihypertensive drugs had an average systolic blood pressure reduction from 134 to 107 mmHg. A second group of twenty-two subjects, with BP well controlled by antihypertensive drugs, had an average systolic blood pressure reduction from 102 to 100 mmHg. A third group of fifteen subjects, with inadequately controlled blood pressure using antihypertensive drugs, had an average systolic blood pressure reduction from 120 to 110 mmHg. The subjects' average drug requirement was reduced to 32% of the original dosages for the second group. In group three, six patients reduced their drug requirement to 29% of the original, seven patients' dosages were unchanged, and two patients required an increased dosage.

Blood pressure is one of the easiest physiological variables to measure. The evidence just presented shows that many patients with moderate hypertension improve with meditation. Because these studies involved different types of meditation, different levels of meditation experience among subjects, and different kinds of measurement, the mechanisms mediating the improvement are uncertain. Most studies indicate that benefits disappear without continued practice [see Frankel (1976) and Patel (1976)]. Nevertheless, a therapeutic approach to hypertension involving meditation has been shown to be effective [see Patel (1977, 1984)].

Other studies examining the effect of various forms of meditation on blood pressure include: Sothers and Anchor (1989), Kuchera (1987), Mills

(1987), Caudill et al. (1987), Benson (1986), Juhl and Strandgaard (1985), Patel et al. (1985), Friskey (1985), Caudill et al. (1984a, 1984b), Muskatel et al. (1984), Benson and Caudill (1984), Lang (1984), Slaughter (1984), English (1981), Bynum (1980), and Benson et al. (1974c, 1974d).

Other Cardiovascular Changes

Evidence that meditation helps relieve certain forms of cardiovascular disease generally conforms to assertions that yoga, tai chi, and other transformational disciplines promote health. Similarly, evidence that meditators recover more quickly from stressful impacts and demonstrate fewer chronic or inappropriate emergency responses than nonmeditators agrees in a general way with teachings about the alert calm and peace of yogic practice or the effortless but appropriate behavior of Zen Buddhist and Taoist adepts.

For contemporary evidence that meditation assists individuals with forms of cardiovascular disease such as hypercholesterolemia and angina pectoris, see Barr and Benson (1984), Benson (1983c), Benson and Goodale (1981), Cooper and Aygen (1979), Zamara et al. (1977), Benson (1976), Benson et al. (1976), Benson and Wallace (1972a), and Tulpule (1971).

Goleman and Schwartz (1976) exposed thirty experienced meditators to a stressor film, and measured responses by skin conductance, heart rate, self-report, and personality scales. The heart rates of both experienced and inexperienced meditators recovered from stressor impacts more quickly than those of control subjects, demonstrating a psychophysiological configuration in stress situations opposite to that seen in stress-related syndromes. In a study by Glueck and Stroebel (1975), meditators demonstrated fewer chronic or inappropriate activations of the emergency response.

The Cortical System

EEG: Alpha Activity

Evidence indicating that meditation leads to an increase in alpha rhythms (slow, high amplitude brain waves extending to anterior channels and ranging in frequency from eight to thirteen cycles per second) is extensive. The following studies, using many types of meditation, with subject groups of one to more than fifty including beginners and Zen masters, reach that conclusion: Delmonte (1984f), Daniels and Fernhall

(1984), Stigsby et al. (1981), Lehrer et al. (1980), Wachsmuth et al. (1980), West (1980a), Dostalek et al. (1979), Corby et al. (1978), Pelletier and Peper (1977b), Elson et al. (1977), Kasamatsu et al. (1957), Kras (1977), Fenwick et al. (1977), Glueck and Stroebel (1975), Tebecis (1975), Williams and West (1975), Woolfolk (1975), Banquet (1973 and 1972), Vassiliadis (1973), Benson et al. (1973a), Wallace et al.(1971c), Akishige (1970), Wallace (1970), Kasamatsu and Hirai (1963, 1966, 1969a, 1969b), Kamiya (1968, 1969a), Anand et al. (1961a), Hirai (1960), Hirai et al. (1959), Bagchi and Wenger (1957), and Das and Gastaut (1955) [see also the EEG research review of Echenhofer and Coombs (1987)].

In contrast, some studies report a decrease in alpha activity during meditation. See Jacobs and Lubar (1989), Warrenburg et al. (1980), and Tebecis (1975). A possible explanation may be found in differences in the initial level of relaxation of subjects.

Gayten (1978) examined the EEGs of tai chi practitioners (a form of moving meditation) using a Medi-Log Ambulatory Monitor and did not find brain-wave patterns similar to those of meditators. After reviewing their own and other studies, Jevning and O'Halloran (1984) concluded that various TM-correlated changes persisted after the cessation of TM practice, particularly EEG changes of the kind reported in the studies we have listed here.

Sim and Tsoi (1992) investigated the effects of three centrally acting drugs (naloxone, diazepam, and flumazenil) on the significant increase in the intermediate alpha frequency of the EEG that accompanied meditation in an experienced meditator. They found no significant changes, which would indicate that the EEG correlates of meditation are not causally related to the rise or fall of endogenous opioid peptides or benzodiazepinelike substances in the brain.

EEG: Theta Activity

A characteristic brain-wave pattern of long-term meditators includes strong bursts of frontally dominant theta rhythms (five to seven cycles per second), during which meditators report peaceful, drifting, and generally pleasant experiences with intact self-awareness. The following studies have reported this pattern: Jacobs and Lubar (1989), Delmonte (1984f), West (1979a), Hebert and Lehmann (1977), Elson et al. (1977), Pelletier and Peper (1977b), Fenwick et al. (1977), Banquet and Sailhan (1977), Ghista et al. (1976), Levine (1976), Tebecis (1975), Glueck and Stroebel (1984),

Krahne and Tenoli (1975), Hirai (1974), Banquet (1972, 1973), Wallace and Benson (1972), Wallace et al. (1971b), Wallace (1971), Kasamatsu and Hirai (1963, 1966), Anand et al. (1961a, 1961b), and Bagchi and Wenger (1958).

EEG: Beta Activity

During deep meditation, experienced subjects sometimes exhibit bursts of high-frequency beta waves (twenty to forty cycles per second). This sudden autonomic activation is often associated by the meditator with an approach of yogic ecstasy or a state of intense concentration; and it is usually accompanied by an acceleration of heart rate. The following studies have reported beta activity: West (1980), Peper and Ancoli (1979), West (1979), Corby et al. (1978), Fenwick et al. (1977), Banquet (1973), Kasamatsu and Hirai (1963, 1966), Anand et al. (1961a), and Das and Gastaut (1955). Surwillo and Hobson (1978) recorded the EEGs of six Protestant adults during prayer to discover whether the pattern was slower than during rest. They did not find any evidence of EEGs slowing during prayer, and in fact found the opposite in the majority of subjects. The authors speculated that this phenomenon was similar to that observed in experienced meditators during deep meditation.

EEG: Hemispheric Synchronization

EEG synchronization/coherence with respect to the distribution of alpha activity between the four anatomically distinct regions of the brain— left, right, anterior, and posterior—may indicate the effectiveness of meditation. It has been positively correlated with creativity (Orme-Johnson et al., 1977b). Such neural ordering has been reported in the following studies: Jevning and O'Halloran (1984), Badawi et al. (1984), Orme-Johnson and Haynes (1981), Dillbeck and Bronson (1981), Dillbeck et al. (1981a), Glueck and Stroebel (1978), Corby et al. (1978), Bennett and Trinder (1977), Orme-Johnson (1977a), Morse et al. (1977), Hebert and Lehmann (1977), Westcott (1977), Haynes et al. (1977), Ferguson and Gowan (1976), Davidson (1976), Levine (1976), Ferguson (1975), Glueck and Stroebel (1975), Banquet and Sailhan (1974), Banquet (1973 and 1972), Wallace et al. (1971c), Wallace (1971), Anand et al. (1961a), and Das and Gastaut (1955).

EEG: Dehabituation

Whether meditation produces a heightened awareness that resists habituation is a significant question, we feel, because many traditional teachings maintain that it does. The Sanskrit *anuraga*, or constant freshness of perception, for example, is said to be a primary result of yoga; Zen Buddhist teachers describe the freedom from "perceptual averaging" that zazen and right living lead to; and Taoist stories accentuate the spontaneity of each moment for those who are wise in the way of the Tao. Such teachings are supported by most modern meditation studies, though a few experiments have failed to replicate their findings. Some religious ecstatics, however, become so absorbed in trance that they inhibit or entirely suppress their responses to the outer world. Early studies by Bagchi and Wenger compared yogis and Zen masters in this regard, and appeared to show significant differences in EEG response between the two kinds of meditation. The yogis they studied habituated to repeated stimuli more rapidly and completely than Zen masters, leading Bagchi and Wenger to speculate that the two types of discipline produced different spiritual results—either inner absorption or heightened awareness of the outer world. The following studies report that meditation leads to a heightened perceptual awareness, in which the EEGs remain responsive to repeated stimuli such as clicks or light flashes instead of habituating to them: Delmonte (1984b), McEvoy et al. (1980), Davidson (1976), Williams and West (1975), Hirai (1974), Wada and Hamm (1974), Banquet (1973), Orme-Johnson (1973), Gellhorn and Kiely (1972), Naranjo and Ornstein (1971), Wallace et al. (1971b), Wallace (1971), Akishige (1970), Kasamatsu and Hirai (1963, 1966), Anand et al. (1961a), and Bagchi and Wenger (1957).

Other studies, however, failed to replicate this finding. Heide (1986) compared seventeen TM meditators and seventeen controls and found no significant differences between groups in the rate of habituation of alpha blocking. Becker and Shapiro (1981) used three groups of Zen, yoga, and TM meditators with five to seven years of experience, and two groups of controls. They found that EEG alpha suppression in response to repeated stimuli did not differ among the five groups. West (1980a) concluded that too few systematic studies of habituation have been made to reach a solid conclusion. Barwood et al. (1978) tested auditory-evoked potentials of eight experienced meditators before, during, and after meditation, and also during light sleep, and found no consistent changes between baseline and meditating or meditating and sleep auditory-evoked potentials.

Specific Cortical Control

Traditional teachers did not have electroencephalographs to study cortical activity, but the findings in modern studies that meditators achieve various kinds of control over specific kinds of brain function conform to the tenet of many contemplative literatures that self-awareness brings self-mastery. As various kinds of functioning are brought to consciousness, their integration can be more deliberately guided, according to most traditional teachings. Several modern studies seem to show that meditators do indeed acquire control of specific brain functions.

Delmonte (1984b) concluded that meditation practice may begin with left-hemisphere activity, which then gives way to functioning characteristics of the right hemisphere, while both left- and right-hemisphere activity are largely inhibited or suspended in advanced meditation.

Pagano and Frumkin (1977) reported strong evidence that meditation enhances functioning in the right hemisphere, with cumulative effects among experienced meditators. Prince (1978) suggested that meditation may inhibit the left hemisphere somewhat, shifting the focus of consciousness to the right hemisphere. Bennett and Trinder (1977) reported that TM meditators had greater flexibility in shifting from one brain hemisphere to the other. Davidson and Goleman (1977) suggested that during periods of intense concentration in meditation, sensory information may become attenuated below the level of the cortex. Earlier, Davidson (1976) reported that during mystical experience cerebral function is dominated by the right hemisphere. Goleman (1976a) stated that meditators showed a significantly increased cortical excitation during meditation and a simultaneous limbic inhibition that delinked the cortex and limbic systems. He also reported that Gurdjieff meditators' brains showed cortical specificity, or the ability to turn on those areas of the brain necessary to the task at hand while leaving the irrelevant areas inactive. Schwartz (1975) stated that meditation practices can lead to heightened cortical arousability plus decreased limbic arousability, so that perception is heightened and emotion is simultaneously reduced, which he described as a "skilled response."

Others reporting cortical specificity of response are Warrenburg (1979), Hirai (1974), Banquet (1973), and Orme-Johnson (1973).

Other Cortical Changes

Persinger (1984) stated that transient, focal, epileptic-like electrical changes in the temporal lobe, without convulsions, have been hypothesized to be primary correlates of religious experiences. He investigated two cases of this kind. The first involved the occurrence of a delta-wave dominant electrical seizure for about ten seconds, from the temporal lobe only, of a TM teacher during a peak experience. The second involved the occurrence of spikes, within the temporal lobe only, during protracted intermittent episodes of glossalalia by a member of a Pentecostal sect. Persinger concluded that religious experiences are natural correlates of temporal-lobe transients that can be detected by routine EEG measures.

Researchers have analyzed EEG differences between meditators and those in stages of sleep, hypnosis, and other self-regulation strategies. Brown et al. (1977-78) were not able to differentiate between EEG data during meditation, sleep, and therapeutic touch healing states. Fenwick et al. (1977) found that EEG results showed TM to be a method of holding the meditators' level of consciousness at stage "onset" sleep. He found no evidence to suggest that TM produced a hypometabolic state beyond that produced by muscle relaxation, nor support for the idea that TM is a fourth stage of consciousness. Pagano et al. (1976) studied the EEGs of five experienced meditators, and found appreciable amounts of sleep stages two, three, and four during meditation. Otis (1974) found during a post-treatment testing session that twenty-three Transcendental Meditators displayed significantly more sleep-stage-one activity than they had in a premeditation rest period, and significantly more sleep than controls. Rao (1965) described meditation as a form of autohypnotism parallel to the state of hypnotic trance or hypnotic sleep. On the other hand, those who have found the EEGs of meditators to be distinct include West (1979a), Wachsmuth (1978), Patey et al. (1977), Dash and Alexander (1977), Banquet and Sailhan (1974), Wallace and Benson (1972), Wallace et al. (1971b), Wallace (1971), Kasamatsu and Hirai (1966), Onda (1967), Anand et al. (1961a), and Bagchi and Wenger (1957).

A few researchers have looked at EEG results in terms of the ergotropic/trophotropic model developed by Gellhorn [see Gellhorn and Kielly (1972)]. Davidson (1976) stated that mystical states may be experienced during either ergotropic (excited) or trophotropic (relaxed) conditions. He suggested that the whirling dances of Sufis and the violent abdominal contractions of Ishiguro Zen monks induce ergotropic conditions, whereas TM and other forms of sitting meditation elicit trophotropic reactions. Sargant (1974) speculated that trophotropic states may occur in the midst of an ergotropically induced experience. Gellhorn and Kielly (1972) observed that physiological changes in meditation are due to a shift in the ergotropic/trophotropic balance in the trophotropic direction—a good strategy for improving mental health. Their model was criticized by Mills and Campbell (1974), because it ignored differences in meditation techniques, left out certain evidence of alpha-blocking differences between yoga and Zen, and provided an ambiguous interpretation of trophotropic/ergotropic effects on the orienting reflex. Emerson (1972) concluded that the religion of the meditator determines the way in which his EEG pattern will change during the course of meditation. Fischer (1971) stated that the mystic may switch between extreme ergotropic and extreme trophotropic forms of mystical experience, a rebound from ecstatic rapture to yogic samadhi in response to intense ergotropic excitation. Das and Gastaut (1955) characterized the mystical state of yogic ecstacy as predominantly ergotropic, where no effect on the EEG pattern as a result of external stimuli was noticed.

Blood Chemistry

Strict comparisons between traditional understandings of bodily change in contemplative practice and modern studies of meditation's effect on blood chemistry are uncertain at best, though the finding in some studies that meditation lowers adrenal hormones, lactates, and cholesterol seems to confirm the repeated discovery that spiritual practice reduces stress and anxiety. This area of research is not as well developed, though, as other areas of meditation research. Only more investigation will reveal the intricate relationships of blood chemistry in contemplative activity.

Adrenal Hormones

Meditation generally produces psychological results opposite from those of stress, yet researchers have been puzzled by the fact that stress-induced adrenal hormone levels do not fall consistently in the blood of meditators. Benson (1983a) studied nineteen subjects who practiced the relaxation response technique twice daily for thirty days. He found increased norepinephrine levels without any increase in heart rate or blood pressure, and concluded that the relaxation response technique reduces central nervous system responsivity to norepinephrine. Or norepinephrine levels rise because less is used up by tissues that ordinarily respond to it. Benson (1989) concluded that reduced norepinephrine end-organ responsivity may be the mechanism through which physiologic changes persist after the elicitation of the relaxation response [see also Morrell (1985)]. Mills et al. (1990) measured functional lymphocyte beta-andrenergic receptors and found lower levels in TM meditators supporting

Benson's hypothesis. Engle (1983), commenting on Benson's work, agreed that the relaxation response is a useful technique to modify physiological functions, but that little is understood about the mechanisms that mediate its effect. Earlier, Hoffman et al. (1982) assessed sympathetic nervous system activity in experimental subjects practicing the relaxation response and in control subjects, all of whom were exposed to graded orthostatic and isometric stress during monthly hospital visits. They found higher concentrations of norepinephrine for experimental subjects and no changes for controls [see the follow-up study by Morrell and Hollandsworth (1986) that supports this conclusion].

Sudsuang et al. (1991) reported decreased cortisol levels measured after meditation in inexperienced meditators. Michaels et al. (1979) studied eight TM meditators and eight controls, and found that cortisol decreased progressively for both groups, aldosterone did not change for either group, and renin increased by 14% for the meditation group, thereby not supporting the hypothesis that TM induces a unique state character- ized by decreased sympathetic activity or release from stress. However, since cortisol concentrations varied more widely for controls than for meditators during the experiment, Michaels concluded that meditators may be less responsive to acute stress. Lang et al. (1979), in a study of ten advanced meditators with over four years of experience and ten medita- tors with over two years of experience, found that catecholamine levels were higher in advanced meditators during the experiment, and concluded that meditation enhances sympathetic activity. Michaels et al. (1976) measured plasma epinephrine and norepinephrine in twelve meditators before, during, and after meditation, and in a control group matched for sex and age who rested instead of meditating, and obtained the same results for both groups, thereby concluding that TM does not reduce stress and the activity of the sympathetic nervous system. Bevan et al. (1976) found significant decreases in plasma and urinary-free cortisol during TM, the effect being cumulative with increased meditation experi- ence. However, no significant effects on catecholamine excretion were noted. He concluded that TM produces an acute and chronic reduction in trophotropic anterior hypothalamic activity but little effect on ergotropic posterior hypothalamic function, and that the mechanisms underlying the practice are not a simple counterpart of the fight-or-flight response.

Other researchers, however, have reported decreases in adrenal hormones during meditation. Werner et al. (1986) evaluated eleven subjects before and during a three-year period after starting the TM-Sidhi program. They found a progressive decrease in serum TSH, growth hormone, and prolactin levels, with no consistent change in cortisol, T4, or T3. Stone and DeLeo (1976) measured plasma dopamine-B-hydroxylase as an index of sympathetic nervous system activity in a six-month controlled trial of simple word meditation in hypertension patients. They noted significant reductions of plasma D-B-H, which was positively correlated with significant reductions of blood pressure. Schildkraut et al. (1990) found a possible common mechanism of action for the drug alprazolam (a triazolobenzodiazepine with antianxiety and antidepressant as well as antipanic effects) and elicitation of the relaxation response that involves decreased catecholamine output. Bujatti and Riederer (1976) found a significant decrease of the catecholamine metabolite VMA (vanillicmandelic acid) in meditators. This decrease was associated with a reciprocal increase of the serotonin metabolite 5-HIAA, which supports, as a feed-back necessity, the rest-and-fulfillment response versus fight and flight. Loliger (1991) also reported an increase in 5-HIAA during the practice of TM and the TM-Sidhi program.

Several studies have found decreased cortisol levels in meditators versus controls with the level of effect increasing with duration of medita-tion practice. See Ahuja et al. (1981), Jevning et al. (1978a, 1978d), Udupa et al. (1975), and Jevning et al. (1975).

Jevning and O'Halloran (1984) stated that adrenocortical activity may be the one parameter sufficient to determine the relationship between TM and sleep, since cortisol secretion is not apparently related to sleep. They reviewed the literature, particularly Jevning, Wilson, and Davidson's study (1978), and concluded that it is unlikely that TM can be the same as sleep, or accounted for as unstylized rest/relaxation, since sharp declines of up to 25% in cortisol during meditation for long-term meditators was measured, whereas insignificant declines were noted in short-term meditators, and no changes were noted in the rest/relaxation control group.

Androgen levels are a well-established correlate of the response to acute stress, and are possibly of adrenocortical origin. Jevning and Wilson (1978) studied testosterone concentration changes during TM and during rest among a group of fifteen TM practitioners with three to five years of experience and a group of fifteen controls. The controls were restudied as practitioners after three to four months of practice. No change in testosterone concentration was found during either rest or TM. Cooper et al. (1985) studied ten experienced Transcendental Meditators and found no clear evidence that meditation suppressed stress-related hormones [see the comments of Davis (1986)].

The serum level of the adrenal androgen, dehydroepiandrosterone sulfate (DHEA-S), is closely correlated with age in humans and has also been associated with measures of health and stress. Levels of DHEA-S decrease with age, stress, and illness. Glaser et al. (1992) found generally higher levels of DHEA-S in TM meditators versus controls suggesting greater health and adaptability for meditators.

Hill (1990) studied ten meditators to investigate the acute autonomic effects of Transcendental Meditation and found that both divisions of the autonomic nervous system are attenuated. The results also provide preliminary evidence to support the hypothesis that TM is associated with acutely reduced hypothalamic and peripheral serotonergic activity.

Thyroid Hormones

Werner et al. (1986), in a study of eleven subjects in the TM-Sidhi program, found decreased TSH, growth hormone, and prolactin levels and no consistent change in cortisol, T3 or T4. Jevning and Wilson (1977) found in a study of TM practitioners that T3, T4, and insulin levels did not change during meditation, but that TSH levels declined dramatically. Decreased TSH, along with stable thyroid hormone levels, may suggest change of the set point for feedback control of TSH secretion during TM and is consistent with primarily neural modulation of TSH secretion. The stability of T3, T4, and insulin make it unlikely that these hormones regulate the acute metabolic changes associated with the meditative state.

Total Protein

Sudsuang et al. (1991) reported increased serum protein levels after six weeks of meditation and speculated that cortisol reduction during meditation practice may be related to an increase in total protein because of reduction of gluconeogenesis and increased total protein synthesis by the liver.

Amino Acids and Phenylalanine

There is some evidence that amino acid metabolism is related to mental states, since alteration of plasma amino acid levels has been correlated with various forms of behavior. Jevning et al. (1977b) measured thirteen plasma neutral and acidic amino acids in twenty-eight subjects, thirteen of whom were controls and fifteen of whom had practiced TM twice daily for three to five years, and found that phenylalanine concentration increased by 23% during TM practice with no change during control relaxation. No significant changes were noted for the other twelve amino acids studied. Jevning speculated that since the liver is the principal utilizer of phenylalanine hydroxylase, reduced blood flow to the liver during meditation [see Jevning (1978c)] might be the cause of increased phenylalanine levels. He also suggested that the brain might utilize less phenylalanine during meditation.

Plasma Prolactin and Growth Hormone

Werner et al. (1986) evaluated the endocrine changes of eleven subjects before and over a three-year period after starting the TM-Sidhi program. A progressive decrease in serum thyroid stimulating hormone (TSH), growth hormone, and prolactin levels occurred over the three years, while no consistent change in cortisol, total thyroxine, or triiodothyronine was observed. Jevning, Wilson, and Vanderlaan (1978b) studied the concentrations of plasma prolactin and growth hormone before, during, and after forty minutes of TM. Twenty-four subjects were studied, including a group of twelve who had regularly practiced TM for three to five years and a group of twelve who had been regular practitioners for three to four months. The short-term practitioner group was studied as controls before, during, and after a forty-minute eyes-closed rest period. Prolactin concentration began to increase toward the end or after meditation in both groups of practitioners, with levels continuing to increase in the post-TM period. The increases were not correlated with sleep occurrence. Prolactin levels were stable in controls throughout the experiment. Growth hormone concentration was unchanged in both TM and rest groups.

Bevan et al. (1979) studied the short-term endocrine changes of five experienced meditators before, during, and after a thirty-minute period of meditation; and restudied the same group under the same experimental conditions, except that instead of meditating they read and talked quietly among themselves. A comparable group of five previously unstudied meditators were examined under the same nonmeditation conditions to offset the "second-experience" effect. A significant 38% reduction in serum hGH occurred during TM. The hGH fall commenced before the onset of meditation and appeared to be a response to anticipation of meditation. Serum hGH concentrations after TM rebounded to 50% above premeditation values. There was no change in the same subjects during a comparable nonmeditation experimental period, and the absence of hGH changes was not due to a second-experience effect. The experienced meditators showed slight decreases in prolactin and cortisol during meditation, which were not statistically significant. There were no statistically significant changes in thyroxine, triiodothyronine, reverse triiodothyronine, hemoglobi, packed cell volume, or total serum protein during the experimental period.

Lactate

High blood lactate concentrations have been associated with anxiety and high blood pressure, and the infusion of lactate in the blood has been found to produce symptoms of anxiety. The following studies have reported significant declines of up to 33% in blood lactate during meditation, and a rate of decline nearly four times faster than the rate of decrease among people resting or in a premeditation period: Bagga et al. (1981), Jevning et al. (1978c), Jevning and Wilson (1977), Benson (1975), Benson et al. (1973a, 1973b), Orme-Johnson (1973), Wallace and Benson (1972), Wallace et al. (1971a), and Wallace (1971).

Other studies have not confirmed a drop in lactate concentrations during meditation. Michaels et al. (1979) studied the plasma concentration of lactates of eight TM meditators before, during, and after twenty to thirty minutes of meditation, and of eight controls who rested quietly. Their failure to observe a change in lactate was consistent with their previously published report (Michaels et al., 1976).

White Blood Cells

Parulkar et al. (1974) studied twelve TM practitioners and found the following average decreases: white blood cell count before TM, 7,100, after TM, 6,813; eosinophil count before TM, 638, after TM, 460; and lymphocyte count before TM, 2,855, after TM, 2,781.

Red Blood Cell Metabolism

Jevning et al. (1983) studied thirty-two TM instructors with at least six years of meditation experience. They found a marked decline of whole blood metabolism during TM, which was accounted for mostly by a decline of red cell glycolite rate. This was correlated with decreased plasma lactate concentration and with relaxation as indicated by electrodermal response.

Cholesterol

Chronic sympathetic nervous system overactivity has been implicated as a factor capable of elevating and maintaining high serum cholesterol levels independent of dietary measures. Bagga et al. (1981) studied forty female medical students who practiced TM and yoga, and reported that their average serum cholesterol decreased from 196.3 mg/dl to 164.7 mg/dl. Cooper and Aygen (1979) measured serum cholesterol levels at the beginning and end of an eleven-month period for twelve hypercholesterolemic subjects who practiced TM. Eleven hypercholesterolemic controls who did not practice the technique were similarly followed for thirteen months. Paired comparisons showed a significant reduction in fasting serum cholesterol levels for those subjects who practiced meditation. The cholesterol mg per 100 ml for the meditation group was 254 at the start and 225 at the end of the period, and for the control group it was 259 at the start and 254 at the end of the period.

The Metabolic and Respiratory Systems

According to most contemplative teachings, the turbulence and distress of ordinary life can be reduced through quiet meditation. The subtle turnings of the mind's substance, the *citta-vritti* as they are described in Patanjali's *Yoga Sutras*, can be quieted so that a clearer and deeper apprehension of inner and outer worlds might ensue. This quieting also results in a growing efficiency of mind and body and a concomitant reduction in the organism's consumption of energy. This picture of contemplative transformation, embedded in Hindu, Buddhist, Taoist, and other teachings, corresponds to the one we find in contemporary studies of meditation's effects on breathing. Some forty studies have shown that oxygen consumption is reduced during meditation, that carbon dioxide elimination and respiration rate are reduced, and that minute volume is lowered. Other studies, moreover, have shown that oxygen consumption was decreased in subjects working at a fixed intensity, and that meditators sometimes suspend breathing longer than control subjects without apparent ill effects. These studies strongly suggest that meditation lowers the body's need for energy and the oxygen to help metabolize it. Such quieting of the organism, however, happens for the most part in quiet meditation of the TM or zazen type, not in active, high-arousal practices such as Ananda Marga Yoga.

Various studies have shown that oxygen consumption is reduced during meditation (in some cases up to 55%), that carbon dioxide elimination is reduced (in some cases up to 50%), that respiration rate is lessened (in some cases to one breath per minute when twelve to fourteen breaths per minute are normal), and that minute volume is also lowered. See Sudsuang et al. (1991), Kesterson (1986), Wolkove et al. (1984), Morse et al. (1984), Singh (1984), Cadarette et al. (1982), Hoffman et al. (1981b), Jevning et al. (1978c), Fenwick et al. (1977), Peters et al. (1977a, 1977b), Hoffman et al. (1981b), Benson et al. (1977a), Dhanaraj and Singh (1977), Elson et al. (1977), McDonagh and Egenes (1977), Corey (1977), Routt (1977), Davidson (1976), Benson et al. (1975c), Glueck and Stroebel (1975), Woolfolk (1975), Beary and Benson (1974), Hirai (1974), Parulkar et al. (1974), Benson et al. (1974a), Kanellakos and Lukas (1974), Benson et al. (1973a), Banquet (1973), Treichel et al. (1973), Wallace and Benson (1972), Russell (1972), Watanabe et al. (1972), Goyeche et al. (1972), Wallace et al. (1971b), Wallace (1971), Allison (1970), Sugi and Akutsu (1968), Karambelkar et al. (1968), Kasamatsu and Hirai (1963, 1966), Anand et al. (1961a), Wenger and Bagchi (1961), Anand and Chhina (1961), and Bagchi and Wenger (1957).

Badawi et al. (1984) observed fifty-two periods of spontaneous respiratory suspension in eighteen subjects during the practice of TM. These periods were correlated with subjective experiences of pure consciousness. Total EEG coherence showed a significant increase during these periods, moreover. Earlier, Farrow and Hebert (1982) observed, over four independent experiments, a significant number of episodes of breath suspension in forty subjects practicing TM, where the frequency and length of the suspension were significantly greater than for control subjects relaxing with eyes closed. This verified a previous study performed by Hebert (1977).

Benson et al. (1978a) reported that oxygen consumption was decreased by 4% in eight subjects working at a fixed intensity (on an electrically braked stationary bicycle ergometer) when the relaxation response was simultaneously elicited.

Vakil (1950) reported the case of a middle-aged yogi who meditated for fifty-six hours in an airtight concrete cubicle, measuring approximately five feet by five feet by eight feet and lined with thousands of three-inch rusty nails. The cubicle was then filled with 1,400 gallons of water through a narrow opening bored in the lid, then resealed, and the yogi remained

The Physical and Psychological Effects of Meditation

immersed for an additional seven hours. The author examined the yogi immediately on his removal, and found his pulse, blood pressure, and respirations normal.

Though it seems clear that meditation produces changes in breathing patterns, a number of studies have found little difference in various metabolic measurements between meditation and other self-regulation strategies. D.H. Shapiro (1982) argued that "the original belief that we would be able to discriminate meditation as a unique physiological state has not been confirmed—on either an autonomic or a metabolic level or in terms of EEG pattern." Puente (1981) compared forty-seven volunteers randomly assigned to TM, Benson's relaxation response, or no treatment, and found that none of the techniques exhibited clear superiority in reducing physiological arousal (measured by respiration rate, heart rate, electromyogram, electroencephalogram, and skin conductance). A similar experiment using TM meditators of varying experience indicated that individuals with 1.5 years of experience exhibited arousal levels similar to individuals with over five years of experience [also see Puente and Bieman (1980)]. Morse et al. (1977) concluded that relaxation, meditation, and relaxation hypnosis yield similar results, all suggestive of deep relaxation. In *The Relaxation Response* (1975), Benson argued that the physiological response pattern found in meditation was not unique to meditation but common to any passive relaxation strategy. See also Boswell and Murray (1979), Cauthen and Prymak (1977), Fenwick et al. (1977), Travis et al. (1976), Curtis and Wessberg (1975-76), and Walrath and Hamilton (1975).

Recently, Jevning, and O'Halloran (1984) summarized the results of their own and others' studies on the metabolic characteristics of TM and its relationship to sleep and unstylized eyes-closed rest/relaxation. They concluded that:

> We have seen, in the course of research into these questions, a clearer delineation of the differences and similarities between TM and other hypometabolic states as more sophisticated studies involving more clearly specified subject groups and more powerful measures have been applied. At present, it seems unlikely that TM is sleep or that it is the same as simple eyes-closed rest. Whether physiological changes accompanying TM might be induced by other stylized means is at present a moot and, in our opinion, a probably unproductive question, in view of the dearth of regularly practiced

techniques. The noncultic relaxation response advocated by Benson et al. (1974b) may deserve further investigation in this regard.

Recently, Jevning et al. (1992) conducted a review of the physiology of meditation, with emphasis on research in which the TM technique was used. They state that:

> Although facts therefore support the relevance of physiology to meditation (and indeed, meditation to physiology), the precise relationship of physiology to the unique subjectivity of meditation remains a primary research question.

Muscle Tension

Muscle tension, like oxygen consumption, has been reduced during recent experiments involving quiet meditation. In the secure calm of meditation, it seems, one comes to feel less need for defensive armoring. One can begin to relax more deeply as conditioned expectations of threat diminish. Such relaxation of the musculature contributes to the body's lowered need for energy, the slowing of respiration, and the lowering of stress-related hormones in the blood.

Credido (1982) tried to find whether a low-arousal relaxation pattern consisting of frontalis EMG decreases and peripheral skin temperature increases could be attained more effectively through biofeedback or meditation training. Thirty female subjects, ranging in age from twenty-one to fifty-nine, were randomly assigned to a patterned biofeedback group, a clinically standardized meditation group, or a control group, and were seen weekly for seven sessions. The meditation group showed significantly lower EMG levels than the other groups. No group had significant temperature increases. The biofeedback group had difficulty patterning the two feedback signals simultaneously, confirming the difficulty revealed by other studies in training individuals to gain voluntary control over more than one physiological modality with biofeedback.

Zaichkowsky and Kamen (1978) studied forty-eight subjects to determine whether EMG biofeedback, TM, or Benson's relaxation response produced decreased muscle tension. They found that all three groups had significant decreases in frontalis muscle tension when compared with a control group. Morse et al. (1977) monitored respiratory rate, pulse rate, blood pressure, skin resistance, EEG activity, and muscle tension for forty-eight subjects divided equally into meditation, hypnosis, relaxation, and control groups. Their results showed significantly better relaxation responses for those practicing a relaxation technique than the control group. There were no significant differences between the relaxation techniques, however, except for the measure of muscle tension, in which meditation was significantly better. Others reporting significantly reduced muscle tension through meditation include Delmonte (1984f), Brandon (1983), Bhalla (1981), Cangelosi (1981), Delmonte (1979), Kemmerling (1978), Miller et al. (1978), Fee and Giordano (1978), Pelletier and Peper (1977b), Haynes et al. (1975), Ikegami (1974), Gellhorn and Kiely (1972), and Das and Gastaut (1955).

Ikegami (1974) compared muscle tension in the lotus position with other relaxed forms of sitting, and found that it was lower than in any other posture except that of lying down.

Citing the work of Cauthen and Prymak (1977), Curtis and Wessberg (1975-1976), and Travis et al. (1976), D.H. Shapiro (1982) pointed out that "most studies have found that the constellation of changes is significantly different between meditation groups and placebo control groups but not between meditation and other self-regulation strategies."

Skin Resistance and Spontaneous GSR

Low skin resistance, as measured by the galvanic skin response test, is generally thought to be a reliable indicator of stress because it is caused in large part by anxiety-induced perspiration. Like respiration rate and muscular tension, it has been affected by meditation in many contemporary experiments. This measure of stress, we believe, fits into the general picture from both traditional and modern accounts that meditation often lowers anxiety.

Increased skin resistance, as well as a lower frequency of spontaneous galvanic skin responses, has been widely reported in the TM literature or in studies of TM groups [see Delmonte (1984c), Bono (1984), Bagga and Gandhi (1983), Orme-Johnson and Farrow (1977), Farrow (1977), Laurie (1977), West (1977), T.R. Smith (1977), Orme-Johnson (1973), Wallace and Benson (1972), Wallace et al. (1971b), and Wallace (1971)]. Other researchers who concluded that meditation increases skin resistance (and sometimes lowers the frequency of spontaneous GSR fluctuations) are Schwartz et al. (1978), Sinha et al. (1978), Pelletier and Peper (1977a), Glueck and Stroebel (1975), Walrath and Hamilton (1975), Woolfolk

(1975), Benson et al. (1973a), Akishige (1970), Akishige (1968), Karambelkar et al. (1968), and Bagchi and Wenger (1957). In addition to increased skin resistance, Wenger and Bagchi (1961) found slow oscillatory skin-resistance waves in the later part of meditation for several subjects.

In reviewing studies of meditation's effect on GSR, Shapiro (1982), said that early first-round studies suggested that skin resistance significantly increased for subjects in Transcendental Meditation groups compared with control groups, but cited more recent studies showing no significant differences in GSR between meditation and other self-regulation strategies, including self-hypnosis, progressive relaxation, and other modes of instructional relaxation [see Lintel (1980), Boswell and Murray (1979), Parker et al. (1978), Morse et al. (1977), Cauthen and Prymak (1977), Travis et al. (1976), Curtis and Wessberg (1975), and Walrath and Hamilton (1975)].

Other Physiological Effects

Brain Metabolism

Using positron emission tomography, measurements of the regional cerebral metabolic rate of glucose are able to delineate cerebral metabolic responses to external or mental stimulation. Using data from PET scans performed in eight members of a yoga meditation group, Herzog et al. (1990-1991) showed the ratios of frontal vs. occipital rCMRGlc were significantly elevated indicating a holistic behavior of the brain metabolism during yogic meditation vs. A normal control state.

Salivary Changes

Morse et al. (1983) studied ten dental patients requiring nonsurgical endodontic therapy on upper anterior teeth who practiced simple word meditation in order to relax. Results showed significant pretest/posttest-meditation anxiety reduction measured by questionnaire, increased salivary volume, reduced salivary protein, increased amylase, and increased salivary pH.

Earlier, Morse et al. (1982) tested the hypothesis that salivary changes from stress to relaxation will be from opaque to translucent and from high to low protein levels, and that salivary bacteria will increase under the condition of stress and decrease under the condition of relaxation. Stress and relaxation of their twelve subjects, all dental students, were evaluated before and after meditation by verbal reports and examination of saliva for opacity, translucency, protein, and bacteria (resazurin dye method). Subjects were taught word meditation and instructed to meditate twice daily for twenty minutes. The study began one week after the subjects learned meditation and continued for six weeks. There were significant anxiety-reduction changes by the end of the meditation sessions as measured by increased salivary translucency, decreased salivary protein, and reduced subjective evaluation of stress. In addition, bacteria levels showed a significant decrease by the end of the meditation sessions. The results support previous findings by Morse in regard to salivary changes as measures of stress reduction mediated by meditation [see Morse et al. (1977, 1981), Morse (1976b, 1977a), and Morse and Hilderbrand (1976)]. The finding of higher bacteria levels under stress and lower bacterial levels under relaxation indicates that stress may contribute to dental caries and relaxation may have an anticaries effect.

McCuaig (1974) studied one male TM practitioner with six months of experience during ten sessions over a two-week period and found that meditation produced a general increase in salivary minerals, especially sodium, 70%; magnesium, 42%; calcium, 36%; inorganic phosphate, 46%; and potassium, 23%. Salivary zinc was not significantly altered. Protein content of the saliva was increased during meditation by 60%. McCuaig stated that salivary changes during TM indicate that extracellular fluid electrolytes may also be altered during this state. Some of the increase in solids is undoubtedly due to water reabsorption and/or the secretion of a more concentrated saliva. According to McCuaig, however, the large difference in the degree of concentration of solids indicates more than an overall change in water concentration. Differing increases in acid-soluble over acid-insoluble protein, moreover, and the fact that the former is decreased ten minutes after meditation while the latter remains elevated, indicate a specific process involving these substances.

Effectiveness in the Treatment of Disease

Meditation has been found to be of benefit in several conditions that may have a mental component to their etiology.

Premenstrual syndrome (PMS) is a disorder for which there is no known cause or consistent treatment. Possible etiological factors include endocrinologic imbalances, dietary deficiencies, and excessive psychological stress. Goodale et al. (1990) found an improvement in physical and emotional symptoms after elicitation of the relaxation response over a five-month period. A suggested mechanism of action was reduction in norepinephrine receptor sensitivity.

Cerpa (1989) found the blood sugar levels of subjects with type II diabetes practicing a meditation-relaxation technique (CSM) were significantly reduced after participating in a six-week program, whereas the blood sugar levels of subjects in a diabetes education program and a control group did not significantly change, indicating meditation-relaxation techniques could be of significant benefit in diabetes control. Contrary to predictions, the state and trait anxiety levels of the three groups remained relatively constant.

A number of studies have concluded that meditation is useful in the treatment of asthma. See: Gong et al. (1986), Goyeche et al. (1982), Corey (1977), and Honsberger and Wilson (1973a, 1973b).

Gaston et al. (1988-1989) found that meditation may be clinically effective for some patients in reducing their psoriasis symptoms.

In a preliminary study, Kaplan et al. (1993) found evidence suggesting a meditation-based stress reduction program is effective for patients with fibromyalgia, a chronic illness characterized by widespread pain, fatigue, sleep disturbance, and resistance to treatment.

Hershfield et al. (1993) found enough evidence of improvement in a pilot study of Crohn's disease patients using meditation to warrant a control study.

Treatment of Cancer

Magarey (1981b, 1983) stated that medical technology has not reduced the death rate from cancer for fifty years, and suggested that a broader, holistic approach involving meditation was needed. He pointed out that meditation is associated with physiological rest and stability, and also with the reduction of psychological stress and the development of a more positive attitude to life, with an inner sense of calmness, strength, and fulfillment.

Meares proposed a form of intensive meditation associated with the regression of cancer (1983); discussed the relationship between stress, meditation, and cancer (1982a, 1982b); reported on a case of regression of recurrence of carcinoma of the breast at a mastectomy site associated with intensive meditation (1981); reported the results of treatment of seventy-three patients with advanced cancer who attended at least twenty sessions of meditation and experienced significant reductions of anxiety and depression (1980a); reported on a case of remission of massive metastasis from undifferentiated carcinoma of the lung associated with intensive meditation (1980b); analyzed meditation as a psychological approach to cancer treatment (1979b); reported on a case of regression of cancer of the rectum after intensive meditation (1979a); analyzed the quality of meditation effective in the regression of cancer (1978a); reported on the regression of osteogenic sarcoma metastases associated with intensive meditation (1978c); looked at the relationship between vivid visualization and dim visual awareness in the regression of cancer after meditation (1978a); raised the issue of atavistic regression, which reportedly occurs in meditation, as a factor in the remission of cancer (1977); and reported on the case of a woman whose breast cancer was alleviated through intensive meditation (1976a).

Gersten (1978) reported the case of a forty-three-year-old patient who used meditation as a treatment of last resort for diplopia and ataxia. Although the reasons for the improvement his patient experienced in these diseases is elusive, Gersten believed that meditation was a significant factor in the healing process. Pelletier (1977b) reported the successful use of meditation and visualization with cancer patients.

Changes in Body Temperature

Studies by Herbert Benson, Elmer Green, and others have shown that Tibetan monks and Indian yogis can raise the temperature of their fingers and toes at will, confirming many written and verbal reports that spiritual adepts often achieve exceptional control of their bodies. A wide range of physiological functions has been brought under some degree of self-control in meditation experiments, showing that traditional accounts have been accurate in this regard.

Benson et al. (1982a) reported that three practitioners of the advanced Tibetan Buddhist meditational practice known as *g Tum-mo* (heat) yoga exhibited the capacity to increase the temperature of their fingers and toes by as much as 8.3°C.

Alleviation of Pain

Kabat-Zinn et al. (1987) studied 225 patients in chronic pain following training in mindfulness meditation. Large and significant overall physical and psychological improvements were recorded with the Pain Rating Index (PRI), measures of negative body image (BPPA), number of medical symptoms (MSCL), and global psychology symptomatology (GSI). Earlier, Kabat-Zinn et al. (1985) trained ninety chronic-pain patients in mindfulness meditation. Statistically significant reductions were observed in measures of present-moment pain; negative body image; and inhibition of activity by pain, symptoms, mood disturbance, and psychological symptom atology, including anxiety and depression. Pain-related drug utilization decreased and activity levels and feelings of self-esteem increased. Improvement appeared to be independent of gender, source of referral, and type of pain. A comparison group of patients in pain did not show significant improvement on these measures after traditional treatment protocols. Still earlier, Kabat-Zinn (1982) presented data on fifty-one chronic-pain patients who had not improved with traditional medical care. The patients experienced low-back, neck, shoulder, and headache pain. Some also experienced facial, angina pectoris, noncoronary chest, and gastrointestinal pain. After practicing mindfulness meditation for ten weeks, 65% of the patients felt less pain [see also Kabat-Zinn et al. (1984b) and Kabat-Zinn and Burney (1981)].

Hustad and Carnes (1988) showed the effectiveness of walking meditation in reductions of EMG readings, muscle tone, and levels of pain and/or anxiety. Mills and Farrow (1981) found that TM increased pain tolerance and reduced distress, while the physiological response to pain remained unchanged. Pelletier and Peper (1977b) studied three adept meditators who voluntarily inserted steel needles into their bodies while such physiological measures as EEG, EMG, GSR, EKG, and respiration were recorded. Although each adept used a different passive attention technique, none reported pain. Lovell-Smith (1985) reported three cases in which TM was successful in reducing migraine headache pain. Buckler (1976) found that TM was effective in relieving muscle-tension pain. Morse et al. (1984), Katcher et al. (1984), Morse et al. (1984c), Morse et al. (1981), Morse and Wilcko (1979), Morse (1977), and Morse (1976b) reported that meditation-hypnosis relieved pain and anxiety during nonsurgical endodontic therapy. Mandle et al. (1990) reported significant reduction in anxiety and pain in patients in which the relaxation response was elicited prior to femoral angiography. Goleman (1976) described an individual, who had not been helped by a wide variety of medical treatments, whose migraine headaches disappeared three days after beginning meditation. Anderson (1984) reported that meditation was used successfully in the treatment of primary dysmenorrhea among sixty-eight women. Benson et al. (1974b) and Benson et al. (1973a) reported that TM was effective in decreasing headache pain. See also Sharma et al. (1990), Fentress et al. (1986), Benson et al. (1984), and Kutz et al. 1983).

Exceptional Body Control

Kabat-Zinn and Beall (1987) and Kabat-Zinn et al. (1984) reported on a mental training program based on mindfulness meditation to optimize performance in collegiate and olympic rowers.

Bono (1984) studied sixteen beginning practitioners of Transcendental Meditation, nine meditators with five years of practice, and twenty control subjects who sat quietly with eyes closed for twenty minutes. He found a slight relationship between meditation and aptitude for changing heart rate, no appreciable difference between groups for changes in skin conductance, and no appreciable differences between groups in their ability to modify spontaneous electrodermal responses. However, the long-term meditators were significantly better than controls in their ability to control phasic electrodermal responses. The author concluded that the meditation groups tended to be slightly better than controls at operant autonomic learning.

A number of researchers have stated that adept meditators have been able to achieve control over various autonomic physiological functions [see Pelletier and Peper (1977a), Pelletier and Garfield (1977), Akishige (1974a), Wallace (1971), Kasamatsu and Hirai (1966), Anand et al. (1961a), Wenger and Bagchi (1961), and Bagchi and Wenger (1957)]. Orme-Johnson and Farrow (1977) and Hjelle (1974) viewed TM as a method of increasing inner control. Hirai et al. (1977) compared twelve Zen priests and disciples with sixteen students with no meditation experience in their ability to control skin potential response using biofeedback. They found that, although the Zen group had greater frequency of potential response, both groups were equally able to produce more spontaneous skin responses during biofeedback periods than during control periods, suggesting that biofeedback training is independent of Zen training.

Earlier, after claims that certain yogis were able to learn cardiac control, and after some even demonstrated a capacity for stopping the heart, Wenger et al. (1961) conducted an extensive investigation with elaborate equipment. Since none of the yogis they studied could stop their heart, the investigators concluded that the disappearance of the heart activity signal was probably an artifact, since the heart impulse is sometimes obscured by electrical signals from contracting muscles of the thorax [see Wallace and Benson (1972)]. Wallace (1971) stated that TM can change a variety of autonomic body functions, including brain waves, rate of respiration, blood pressure, oxygen consumption, spontaneous galvanic skin response, blood pH, and lactate, and these changes persist after meditation has ended, which may account for reports of an afterglow effect in the waking state after meditation. Wenger and Bagchi (1961) observed yogis who could perspire from the forehead on command, regurgitate at will, defecate at will, and draw water into the bladder using a tube. They concluded, however, that such direct voluntary control was achieved by employing intervening voluntary mechanisms. Bagchi and Wenger (1957) believed that the superb respiratory control that yogis exhibited was due to the importance of breathing exercises used in almost all forms of meditation.

CHAPTER 3

Behavioral Effects
by Michael Murphy and Steven Donovan

*[Since the 1930s Western psychology has been gripped with the frenzy
that it is a behavioral science, meaning that what good scientific
psychologists should study is only overtly measurable behavior. Historically, this was due to the inordinately excessive influence that animal
learning theory, particularly classical and operant conditioning, exerted
over American academic laboratory psychology, roughly from the 1930s
to the 1960s. Large-scale studies of the white rat proliferated to such
an extent that they took over all other forms of psychology—causing
B.F. Skinner to declare that the term psychology, at that time believed
to be outmoded, had finally been displaced by the more precise phrase
'behavior science.' Following suit, federal and private grant funding
agencies took up the phrase, renaming all their departments, causing
the word psychology to fall out of scientific vogue for several decades.
Everything termed psychological was then termed behavioral. While the
hegemony of the behaviorists ended in the 1960s and was replaced by
the cognitive revolution in psychology, cognitivists have retained a large
portion of the principles of classical and operant behavior, which they
apply to a study of internal mental events. Thus, the term behavioral is
now often used synonymously with the word psychological, although the
field of psychology contains many more humanistic pastures. Ed.]*

Perceptual and Cognitive Abilities

Many traditional schools maintain that sensory, perceptual, and
cognitive abilities are enhanced by meditation. Some Eastern schools,
including Theravada and Zen Buddhism, Vedanta, and yoga, offer systematic
ways to cultivate a clarity, flexibility, efficiency, and broadened range of
mental functions similar to the meditation results reviewed in the six sub-
sections below. The perceptual and cognitive abilities that seem to have
been enhanced during modern experiments correspond with various
capacities described in the Hindu-Buddhist traditions as *siddhis* (exceptional powers), *vibhutis* (perfections), and *riddhis* (psychically prosperous
states). *Smritritwa*, for example, is a highly developed form of memory
enhancement reported in contemporary studies. *Adwani siddhi*, the ability
to withstand misleading or destructive suggestions from other minds,

resembles the good judgment and perception associated with field independence (below). *Vijnamaya vidya siddhi*, a supernormal agility of mind, includes many of the mental improvements being reviewed here. Other capacities such as these, according to the traditional teachings, could also be included in such comparisons.

Perceptual Ability

Brown et al. (1984a, 1984b) studied the relationship between meditation and visual sensitivity, and summarized their findings as follows:

> Practitioners of the mindfulness form of Buddhist meditation were tested for visual sensitivity before and immediately after a three-month retreat during which they practiced mindfulness meditation for sixteen hours each day. A control group composed of the staff at the retreat center was similarly tested. Visual sensitivity was defined in two ways: by a detection threshold based on the duration of simple light flashes and a discrimination threshold based on the interval between successive simple light flashes. All light flashes were presented tachistoscopically and were of fixed luminanoe. After the retreat, practitioners could detect shorter single-light flashes and required a shorter interval to differentiate between successive flashes correctly. The control group did not change on either measure. Phenomenological reports indicate that mindfulness practice enables practitioners to become aware of some of the usually preattentive processes involved in visual detection. The results support the statements found in Buddhist texts on meditation concerning the changes in perception encountered during the practice of mindfulness.

McEvoy et al. (1980) measured brainstem auditory-evoked potentials in five advanced practitioners of TM to determine whether such responses would reflect reported increases in perceptual acuity to auditory stimuli following meditation. No pre-, postmeditation differences for experimental subjects were observed at low stimulus intensities (0—35dB). At moderate intensities (40—50dB) latency of the inferior collicular wave increased following meditation, but at higher stimulus intensities (55—70dB) latency of this wave was slightly decreased. The authors concluded that a comparison of slopes and intercepts of stimulus intensity-latency functions indicates a possible effect of meditation on brainstem activity. Earlier, Wandhofer and Plattig (1973) reported that cortical auditory-evoked

The Physical and Psychological Effects of Meditation

potentials were of significantly shorter latency in TM practitioners compared with controls. McEvoy et al. (1980) pointed out that these results were consistent with earlier reports of increased auditory acuity in meditators versus nonmeditators, as well as decreased sensory thresholds following a period of meditation [see Clements and Milstein (1977) and Pirot (1977)]. Such findings have been interpreted to indicate a beneficial central nervous system effect of TM on factors underlying sensory and perceptual processing [see Pelletier (1977b) and Pelletier and Garfield (1977)]. Keithler (1981) found that TM meditators had significantly lower auditory thresholds than controls using a method-of-limits test, and had no significant differences using a forced-choice absolute threshold test.

Meissner and Pirot (1983) tested twenty males (ten TM meditators and ten controls) with a strong right-hand preference, with 120 time trials to a 500 hz auditory stimulus presented to right, left, and both ears. Before meditation, when the ears were compared to each other, a significant right-ear advantage occurred in all relaxation conditions for both groups. After meditation, however, the TM group demonstrated no right-ear advantage. The authors concluded that TM is an attentional strategy that disrupts the usual biases of the brain.

Heil (1983) concluded that the practice of meditation enhances visual imagery ability. Shapiro (1980a) and Shapiro and Giber (1978) reported enhanced perceptual sensitivity. Walsh (1978) reported that meditation reduced perceptual noise. Blasdell (1977), Orme-Johnson et al. (1977a), and Orme-Johnson (1973) found that TM increased perceptual motor performance. Linden (1973) found that regular practice of meditation is associated with a significant enhancement of attentive ability, as assessed by the Embedded Figures Test and the Rod and Frame Tests. Williams and Herbert (1976), however, conducted a study that found no differences in perceptual motor ability within subjects practicing meditation. Domitor (1978) found no support for the hypothesis that meditation favorably affects perceptual change as measured by the Holtzman Inkblot Test and the Embedded Figures Test.

Dillbeck (1977b) investigated the effects of the regular practice of TM on habitual patterns of visual perception and verbal problem solving. He hypothesized that two weeks of TM practice would tend to free the subjects from inhibitory effects of those patterns, while allowing an improvement in their efficient use when appropriate. The subjects in this study were sixty-nine university students who either practiced TM, relaxed, or added nothing to their daily schedule for two-week periods. The general hypothesis was supported for tasks involving a tachistoscopic identification of card-and-letter sequence stimuli, but not for a verbal problem-solving task involving anagram solutions.

Pagano and Frumkin (1977) reported that TM meditators demonstrated enhanced ability to remember and discriminate musical tones. Shaw and Kolb (1977), Davidson et al. (1976a, 1976b), and Udupa (1973) also reported that meditators seemed to have better auditory receptivity and perceptual discrimination than controls. Martinetti (1976) concluded that practitioners of TM may have learned to focus their attention to a level at which thresholds for pertinent perceptual cues such as binocular disparity may be lowered. He stated that the concomitant increase in response sensitivity would account for the superiority of meditators at signal detection in the Ames Trapezoid Illusion, where meditators were twice as sensitive as controls. Nolly (1975) found that meditating subjects perceived a greater number of objects on a stimulus slide than did nonmeditating controls.

Reaction Time and Perceptual Motor Skill

Jedrczak et al. (1986) found that the number of months of practice of the TM-Sidhi program significantly predicted higher performance on two measures of perceptual motor speed. Robertson (1983) assessed fractionated reaction time for fourteen subjects to determine the short- and long-term effects of TM on neuromuscular integration. Results indicated no significant immediate pre- to posttreatment effect, but a significant cumulative effect over days. Faster total reaction time was noted due to a decrease in premotor time, although an increase in motor time was also observed. Warshall (1980) found a significant reduction in reflex latency and reflex motor time in TM practitioners, indicating increased peripheral neurological efficiency. Holt et al. (1978) reported that TM increased the speed of visual-choice reaction time. Sinha et al. (1978) found a consistent decline in reaction time following *vipashyana* meditation for three groups of police officers. Shaw and Kolb (1977), Blackwell et al. (1976), Appelle and Oswald (1974), and Wandhofer and Plattig (1973) concluded that the increased alertness developed through meditation resulted in improvement of reaction time.

On the other hand, Wood (1983 and 1986) tested sixteen TM meditators with three or more years of experience against a group of controls and found that there was no significant difference between groups on the pursuit rotor task. Williams and Herbert (1976) had similar findings when they compared thirty TM meditators and thirty nonmeditators on the pursuit rotor task, reporting that meditators did not perform better, did not exhibit less intraindividual variability, and were not more resistant to the accumulation of reactive inhibition. In fact, it appeared that the meditators were a little more susceptible to the cumulative effects of reactive inhibition. Williams and Vickerman (1976) gave forty-six college female volunteers sixty-six ten-second trials on the pursuit rotor task in three practice sessions (eighteen, thirty, and eighteen trials per session). After the first eighteen trials, the twenty-three subjects who were practiced Transcendental Meditators meditated for a twenty-minute period followed by a five-minute waking phase prior to performing a further thirty trials on the rotor. A four-minute rest was taken before resuming practice for the final eighteen trials. The other twenty-three subjects, who were not meditators, followed the same procedures, except instead of meditating they sat quietly with closed eyes. In terms of performance, learning, reminiscence, and intra-individual variability, the two groups were similar. These results were not in accordance with the expectations that these parameters would reflect the facilitative effects of Transcendental Meditation on alertness, awareness, consistency, and resistance to stress. While Williams and Vickerman concluded that the practice of Transcendental Meditation does not appear to benefit acquisition of fine perceptual motor skill, they suggested that more investigation might produce a better understanding of meditation's effects on perceptual motor behavior.

In a ten-day trial, Dhume and Dhume (1991) compared the performance of balance on a balance board in three groups: controls, subjects given dextroamphetamine, and yogic meditators. The group given dextroamphetamines scored significantly worse than the control group, and the yogic meditation group scored significantly better than the control group.

Deautomatization

Deikman (1966a) hypothesized that mystical phenomena were a consequence of deautomatization, i.e., an increased flexibility of perceptual and emotional responses to the environment. He suggested that meditation is a manipulation of attention that produces deautomization. He also suggested that deautomization was a regression to the perceptual and cognitive state of the child or infant, and that it explained the five principal features of the mystic experience: intense realness, unusual sensations, unity, ineffability, and trans-sensate experiences.

Field Independence

Bono (1984) studied sixteen beginning TM meditators and found that the meditators made a significant shift toward field independence after six months of TM practice. However, a group of twenty control subjects tested simultaneously also made a significant shift toward field independence after merely sitting quietly with eyes closed for twenty minutes. The author concluded that relaxation and calmness are crucial factors involved in the fluctuation of this perceptual style, perhaps along with a practice effect. And while meditation is a sufficient cause of these quieting responses, it is not a necessary one. Bono also measured autokinetic effect, which Pelletier (1974b) considered a measure of field independence, and found that control subjects demonstrated greater autokinetic effect than meditators when observed before and after the six-month control period. Although meditators showed a slight shift toward greater perceived autokinesis after the two control periods, while control subjects moved slightly in the opposite direction, no significant differences were found. Five-year meditators were not found to be appreciably different from control subjects in reported autokinetic effect. However, the difference between long- and short-term meditators approached significance, with long-term meditators perceiving more autokinesis.

The following researchers have found that measures of field dependence/independence, such as the Embedded Figures Test and the Rod and Frame Test, have shown that meditators become more field independent following periods of meditation: Fergusson (1993), Fergusson (1992), Jedrczak and Clements (1984), Shapiro and Giber (1978), Orme-Johnson and Granieri (1977), Abrams (1977b), Goleman and Schwartz (1976), Smith (1975b), Pelletier (1974, 1977b), and Linden (1973). But Goldman et al. (1979) found no change in field independence among Zen meditators.

MacRae (1983) studied forty-five experienced meditators and forty-five controls using the Time Metaphor Test and the Human Field Motion Test. There was a significant difference in scores between meditators reporting deeper meditative experiences and controls, indicating that meditators experienced greater human field motion.

Hjelle (1974) investigated the effects of TM on locus of control and found that meditators demonstrated increased internal locus of control on the Rotter I-E scale.

Concentration and Attention

Sabel (1980) assigned sixty practitioners of TM to two treatment groups. One group meditated for twenty minutes while the other read a text quietly. Both groups were tested before and after treatment to measure their concentration ability. Meditation had no measurable short-term effect on concentration and the subjects' experience of meditation was not correlated with their concentration score.

Spanos et al. (1980a) pretested eighty-one male students on absorption and three measures of hypnotic responsiveness, then randomly assigned them to three treatment groups, one that meditated for eight sessions, a second that listened analytically to lectures about hypnosis for eight sessions, and a third that was not treated. All students were then posttested on absorption and hypnotic responsivity measures. Meditating subjects were much more likely than those who listened to lectures to report intrusions into their attending. Neither the meditation nor the listening treatments enhanced hypnotic responsivity or absorption.

Earlier, Spanos et al. (1979) studied four groups of trained meditators differing in amount of meditation practice, and a group of nonmeditators, all of whom were assigned to attend nonanalytically to a mantra in two meditation sessions. Meditators signaled fewer intrusions and reported "deeper" levels of meditating than nonmeditators. However, meditators and nonmeditators did not differ on hypnotic susceptibility, absorption, or indices of psychopathology. Previously, Spanos et al. (1978) found a significant negative correlation between the number of irrelevant thoughts that subjects reported as intruding into their meditating and hypnotic susceptibility.

Other researchers have reported that meditation trains the capacity to attend, that meditators report more instances of total intentional involvement, or that meditators have fewer intrusions of irrelevant thoughts [see Moretti-Altuna (1987), Tomassetti (1985), Williams (1985), Sinha et al. (1978), Kelton (1978), Goleman (1976), Davidson et al. (1976a, 1976b), Walrath and Hamilton (1975), Orme-Johnson and Granieri (1977), Pelletier (1974), Van Nuys (1973), Deikman (1971), Tart (1971), and Maupin (1965)].

Memory and Intelligence

Jedrczak et al. (1986) found that the number of months of practice of the TM-Sidhi program predicted higher performance on two tests of nonverbal intelligence.

Verma et al. (1982) gave twenty-three TM practitioners and fifteen controls ten cognitive psychological tests. Statistically significant improvements were noted in the coding, time factor, and Raven standard progressive matrices tests, with improvement in the arithmetic test falling just short of significance. On the other tests, which measured less complicated mental functions, such as number 9 cancellation and digit span, the influence of TM on performance was negligible.

Fiebert and Mead (1981) randomly assigned twenty students in an introductory psychology class to an experimental group that was taught "actualism" meditation and asked to practice before studying and before exams, and a control group that was taught the technique but asked to practice at other times. There were no differences between the groups in mean weekly study time, but the experimental group performed significantly better on examinations than the control group.

Yuille and Sereda (1980) studied sixty-six females and seventy males who responded to ads in a university newspaper. All subjects were given pretests and posttests of short- and long-term memory, attention, reading skills, and intelligence. After the pretest, each subject was given individual training in TM, Shavasana yoga, or pseudomeditation, and was asked to practice meditation twice a day, monitoring his or her practice with individual diaries. The practice of meditation had no systematic effect on the variables assessed.

Kindler (1979) studied 230 subjects in forty-six five-person teams in group problem-solving effectiveness, and found that meditation teams improved more from pretest to posttest than control teams and that meditators felt less tense and had a greater sense of effective teamwork than control teams.

Nidich (1976) measured ninety-six TM meditators of various lengths of experience using Lawrence Kohlberg's Moral Judgement Review, and found a positive relationship between the practice of TM and moral development.

The TM literature generally reports improvement in intelligence, school grades, learning ability, and short- and long-term recall [see

The Physical and Psychological Effects of Meditation

Cranson et al. (1991), Dillbeck et al. (1986), Jedrczak et al. (1985), Lewis (1978a), Orme-Johnson and Granieri (1977), Abrams (1977a,b), Heaton and Orme-Johnson (1977a, 1977b), Collier (1977), Levin (1977), Glueck and Stroebel (1975), and Tjoa (1975)].

Rorschach Shifts

Brown and Engler (1984) studied five groups of meditation practitioners who practiced Buddhist Vipassana or mindfulness meditation. Teacher ratings were used as the primary criteria to delineate a subject's experience level.

A "beginners' group" consisted of fifteen subjects whose Rorschachs were collected immediately after three months of intensive meditation. These subjects received a mean rating of six or more by their teachers on the scale of Emotional Problems. Their Rorschachs were not especially different from Rorschachs they took just before the meditation retreat. The only differences were a slight decrease in productivity across subjects and a noticeable increase in drive-dominated responses for some subjects.

A second group consisted of thirteen subjects who met the dual criteria of receiving a mean rating of six or more by their teachers on the scale of Emotional Problems and who reported "sometimes" on the POME (Profile of Meditation Experience) questions concerning concentration and samadhi. The most outstanding characteristic of their Rorschachs was their unproductivity and paucity of associative elaboration. In addition, many of their images were fluidly perceived and they made many comments on the pure perceptual features of the inkblot.

A third group consisted of three subjects who met the dual criteria of receiving a mean rating of six or more by their teachers on the scale of Emotional Problems and who reported "sometimes" on the POME questions concerning concentration and samadhi. Their teachers also believed that they had progressed to the more advanced "insight" stages as classically defined. The Rorschachs of this group point in a direction nearly opposite to that of the second group, in that they are primarily characterized by increased productivity and richness of associative elaborations.

A fourth group consisted of four advanced Western meditators judged by their teachers to have reached at least the first of the four stages of enlightenment recognized by their school of meditation practice.

Their Rorschachs were not collected after a period of intensive meditation and they appear to be more like the Rorschachs of the beginners' group. The most unusual feature of their responses was the degree to which they perceived the inkblots as an interaction of form and energy or form and space.

A fifth classification consisted of a single South Asian individual recognized as an *ariyas* or "one worthy of praise," who is alleged to have attained all but one of the four levels of enlightenment and to have undergone a cognitive-emotional restructuring that has completely or almost completely eliminated suffering from his experience. Analysis of this Rorschach opens up all the complicated issues of cross-cultural Rorschach interpretation, though it revealed two notable facts. First, the subject demonstrated a shift in perspective, seeing the inkblot as a projection of mind, whereas most subjects accept the physical reality of an inkblot and then project their imagings onto it. Second, the subject integrated all ten Rorschach cards in a single associated theme representing a Buddhist discourse on the alleviation of suffering.

The authors concluded that these Rorschach protocols supported the belief that the classical subjective reports of meditation stages are more than religious belief systems. Such reports, the authors maintain, are valid accounts of the perceptual changes that occur with intensive meditation that seeks understanding and relief from suffering.

Earlier, Maupin (1965) conducted a Rorschach study of twenty-eight inexperienced meditators who were instructed in a Zen Buddhist-related concentration exercise, concluding that these subjects experienced an increase in primary process thinking along with a greater capacity to tolerate it. Kasamatsu and Hirai (1963) found relatively higher scores of whole responses, relatively higher scores of Human Movement Reaction, and relatively lower total color responses and differentiated texture reactions among Zen practitioners.

Empathy

Every enduring school of spiritual practice, no matter how world denying, has emphasized concern for the condition of others. Nearly all their disciplines seek to promote an empathy with created things that leads toward oneness with them. *Tat tvam asi*, thou art that, perhaps the most famous Indian spiritual assertion, refers to our fundamental identity with the Ground of Being, which we can realize through the practice of Vedantic yoga. The cessation of the mind's subtle turbulence, the *citta-vritti-nirodh* described in Patanjali's sutras, reveals the essential unity we have with the universe. Given the pervasiveness of this teaching in so many traditions, it is not surprising that several contemporary studies show that meditation increases empathy for others.

Lesh (1970a,c), for example, studied Zen meditation and the development of empathy in counselors. He used Carl Rogers' characterization of empathy as a twofold process involving both the capacity of the counselor to sense what the client is feeling and the ability to communicate this sensitivity at a level attuned to the client's emotional state. Three groups were studied. The first consisted of sixteen students who were taught zazen. The second consisted of twelve students who volunteered to learn zazen but were not actually taught. The third consisted of eleven students who were opposed to learning meditation. All subjects were pretested and posttested four weeks later using the Affective Sensitivity Scale, the Experience Inquiry, and the Personal Orientation Inventory, with the following findings:

•The group that practiced zazen improved significantly in empathic ability. The two control groups did not.

•The level of concentration reached in zazen is not related to the degree of empathy achieved.

•Zazen is most effective in improving empathic ability in people who start out low in this ability.

•Openness to experience is related to empathic ability. The more open to experience, the more empathic a person seems to be.

•Empathic ability is related to the degree of self-actualization a person has achieved. The more self-actualizing, the more empathic a person seems to be.

•People less open to experience seem to be unwilling to practice zazen, and they are less empathic than those who are open to experience.

Sweet and Johnson (1990) have developed a meditation-based program for developing empathy called MEET (Meditation Enhanced

Empathy Training) for use in training of mental health professionals and in treatment protocols. Anecdotal reports of effectiveness have been positive and confirmatory research is planned.

Other researchers have concluded that meditation increases empathy and sensitivity [see Reiman (1985), Shapiro (1980b), Kornfield (1979), Walsh (1978), Kohr (1977a, 1977b), Shapiro and Giber (1978), Pelletier (1976b, 1978), Davidson et al. (1976a, 1976b), Griggs (1976), Kubose (1976), Van den Berg and Mulder (1976), Leung (1973), Udupa (1973), Osis et al. (1973), Banquet (1973), Van Nuys (1973), Nidich et al. (1973), Deikman (1966a), and Maupin (1965)].

Regression in the Service of the Ego

The legend that Gautama Buddha witnessed his past lives before he attained enlightenment can be interpreted as a parable of meditation's cathartic power, which facilitates liberation from unconscious effects of early experience on present consciousness and behavior. The *Yoga Sutras* of Patanjali suggest a similar process (see Book III, verse 18). Modern studies also suggest that meditation stimulates a regression to early fixation points so that they may be understood and mastered.

Shafii (1973b), for example, stated that in meditation controlled regression returns an individual to early fixation points, and to the reexperience of minute and silent traumas of the separation and individuation phase on a silent and nonverbal level. This revisit and reexperience frees psychic energy, he suggested, providing more freedom from earlier patterns of behavior and more openness to all forms of learning. Maupin (1965) reported that Rorschach test results indicated that meditation brings about a sequence of regressive states. Others who have reported that meditation increases adaptive regression include Kornfield (1979), Pelletier (1976a, 1978), Moles (1977), Lesh (1970a), and Alexander (1931).

Creativity and Self-Actualization

Studies that have tried to measure these two aspects of personal functioning have produced mixed results, making comparison with traditional ideas about them extremely difficult. Both creativity and self-actualization, moreover, as they are defined for psychological study, are complex entities consisting of various traits and capacities, such as perceptual skill, ideational fluency, openness to experience, emotional flexibility, empathy, and adaptive regression. In some studies, one or more of these traits have improved while others have not, clouding the picture of meditation's result on the category as a whole. Furthermore, the psychologies on which traditional contemplative disciplines were based did not use the same personality categories. In the two sections that follow, therefore, we have not tried to compare the results of contemporary studies with traditional accounts of contemplation's effect on personality development as a whole.

Creativity

O'Haire and Marcia (1980) used three groups to study personality characteristics associated with Ananda Marga Meditation: thirty-two subjects with interest but no experience in meditation, seventy-eight subjects with six months to three years of meditation experience, and thirty-six subjects with more than three years of meditation experience. Autobiographical information was collected from the subjects and the following measures were taken: Torrance Tests of Creative Thinking, Barron's Ego Strength Scale, Myers-Briggs Type Indicator, Eysenck Personality Inventory, and frequency of lateral eye movement. No relationship between creativity and experience in meditation was found. This conclusion supported the research of Domino (1977), Otis (1974), Schwartz (1974), and Cowger (1974a).

Cowger and Torrance (1982), however, studied twenty-four college undergraduates who experienced Zen meditation and ten who experienced similar training in relaxation. Both groups were administered pre- and posttests of the Torrance Tests of Creative Thinking. The meditators attained statistically significant gains in heightened consciousness of problems, perceived change, invention, sensory experience, expression of emotion/feeling, synthesis, unusual visualization, internal visualization, humor, and fantasy. Those experiencing relaxation training manifested statistically significant drops in verbal fluency, verbal originality, figural fluency, and figural originality; and statistically significant gains in sensory experience, synthesis, and unusual visualization. When the Linear Models Procedure was used to compare the changes registered by the meditation and relaxation groups, it was found that the change of the meditation group exceeded those of the relaxation group on perceived change resulting from new conditions, expression of emotion, internal visualization, and imagery.

Earlier, Kubose and Umemoto (1980) pointed to various similarities between creative problem solving and Zen koan study. They found that both involved the elimination of prior interfering approaches, satiation effects resulting from prolonged concentration, a unification of contradictory events, and more right-brain than left-brain hemispheric functioning. They also noted that both involved common psychological processes, including stages of preparation, incubation, illumination, and evaluation.

Several TM researchers have claimed that meditation and creativity are linked. Ball (1980) stated that students participating in the TM-Sidhi program showed significant increases in creativity. Ball (1980) also compared a group of TM practitioners with a group of students taking a developmental psychology class and found that TM improved verbal originality and originality on the sounds and images test. Orme-Johnson and Granieri (1977) reported significant increases in originality and fluency of visuo-spatial creativity using the Torrance Test of Creative Thinking. They concluded that their subjects improved significantly on the fluency and creativity subscales of the Torrance Test of Creative Thinking, and that these improvements were significantly correlated with the number of experiences of siddhis. They stated that at least one type of competence—superior performance on the Torrance Tests of Creativity—has been found to correlate significantly with subjective reports of transcendental consciousness. Shecter (1977) reported increased creativity in the classroom [see also Margid (1986), Stamatelos (1986), Garfield (1985a, 1985b), and Jedrczak et al. (1985)].

Self-Actualization

According to Sallis (1982), Abraham Maslow and meditation philosophy share a view that humans are endowed with potentials for growth that are obstructed by social conditioning and fears. Although meditation teachers teach that self-actualization is an intermediate step on the meditator's path, and that man's true potential far exceeds the imagination of most Westerners, psychotherapists might profitably explore the practice of meditation as a means of enhancing the growth process, and a consideration of meditation theory may add new dimensions to the conceptions of growth and human potential [see also Compton (1984), who stated that Sallis failed to differentiate between the various levels of meditation practice].

Compton and Becker (1983) tested the hypothesis that the inconsistencies found in research on the relationship between Zen meditation and self-actualization were due in part to the existence of a learning period for Zen meditation. Using the Personal Orientation Inventory, they tested thirty-six students of Soto Zen and thirty-four undergraduate students who had never meditated. They found that the learning period was approximately twelve months, during which time there was no increase in group self-actualization. After that time, a significant increase in group self-actualization was noted.

The following section summarizes reports on the effect of various types of meditation (primarily TM) on measures of self-actualization:

Alexander et al. (1991) The authors performed a statistical meta-analysis of all existing studies (42 treatment outcomes) on the effects of TM and other forms of meditation and relaxation on self-actualization. The effect size of TM on overall self-actualization was approximately three times as large as that of other forms of meditation and relaxation. Factor analysis of the Personal Orientation Inventory revealed three independent factors: effective maturity, integrative perspective on the self and world, and resilient sense of self.

Gelderloos et al. (1990b) The authors investigated the nature of the relationship between experiences of transcendental consciousness and psychological health, and found that experience with TM and the TM-Sidhi program was positively related to a general measure of psychological health.

Zika (1987) This study compared hypnosis with two forms of meditation and a placebo treatment for their effects on the Personal Orientation Inventory (POI). Hypnosis and TM were significantly more effective in facilitating self-actualization with hypnosis showing a slightly stronger effect. Findings support research suggesting that hypnosis and meditation are similar in promoting psychological health.

Bono (1984) This study measured the self-concept (the relationship between one's real and ideal self) of sixteen subjects practicing Transcendental Meditation and twenty control subjects, and found that the meditators showed a dramatic increase in self-regard. There was no meaningful difference between long- and short-term meditators, however. Since the meditators had a significantly lower score on self-concept than controls before TM instruction, the author speculated that those choosing to practice TM have greater dissatisfaction with self and are more ready for a change; in this they resemble individuals seeking psychotherapy or other forms of help, so other disciplines of self-improvement may work as well as TM in improving their self-esteem.

Turnbull and Norris (1982) The authors studied seven subjects who learned and practiced TM and seven controls. They were given a role construct repertory grid and an Eysenck Personality Questionnaire once before and twice after starting to practice TM. Initially the two groups differed only in that meditation subjects tended to judge other people to be more unlike their ideal selves than did comparison subjects. This difference was maintained. With meditation subjects the grid results showed a systematic pattern of significant changes over the three tests. Meditators came to perceive their actual selves as being increasingly similar to their ideal and social selves, and they developed a more strongly defined concept of their actual selves. The authors concluded that TM has therapeutic value.

Kline et al. (1982) The MMPI and Tennessee Self-Concept Scale were administered to volunteers in an experimental group consisting of recovering alcoholics and individuals with general emotional problems participating in a three-month program of TM, and to a control group from the same population. Experimental and control groups were not significantly different on any of the pretest measures, and at posttest no significant differences were found.

Turnbull and Norris (1982) In this study a role construct repertory grid and an Eysenck Personality Questionnaire were completed by TM subjects, once before and twice after starting the regular practice of TM. Controls did not learn TM and were assessed in the same way at the same times. With meditation subjects the grid results showed a systematic pattern of significant changes over the three tests. These changes indicate that meditators came to perceive their actual selves as being increasingly similar to their ideal (as they ideally want to be) and their social selves (as they are envisaged by others), and that they developed a more strongly defined concept of their actual selves that involved increased self-acceptance. Controls did not show consistent or significant changes between tests on any measure.

Hart and Means (1982) Ten undergraduate students in social work were administered the Shostrom Personal Orientation Inventory and were taught Benson's relaxation response meditation technique or instructed to read relevant material for thirty minutes per day. After three weeks, the two groups switched practices. A positive effect of meditation on self-actualization was reported.

Throll (1982) The Eysenck Personality Inventory, the State Trait Anxiety Inventory, and two questionnaires on health and drug usage were administered to thirty-nine subjects before they learned TM or progressive relaxation. All subjects were tested immediately after they had learned either technique and then retested five, ten, and fifteen weeks later. There were no significant differences between groups for any of the psychological variables at pretest. However, at posttest the TM group displayed more significant declines in neuroticism and drug use than the progressive relaxation group. Both groups demonstrated significant decreases in state and trait anxiety. The more pronounced results for meditators were explained by the greater amount of time they spent meditating.

Delmonte (1981a) Ninety-four prospective meditators were administered two fourteen-item questionnaires to ascertain their present self-perceptions and their expectations of TM, on three occasions: just before two introductory talks on meditation, just after these talks, and seven months later on follow-up. Thirty-six subjects decided against taking up meditation. Analysis of variance showed that those who took up meditation were older, with more negative self-perceptions and higher expectations of the positive effects of meditation. Frequent practice was related to improved self-perception and increased expectation scores on follow-up. Younger subjects appeared to be more suggestible; they meditated more frequently, perceived themselves more positively, and were more likely to report an improved perception of self compared with their initial pretalk scores than older subjects.

Davidson and Goleman (1977) Individuals who practiced meditation scored higher on various indices of psychological well-being and on hypnotic susceptibility. The authors concluded, however, that similar previous results may reflect selective volunteering for or selective attrition from meditation.

Fehr et al. (1977) Forty-nine subjects practicing the TM technique were given the Freiburger Personality Inventory and were found to be less nervous, less aggressive, less depressed, less irritable, more sociable, more self-confident, less domineering, less inhibited, more emotionally stable, and more self-reliant than a comparison group constructed from available age and sex norms. They were normally extroverted.

Fehr (1977) The Freiburger Personality Inventory was administered to a group of thirty-seven subjects three times: before they learned the TM technique, approximately seven weeks later, and approximately fifty-five weeks later. At the time of the last testing, twelve subjects had discontinued meditation and were treated as a control group. At the third testing, the twenty-five meditating subjects showed significantly better scores than the control group on the following five scales: nervousness, depression, irritability, inhibition, and neuroticism.

Davies (1977) Spielberger's State-Trait Anxiety Inventory and Shostrom's Personal Orientation Inventory were completed by three groups of undergraduates a few days before they began a program of TM or a parallel program of progressive relaxation, or before acting as controls. Seven weeks later both inventories were readministered to all groups. Only the subjects who practiced TM showed a significant reduction in trait anxiety scores, while subjects who practiced TM or progressive relaxation showed a significant improvement in self-actualization.

Shapiro, J. (1977) Two hundred eleven subjects were tested with the Northridge Development Scale and the Spielberger Trait

Anxiety scale before learning TM. A significant increase in self-actualization was observed among the 180 of these subjects who completed a posttest seventeen weeks later.

Orme-Johnson and Duck (1977) The Personal Orientation Inventory profile of Maharishi International University students who practiced TM was compared with profiles presented in the POI manual for a group of college students and for a group of relatively self-actualized people. MIU students scored significantly higher than nonmeditating college students on eight of the twelve POI scales, indicating that the MIU students were generally more self-actualized than other college students. MIU students also scored significantly higher than a group of people judged to be relatively self-actualized on two of the POI scales (Self-Regard and Nature of Man Constructive) and scored as high as the self-actualized people on five of the POI scales (Time Competent, Self-Actualizing Value, Feeling Reactivity, Spontaneity, and Synergy). On the remaining five POI scales, MIU students scored significantly lower than those judged to be self-actualized.

Nystul and Garde (1977) The Tennessee Self-Concept Scale was administered to fifteen Australian subjects who had been practicing Transcendental Meditation for a mean of three years and to fifteen Australian subjects who had never practiced. A "t" test showed that meditators had significantly more positive self-concepts on seven of the twenty-nine test scores: Total Positive, Identity, Self-Satisfaction, Personal Self, Personality Disorder, Distribution Subscore 2, and Moral Ethical Self.

Van den Berg and Mulder (1976) Two studies were undertaken to examine changes in personality brought about by the practice of TM. First, short-term meditators were compared with nonmeditating controls on the Netherlands Personality Inventory. Significant reductions in physical and social inadequacy, neuroticism, depression, and rigidity were found in short-term meditators, whereas no change occurred in controls. The second study compared long-term meditators with nonmeditating students on the Netherlands Personality Inventory, Quality Inventory, Self-Esteem Inventory, Self-Actualization Inventory, and Ego Strength

Scale. Long-term meditators showed remarkably higher levels of self-esteem, satisfaction, ego strength, self-actualization, and trust in others, as well as improved self-image as measured by the Self-Ideal Self Scale of the Quality Inventory.

Ferguson and Gowan (1976) This study found that the practice of TM twice a day for about twenty minutes facilitated self-actualization for an experimental group of thirty-three short-term meditators and sixteen long-term meditators, versus a group of nineteen nonmeditators, as indicated by their improved scores on the Northridge Development Scale, the Cattell Anxiety Scale, and the Spielberger State-Trait Anxiety Inventory.

Hjelle (1974) Fifteen experienced TM meditators and twenty-one novice meditators were administered Bendig's Anxiety Scale, Rotter's Locus of Control Scale, and Shostrom's Personal Orientation Inventory of self-actualization. Experienced meditators were significantly less anxious and more internally controlled than beginning meditators, and they were more self-actualized on seven of Shostrom's twelve subscales.

Nidich et al. (1973) Shostrom's Personal Orientation Inventory was administered two days before the beginning of a TM program and readministered ten weeks later to an experimental group of nine and a nonmeditating control group of nine. The control group took the tests during the same period of time, with no significant difference on any POI variables. For ten of the twelve variables, significant differences between experimental and control subjects appeared in the direction of self-actualization.

Stek and Bass (1973) Using the Internal/External Control of Reinforcement Scale and the Personal Orientation Inventory, the authors found that individuals interested in TM were neither more self-actualized nor more externally controlled than average.

Seeman et al. (1972) Shostrom's Personal Orientation Inventory was administered to an experimental group of fifteen people two days before the beginning of a TM program. The control group consisted of twenty nonmeditators. Experimental and control subjects did not differ significantly on any of the POI scales on the first administration. Two months later, following regular meditation sessions by the experimental subjects, the POI was again administered to both groups. For six of the POI variables there were differences between experimental and control subjects in the direction of self-actualization.

For other studies examining the relationship between meditation and self-actualization, see: Greene and Hiebert (1988), Thomas (1987), Coffelt (1986), Warner (1986), deSantis (1986), Hungerman (1985), Rhyner (1985), Delmonte (1984d), Ray (1984), Burrows (1984), Oldfield (1982), Trausch (1981), Dice (1979), Joseph (1979), Bartels (1976), Joscelyn (1979), Maher (1979), Pelletier (1976a, 1978), Lewis (1978), Kongtawng (1977), Scott (1977), Bartels (1976), Weiner (1977), Denmark (1976), J. Shapiro (1975), Valois (1976), Walder (1976), and Willis (1975).

Hypnotic Suggestibility

Hypnotic suggestibility is influenced by a number of personal attributes, among them the capacity for concentration, the ability to surrender one's attention to commanding images, the tolerance of unusual experiences, and the trust of the hypnotist or induction program involved. Because meditation depends in large part on concentration[34] and the tolerance of unusual experiences, it is not surprising that several contemporary studies have shown a relationship between it and suggestibility.

Delmonte (1981b) tested thirty-six subjects using Barber's Scale for Hypnotic Suggestibility during both meditation and rest, with subjects acting as their own controls, and found that during meditation subjects were significantly more suggestible. This finding was similar to one made by Davidson et al. (1976a), who reported that higher absorption scores among meditators was due to the practice of meditation.

Walrath and Hamilton (1975) reported that there is some indication that TM is related to hypnotic susceptibility. In their study, although only 44% of the non-TM volunteer subjects were rated as highly susceptible, with scores of 10 or higher on the Stanford Hypnotic Susceptibility Scale, 100% of the TM practitioners received scores of 11 or 12 on the Stanford Scale. Walrath and Hamilton concluded that either the practice of TM increases susceptibility to hypnosis or only highly susceptible subjects find sufficient reinforcement in the technique to continue its practice. Using the Harvard Group Scale of Hypnotic Susceptibility and the Field Depth of

Hypnosis Inventory to test hypnosis, Van Nuys (1973) also found that hypnotic susceptibility correlated with subjects' initial skill at meditating.

On the other hand, Rivers and Spanos (1981) assessed 147 students on absorption, hypnotic susceptibility, three measures of psychological well-being, and their response to meditation, concluding that differences between meditators and nonmeditators may be due to self-selection. Earlier, Spanos et al. (1980a) and Spanos et al. (1978) found that hypnotic susceptibility correlated significantly with subjects' initial skill at meditating.

Anxiety

Recent studies have shown that meditation and practices such as progressive relaxation reduce both acute and chronic anxiety. This finding agrees with the assertion in nearly all traditional teachings that contemplation reduces unwarranted fear. The various traditions give somewhat different (though related) reasons for this, however. For example, Buddhism maintains that the eight-fold path or its variations relieve suffering (including fear) by eliminating egotism and desire; Vedanta and Samkhya claim that yoga removes the anxieties born of false attachments; and some Christian mystics say that union with God drives away the concerns of the world. Contemporary studies, on the other hand, interpret meditation's success in reducing anxiety with clinical terms such as lowered arousal of the sympathetic system or the reduction of cognitive dissonance. Modern and traditional understandings of the matter do share certain features, though, among them the observations that calming mental activity helps produce calmer bodies, that concentration helps unify scattered feelings and thoughts, that introspection facilitates catharsis, that self-mastery builds a self-confidence that mitigates fear.

It is important, however, to note a fundamental difference between the aims of modern therapy and most spiritual traditions, namely that the latter generally aim to remove suffering rather than alleviate it. In this, they often regard affliction as an aid to spiritual transformation and therefore something to be learned from. Even when therapies try to deepen self-awareness through continued focus on presenting symptoms, they do not seek the deep liberation that the great ways of enlightenment promote. On the other hand, by promoting liberation, contemplation may eliminate symptoms automatically.

Delmonte (1985b) reviewed the literature on meditation and anxiety reduction, and concluded that those who practice meditation regularly tend to show significant decreases in anxiety, although meditation does not appear to be more effective than other types of intervention, such as hypnosis [see Edwards (1991) and Eppley et al. (1989)].

Davidson and Schwartz (1984) argued that different relaxation techniques (progressive relaxation, hypnotic suggestion, autogenic training, and meditation) activate different major modes or systems, and that the effects of a particular relaxation technique can be meaningfully understood only after determining the type of dependent variable employed. For example, progressive relaxation, a somatic technique, was significantly superior to hypnotic relaxation, a cognitive technique, on a number of somatic measures, while the results on a cognitive measure yielded no significant differences. They demonstrated that the cognitive and somatic contributions to anxiety can be meaningfully separated, and they stated that two general principles pertaining to relaxation and anxiety reduction apply: first, that self-regulation of behavior (including voluntary focusing of attention) in a given mode will reduce (or inhibit) unwanted activity in that specific mode; and second, that self-regulation of behavior in a given mode may, to a lesser degree, reduce unwanted activity in other modes.

These researchers hypothesized that forms of Zen meditation that require that the person count breaths or say a mantra in synchrony with breathing are particularly effective because they simultaneously attenuate both cognitive and somatic anxiety. They suggested that meditation involving the generation of cognitive events (TM's mantra) should elicit greater changes on measures of cognitive processing than meditation on somatic events (breathing), which would result in greater changes on measures of somatic activation. They concluded that it is valuable to assess anxiety in a more systematic way so as to uncover the specific modes in which the unwanted behavior is occurring. Only then will it be possible to determine which relaxation technique might be most effective in reducing anxiety for a given patient in a given state. In addition, the procedure selected must be acceptable to the patient, since his or her motivation to faithfully practice a given technique is crucial to the outcome of treatment.

The following studies have analyzed the relationship between meditation and anxiety:

Kabat-Zinn et al. (1992) Twenty-two study participants were screened with a structured clinical interview and found to meet the DSM-III-R criteria for generalized anxiety disorder or panic disorder with or without agoraphobia. The subjects participated in an eight-week meditation-based stress reduction and relaxation program with a three-month follow-up period. The study found significant reductions in anxiety and depression scores and a reduction in panic symptoms after treatment for twenty of the subjects—changes that were maintained at follow-up.

Edwards (1991) A meta-analysis was conducted to determine the effects of meditation and hypnosis techniques on psychometric measures of anxiety. The chief measure employed in the evaluated research was the State-Trait Anxiety Inventory (Spielberger, 1970; 1983). The analysis included twenty-one hypnosis studies and fifty-four meditation studies. Both techniques were effective in reducing measures of state anxiety. However, for measures of trait anxiety, meditation was more effective.

Steptoe and Kearsley (1990) This study evaluated the influence of meditation and physical exercise on cognitive and somatic anxiety, using 340 meditators, competitive athletes, recreational exercisers, and sedentary controls. Results did not confirm that meditation is associated with reduced cognitive anxiety or that exercise is linked with lower somatic anxiety.

Eppley et al. (1989) The authors conducted a meta-analysis of studies on the effects of relaxation techniques on trait anxiety. Effect sizes for the different treatments (e.g. progressive relaxation, biofeedback, meditation) were calculated. Most treatments produced similar effect sizes, although Transcendental Meditation produced a significantly larger effect size than other forms of meditation and relaxation. A comparison of the content of the treatments and their differential effects suggests that this may be due to the lesser amount of effort involved in TM. Meditation that involved concentration had a significantly smaller effect than progressive relaxation.

Muskatel et al. (1984) Fifty-two undergraduates who had volunteered to receive meditation training were placed into either high or low time-urgency groups based on their scores on Factor S of the Jenkins Activity Survey. Subjects then either received training in Clinically Standardized Meditation followed by three-and-one-half weeks of practice or waited for training during that period. Analyses of scores on a time-estimation task and of self-reported hostility during an enforced waiting task indicated that meditation significantly altered subjects' perceptions of the passage of time and reduced impatience and hostility resulting from enforced waiting.

Beiman et al. (1984) Fifty-two respondents to an ad for anxiety reduction therapy were randomly assigned to TM, behavior therapy, self-relaxation, or a waiting-list control group. They were evaluated before and after treatment on multiple self-report and psychophysiological measures. The results of multivariate analyses of variance indicated there were no significant differerential treatment effects. The results of stepwise multiple regression analyses performed separately for each experimental condition indicated that client characteristics accounted for significant portions of the variance in one or more of the dependent variables for each treatment. Clients who reported perceiving more internal locus of control benefited more from TM than clients who reported greater external locus of control.

Heide and Borkovec (1983) This study was designed to document the occurrence of relaxation-induced anxiety. Fourteen subjects suffering from general tension were given one session of training in each of two relaxation methods, progressive relaxation and mantra meditation. Four subjects, plus one other who terminated prematurely, displayed clinical evidence of anxiety reaction during a preliminary practice period, while 30.8% of the total group under progressive relaxation and 53.8% under focused relaxation reported increased tension due to the relaxation session. Progressive relaxation produced greater reductions in subjective and physiological outcome measures and less evidence of relaxation-induced anxiety.

Kindlon (1983) Thirty-five undergraduate volunteers were randomly assigned to either a meditation group or a sleep/rest control group balanced for expectancy to compare the function of these treatments in the alleviation of test anxiety. Self-report, performance, and physiological indices were assessed, as moderated by gender, Scholastic Aptitude Test score, frequency of practice, repression, and expectancy of relief. The treatments were equally effective in reducing test anxiety.

Lehrer et al. (1983) Physiological and self-report data were collected on sixty-one anxious subjects who were recruited from newspaper ads and randomly assigned to a progressive relaxation, mantra meditation, or control group. Both progressive relaxation and meditation generated positive expectancies and produced decreases in a variety of self-reported symptoms and on EMG, but no skin conductance or frontal EEG effects were observed. Progressive relaxation produced bigger decreases in forearm EMG responsiveness to stressful stimulation and a generally more powerful therapeutic effect than meditation. Meditation produced greater cardiac-orienting responses to stressful stimuli, greater absorption in the task, and better motivation to practice than progressive relaxation, but it also produced more reports of increased transient anxiety.

DeBerry (1982) Thirty-six female volunteers ranging in age from sixty-three to seventy-nine years participated in a twenty-week study designed to evaluate the effects of meditation/relaxation on symptoms of anxiety and depression. Subjects, 83% of whom were widows, were selected because of complaints of anxiety, nervousness, tension, fatigue, insomnia, sadness, and somatic complaints. Subjects were randomly assigned to one of three groups: (1) relaxation/meditation, (2) relaxation/meditation with a ten-week follow-up consisting of practice on a daily basis using relaxation/meditation tapes, and (3) a pseudorelaxation control group (N=12 per group). The treatment groups received one week of baseline evaluation, ten weeks of weekly thirty-minute training sessions, and a ten-week follow-up, with taped relaxation sessions for group 2. The control group followed an identical schedule for ten weeks but did not participate in the follow-up. The Spielberger Self-Evaluation Questionnaire and the Zung Self-Rating Depression Scale were administered before treatment, at the end of the ten weeks of training, and again at the end of the follow-up period (for the treatment groups). In comparison to the control group, the treatment groups manifested a significant pre- to posttreatment decrement for both state and trait anxiety. When the treatment groups were compared as to the efficacy of the follow-up practice sessions, it was found that the practice group continued to show a decrement in state anxiety while the nonpractice group exhibited a return toward baseline levels. However, trait anxiety continued to decrease for both groups. In terms of depression, there was a tendency toward a decrease in mean symptom scores that failed to reach significance. Yet, when questions that correlated highly with anxiety and somatic symptoms were removed and analyzed separately, a significant pre- to posttreatment decrement was noted.

Woolfolk et al. (1982) Thirty-four subjects were recruited from advertisements in local newspapers and received training in meditation or progressive relaxation, or were assigned to a control group. Subjects were tested using the SCL-90, IPAT Anxiety Inventory, and the Lehrer-Woolfolk Anxiety Symptom Questionnaire. Their behavior was also rated weekly by a spouse or roommate. The progressive relaxation and meditation treatments resulted in a significant reduction of stress symptomatology over time.

Fling et al. (1981) Sixty-one undergraduate volunteers were randomly assigned to clinically standardized meditation, quiet sitting, or waiting-list groups. Nineteen others were assigned either to a group practicing "open focus," a technique that begins with awareness exercises focusing on bodily spaces and continues to an expanded awareness of space permeating everything, or to a waiting list. All subjects were tested before training and again eight weeks later. All groups except the waiting list decreased significantly on Spielberger's Trait Anxiety.

Throll (1981) The Eysenck Personality Inventory, the State-Trait Anxiety Inventory, and two questionnaires on health and drug usage were administered to thirty-nine subjects before they learned TM or progressive relaxation. All subjects were tested immediately after they had learned either technique and then retested five, ten, and fifteen weeks later. There were no significant differences between groups for any of the psychological variables at pretest. However, at posttest the TM group displayed more significant and comprehensive results (decreases in Neuroticism/Stability, Extraversion/Introversion, and drug use) than did the progressive relaxation group. Both groups demonstrated significant decreases in State and Trait Anxiety. The more pronounced results for meditators were explained primarily in terms of the greater amount of time that they spent on their technique, plus the differences between the two techniques themselves.

Carrington et al. (1980) The authors studied 154 New York Telephone employees, self-selected for stress, who learned one of three techniques—clinically standardized meditation, respiratory one method meditation, or progressive relaxation—or who served as waiting-list controls. At 5.5 months, the treatment groups showed clinical improvement in self-reported symptoms of stress using the SCL-90-R Self-Report Inventory, but only the meditation groups showed significantly more symptom reduction than the controls. The authors concluded that meditation training has considerable value for stress-management programs in organizational settings.

Lehrer et al. (1980) Thirty-six volunteer subjects were assigned to a progressive relaxation group, a clinically standardized meditation group, or a waiting-list control group asked to relax daily without specific instructions. Subjects were given the state and trait scales of the State-Trait Anxiety Inventory and the IPAT Anxiety Inventory two times, separated by five weeks, during which the two treatment groups received four weekly sessions of group training. At the end of the five-week period all subjects were tested in a psychophysiology laboratory where they were exposed to five very loud tones. Using the techniques they had learned while anticipating the loud tones, the meditation group exhibited higher heart rates and higher integrated frontalis EMG activity. However, they also showed greater cardiac decelerations

The Physical and Psychological Effects of Meditation

following each tone, more frontal alpha, and fewer symptoms of cognitive anxiety than the other two groups, according to the two inventories.

Raskin et al. (1980) Thirty-one chronically anxious subjects were studied to compare their responses to muscle biofeedback, TM, and relaxation therapy. The study consisted of a six-week baseline period, six weeks of treatment, a six-week posttreatment observation period, and later follow-up. Each subject was ranked according to the degree of improvement on five anxiety variables: Taylor Manifest Anxiety Scale Score, Mean Current Mood Checklist score, situational anxiety, symptomatic distress, and sleep disturbance. The results indicate that neither EMG feedback nor TM is any more effective in alleviating the symptoms of chronically anxious patients than relaxation therapy. Additionally, the three treatments were similar with respect to both the time course for obtaining therapeutic results and the subjects' ability to maintain these results once they were obtained.

Kirsch and Henry (1979) This study examined the effect of self-desensitization and meditation in the reduction of public speaking anxiety. Thirty-eight speech-anxious students were assigned to a control group or one of the following self-administered treatment conditions: systematic desensitization, desensitization with meditation replacing progressive relaxation, or meditation only. The results indicated that the three treatments were equally effective in reducing anxiety, and all of them produced a greater reduction in self-reported (but not behavioral) anxiety than that found in untreated subjects. Reliable changes in physiological manifestations of anxiety were found only in those subjects who rated the treatment rationale as highly credible. High credibility ratings were also associated with significantly greater reductions in self-reported anxiety.

Benson et al. (1978b) This study explored the efficacy of two nonpharmacological techniques for therapy of anxiety: a simple, meditational relaxation technique and a self-hypnosis technique. Thirty-two patients were divided into two groups and instructed to practice the assigned technique daily for eight weeks. Change in anxiety was determined by psychiatric assessment, physiological testing, and self-assessment. There was essentially no difference between the two techniques in therapeutic efficacy according to these evaluations. Psychiatric assessment revealed overall improvement in 34% of the patients, while self-rating assessment indicated improvement in 63% of them.

Thomas and Abbas (1978) Using the Middlesex Hospital Questionnaire (which measures free-floating anxiety and obsessions) and the Spielberger State-Trait Anxiety Inventory, this study found TM and progressive relaxation to be equally effective in reducing anxiety among a group of anxious subjects. The authors suggested that the only way to evaluate claims made by TM practitioners was to compare them with others who are using alternative treatments (or coping mechanisms) with measurement criteria strictly defined.

Davies (1977) Spielberger's State-Trait Anxiety Inventory and Shostrom's Personal Orientation Inventory were completed by three groups of undergraduates. A group of twenty-five was taught TM, a group of forty was taught progressive relaxation, and a group of twenty-seven acted as controls. Seven weeks later, both inventories were readministered to all groups. Only the subjects who regularly practiced TM showed a significant reduction in trait-anxiety scores compared with controls.

Stern (1977) The Trait Anxiety Scale of Spielberger's State-Trait Anxiety Inventory was administered to an experimental group of thirty-seven subjects practicing the TM technique and to a control group of fifteen subjects not practicing TM. The meditators were found to be significantly less anxious than the nonmeditators.

Lazar et al. (1977) Four weeks after learning the TM technique, eleven subjects showed a significant decrease in mean anxiety scores on Campbell and Stanley's Recurrent Institutional Cycle Design and the IPAT Anxiety Scale Questionnaire. Similar results were obtained in a second experiment.

Ross (1977) Seventeen students who practiced TM regularly and thirteen who learned TM but did not practice it regularly were given the IPAT Anxiety Scale and the Psychoticism, Neuroticism, Extroversion, and Lie scales of the PENL before and three to four months after starting the TM program. Analyses of covariance showed that neuroticism declined significantly more among the regular meditators. There was a similar trend of greater decreases for the regular meditators in anxiety and psychoticism, although these differences in changes over the three- to four-month period only approached significance. No changes were observed in the other scales.

Kanas and Horowitz (1977) This study experimentally tested the claimed stress-reducing effects of TM. Two stress films were shown to a group of sixty meditators and nonmeditators. Stress response was observed through the use of cognitive and affective measures, employing content analysis techniques and self-ratings. On several self-rating scales, a group of subjects who had signed up to be initiated into TM rated themselves significantly more emotionally distressed than either a control group pr other meditators. There was a trend for meditators who meditated during the experiment to show less stress response to the films than meditators who were told not to meditate. However, this difference was significant on only one measure, a subjective stress scale.

Shapiro (1976b) This study combined the self-control techniques of Zen meditation and behavioral self-management, and applied them to a case of generalized anxiety. The subject was a female undergraduate student who complained of "free-floating anxiety" and who described her feelings of loss of self-control and anxiety as an "overpowering feeling of being bounced around by some sort of all-powerful forces." Intervention consisted of training in behavioral self-observation and functional analysis, a weekend of Zen experience, and three weeks of formal and informal meditation. Results indicated a significant decrease in daily feelings of anxiety and stress during the intervention phase.

Nidich et al. (1973) The State-Trait Anxiety Inventory A-State Scale was administered to eight experimental subjects and nine control subjects two days before the experimental subjects began the practice of TM. Six weeks later the subjects were asked to carry out a demanding task, after which the control group was instructed to sit with eyes closed and the experimental group was instructed to meditate for fifteen minutes. The anxiety scale was then readministered. Mean anxiety scores for the two groups were not significantly different on the first administration of the test. The reduction in anxiety between the two tests was significantly greater for the meditators than for the nonmeditators. Since both groups were exposed to knowledge about the TM program but only the experimental group was instructed in the technique, it appeared that the reduced anxiety in the meditators was due to the experience of TM rather than knowledge about it.

Puryear et al. (1976) One hundred fifty-nine Association for Research and Enlightenment members were randomly assigned to either a treatment or control group, with the former learning a new meditation technique (Edgar Cayce's approach) and the latter continuing their customary daily pattern. Analysis of variance was used to compare group means of the scale scores yielded by the IPAT Anxiety Scale and the Mooney Problem Check List. Unlike the control group, the treatment group reported highly significant reductions on the IPAT Anxiety Scale scores after twenty-eight days of meditation with the new approach. No significant differences were found on the checklist variables for either the treatment or control group.

Davidson et al. (1976a, 1976b) Attentional absorption and trait anxiety in fifty-eight subjects divided into four groups: controls who were interested in but did not practice meditation, beginners who had meditated for one month or less, short-term meditators who had practiced regularly for one to twenty-four months, and meditators who had practiced for more than two years. Subjects were administered the Shor Personal Experiences Questionnaire, the Tellegen Absorption Scale, and the Spielberger State-Trait Anxiety Inventory. The results indicated reliable increases in measures of attentional absorption, in conjunction with a reliable decrement in trait anxiety across groups as a function of length of time meditating.

The Physical and Psychological Effects of Meditation

Goleman and Schwartz (1976) This study compared meditation and relaxation for their ability to reduce stress reactions in a
laboratory threat situation. Thirty experienced meditators and
thirty controls either meditated or relaxed, with eyes closed or
with eyes open, then watched a stressor film. Stress response was
assessed by phasic skin conductance, heart rate, self-report, and
personality scales. Meditators habituated heart rate and phasic
skin-conductance responses more quickly to the stressor impacts
and experienced less subjective anxiety (as indicated by the
Activity Preference Questionnaire, State-Trait Anxiety Inventory,
and Eysenck Personality Inventory).

Smith (1975c) In this study, two experiments were conducted
to isolate the trait-anxiety-reducing effects of TM from expectation of relief, and the concomitant ritual of sitting twice daily.
Experiment 1 was a double-blind study in which forty-nine
anxious college student volunteers were assigned to TM and fifty-
one were assigned to a control treatment, "periodic somatic
inactivity" (PSI). PSI matched form, complexity, and expectation-
fostering aspects of TM, but incorporated a daily exercise that
involved sitting twice daily rather than sitting and meditating. In
experiment 2, two parallel treatments were compared, both
called "cortically mediated stabilization" (CMS). Twenty-seven
volunteers were taught CMS 1, a treatment that incorporated a
TM-like meditation exercise, and twenty-seven were taught CMS
2, an exercise designed to be the near antithesis of meditation
(deliberate cognitive activity). The dependent variables were self-
reported trait anxiety measured by the State-Trait Anxiety
Inventory A-Trait Scale and anxiety symptoms of striated muscle
tension and autonomic arousal as measured by the Epstein-Fenz
Manifest Anxiety Scale. Results show six months of TM and PSI to
be equally effective and eleven weeks of CMS 1 and CMS 2 to be
equally effective. Differences between groups did not approach
significance. The results strongly support the conclusion that the
crucial therapeutic component of TM is not the TM exercise.

Girodo (1974) In this study, nine patients diagnosed as anxiety
neurotics were monitored for anxiety symptoms with an anxiety
symptom questionnaire before practicing yoga meditation at each

training session. After approximately four months of practice, five patients improved significantly, while the other four failed to show any appreciable decline in anxiety symptoms. These four then meditated while engaged in imaginal flooding, where they imagined the worst thing that could happen to them. During meditation and imaginal flooding a decrement in anxiety occurred. Analysis of patient characteristics suggested that yoga meditation was beneficial for patients with a short history of illness and that flooding was effective for those with a long history.

Hjelle (1974) Fifteen experienced TM meditators and twenty-one novice meditators were administered Bendig's Anxiety Scale, Rotter's Locus of Control scale, and Shostrom's Personal Orientation Inventory of self-actualization. As predicted, experienced meditators were significantly less anxious and more internally controlled than beginning meditators. Likewise, experienced meditators were significantly higher, i.e., more self-actualized, on seven of Shostrom's twelve subscales.

Nidich et al. (1973) The State-Trait Anxiety Inventory A-State Scale was administered to eight experimental subjects and nine control subjects two days before the experimental subjects began learning the TM technique. Six weeks later the subjects were asked to carry out a demanding task; immediately afterward the control group was instructed to sit with eyes closed and the experimental group to meditate for fifteen minutes. The anxiety scale was then readministered. Mean anxiety scores for the two groups were not significantly different on the first administration of this test. At the second administration of the test, however, the reduction in anxiety was significantly greater for the meditators.

Vahia et al. (1973) In this study, ninety-five outpatients, diagnosed as psychoneurotic, acted as subjects. All of them had failed to show improvement as a result of previous treatments. Half were taught yoga and meditation, and they practiced these techniques for one hour a day for four to six weeks. The other half, the controls, were given a pseudotreatment consisting of exercises resembling yoga asanas (postures) and pranayamas (breathing exercises). Control subjects were asked to write down

The Physical and Psychological Effects of Meditation

all the thoughts that came into their minds during treatment, and they followed the same daily schedule as the experimental group. Both groups were given the same support, reassurance, and placebo tablets, and were assessed clinically before, during, and after treatment. Following treatment, the experimental group exhibited a significant mean decrease in anxiety, measured on the Taylor Manifest Anxiety Scale. The control group exhibited no significant change on this scale. Overall, 74% of the experimental group were judged to be clinically improved after treatment as against only 43% of the control group (improvement in the control group being attributed to a combination of involvement in research and therapist's time). The authors concluded that meditation and yoga are significantly more effective than a pseudotherapy in the treatment of psychoneurosis.

For other studies examining the relationship between meditation and anxiety, see: Alexander et al. (1993), Weinstein and Smith (1992), Snaith et al. (1992), Fulton (1990), Coleman (1990), Traver (1990), DeBerry et al. (1989), Soskis et al. (1989), Collings (1989), Agran (1989), Kalayil (1989), Jangid et al. (1988a), Sawada and Steptoe (1988), Delmonte and Kenny (1987), Delmonte (1986a), Shaw (1986), Benson (1986), Callahan (1986), DeLone (1986), van Dalfsen (1986), Benson (1985a), Blevens (1985), Kutz et al. (1985a,b), Delmonte and Kenny (1985), Delmonte (1985a, 1985d), Hungerman (1985), Gilmore (1985), Norton et al. (1985), Scardapane (1985), Steinmiller (1985), Maras et al. (1984), Benson (1984b), Clark (1984), Cummings (1984), Gitiban (1983), Hirss (1983), Goldberg (1982), Kindlon (1982), Schuster (1982), Borelli (1982), DeBlassie (1981), Jones (1981), Denny (1981), Zeff (1981), Curtis (1980), Gordon (1980), Bridgewater (1979), Joseph (1979), Diner (1978), Bahrke (1978), Comer (1978), Goldman (1978), Hendricksen (1978), Lewis (1978a), Pelletier (1976b, 1978), Scuderi (1978), Wampler (1978), Wood (1978), Berkowitz (1977), Traynham (1977), Weiner (1977), Fabick (1976), Schecter (1975), and J. Shapiro (1975).

Psychotherapy and Addiction

Psychotherapy as we know it now did not exist when the major contemplative traditions developed, so comparisons between its effects and those of meditation cannot be made precisely. Contemplative activity, however, has generally been said to have a healing effect on mind and body.

More than fifty contemporary studies argue for this connection, showing that meditation has helped relieve addiction, neurosis, obesity, claustrophobia, headache, anxiety, and other forms of distress. It is important to remember that, although traditional contemplative teachings may give the same reasons for these healing effects that contemporary psychology and medicine do, they generally aim at a more radical liberation from suffering.

Craven (1989) suggests there are several factors that need to be kept in mind when evaluating various studies. These include: the length of time and training of meditation; the context within which it is practiced; personality differences between meditators and the general population; variability in outcome measures and the difficulty in operationalizing psychotherapeutic change. Another variable that should be considered is that various meditation practices may produce different psychological effects. Epstein (1990a) discusses meditation as involving two distinct attentional strategies (Goleman, 1977), the first being concentration on a single object and the second moment-to-moment awareness of changing objects of perception (mindfulness). The concentration practices are used to provide enough stability of mind to attempt the second type of practice (mindfulness). Like free-association and evenly suspended attention, mindfulness practices encourage the development of an observing self and initially promote the emergence of unconscious material. As meditation progresses, however, emphasis shifts from intrapsychic content to intrapsychic process, and proceeds to illuminating the actual representational nature of the inner world. In very advanced mindfulness meditation, one can become aware of the relationships between one's behavior, physiological functioning, and mental activity. See Delmonte (1990b) for a discussion of the effects of concentration and mindfulness practices. As can be seen from the discussion above, there is a developmental aspect to meditation practice, therefore, psychological effects can vary with length of practice. See Shapiro (1992a, 1992b) and Epstein (1990a, 1990b).

Psychiatry and Psychotherapy

Delmonte and Kenny (1987) evaluated meditation as an adjunct to psychotherapy. They concluded that meditation practice may be associated with the acquisition of useful skills (focused attention) and may be physiologically relaxing. They also concluded that meditation may decrease anxiety, insomnia, and drug usage, while enhancing hypnotic induction and self-actualization. However, they concluded that there is still no compelling evidence that meditation practice is associated with unique state effects

The Physical and Psychological Effects of Meditation

compared with other relaxation procedures. Furthermore, they concluded that the long-term objectives of meditation are not generally congruent with those of mainstream psychotherapy, since they go beyond therapeutic gain in the clinical sense [see also Delmonte and Kenny (1985)]. Earlier, Delmonte (1986a) concluded that meditation as an intervention strategy was successful with anxiety and hypertension, but of doubtful effectiveness in the treatment of most other therapeutic disorders.

Kutz et al. (1985a) presented a framework for the integration of meditation and psychotherapy. The authors saw a synergistic advantage in the combination of the two practices:

> The intensification of the psychotherapeutic process by this ancient/new mind-body discipline should not be viewed as a revolution in psychotherapy but as an evolution of the ideas of its founders. Freud and Jung were each searching for more direct ways of expanding consciousness and self-awareness. With the information available in their time, they both were justified in disqualifying the nonselective acceptance of mystical teachings. Such a cultural transformation is as incompatible with the world view of our time as it was with theirs. However, today the hindsight of more than half a century and its accumulated alteration of our biological and psychological perspectives offers a unique vantage point for synthesizing disparate existing con-structs into more comprehensive models of self-exploration in the same way that Freud and Jung used the knowledge blocks available in their era.[35]

Epstein (1990a) finds that meditation can be used in the therapeutic setting as an aid to relaxation, as an adjunct to psychotherapy, as a self-control strategy, for promoting regression in service of the ego, and for encouraging greater tolerance of emotional states.

Shapiro (1992a) sees meditation as being therapeutic in a number of ways including:

1. A self-regulation strategy in addressing stress and pain manage-ment and enhancing relaxation and physical health (Benson, 1975; Shapiro and Zifferblatt, 1976; Shapiro and Giber, 1978; Kabat-Zinn et al., 1992, 1985, 1986; Orme-Johnson, 1987);

2. A self-regulation strategy (cf. Ellis, 1984) comparable to other

cognitive focusing, relaxation, and self-control strategies such as guided imagery, hetero-hypnosis, biofeedback, progressive relaxation, and autogenic training (Shapiro, 1982, 1985; Holmes, 1984; Dillbeck and Orme-Johnson, 1987);

3. An adjunct to psychotherapy (Goleman, 1981; Kutz et al., 1985b). Psychodynamic therapists have used meditation for controlled regression in service of the ego and as a means to allow repressed material to come forth from the unconscious (Carrington and Effron, 1975b; Shafii, 1973b). Humanistic psychologists have used it to help individuals gain a sense of self-responsibility and inner directedness (e.g., Keefe, 1975; Schuster, 1975-1976; Lesh, 1970c). Behaviorists have used it for stress management and self-regulation (e.g., Stroebel and Glueck, 1977; Shapiro, 1985; Woolfolk and Franks, 1984).

Recently several researchers have reviewed previous studies and evaluated the use of meditation in psychotherapy practice. See Bogart (1991), Delmonte (1990b), and Craven (1989).

Earlier, West (1979b) observed that meditation has become increasingly popular as a therapy and that a number of theoretical papers have appeared in journals comparing Zen and psychotherapy, including: Dean (1973), Haimes (1972), Van Dusen (1961), Becker (1961), Fromm (1959), and Sato (1958). Single case studies have also been published describing the use of meditation; for paranoia (Boorstein, 1983); for obesity (Weldon and Aron, 1977, and Berwick and Ozeil, 1973); for claustrophobia (Boudreau, 1972); for insomnia (Miskiman, 1977b and 1977d, and Woolfolk et al., 1976); for hypertension (see previous section); for headache (Benson et al., 1973a); and for anxiety (see previous section).

C.P. Allen (1979) and McIntyre et al. (1974) reported that stutterers were helped by TM. More detailed cases of the use of meditation as an adjunct to psychotherapy have been done by Carrington (1977), Carrington and Ephron (1975c), and Shafii (1973a). West (1979b) cited the work of Vahia et al. (1973) as an example of a well-controlled study in which meditation and yoga were shown to be significantly more effective than a pseudotherapy in the treatment of psychoneurosis. West (1979b) argued that most recent investigations of meditation's use in the psychiatric setting were inadequately controlled and conducted [studies by Candelent and Candelent (1976) and Glueck and Stroebel (1975), which used meditation in psychiatric hospitals, might be cases in point, because in both cases meditation was taught indiscriminately to patients representing a broad range of diagnostic categories].

The usefulness of meditation in psychotherapeutic practice has been much debated, and studies indicate that whereas it may be helpful in some conditions it is contraindicated in others. Several researchers warn that meditation is probably not useful for some patients. Craven (1989) states that meditation may be contraindicated for patients who are likely to be overwhelmed and decompensate with the loosening of cognitive controls on the awareness of inner experience. This would include patients with a history of psychotic episodes or dissociative disorder. Delmonte (1990b) states that meditation may not be suitable for patients who are withdrawn or disengaged from daily activities such as depressed, schizoid, or psychotic individuals. Engler (1984) believes that meditation will only be effective when a patient has a relatively intact, coherent, and integrated sense of self, and thus would not be helpful for autistic, psychotic, schizophrenic, borderline, or narcissistic conditions.

Miller (1993) warns of the possibility of emergence of hitherto repressed traumatic memories of abuse in individuals referred to stress-reduction programs which utilize meditative techniques.

For a discussion of the potential misuses of meditation by the person who meditates and possible psychotherapeutic treatment strategies, see Gregoire (1990). See also Epstein (1989, 1990b), Wilber, Engler, and Brown (1986), and Epstein and Lieff (1981) for discussions of psychiatric complications of meditation practice.

It has been suggested that meditation may have benefits for therapists as well as patients. Studies suggest that meditation is useful in developing empathy and a quality of listening ability that emphasizes a detached wide-focus attention as well as other qualities that may be helpful in therapeutic practice. See Dubin (1991), Delmonte (1990b), Dreifuss (1990), Sweet and Johnson (1990), Walker (1987), Rubin (1985), Keefe (1975), and Leung (1973)

These studies also examined the usefulness of meditation in psychiatry and psychotherapy:

Kutz et al. (1985b) The authors studied the effect of a ten-week meditation program on twenty patients who were undergoing long-term individual explorative psychotherapy. Results obtained from patients' self-ratings (Hopkins Symptoms Checklist, Profile of Mood States, and the Table of Level of Activity Interference), and the therapists' objective ratings (Clinical Rating Scale and an open-ended questionnaire) demonstrated substantial improvement in most measures of psychological well-being.

Woolfolk (1984) The author reported the case of a twenty-six-year-old construction worker who suffered from chronic and debilitating anger. He was taught to meditate twice a day for fifteen minutes and to employ one or two minutes of self-control meditation whenever anger might be forthcoming. The overall pattern of results suggested that the client's ability to cope with anger was unaffected by meditation practiced in the standard twice-a-day fashion. On the other hand, self-control meditation seemed to result in substantial alterations in the client's anger. The author concluded that brief meditation employed within a self-control framework may be of great clinical value.

Woolfolk and Franks (1984) The authors see great potential for cross-fertilization between behavior therapy and meditation research. However, they believe there is a necessity to divest the scientific study of meditation from the "shrouds of mystery" that are part of its origin. Removing meditation from the arcane might enable it to become an integral part of behavior therapy.

Jichaku et al. (1984) The authors examined the relationship between the Zen koan and the double-bind theory of schizophrenia, and suggested that koan practice creates a psychological state in which an individual can reorganize inner psychological complexities. Meditation's beneficial effects in this regard indicate that perhaps other pathogenic double-bind contexts might be transformed to beneficent ones.

Muskatel et al. (1984) The authors studied fifty-two undergraduates who had volunteered to receive meditation training and who were placed into either high or low time-urgency groups based on their scores on Factor S of the Jenkins Activity Survey. Subjects then received training in Clinically Standardized Meditation followed by three-and-one-half weeks of practice or waited for training during that period. Analyses of scores on a time-estimation task and of self-reported hostility during an enforced waiting task indicated that meditation significantly altered subjects' perceptions of the passage of time and reduced impatience and hostility resulting from enforced waiting.

Ellis (1984) The author suggested that meditation can be seen as one of many cognitive behavioral methods that are employed in cognitive behavior therapy and rational emotive behavior. He described it as a mode of cognitive distraction or diversion that enables one to temporarily interfere with anxiety, self-damnation, depression, or hostility. He described it as "profoundly therapeutic." He warned, however, against meditation as a form of spiritual discipline, since it might interfere with an individual's acceptance of the true human condition, which is "fallible, screwed-up."

Delmonte (1984g) The author administered tests to outpatients before learning meditation. High pretest scores on sensitization, suggestibility, introversion, neuroticism, and perceived symptomatology predicted a low practice frequency. Gender, expectation, credibility, locus of control and self-esteem were unrelated to outcome. By two years, 54% had stopped meditating. Meditation appeared to be more rewarding for subjects with milder complaints.

Delmonte (1980) The author conducted a prospective study in which personality scores taken prior to meditation initiation were used to predict responses to meditation. Eysenck's Personality Inventory, Byrne's Repression-Sensitization Scale, Rotter's Locus of Control, and Barber's Suggestivity Scale were completed by fifty-five prospective meditators. Subjects were recontacted after eighteen months and grouped according to how frequently they meditated as "regulars," "irregulars," and "drop-outs." Eight subjects remained "uninitiated." Statistical analysis of preinitiation scores and frequency of meditation practice showed: (1) Frequency of meditation was negatively correlated with both neuroticism and sensitization. (2) Neuroticism and sensitization were positively correlated independent of meditation practice. (3) Prospective dropouts scored significantly higher on both neuroticism and sensitization than prospective regular meditators and uninitiated subjects, and were significantly more neurotic than Eysenck's norms. (4) Scores of regular meditators and uninitiated subjects were not significantly different from Eysenck's norms for neuroticism. (5) Regular meditators and uninitiated subjects did not differ significantly with regard to neuroticism and sensitization. (6) Meditators-to-be were significantly more neurotic than uninitiated subjects and than Eysenck's norms. No significant differences were found for extraversion, locus of control, and suggestivity. The maintenance of the practice of meditation was not related to one's gender, but dropouts tended to be younger. More recently, Delmonte (1983a) concluded that there was no evidence to support the claim that the "it" between mantra and meditator is of central importance to the effects of meditation practice.

Zuroff and Schwarz (1980) The authors conducted a questionnaire survey to measure the outcome among twenty students randomly assigned to muscle relaxation training and nineteen assigned to Transcendental Meditation at one year and two-and-one-half years. At both follow-ups there were no differences between the groups in frequency of practice or satisfaction. In both groups, less than 25% reported more than moderate satisfaction, and less than 20% practiced as much as once per week. Subjects' expectancies at nine weeks predicted their satisfaction and frequency of practice at two-and-one-half years. The authors concluded that, although some subjects (15-20%) do enjoy and continue to practice Transcendental Meditation, it is not universally beneficial.

Solomon and Bumpus (1978) The authors studied the combination of slow, long-distance running with Transcendental Meditation as a way of enhancing peak experiences and altered states of consciousness, and suggested that this combination could be used as an adjunct to formal individual and group psychotherapy.

Lazarus (1976) The author stated that, although TM proves extremely effective when applied to properly selected psychiatric cases, there are clinical indications that the procedure can precipitate serious psychiatric problems such as depression, agitation, and even schizophrenic decompensation.

Smith (1975b) The author claimed that research on meditation has yielded three sets of findings: (1) experienced meditators who are willing to participate without pay in meditation research appear happier and healthier than nonmeditators, (2) beginning meditators who practice meditation for four to ten weeks show more improvement on a variety of tests than nonmeditators tested at the same time, and (3) persons who are randomly assigned to learn and practice meditation show more improvement over four to ten weeks than control subjects assigned to some form of alternate treatment. However, he suggested that meditation's benefits might come from expectation of relief or from simply sitting on a regular basis.

For other studies examining the relationship between meditation and psychiatry/psychotherapy, see: Dua and Swinden (1992), Compton (1991), Castillo (1990), Delmonte (1990b), Kokoszka (1990), Delmonte (1989), Driskill (1989), Aranow (1988), Epstein (1988), Boerstler and Kornfield (1987), Delmonte (1987), Burnard (1987), Bleick (1987), Bowman (1987), Dubs (1987a, 1987b), Boerstler (1986), Delmonte (1986b), Deikman (1986), Ellis (1986), Seer (1986), Kokoszka (1986), Nespor (1985), Choudhary (1985), Kahn (1985), Chen (1985), Finney and Malony (1985), Levy (1986), Shafii (1985), Simon (1985), Zika (1985), Rosenbluh (1984), Assad (1984), Claxton (1984), Goodpaster (1984), Chriss (1984), Fenwick (1984), Engler (1984), Finney (1984), O'Connell (1984), Sagert (1984), Vassallo (1984), Fertig (1983), Harvey (1983), Norwood (1983), Rhead and May (1983), Alexander (1982), Aron and Aron (1982b), Lester (1982), Rachman (1981), Bacher (1981), Kobayashi (1982), Ling (1982), West (1980b, 1980c), Fritz (1980), Hattauer (1981), Progoff (1980), Green (1980), King (1979), Lourdes (1978), Glueck and Stroebel (1978), Bunk (1979), Handmacher (1978), S.J. Marcus (1978), Pelletier (1978), Benson et al. (1977b), MacMuehlman (1977), Orme-Johnson et al. (1977d), Bloomfield (1977), Fehr (1977), Avila and Nummela (1977), Carpenter (1977), Jackson (1977), Tsakonas (1977), Kline (1976), Reed (1976), Schmidt (1976), Williams, Francis and Durham (1976), Carson (1975), Hirai (1975), Keefe (1975), Hendricks (1975), Mayer (1975), J. Shapiro (1975), Smith (1975b),

West (1975), Murase and Johnson (1974), Timmons and Kanellakos (1974), Chang (1974), Neki (1973), Gellhorn and Kiely (1972), Seeman et al. (1972), Veith (1971), Goleman (1971), Gattozzi and Luce (1971), Lesh (1970b), Timmons and Kamiya (1970), Kretschmer (1969), Malhotra (1962), Becker (1961), Fromm et al. (1960), and Kondo (1958).

Addiction and Chemical Dependency

The following studies have evaluated meditation's effectiveness in treating various types of addictions and drug use:

Gelderloos et al. (1991) The researchers reviewed twenty-four studies on the benefits of TM in treating and preventing misuse of chemical substances. All the studies showed positive effects of the TM program. The authors speculate that the results of these studies and other studies indicate the TM program simultaneously addresses several factors underlying chemical dependence providing not only immediate relief from distress but also long-range improvements in well-being, self-esteem, personal empowerment, and other areas of psychophysiological health. Psychological and physical mechanisms that might be involved in the effects of TM on substance usage are discussed.

Royer-Bounouar (1989) This study examined the effect of practice of the TM technique on smoking behavior during a period of twenty months. Of 7,070 subjects who attended introductory lectures on the TM technique, 13% learned the TM technique and 87% did not. When quit and decrease rates were combined, it was found that 90% of those who practiced TM twice each day had quit or decreased smoking by the end of the study vs 71% for the once each day TM meditators, 55% for those who were irregular or no longer practiced TM, and 33% for the non-TM group.

Klajner et al. (1984) This survey reviewed the efficacy of relaxation training as a treatment for alcohol and drug abuse. The authors concluded that the anxiety that precipitates substance abuse is limited in interpersonal-stress situations involving diminished perceived personal control over the stressor, and that alcohol and other drugs are often consumed for their euphoric rather than tranquilizing effects. Consequently, the empirical

The Physical and Psychological Effects of Meditation

support for the effectiveness of relaxation training as a treatment for substance abuse in general is equivocal. As well, the existing outcome studies suffer fron numerous methodological and conceptual inadequacies. In cases of demonstrated effectiveness, increased perceived control is a more plausible explanation than is decreased anxiety.

Marlatt et al. (1984) In this study, potential subjects were recruited by administering a Drinking Habits Questionnaire to 1,200 undergraduate students at the University of Washington. One hundred thirty males who qualified as high-volume drinkers were invited to attend a meeting at which the purpose of the study was presented. Forty-four agreed to participate and forty-one of them completed the treatment phase of the study, which was divided into three phases: a baseline period of two weeks, a treatment period of six weeks, and a follow-up period of seven weeks. After baseline-period laboratory tests for taste rating and personality testing using the Spielberger State-Trait Anxiety Inventory, the subjects were randomly divided into four groups: meditation (ten), progressive relaxation (eight), attention-placebo control (bibliotherapy) (nine), and no-treatment control (four-teen). The results showed that the regular practice of a relaxation technique (all three of the above) led to a significant decline in alcohol consumption for subjects who were heavy social drinkers. Of all the personality measures administered, only locus of control showed a significant change (toward the internal side of the scale for all three relaxation groups). Although all three relaxation procedures were equally effective, the meditation group subjects continued the practice more faithfully during the follow-up period, and the authors concluded that meditation is a more intrinsically reinforcing or satisfying procedure than the other techniques.

Wong et al. (1981) In this study, a non-self-selected sample of 200 chemically dependent people was instructed in the practice of meditation as part of an ongoing rehabilitation program, and compared with a noninstructed control group, both at the termination of training and six months later. Differences estab-lished upon termination were no longer evident in the instructed group after six months. Subjects who reported continuing at least minimal meditative practices, however, showed improvements in social adjustment, work performance, and use of drugs and alcohol when compared with nonpractitioners. These differences were more pronounced than those established for ongoing Alcoholics Anonymous members.

Parker and Gilbert (1978) The authors investigated the effects of progressive relaxation training and meditation on generalized arousal in alcoholics. Thirty subjects were selected from an in-patient alcohol treatment unit of a Veterans Administration hospital, and randomly assigned to progressive relaxation training, meditation, or a quiet-rest control group. The groups met three times per week for three weeks. The measures of arousal employed were state-anxiety tests (Spielberger, Gorsuch, and Lushene), systolic and diastolic blood pressure, heart rate, and spontaneous GSR. These measures of generalized arousal were collected once each week at a specified time for all subjects. Of the measures taken, only systolic and diastolic blood pressure was significantly different across the groups. Although the progressive relaxation and meditation training groups remained approximately the same on the systolic blood pressure measures across trials, the quiet-rest group increased significantly prior to the second measurement period. On the diastolic measures across trials, the quiet-rest group again increased significantly prior to the second measurement period, while the progressive relaxation and meditation groups showed significant decreases before the end of the training period. The authors believe that the therapeutic potential of this finding is significant, since level of anxiety at the point of discharge from an in-patient substance-abuse program may be related to rehabilitation success rates.

Anderson (1977) In this study, a population of 115 admitted heroin users in the military was studied. Most were weekend users and none were physiologically addicted. After the subjects spent five to seven days in a ward for detoxification, eighty-nine were returned to duty and twenty-six discharged for repeated drug abuse. All of the subjects volunteered to participate in a study, where they were taught TM and asked to practice for

The Physical and Psychological Effects of Meditation

fifteen to twenty minutes twice each day. Of the eighty-nine subjects who returned to duty, none continued TM and all continued some form of drug abuse almost immediately. Of the twenty-six subjects who returned to civilian life, two returned questionnaires, and they indicated that they were continuing to meditate and refraining from drug use.

Winquist (1977) In this study, a questionnaire requesting information on amount and type of drug use before and after beginning the practice of TM was distributed to 525 subjects attending an advanced course on TM. Of 143 subjects who had been regular users of marijuana, hallucinogens, or "hard drugs" before beginning TM, 119 had discontinued all drug use and twenty-two had reduced drug use 50% or more, while only two continued regular drug use.

Brautigam (1977) In this study, ten experimental and ten control subjects matched for past drug use were monitored for drug consumption over a three-month period. Subjects in the experimental group, who were instructed in the TM technique, showed a marked decrease in drug usage, while the control subjects maintained a high usage level. Psychological tests administered to both groups indicated that the meditators showed increased self-acceptance, increased satisfaction, increased ability to adjust, and decreased anxiety in comparison to the nonmeditating controls. The meditating group expressed increased joyfulness and fulfillment, moreover, as well as improved mental and physical well-being.

Lazar et al. (1977) In this study, an anxiety test and a questionnaire concerning drug use, cigarette smoking, and alcohol consumption were administered once to a control group of twenty-four a few days before they received instruction in TM and to experimental groups before and again either four weeks (N=13), eight weeks (N=9), or twelve weeks (N=14) after instruction in TM. The meditators sharply and significantly decreased their use of drugs, their use of marijuana, their cigarette smoking, and their alcohol consumption. Analysis suggested an initial rapid decrement in drug use followed by a continuing but more gradual decline. Those subjects who meditated regularly showed substantially greater reductions in anxiety and drug use than those who were irregular in their practice. The subjects' decreased anxiety was correlated with their decreased use of drugs.

Katz (1977) In this study, a drug history questionnaire was distributed to 269 high school and college students who had decided to learn the TM technique and to a control group of 198 subjects matched by age and sex. After the experimental group received instruction in the TM technique, identical questionnaires were administered three times to both groups at two-month intervals. Subjects practicing the TM technique significantly decreased their use of marijuana, hashish, wine, beer, and hard liquor in comparison with the control group. Fewer TM subjects who were initially nonusers of marijuana and hashish subsequently began the use of these drugs than did nonmeditating subjects who were initially nonusers. Subjects regularly practicing TM decreased their use of marijuana, hashish, wine, beer, and hard liquor to a greater degree than did subjects who practiced the TM technique irregularly.

Schenkluhn and Geisler (1977) A longitudinal study of seventy-six subjects at a drug rehabilitation center in Germany confirmed the positive results of several previous retrospective studies concerning the influence of the TM program on drug abuse. A significant reduction in drug abuse in various categories was observed among those participating in the TM program.

Shafii et al. (1975) The authors of this study surveyed the frequency of alcohol use in 126 individuals identified as practitioners of TM and a matched control group of ninety. No control subjects reported discontinuation of beer and wine use, while 40% of the subjects who had meditated for more than two years reported discontinuation within the first six months. After twenty-five to thirty-nine months of meditation, this figure increased to 60%. In addition, 54% of this group, versus 1% of the control group, had stopped drinking hard liquor.

Shafii et al. (1974) In this study, the effect of TM on subjects' use of marijuana was analyzed using a questionnaire survey. While only 15% of a nonmeditating control group had decreased or stopped their use of marijuana during the preceding three months, one-half to three-quarters of the meditators (depending on the length of time since their initiation) had decreased or stopped their use during the first three months after their introduction to meditation. The authors found that the longer a person had practiced meditation the more likely it was that he or she had decreased or stopped the use of marijuana.

Marcus (1974) After summarizing research concerned with TM and drugs, Marcus argued that the release of stress and tension in the nervous system and the physical and mental well-being produced thereby are apparently responsible for the very encouraging reduction in drug abuse among meditators.

Benson and Wallace (1972b) In this study, questionnaires given to 1,862 subjects who had practiced TM for at least three months revealed that since they had started TM these subjects used and sold fewer drugs and tended to discourage others from doing so. They had decreased their consumption of "hard" alcoholic beverages, moreover, and smoked fewer cigarettes. The magnitude of these changes increased with the length of time that the subject had practiced TM.

West (1979b) pointed out a number of methodological problems associated with studies of meditation and addiction, suggesting that since many of the studies involved TM, whose practitioners are required to abstain from nonprescribed drugs for fifteen days prior to learning the technique, the samples in these studies have been biased. For those who take up TM may have a predisposition to reduce their drug usage anyway. And since many such studies use retrospective questionnaires administered during TM training courses at TM centers, subjects are exposed to social pressure to give up (or not admit) drug usage. Shapiro and Giber (1978) felt that research studies using retrospective sampling in the form of questionnaires were subject to three possible problems: subjects' reports on a paper-and-pencil questionnaire may be inadvertently inaccurate, subjects' memory may be faulty, and subjects may try to deceive the experimenters to gain experimenter approval. In addition, since the questionnaires were given only to long-term meditators and not to the 30% who dropped out, there may have been a subject selection bias.

Shapiro and Giber (1978) pointed out that more recent studies, because of methodological problems in retrospective sampling, have employed longitudinal designs. Although this method is an improvement, it is not definitive because other methodological problems exist, including self-reporting without concurrent validity, combination treatments, lack of control for demand characteristics, expectation effects, and subjects' motivation. Furthermore, the studies often suffer from a lack of clear theoretical rationale between the independent and the dependent variables.

Maliszewski (1978) investigated the relationship between meditation and an organism's need for stimulation using the sensation-seeking scale, the kinesthetic after-effects test, and the magnitude estimation task for auditory intensities. This investigation tested the hypothesis that meditators may reduce stress and the intake of substances that stimulate the organism physically and psychologically. He found that no significant changes in need for stimulation were observed over time between beginning meditators and nonmeditators.

For other studies examining the relationship between meditation and chemical dependency, see: O'Connell (1991), Clements et al. (1988), Delmonte and Kenny (1987), Delmonte (1986b), Murphy et al. (1986), Towers (1986), Delmonte and Kenny (1985), Ganguli (1985), Cohen (1984), Jewell (1984), Matheson (1982), Neurnberger (1977), Parker (1977), and Ottens (1975).

Sleep

Zen Buddhism and other traditions clearly differentiate various degrees of wakefulness, in both ordinary activity and meditation (though they did not have electroencephalographs to measure the differences between them), maintaining that awareness of them was crucial to spiritual growth. The contemporary Zen Buddhist teacher Suzuki Roshi, for example, taught his students to sit through episodes of sleep that appeared during their meditation, holding the half-lotus position while maintaining as much awareness as they could until their drowsiness and dreaming "cleared up." In one Vedantic classification, four states of consciousness were distinguished: *jagrat*, the ordinary waking state, *swapna*, dreaming, *sushupti*, dreamless sleep, and *turiya*, union with the Brahman. And in some schools, such as Gurdjieff's, ordinary consciousness itself was regarded as a form of sleep from which we must awake to achieve true awareness.

In the contemporary studies we review below, drowsiness or light sleep has been compared with meditation. In some of them, the difference is determined when skilled EEG researchers rate EEG records to identify which represent drowsiness and which represent meditation.

West (1980) The author reviewed previous research on meditation and the EEG and concluded that, on the basis of existing EEG evidence, there is some reason for differentiating between meditation and drowsing. He suggested that meditation is, psychophysiologically, a finely held hypnagogic state. He felt, however, that more precisely formulated research was needed.

Banquet and Sailhan (1977) The authors analyzed the results of Banquet's (1973) study using computerized spectral analyses and qualitative reports, and found differences in EEG records between TM, various sleep stages, and wakefulness in meditators and controls.

Fenwick et al. (1977) A consultant neurophysiologist, when asked to allocate the EEG records of twenty-four subjects, correctly identified thirteen records and incorrectly identified eleven control records as meditation. This result would have been expected by chance, and the authors concluded that there was no evidence that EEG changes were different from those observed in stage "onset" sleep. The authors did report, however, that myoclonic jerks observed during meditation are different from those seen in normal drowsing, the former being repetitive, large, well-organized bodily movements, usually confined to a limb or the trunk, whereas in drowsing the jerks are usually single, stereotyped, and simple. They also reported that four subjects displayed a significant increase in abnormal paroxysmal theta bursts during meditation.

Hebert and Lehmann (1977) The authors found that twenty-one out of seventy-eight advanced practitioners of meditation demonstrated intermittent prominent bursts of frontally dominant theta activity during meditation. The subjects' reports suggested that these theta bursts were not related to sleep. During relaxation and sleep onset, fifty-four nonmeditating controls showed no similar theta bursts. The authors suggested that these theta bursts might be evidence of a state adjustment mechanism that comes into play during prolonged low-arousal states. They hypothesized that this mechanism might prevent the drift into sleep by widespread, brief, rhythmic neural activation.

Elson et al. (1977) The authors reported that meditation may be the art of postponing the moment of sleep or freezing the hypnagogic process at later and later stages. They studied eleven Ananda Marga meditators and eleven controls. Six of the controls fell asleep despite a charge to remain in a state of relaxed wakefulness. The meditators did not fall asleep, but entered a nondescending theta state, with the most advanced meditator showing the greatest predominance of theta brainwaves.

Miskiman (1977a, 1977b, 1977d) Subjects in control and experimental groups (N=5 for each group) were deprived of one night's sleep and, as an index of recovery, were tested for para-doxical (REM) sleep on the two following nights. The experimen-tal groups practiced the TM technique for twenty minutes twice a day, and the control group sat with eyes closed and rested for the same period. Meditators showed a much lower total amount of paradoxical sleep on both nights following sleep deprivation and returned to their predeprivation level on the second recovery night, indicating a rapid elimination of fatigue through the practice of TM.

Pagano et al. (1976) The authors studied the EEGs of five experienced practitioners of TM and found that the subjects spent considerable parts of meditation sessions in sleep stages two, three, and four. The time spent in each sleep stage varied both between sessions and between subjects. In addition, the authors compared EEG records made during meditation with those made during naps taken at the same time of day. The range of states observed during meditation did not support the view that meditation produces a single, unique state of consciousness.

Younger et al. (1975) The authors recorded EEGs and EOGs during TM for eight experienced subjects. The records, scored blind, showed that all but two subjects spent considerable portions of their meditation periods in unambiguous physiological sleep.

Banquet and Sailhan (1974) The authors measured the EEG during TM for a group of fifteen meditators and a group of controls, and found significant differences in the amount of wakefulness between the meditation group and the control group as measured by the proportion of alpha to delta waves. The meditators appeared to remain wakeful during meditation, while the controls drifted toward sleep during a comparable period of rest.

Otis (1974) The author recorded the EEGs of twenty-three TM meditators and twenty-one controls who received no training. After learning TM, the TM group displayed significantly more sleep stage-one activity during meditation than they had displayed in a premeditation rest period, and significantly more than the controls. There were no baseline differences between the groups prior to the TM group learning meditation.

Banquet (1973) The author studied twelve TM practitioners and twelve controls who were about to learn TM. He found that subjects practicing TM had distinctive EEG changes, including slow high-amplitude alpha activity extending to anterior channels, theta activity different from sleep, rhythmic amplitude-modulated beta waves present over the whole scalp, and synchronization of anterior and posterior channels.

Fenwick et al. (1977) The author compared meditation and drowsing by having three experienced EEG researchers rate the records of twelve subjects. The most experienced rater achieved the best score, with ten out of twelve records being correctly identified. The least experienced rater correctly identified eight out of twelve records. Overall, the success rate was twenty-seven correctly identified records and nine incorrectly identified records. The raters identified one of the main differences as the relative stability of the alpha rhythm during meditation. The author concluded that the success rate suggests there are clear differences between the EEG records of those meditating and those drowsing.

Sex-Role Identification

D.H. Shapiro et al. (1982) assessed the impact of a three-month meditation retreat on fifteen respondents' self-perceived masculinity and femininity using the Bem Sex-role Inventory before and after the retreat. As hypothesized, male and female subjects, who on pretest perceived themselves to be more stereotypically feminine than normative samples, on posttest reported a significant shift to even greater endorsement of feminine and less endorsement of masculine adjectives.

We may account for such shifts in attitude, among men at least, by assuming that meditation helps its practitioners accept a fuller range of their potentialities. Such an increase in self-acceptance, perhaps, facilitates the development of attributes normally excluded by common stereotypes of masculinity. Qualities such as surrender, empathy, and sensitivity, more often associated with women than men, have been cultivated in most contemplative traditions, some of which even hold up the androgyne as a symbol of spiritual perfection, e.g., in the legend of the Buddha's sixty-four attributes, of which half are male and half female, or in various Gnostic visions of Christ.[36] The ideal of completion through sexual biunity appears in Greek myth and Hindu-Buddhist imagery, and was highly developed during the Middle Ages by men and women in the Christian Monastic tradition. Both Anselm of Canterbury and the anchoress Julian of Norwich spoke of "mother Jesus." In the last century, Mary Baker Eddy wrote of "Father-Mother God" at the same time that the Indian saint Sri Ramakrishna underwent the discipline of identifying with the feminine aspect of the divine. And Tantric ritual, ancient and modern, emphasizes the creation of male-female fullness, rather than seeking relief from it.

CHAPTER 4

Subjective Reports
by Michael Murphy and Steven Donovan

[Subjective report, traditionally rejected as a viable source of scientific information by the reductionists, holds a central place in phenomenology and the new movement in the social sciences emphasizing qualitative methods. The subject matter included here clearly challenges the epistemology of traditional definitions of experimentalism and, to an even greater extent than in 1988 when the first edition appeared, presages the outline of a potential psychology to come. Ed.]

Equanimity

Equanimity is regarded in many contemplative traditions as both a first result of meditation and as a necessary basis for spiritual growth. There are various stages of its development, though, and like empathy and detachment it deepens with practice into states and qualities that require various names to identify them. The philosopher Sri Aurobindo, for example, has written at length about its cultivation, differentiating its various aspects.[37]

Contemporary researchers, however, have only begun to chart the gradations and varieties of such experience. Kornfield (1979), for example, reported that mindfulness practice frequently enhances adaptation to a large range of fluctuating experiences. Goleman (1978-79 and 1976a), Pelletier (1976a, 1978), Walsh (1977), and Davidson (1976) discussed the tranquility of mind and body, the detached neutrality, the experience of global desensitization, and the greater behavioral stability reported by meditators. Other studies have reported similar findings [see Pickersgill and White (1984a,b), Kornfield (1979), Davidson and Goleman (1977), Woolfolk (1975), Hirai (1974), Boudreau (1972), Kasamatsu and Hirai (1966), and Anand et al. (1961a)].

Detachment

Contemporary meditation researchers have described the detachment experienced during meditation, characterizing it as disidentification from pain or inner dialogue, sensory detachment from the external world, full awareness of the outside world while remaining unaffected by it, paring away of attachments, or a growing sense of being the witness. Brown et al.

(1982-1983) compared the phenomenological differences among 122 subjects engaged in meditation, self-hypnosis, and imaging, and reported that the meditators' mental processes seemed to slow down, and awareness assumed an impersonal quality [see Goldstein (1982), Pelletier (1976b, 1978), Goleman (1977), Walsh (1977), Davidson (1976), and Mills and Campbell (1974)].

Such reports resemble the descriptions of holy indifference and nonattachment made by contemplative masters of the past. The Taoist sage Chuang Tzu said, for example:

> By a man without passions I mean one who does not permit good or evil to disturb his inward economy, but rather falls in with what happens and does not add to the sum of his morality.[38]

Or St. John of the Cross:

> Disquietude is always vanity, because it serves no good. Yes, even if the whole world were thrown into confusion and all things in it, disquietude on that account would be vanity.[39]

Or St. Catherine of Genoa:

> We must not wish anything other than what happens from moment to moment all the while, however, exercising ourselves in goodness.[40]

Or the Bhagavad-Gita:

> Not shaken by adversity,
> Not hankering after happiness:
> Free from fear, free from anger,
> Free from the things of desire.
>
> I call him a seer, and illumined.[41]

Like equanimity, detachment from the contents of our mind and from the contradictory impacts of the external world conforms us more closely to the unbroken wholeness of our spiritual ground. It enables us to approach and become the internal freedom we seek.

Ineffability

Meditators often report experiences so different from ordinary experience that they defy description [see Goldstein (1982), Kornfield (1983 and 1979), Pelletier (1976a, 1978), Shapiro (1978d), Goleman (1978-79), Walsh (1978), Welwood (1976), Davidson (1976), Schmidt (1976), Woolfolk (1975), Shafii (1973b), and Murphy (1973)].

The ineffability of mystical experience has been noted by philosophers and contemplative masters since ancient times. William James wrote, for example, that:

> The handiest of the marks by which I classify a state of mind as mystical is negative. The subject of it immediately says that it defies expression, that no adequate report of its contents can be given in words. It follows from this that its quality must be directly experienced; it cannot be imparted or transferred to others.[42]

And Lao Tzu:

> It was from the Nameless that Heaven and Earth sprang; the named is but the mother that rears the ten thousand creatures, each after its kind.[43]

And St. John of the Cross:

> A man, then, is decidedly hindered from the attainment of this high state of union with God when he is attached to any understanding, feeling, imagining, opinion, desire, or way of his own, or to any other of his works or affairs, and knows not how to detach and denude himself of these impediments. His goal transcends all of this, even the loftiest object that can be known- or experienced. Consequently, he must pass beyond everything to unknowing.[44]

And the contemporary Indian sage Ramana Maharshi:

> Strictly speaking, there can be no image of God, because He is without any distinguishing mark.[45]

Bliss

West (1980b, 1980c) said his subjects used these terms to describe their meditative state: feelings of quiet, calmness, and peace; pleasant feelings; warm contentedness; relaxation beyond thought; and a feeling of being suspended in deep warmth. Kornfield (1979) said that rapture and bliss states are common at insight meditation retreats and are usually related to increased concentration and tranquility. Goleman (1978-79) said that meditation brings about rapturous feelings that cause goose flesh, tremor in the limbs, the sensation of levitation, and other attributes of rapture. He said that sublime happiness sometimes suffused the meditator's body, accompanied by an unprecedented never-ending bliss, which motivates the meditator to tell others of this extraordinary experience. Farrow (1977) said that during the deepest phases of meditation, subjects report that thinking settles down to a state of pure awareness or unbounded bliss, accompanied by prolonged periods of almost no breathing.

These reports by contemporary researchers echo many traditional accounts of meditation's delight. The Vedas, for example, claim that through spiritual discipline "Man rises beyond the two firmaments, Heaven and Earth, mind and body ... to the divine Bliss. This is the 'great passage' discovered by the ancient Rishis."[46] Elsewhere Aurobindo writes that "A Transcendent Bliss, unimaginable and inexpressible by the mind and speech, is the nature of the Ineffable. That broods immanent and secret in the whole universe. It is the purpose of yoga to know and become it."[47]

And in the Taittiriya Upanishad it is said that "For truly, beings here are born from bliss, when born, they live by bliss and into bliss, when departing, they enter."[48]

Energy and Excitement

Kornfield (1979) reported that spontaneous body movements, often described as unstressing and releasing, along with intense emotions and mood swings, are common during insight meditation retreats. Shimano and Douglas (1975) described a remarkable build-up of energy during zazen that often became apparent after several days of a meditation retreat. Others have reported the increased energy released by meditation [see Kornfield (1979), Krippner and Maliszewski (1978), Piggins and Morgan (1977-78), Davidson (1976), and Maupin (1965)].

Altered Body Image and Ego Boundaries

Kornfield (1979, 1983) reported that during insight meditation some people experienced an altered body image. Goleman (1978-79) stated that by continually focusing on the object of meditation, one sometimes makes a total break with normal consciousness. The mind sinks into the object and remains fixed in it, and the awareness of one's body vanishes. Woolfolk et al. (1976) noted that certain subjects experienced a complete loss of body feeling. Deikman (1966a) reported that meditators sometimes experienced alterations in ego boundaries, all in the direction of fluidity and breakdown of the usual subject-object differentiation. Others have commented on these phenomena [see Shapiro (1978a), Krippner and Maliszewski (1978), and Piggins and Morgan (1977-78)].

Again, we can find countless descriptions like these in the traditional contemplative literature. The *sukshma sharira*, or "experience body," of certain Hindu schools was distinguished from the *shtula sharira*, the body observed through our exteroceptors. In meditation, it was said, the *sukshma sharira* passed through many shapes, sizes, and densities. The "experience body" in this sense was often equated with the *koshas* or *kayas* (subtle bodies) of Hindu-Buddhist teachings,[49] which could be more easily altered during spiritual practice than the physical frame. The experience of boundary loss and boundary flexibility from which these doctrines arise strongly resemble the altered body images reported in contemporary studies.

The sense of ego or body image may disappear completely during intense realizations, moreover, as it did for the Indian saint Ramakrishna's disciple Narendra:

> During his second visit, about a month later, suddenly, at the touch of the Master, Narendra felt overwhelmed and saw the walls of the room and everything around him whirling and vanishing. "What are you doing to me?" he cried in terror. "I have my father and mother at home." He saw his own ego and the whole universe almost swallowed in a nameless void. With a laugh the Master easily restored him. Narendra thought he might have been hypnotized, but he could not understand how a monomaniac could cast a spell over the mind of a strong person like himself. He returned home more confused than ever, resolved to be henceforth on his guard before this strange man.[50]

Hallucinations and Illusions

Kornfield (1979, 1983) noted that there was a strong correlation between student reports of higher levels of concentration during insight meditation, when the mind was focused and steady, and reports of altered states and perceptions. He reported that unusual experiences, such as visual or auditory aberrations and hallucinations, and unusual somatic experiences, are the norm among practiced meditation students. Walsh (1978) reported that he experienced hypnagogic hallucinations, and Goleman (1978-79) reported visionary experiences during deep meditation. Shimano and Douglas (1975) reported hallucinations similar to toxic delirium during zazen.

The studies of both Kohr (1977a, 1977b) and Osis et al. (1973) reported that there was almost no correlation between meditators' moods before and after meditating, indicating that meditation produced a different state of consciousness. Kubose's (1976) data revealed that meditators categorized most of their thoughts along a present-time dimension, whereas control subjects categorized their thoughts as past or future. In an unpublished paper Deikman has described vivid, autonomous, hallucinatory perceptions during meditation. Earlier, Deikman (1966a) reported that during meditation on a blue vase, his subjects' perception of color became more intense or luminous, and that for some of them the vase changed shape, appeared to dissolve, or lost its boundaries. Maupin (1965) reported that meditators sometimes experience "hallucinoid feelings, muscle tension, sexual excitement, and intense sadness."

The contemplative literature contains numerous descriptions of the perceptual distortion produced by meditation. It is called *makyo* in Zen Buddhist sources, and is characterized in some schools as "going to the movies," a sign of spiritual intensity but a phenomenon that is regarded to be distinctly inferior to the clear insight of settled practice. In some Hindu schools it is regarded as a product of the *sukshma sharira*, or "experience body," in its unstable state, and in that respect is seen to be another form of *maya*, which is the illusory nature of the world as apprehended by ordinary consciousness.

In a similar manner, St. John of the Cross described the false enchantments that may lure the aspirant in prayer, warning that "devils may come in the guise of angels."[51] In his allegory of the spiritual journey, *The Pilgrim's Progress*, John Bunyan described Christian's losing his way by following a man who says he is going to the Celestial City but instead leads him into a net. In all the great contemplative manuals, one is taught that detachment, equanimity, and discrimination are required for spiritual balance once the mind has been opened and made more flexible by prayer and meditation. Illusions and hallucinations, whether they are troubling or beatific, are distractions—or signposts at best—on the way to enlightenment or union with God.

Dreams

Kornfield (1979, 1983) reported that exceptionally vivid dreams and nightmares are common during insight meditation retreats, along with a general increase in awareness before, during, and immediately following sleep. Faber et al. (1978) compared the dreams of seven experienced meditators with a group of matched control subjects on measures of dream recall, amount of dream material, and archetypal dream content. The dreams of meditators contained significantly more archetypal elements, reflecting universal moral themes, than did those of the nonmeditators, which were characterized by personal and everyday issues. The researchers also found a significantly higher recall rate and amount of content in the dreams of meditators. Meditators' archetypal dreams, moreover, were longer than their nonarchetypal dreams. Reed (1978) analyzed the effect of meditation on the completeness and vividness of intentional dream recall, using approximately 400 subjects who recorded dreams for twenty-eight consecutive days and voluntarily recorded the results. He found that when subjects meditated the day before dreaming, they had significantly greater completeness of dream recall on the following morning. The regularity of a subject's meditation was also associated with improved dream recall. On the other hand, Banquet and Sailhan (1977) reported that dream phases become shorter or less frequent in practitioners of TM. Fuson (1976) observed that subjects practicing TM reported improved quality of sleeping and dreaming. The discovery that awareness of dreams is enhanced by meditation conforms to assertions by traditional teachers that contemplative activity introduces fuller consciousness into sleep. Sri Aurobindo, for example, wrote:

> As the inner consciousness grows ... dream experiences increase in number, clearness, coherency, accuracy and after some growth of experience ... we can come to understand them and their significance to our inner life. We can by training become so

conscious as to follow our own passage, usually veiled to our awareness and memory, through many realms and the process of the return to the waking state. At a certain pitch of this inner wakefulness this kind of sleep, a sleep of experience, can replace the ordinary subconscious slumber.[52]

Awakening consciousness during sleep is part of the more general process in spiritual practice by which awareness is enhanced in all activities. Traditional teachings maintain that we can reclaim that full and eternal awareness that is our fundamental ground and source, in all of our experience.

Synesthesia

Walsh (1978) reported that meditators sometimes experience synesthesia, or cross-modality perception, where a sight is smelled or a sound is felt. His report resembles many accounts by contemplatives that their perception blossomed through prayer and meditation so that epiphanies were triggered by the slightest sensory impact.

Extrasensory Experiences

Lesh (1970c) reported that certain experiences occur during the practice of meditation that seem to be either unexplainable or indicative of a higher potential of perception, bordering on the extrasensory or parapsychological. As we have already pointed out, many of the siddhis or supernormal powers, and vibhutis, or perfections, of Hindu Buddhist practice are paranormal. Similar powers have long been reported in the Christian tradition, in Taoism, in Sufism, and in other contemplative traditions.[53]

Clearer Perception

Forte et al. (1984-1985) studied seven advanced meditators and reported that the practice of mindfulness meditation enabled them to become aware of some of the visually preattentive processes involved in visual detection. Unusual perceptual effects were also reported.

Brown et al. (1982-1983) compared the phenomenological differences among 122 subjects engaging in meditation, self-hypnosis, and imaging. They reported that meditators learn greater awareness of bodily processes and experience changes in the perception of time and self.

Kornfield (1979, 1983) noted the increased frequency of mindfulness as an insight meditation retreat continued, through which meditators became aware of greater sensory and mental detail. Goleman (1978-79) reported that meditators reach a state in which every successive moment is clear and distinct. Walsh (1977) reported that he was more mindful of all primary sensations and more sensitive to neurocybernetic signals, and that his intellectual understanding was deepened. Kornfield (1983) suggested that meditators begin to clarify their perceptions of their own motivation and behavior.

Such experience is a fundamental aspect of all contemplative practice. Because the enhancement of awareness is central in all forms of meditation, and because it is part of the goal all contemplatives seek, the traditional literature is filled with statements describing clarities of perception like those reported by contemporary meditation researchers. As William Blake wrote, "If we would cleanse the doors of perception, we would see things as they are, Infinite."

Negative Experiences

Otis (1984) described a study done at Stanford Research Institute in 1971 to determine the negative effects of Transcendental Meditation. SRI mailed a survey to every twentieth person on the Students International Meditation Society (TM's parent organization) mailing list of 40,000 individuals. Approximately 47% of the 1,900 people surveyed responded. The survey included a self-concept word list (the Descriptive Personality List) and a checklist of physical and behavioral symptoms (the Physical and Behavioral Inventory). It was found that dropouts reported fewer complaints than experienced meditators, to a statistically significant degree. Furthermore, adverse effects were positively correlated with the length of time in meditation. Long-term meditators reported the following percentages of adverse effects: antisocial behavior, 13.5%; anxiety, 9.0%; confusion, 7.2%; depression, 8.1%; emotional stability, 4.5%; frustration, 9.0%; physical and mental tension, 8.1%; procrastination, 7.2%; restlessness, 9.0%; suspiciousness, 6.3%; tolerance of others, 4.5%; and withdrawal, 7.2%. The author concluded that the longer a person stays in TM and the more committed a person becomes to TM as a way of life, the greater is the likelihood that he or she will experience adverse effects. This contrasts sharply with the promotional statements of the various TM organizations.

Ellis (1984) stated that meditation's greatest danger was its common connection with spirituality and antiscience. He said that it might encourage some individuals to become even more obsessive-compulsive than they had been and to dwell in a ruminative manner on trivia or nonessentials. He also noted that some of his clients had gone into "dissociative semi-trance states and upset themselves considerably by meditating." Ellis views meditation and other therapy procedures as often diverting people from doing that which overcomes their disturbance to focusing on the highly palliative technique itself. Therefore, although individuals might feel better, their chances of acquiring a basically healthy, nonmasturbatory outlook are sabotaged.

Walsh (1979) reported a number of disturbing experiences during meditation, such as anxiety, tension, and anger. Walsh and Rauche (1979) stated that meditation may precipitate a psychotic episode in individuals with a history of schizophrenia. Kornfield (1979 and 1983) reported that body pain is a frequent occurrence during meditation, and that meditators develop new ways to relate to their pain as a result of meditation. Hassett (1978) reported that meditation can be harmful. Carrington (1977) observed that extensive meditation may induce symptoms that range in severity from insomnia to psychotic manifestations with hallucinatory behavior. Lazarus (1976) reported that psychiatric problems such as severe depression and schizophrenic breakdown may be precipitated by TM. French et al. (1975) reported that anxiety, tension, anger, and other disturbing experiences sometimes occur during TM. Carrington and Ephron (1975c) reported a number of complaints from TM meditators who felt themselves overwhelmed by negative and unpleasant thoughts during meditation. Glueck and Stroebel (1975) reported that two experimental subjects made independent suicide attempts in the first two days after beginning the TM program. Kannellakos and Lukas (1974) reported complaints from TM meditators. Otis (1974) reported that five patients suffered a reoccurrence of serious psychosomatic symptoms after commencing meditation. Maupin (1969) stated that the deepest objection to meditation has been its tendency to produce withdrawn, serene people who are not accessible to what is actually going on in their lives. He said that with meditation it is easy to overvalue the internal at the expense of the external.

These and other negative meditation outcomes are described in traditional sources. The path is "sharp like a razor's edge" says the Katha Upanishad.[54] St. John of the Cross wrote an entire book about the dark

The Physical and Psychological Effects of Meditation

night of the soul.[55] Several hundred pages of Sri Aurobindo's collected works deal with the problems and dangers of his integral yoga.[56] A large part of Aldous Huxley's *The Perennial Philosophy* consists of admonitions from various spiritual masters about the difficulties encountered in contemplative practice,[57] and William James explores the negative side of religious life in *The Varieties of Religious Experience*.[58] These and other sources provide a wide array of warnings and directions for those entering a path of meditation. Though the rewards of contemplative practice can be great, they do not come easily.

Endnotes

1. For analysis of some cultural forces supporting this interest, see E.I. Taylor. "Desperately Seeking Spirituality." Psychology Today, Nov.-Dec. 1994, p. 56.

2. Monier Monier-Williams, A Sanskrit-English Dictionary: Etymologically and Philogically Arranged with Special Reference to Cognate Indo-European Languages. Oxford: Clarendon Press, 1951 ed., establishes the feminine root dhya as generic to the Vedic, Classical, and Buddhist hybrid Sanskrit traditions, p. 521. Dharana, dhyana, and samadhi are characterized as samyama, the three-fold tool, in The Yoga Sutras.

3. H. Zimmer. The Philosophies of India. New York: Pantheon, 1951.

4. Mircea Eliade. Shamanism: Archaic Techniques of Ecstasy. Translated from the French by Willard R. Trask. New York: Bollingen Foundation; distributed by Pantheon Books, 1964; H. Ellenberger. Discovery of the Unconscious. New York: Basic Books, 1970.

5. Mircea Eliade and Joseph M. Kitagawa, eds. The History of Religions: Essays in Methodology. Chicago: University of Chicago Press, 1959.

6. Frederick J. Streng. Understanding Religious Life. 2d ed. Encino, CA: Dickenson Pub. Co., 1976.

7. See, for instance, Studia Mysticorum, Newsletter of the Mysticism Study Group within the American Academy of Religion (Published by The Essene Press for The Cambridge Institute of Psychology and Religion, 98 Clifton Street, Cambridge MA 02140).

8. The following section has been complied from E.I. Taylor. "Asian Interpretations: Transcending the Stream of Consciousness." In K. Pope and J. Singer, eds. The Stream of Consciousness: Scientific Investigations into the Flow of Human Experience. New York: Plenum, 1978, 31-54. Reprinted in J. Pickering and M. Skinner, eds. From Sentience to Symbol: Readings on Consciousness. London: Harvester-Westsheaf, and Toronto: University of Toronto Press, 1990; E.I. Taylor. "Psychology of Religion and Asian Studies: The William James Legacy." Journal of Transpersonal Psychology, 10:1, 1978, 66-79; E. I. Taylor, "Contemporary Interest in Classical Eastern Psychology." In A. Paranjpe, D. Ho, and R. Rieber, eds. Asian Contributions to Psychology. New York: Praeger, 1988, 79-122; E. I. Taylor. "Our Roots: The American Visionary Tradition." Noetic Sciences Review, Autumn 1993 (Twentieth Anniversary Issue), 6-17; and E. I. Taylor. The Great Awakening: Folk-Psychology and the American Visionary Tradition. In preparation.

9. Charles Alexander. Maharishi International School of Management, 1996 (personal communication).

10. The following is based on interviews with Jon Kabat-Zinn and his colleague Ann Massion, March 1996.

11. William Mikulas. "Behaviors of the Mind." Unpublished course materials, Department of Psychology, University of West Florida, March 1995.

12. See, for instance, W.L. Mikulas. Concepts in Learning. Philadelphia: W. B. Saunders; 1974; W.L. Mikulas. Behavior Modification. New York: Harper and Row, 1978; W.L. Mikulas "Four Noble Truths of Buddhism Related to Behavior Therapy." Psychological Record 28 (1978): 59-67; W.L. Mikulas. Skills of Living. Lanham, MD: University Press of America, 1983; W.L. Mikulas. "Self-Control: Essence and Development." Psychological Record 36 (1986) 297-308; W.L. Mikulas. The Way Beyond. Wheaton, IL: Theosophical Publishing House, 1987; W.L. Mikulas. "Mindfulness, Self-Control, and Personal Growth." In M.G.T. Kwee, ed. Psychotherapy, Meditation, and Health. London/The Hague: East-West Publications, 1990; W.L. Mikulas. "Eastern and Western

Psychology: Issues and Domains for Integration." *International Journal of Integrative and Eclectic Psychotherapy* 10 (1991) 29-40.

13.See, for instance, M. Epstein. *Thoughts Without a Thinker: Psychotherapy from a Buddhist Perspective.* Foreword by the Dalai Lama. New York: Basic Books, 1995.

M.G.T. Kwee, ed. *Psychotherapy, Meditation, and Health.* London/The Hague: East-West Publications, 1990; M.A.West, ed. *The Psychology of Meditation.* Oxford: Clarendon Press, 1987; D.H. Shapiro Jr. and Roger N. Walsh, eds. *Meditation, Classic and Contemporary Perspectives.* New York: Aldine Pub. Co., 1984; D. Goleman. *The Meditative Mind: Varieties of Meditative Experience.* Los Angeles: Tarcher, 1988.

14. Dean Ornish. *Stress, Diet, and Your Heart.* New York: Holt, Rinehart, and Winston, 1982; D. Ornish. *Eat More, Weigh Less.* New York: HarperCollins, 1993.

15. As another example, one of the largest pain clinics in the world, the Diamond Headache Clinic in Chicago, utilized a unique approach of non-pharmacologic techniques from behavioral medicine in combination with advanced pharmacologic interventions to accelerate response to pain reduction. Non-pharmacologic interventions included regimes such as relaxation, meditation, and biofeedback. See S. Diamond, F.C. Freitas, and M. Maliszewski. "Inpatient Treatment of Headache: Long-term Results." *Headache,* 26(4) 1986, 189-197.

16. Published by InnoVision Communications, 101 Columbia, Aliso Viejo CA 92656 (800-899-1712).

17. East-West Center for the Healing Arts, 561 Berkeley Avenue, Menlo Park CA 94025

18. Investigations of Qi Gong are being carried out in Korea and Japan as well. See, for instance, H. Ryu, C.D. Jun, B.S. Lee, B.M. Choi, H.M. Kim, and H. Chung. "Effect of Qi Gong Training on Proportions of T Lymphocyte Subsets in Human Peripheral Blood." *American Journal of Chinese Medicine,* XXII, No. 1, 1995: 27-36; and Yasuo Yuasa. "Traditional Eastern Philosophy and Scientific Technology Today." *Obirin Review of International Studies,* 3, 1991; 23-40.

19. Yoga Biomedical Trust, PO Box 140, Cambridge CB4 3SY. (Tel. +44-1223-67301).

20. H. R. Jarrell. *International Meditation Bibliography, 1950-1982.* Metuchen, NJ: The Scarecrow Press, 1985.

21. In addition to this international bibliography, forthcoming, and an unexpected boon to future experimental investigations, will be Y. Haruki's *Meditation Researchers around the World: An International Overview,* published by the Masara Ibuka Foundation and the Advanced Research Center for Human Sciences at Waseda University in Tokyo. In press.

22. American Psychiatric Association, unsigned statement. *American Journal of Psychiatry,* 134 (1977): p. 720.

23. Now, in a forthcoming lead article in the *American Psychologist* Shapiro, Schwartz, et al. present an even more detailed picture of meditation in the context of cognitive strategies for self-control. D.H. Shapiro, C.E. Schwartz, and J. A. Austin. "Controlling Ourselves, Controlling our World." *American Psychologist* (Accepted for publication 3/25/96). In press.

24. Daniel Druckman and John A. Swets, eds. *Enhancing Human Performance: Issues, Theories, and Techniques* (1988) and Daniel Druckman and Robert A. Bjork, eds. *In the Mind's Eye: Enhancing Human Performance.* Washington, DC: National Academy Press, 1991.

25. This lone researcher had originally based his own conclusions on only 300 of the 1,253 entries he had taken from Murphy and Donovan's first edition. For an analysis of their analysis, see E. I. Taylor. "Radical Empiricism and the Conduct of Research." In Willis Harman and Jane Clark, eds. *New Metaphysical Foundations of Modern Science.* Sausalito, CA: Institute of Noetic Sciences, 1994.

26. NIH Technology and Assessment Panel. *The Integration of Behavioral and Relaxation*

Approaches into the Treatment of Chronic Pain and Insomnia. Bethesda, MD: NIH, 1995.

27. Ibid., p. 5

28. Wenger and Bagchi, 1961. Wenger, Bagchi, and Anand guessed that these three subjects used the Valsalva maneuver, consisting of strong abdominal contractions and breath arrest, to reduce venous return to the heart. "With little blood to pump the heart," they wrote, "sounds are diminished ... and the palpable radial pulse seems to disappear. High amplification finger plethysmography continued to show pulse waves, however; and the electrocardiograph showed heart [contractions]." During such breath retention, moreover, their subjects' hearts changed position so that the potentials in one of their EKG leads decreased, which led Wenger and Bagchi to suggest that Brosse's earlier demonstration of complete heart cessation might have resulted from her use of a single EKG lead that lost its potentials when her subject's heart position shifted.

29. Satyanarayanamurthi and Shastry, 1958. Anand and Chhina, again, investigated three yogis who said they could stop their hearts. They found that to accomplish this, all three increased their intrathoracic pressure by forceful abdominal contractions with closed glottis after inspiration or expiration. Like Bagchi and Wenger, they discovered that their subjects' heartbeats could not be detected with a stethoscope after such a maneuver and that their arterial pulse could not be felt, though EKGs showed that their hearts were contracting normally with a deviation of axis to the right when the subjects held their breath after inspiration, and a deviation to the left after expiration. Furthermore, X-ray examinations showed that each subject's heart became narrower in transverse diameter and somewhat tubular while he was trying to stop it. The three yogis "could not stop ... their heart beats," Anand and Chhina wrote, "[but] they greatly decreased their cardiac output by decreasing venous return [and] the decrease in cardiac output is responsible for the imperceptible arterial pulse. This practice of yogis is identical with the Valsalva maneuver." Like Bagchi and Wenger, they suggested that Brosse's experiment had been flawed because she had used a single EKG lead with her subject.

30. Anand et al., 1961. A second study with an airtight box reported by P.V. Karambelkar and associates compared the reactions of an accomplished yogi, a yoga student, and two controls during confinements ranging from 12 to 18 hours. The box used in this experiment was closely monitored for oxygen and carbon dioxide content, having been thoroughly tested for leakage, and the subjects were attached to an EKG, a respiratory strain gauge belt, an EEG, a blood pressure recording device, and a measure of their galvanic skin response. Each subject stayed in the box until its CO_2 level caused him discomfort. The yogi remained for 18 hours, until the air he was breathing reached 7.7% CO_2, while the other three stayed from 12 1/2 to 13 3/4 hours, when their CO_2 levels reached 6.6 to 7.2.%. The yogi stayed longer, the authors suggested, because he was habituated to such situations. But their yoga student, not their professional yogi, showed the least reduction in oxygen consumption as his CO_2 levels increased. He could withstand higher levels of CO_2, the authors argued, because for three years he had practiced the kumbhaka or breath-holding exercise of pranayama, which had trained his body to function with the increased alveolar CO_2 the exercise produces. Subsequently, the professional yogi increased his pranayama practice and exhibited improved adaptation to CO_2 (Karambelkar, Vinekar, and Bhole, 1968; and Bhole et al., 1967).

31. I.K. Taimni, Patanjali's "Yoga Sutras," Book I, verses 2-4. In *The Science of Yoga.* Wheaton, IL: Theosophical Publishing House, 1975.

32. Swami Nikilananda, tr. *The Gospel of Sri Ramakrishna.* New York: Ramakrishna-Vivekananda Center, 1977. See especially Swami Nikhilananda's introduction for descriptions of Sri Ramakrishna's ecstasies and their physical manifestations.

33. Ibid., 798.

34. In the Sutras of Patanjali, for example, it is said that success in yoga requires *dharana*, a term derived from the Sanskrit root *dhr*, to grasp or seize, and *dhyana*, a flowing into the object that is grasped, which results in *samadhi*. In the *Visuddhimagga*, one of the great texts of Theravada Buddhism, a similar emphasis is placed on *ekagrata*, one-pointed attention, as the basis of higher states attained in meditation. And for the Christian "prayer of quiet," during which one apprehends the simple unity of God, single-minded attention is the fundamental requirement. All the great books of contemplative activity emphasize this effect of meditation practice.

35. [Freud and Jung were, of course, not the originators of psychotherapy. Their immediate precursors were the French psychopathologists, such as Charcot, Ribot, Binet, Janet, and Bernheim. See H. Ellenberger. *Discovery of the Unconscious*. New York: Basic Books, 1970. Ed.]

36. John S. Anson. "The Female Transvestite in Early Monasticism: The Origin and Development of a Motif," in *Viator, Medieval and Renaissance Studies*, Vol. 5. Berkeley: University of California Press, 1974. Caroline Walker Bynum. *Jesus as Mother: Studies in the Spirituality of the High Middle Ages*. Berkeley: University of California Press, 1982. In the Middle Ages there developed a theology of "mother Jesus" that is seen in the religious writings of both men and women, "especially the sophisticated theology developed around it by the anchoress Julian of Norwich" (p. 111). It is possible that the Cistercians "borrowed the idea of mother Jesus from the Benedictine Anselm of Canterbury"(p. 112). Stella Kramrisch. *Manifestations of Shiva*. Philadelphia: Philadelphia Museum of Art, 1981, p. 18. Ardhanarisvara (Siva, the Lord Whose Half is Woman). "He reveals himself through the symbol of sexual biunity as beyond the duality of Siva and Sakti (his power), for both are within him. They are the symbols of the seed and the womb of the universe through whom the Great God Playfully creates, preserves and reabsorbs it." Philip Rawson. *The Art of Tantra*. New York: Oxford University Press, 1973. Rawson discusses the identification of the male participant with the male deity (e.g., Siva) and the female with the Goddess (e.g., Devi or Kali). The more complex, "solitary, interior meditative ritual, may combine the subtle body of both sexes within the sadhaka's single body" (p. 92). The emphasis in the tantric ritual is on the creation of the male-female tension of fullness, rather than seeking relief from that tension. Elemire Zola. *The Androgyne: Reconciliation of Male and Female*. New York: Crossroad, 1981. Zola discusses world religions, legends, and examples from history that are concerned with the ideal of androgyny. Androgyny is a means (and symbol) of completion within one being, containing both the male and female, and is a sign of unity.

37. Sri Aurobindo. *Collected Works*. Pondicherry, India: Sri Aurobindo Ashram, 1976. Volume 30 contains an index with many references to "equality" and "equanimity."

38. Aldous Huxley. *The Perennial Philosophy*. New York: Harper and Row, 1970, chap. 6.

39. Ibid.

40. Ibid.

41. Swami Prabhavananda and Christopher Isherwood, tr. *The Song of God: The Bhagavad-Gita*, with an introduction by Aldous Huxley. New York and Scarborough, Ontario: New American Library, 1944.

42. William James. *The Varieties of Religious Experience*. New York: Longman's, 1902, 371.

43. Huxley. Ibid., 24.

44. Huxley. Ibid., 114.

45. T.M.P. Mahadevan. *Ramana Maharshi: The Sage of Arunacala*. London: Unwin Paperbacks, A Mandala Book, 1977.

46. Sri Aurobindo. Ibid., vol. 10, 43.

47. Sri Aurobindo. Ibid., vol. 21, 568.

48. S. Radhakrishnan, tr. *The Principal Upanishads*. New York: Humanities Press, 1978, 557.

The Physical and Psychological Effects of Meditation

49. Sri Aurobindo. Ibid., vol. 12: 450; vol. 18: 220, 259-60; vol. 19: 749; vol. 20: 12, 435; vol. 21: 668; vol. 23: 1018; vol. 26: 497; vol. 27: 217.

50. Swami Nikhilananda, tr. *The Gospel of Sri Ramakrishna.* New York: Ramakrishna-Vivekananda Center, 1977, 57.

51. St. John of the Cross. *The Collected Works of St. John of the Cross,* trans. Kieran Kavanaugh, and Otilio Rodriquez, with introduction by Kiernan Kavanaugh (Washington, DC: Institute of Carmelite Studies, ICS Publications, 1979). "When there is a question of imaginative visions of other supernatural communications apprehensible by the senses and independent of a man's free will, I affirm that . . . an individual must not desire to give them admittance, even though they come from God . . . by doing so a person frees himself from the task of discerning the true visions from the false ones and deciding whether his visions come from an agent of light or of darkness" (p. 158).

"One of the means with which the devil readily catches uncautious souls, and impedes them in the way of spiritual truthfulness, is the supernatural and extraordinary phenomena he manifests through images, either through the material and corporal ones the Church uses, or through those he fixes in the phantasy in the guise of a particular saint. He transforms himself into an angel of light for the sake of deception. . . . The good soul should conse- quently be more cautious in the use of good things, for evil in itself gives testimony to itself" (p. 279).

"Since the devil transforms himself into an angel of light, he seems to be light to the soul. But this is not all. In the true visions from God, he can also tempt in many ways, by causing inordinate movements of the spiritual and sensory appetites and affections toward these visions. If the soul is pleased with these apprehensions, it is very easy for the devil to occasion an increase of its appetites and affections and a lapse into spiritual gluttony and other evils" (p. 228).

Louis J. Puhl. *The Spiritual Exercises of St. Ignatius.* Chicago: Loyola University Press, 1951. "It is a mark of the evil spirit to assume the appearance of an angel of light. He begins by suggesting thoughts that are suited to a devout soul, and ends by suggesting his own. For example, he will suggest holy and copious thoughts that are wholly in conformity with the sanctity of the soul. Afterwards, he will endeavor little by little to end by drawing his soul into his hidden snares and evil designs" (p. 148).

John Bunyan. *The Pilgrim's Progress.* New York: Washington Square Press, 1961. "Now do I see myself in error. Did not the Shepherds bid us beware of the flatterers?" Christian cries (p. 128). But along comes "a Shining One" carrying "a whip of small cord in his hand." Christian tells him what happened, that he was led astray by "a black man, clothed in white." The Shining One says, "It is Flatterer, a false apostle, that hath transformed himself into an angel of light." He set them free, chastised them, taught them "the good way wherein they should walk" (p. 129).

THE BIBLIOGRAPHY
by Michael Murphy, Steven Donovan, and Eugene Taylor

Abbott, T. Review of *On Being Mindless: Buddhist Meditation and the Mind-Body Problem* by P. Griffiths. *Journal of Asian Studies* 47, no. 1 (1988): 178-179.

Abdullah, S. and H. Schucman. "Cerebral Lateralization, Bimodal Consciousness, and Related Developments in Psychiatry." *Research Communications in Psychology, Psychiatry and Behavior* 1 (1976): 671-679.

Abrams, A.I. "The Effects of Meditation on Elementary School Students." *Dissertation Abstracts International* 37, no. 9-A (1977a): 5689.

Abrams, A.I. "Paired-Associate Learning and Recall: A Pilot Study of the Transcendental Meditation Program." In *Scientific Research on the Transcendental Meditation Program: Collected Papers*, Vol. 1, eds. D.W. Orme-Johnson and J.T. Farrow. New York: M.E.R.U. Press, 1977b: 377-381.

Abrams, A.I., and L.M. Siegel. "The Transcendental Meditation Program and Rehabilitation at Folsom State Prison: A Cross Validation Study." *Criminal Justice and Behavior* 5, no. 1 (1978): 3-20.

Agarwal, B., and A. Kharbanda. "Effect of Transcendental Meditation on Mild and Moderate Hypertension." *Journal of the Association of Physicians of India* 29 (1981): 591-596.

Agran, J.L. "The Effects of Relaxation-Meditation Procedures on Federal Supervisors: A Case Study." *Dissertation Abstracts International* 49, no. 9-B (1989): 4062.

Ahlstrom, H.H. "Transcendental Meditation, Adaptation Mechanisms and Valuations." *Dissertation Abstracts International* 52 no. 9 (1992): 5008.

Ahmad, S., H. Ahmad, and S.S. Sumboo. "Personality Study of Individuals Regularly Practicing Transcendental Meditation Technique." *Journal of Personality and Clinical Studies* 4, no. 1 (1988): 89-92.

Ahuja, M.M.S., M.G. Karmarkar, and S. Reddy. "TSH, LH, Cortisol Response to TRH and LH-RH and Insulin Hypoglycemia in Subjects Practicing Transcendental Meditation." *Indian Journal of Medical Research* 74 (1981): 715-720.

Ajaya, S. *Meditational Therapy*. Glenview, IL: Himalayan International Institute of Yoga Science and Philosophy, 1977.

Akers,T.K., D.M.Tucker, R.S. Roth, et al. "Personality Correlates of EEG Change during Meditation." *Psychological Report* 40, no. 2 (1977): 439-442.

Akhilanada, Swami. *Hindu Psychology: Its Meaning for the West.* New York: Harper, 1946.

Akishige,Y., ed. *Psychological Studies on Zen.*Tokyo: Zen Institute of the Komazawa University, 1970.

Akishige,Y. "Historical Survey of the Psychological Studies of Zen." *Bulletin of the Faculty of Literature of Kyushu University* 5 (1974a): 1-57.

Akishige,Y. "The Principles of Psychology of Zen." In *Meditation: Classic and Contemporary Perspectives*, eds. D.H. Shapiro and R.N.Walsh. New York:Aldine, 1974b: 686-690.

Akishige,Y. *Psychological Studies of Zen: II.*Tokyo: Komazawa University, 1977.

Albert, I.B., and B. McNeece. "The Reported Sleep Characteristics of Meditators and Nonmeditators." *Bulletin of the Psychonomic Society* 3, no. 1-B (1974): 73-74.

Alexander, C.N. "Ego Development, Personality and Behavioral Change in Inmates Practicing the Transcendental Meditation Technique or Participating in Other Programs: A Cross-Sectional and Longitudinal Study." *Dissertation Abstracts International* 43, no. 2-B (1982): 539.

Alexander, C.N. "Is Lucid Dreaming Related to Higher States of Consciousness?" *Lucidity Letter* 9, no. 2 (1991): 70-73.

Alexander, C.N., and R.W. Boyer. "Seven States of Consciousness." *Modern Science and Vedic Science* 2, no. 4 (1989): 325-372.

Alexander, C.N., and D.P. Heaton. "Promoting Adult Psychological Development: Implications for Management Education." *Proceedings of the Association of Management.* (1992)

Alexander, C.N., and E.J. Langer, eds. *Higher Stages of Human Development: Perspectives on Adult Growth.* New York: Oxford University Press, 1990.

Alexander, C.N., and W.E. Larimore. "Distinguishing Between Transcendental Meditation and Sleep According to Electrophysiological Criteria." In *Scientific Research on Maharishi's Transcendental Meditation and TM-Sidhi Program: Collected Papers.* Vol. 3, eds. R.A. Chalmers, G. Clements, H. Schenkluhn.Vlodrop,The Netherlands: MVU Press, 1989: 1712-1719.

Alexander, C.N., and D. Sands. "Meditation and Relaxation." In *McGill's Survey of the Social Sciences: Psychology.*, ed. R.H. McGill. Pasadena, CA: Salem Press, 1993: 1499-1504.

Alexander, C.N., R.W. Cranson, R.W. Boyer, and D.W. Orme-Johnson. "Transcendental Consciousness: A Fourth State of Consciousness Beyond Sleep, Dreaming and Waking." In *Sleep and Dreams: A Sourcebook.*, ed. J. Gackenbach. New York: Garland, 1987: 282-312.

Alexander, C.N., E.J. Langer, R.I. Newman, H.M. Chandler, and J.L. Davies. "Transcendental Meditation, Mindfulness, and Longevity: An Experimental Study with the Elderly." *Journal of Personality and Social Psychology* 57, no. 6 (1989a): 950-964.

Alexander, C.N., T.M. Nader, K.L. Cavanaugh, et al. "The Effects of the Maharishi Technology of the Unified Field on the War in Lebanon: A Time Series Analysis of the Influence of International and National Coherence Creating Assemblies." In *Scientific Research on Maharishi's Transcendental Meditation and TM-Sidhi Program: Collected Papers.* Vol. 4, eds. R.A. Chalmers, G. Clements, H. Schenkluhn, and M. Weinless. Vlodrop, The Netherlands: MVU Press, 1989b: 2687-2714.

Alexander, C.N., J.L. Davies, C. Dixon, et al. "Growth of Higher Stages of Consciousness: Maharishi's Vedic Psychology of Human Development." In *Higher Stages of Human Development: Perspectives on Adult Growth.* eds. C.N. Alexander and E.J. Langer. New York: Oxford University Press, 1990a: 286-341.

Alexander, C.N., S. Druker, and E.J. Langer. "Major Issues in the Exploration of Adult Growth." In *Higher Stages of Human Development: Perspectives on Adult Growth,* eds. C.N. Alexander and E.J. Langer. New York: Oxford University Press, 1990b: 3-34.

Alexander, C.N., M. Rainforth, and P. Gelderloos, "Transcendental Meditation, Self-actualization, and Psychological Health: A Conceptual Overview and Statistical Meta-analysis. Special Issue: Handbook of Self-actualization." *Journal of Social Behavior and Personality* 6, no. 5 (1991): 189-248.

Alexander, C.N., G.C. Swanson, M.V. Rainforth, et al. "Effects of the Transcendental Meditation Program on Stress Reduction, Health, and Employee Development—A Prospective Study in 2 Occupational Settings." *Anxiety, Stress, and Coping* 6, no. 3 (1993): 245-262.

Alexander, C.N., D. Heaton, and H.N. Chandler. "Advanced Human Development in the Vedic Psychology of Maharishi Mahesh Yogi: Theory and Research." In *Transcendence and Mature Thought in Adulthood,* eds. M. Miller and S. Cook-Greuter. Lanham, MD: Roman and Littlefield, 1994a, 41-70.

Alexander, C.N., P. Robinson, D.W. Orme-Johnson, et al. "Effects of Transcendental Meditation Compared to Other Methods of Relaxation and Meditation in Reducing Risk Factors, Morbidity, and Mortality." *Homeostasis* 35, nos. 4-5 (1994b): 243-263.

Alexander, C. N., P. Robinson, and M. Rainforth. "Treating and Preventing Alcohol, Nicotine, and Drug Abuse through Transcendental Meditation: A Review and Statistical Meta-analysis." *Alcoholism Treatment Quarterly* 11, no. 1-2 (1994c): 13-87.

Alexander, C.N., V. Barnes, R.H. Schneider, et al. "A Randomized Controlled Trial of Stress Reduction on Cardiovascular and All-Cause Mortality: Results of 8-Year and 15-year Follow-ups." *Circulation* 93, no. 3 (1996a): 629.

Alexander, C.N., R.H. Schneider, F. Staggers, et al. "A Trial Of Stress Reduction For Hypertension In Older African Americans (Part II): Gender And Risk Subgroup Analysis." *Hypertension* 28, no. 1 (1996b): 228-237.

Alexander, F. "Buddhistic Training as an Artificial Catatonia (The Biological Meaning of Psychic Occurrences)." *Psychoanalytic Review* 18 (1931): 129-145.

Allen, C.P. "Effects of Transcendental Meditation, Electromyographic (EMG) Biofeedback Relaxation, and Conventional Relaxation on Vasoconstriction, Muscle Tension, and Stuttering: A Quantitative Comparison." *Dissertation Abstracts International* 40, no. 2-B (1979): 689.

Allen, D. "TM at Folsom Prison: A Critique of Abrams and Siegel." *Criminal Justice and Behavior* 6, no. 1 (1979): 9-12.

Allison, J. "Respiratory Changes during Transcendental Meditation." *Lancet* 1, no. 7651 (1970): 883.

Almy, T.P. "Meditation on a Forest Path." *New England Journal of Medicine* 297, no. 3 (1977): 165-167.

Alvarado, C.S., and N.L. Zingrone. "Individual Differences in Aura Vision: Relationships to Visual Imagery and Imaginative-fantasy Experiences." *European Journal of Parapsychology*, 10 (1994): 1-30.

American Psychiatric Association. "Position Statement on Meditation." *American Journal of Psychiatry* 134, no. 6 (1977): 720.

Amodeo, J. "Focusing Applied to a Case of Disorientation in Meditation." *Journal of Transpersonal Psychology* 13, no. 2 (1981): 149-154.

Anand, B.K., and G.S. Chhina. "Investigations on Yogis Claiming to Stop Their Heart Beats." *Indian Journal of Medical Research* 49 (1961): 90-94.

Anand, B.K., G.S. Chhina, and B. Singh. "Some Aspects of EEG Studies in Yogis." *Electroencephalography and Clinical Neurophysiology* 13 (1961a): 452-456.

Anand, B.K., G.S. Chhina, and B. Singh. "Studies on Shri Ramanand Yogi during His Stay in an Airtight Box." *Indian Journal of Medical Research* 49 (1961b): 82-89.

Anderson, D.A. "Meditation as a Treatment for Primary Dysmenorrhea among Women with High and Low Absorption Scores." *Dissertation Abstracts International* 45, no. 1-B (1984): 341.

Anderson, D.J. "Transcendental Meditation as an Alternative to Heroin Abuse in Servicemen." *American Journal of Psychiatry* 134, no. 11 (1977): 1308-1309.

Anklesaria, F. "A New Approach to Offender Rehabilitation: Maharishi's Integrated System of Rehabilitation." *Journal of Correctional Education* 43, no. 1 (March 1992): 6-13.

Anklesaria, F. *New Horizons in Criminology and Penitentiary Science: The Maharishi Unified Field Based Integrated System of Rehabilitation in Senegalese Prisons.* Vlodrop, The Netherlands: Maharishi Vedic University Press. 1990.

Anthony, Walter, Jr. "An Evaluation of Meditation as a Stress Reduction Technique for Persons with Spinal Cord Injury." *Dissertation Abstracts International* 46, no. 11-A (1985): 3251.

Appelle, S., and L.E. Oswald. "Simple Reaction Time as a Function of Alertness and Prior Activity." *Perceptual and Motor Skill* 38 (1974): 1263-1268.

Aranow, P.T. "Psychoanalytic Theories of the Self: A Review and Critique from a Buddhist Perspective." Vol. I and II, *Dissertation Abstracts International* 49, no. 9-B (1988): 3992.

Aron, E., and A. Aron. "The Transcendental Meditation Program and Stress: Immunization and Treatment." *Sociological Abstracts* 79, supplement (1978): 39.

Aron, E., and A. Aron. "The Transcendental Meditation Program for the Reduction of Stress-related Conditions." *Journal of Chronic Disease and Therapy Research* 3, no. 9 (1979): 11-21.

Aron, A., and E. Aron. "The TM Program's Effect on Addictive Behavior." *Addictive Behavior* 5, no. 1 (1980): 3-12.

Aron, E., and A. Aron. "An Introduction of Maharishi's Theory of Creativity: Its Empirical Base and Description of the Creative Process." *Journal of Creative Behavior* 16 (1982a): 29-49.

Aron, E., and A. Aron. "Transcendental Meditation Program and Marital Adjustment." *Psychological Reports* 51 (1982b): 887-890.

Aron, E., and A. Aron. *The Maharishi Effect: A Revolution Through Meditation.* Walpole, NH: Stillpoint, 1986.

Aron, A., D.W. Orme-Johnson, and P. Brubaker. "The TM Program in the College Curriculum: A Four-year Longitudinal Study of Effects on Cognitive Affective Functioning." *College Student Journal* 15, no. 2 (1981): 140-146.

Armstrong, R.M. "The Psychology of Inner and Outer Space." *Pastoral Psychology* 37, no. 3 (1989): 161-164.

Assad, Richard M. "The Archetypal Symbology of the Tarot, Meditation and Psychological Change." *Dissertation Abstracts International* 45, no. 3-A (1984): 787.

Assimakis, R.D. "Change in the Quality of Life in Canada: Intervention Studies of the Effect of the Transcendental Meditation and TM-Sidhi Program." *Dissertation Abstracts International* 50, no. 5-B (1989): 2203.

Avila, D., and R. Nummela. "Transcendental Meditation: A Psychological Interpretation." *Journal of Clinical Psychology* 33, no. 3 (1977): 842-844.

Avorn, J., and H. Benson. "Decreased Variability of Plasma Cortisol in Subjects Practicing a Relaxation Technique." *Clinical Research* 21 (1973): 959.

Bache, C. "On the Emergence of Perinatal Symptoms in Buddhist Meditation." *Journal for the Scientific Study of Religion* 20 (1981): 339-350.

Bacher, P.G. "An Investigation into the Compatibility of Existential-Humanistic Psychotherapy and Buddhist Meditation." *Dissertation Abstracts International* 42, no. 6-A (1981): 2565-2566.

Badaracco, M.R. "Psychoanalysis as Altering States of Consciousness." *Journal of the American Academy of Psychoanalysis* 3 (1975): 205-210.

Badawi, K., R.K. Wallace, D. Orme-Johnson, et al. "Electrophysiologic Characteristics of Respiratory Suspension Periods Occurring during the Practice of the Transcendental Meditation Program." *Psychosomatic Medicine* 46, no. 3 (1984): 267-276.

Bagchi, B.K. "Mental Hygiene and the Hindu Doctrine of Relaxation." *Mental Hygiene* 20 (1936): 424-440.

Bagchi, B.K., and M.A. Wenger. "Electrophysiological Correlates of Some Yogi Exercises." *Electroencephalography and Clinical Neurophysiology* 7 (1957): 132-149.

Bagchi, B.K., and M.A. Wenger. "Simultaneous EEG and Other Recordings during Some Yogic Practices." *Electroencephalography and Clinical Neurophysiology* 10 (1958): 193.

Bagchi, B.K., E.T. Righey, K.C. Das, and M. Erden. "Non-specific and Aberrant EEG Signs in 200 Hydrocephalic Cases." *Electroencephalography and Clinical Neurophysiology* 26, no 1 (1969): 115.

Bagga, O.P., and A. Gandhi. "A Comparative Study of the Effect of Transcendental Meditation and Shavasana Practice on the Cardiovascular System." *Indian Heart Journal* 35, no. 1 (1983): 39-45.

Bagga, O.P., A. Gandhi, and S. Bagga. "A Study of the Effect of Transcendental Meditation and Yoga on Blood Glucose, Lactic Acid, Cholesterol and Total Lipids." *Journal of Clinical Chemistry and Clinical Biochemistry* 19, no. 8 (1981): 607-608.

Bahrke, M.S. "Influence of Acute Physical Activity and Non-cultic Meditation on State Anxiety." *Dissertation Abstracts International* 38, no. 10-A (1978): 5987.

Bahrke, M.S. "Exercise, Meditation and Anxiety Reduction: A Review." *American Corrective Therapy Journal* 33, no. 2 (1979): 41-44.

Bahrke, M.S., and W.P. Morgan. "Anxiety Reduction Following Exercise and Meditation." *Cognitive Therapy and Research* 2, no. 4 (1978): 323-333.

Baker, D., and C. Hansen. *Superconsciousness through Meditation.* Wellingborough: Aquarian Press, 1978.

Bakker, R. "Decreased Respiratory Rate during the Transcendental Meditation Technique: A Replication." In *Scientific Research on the Transcendental Meditation Program: Collected Papers.* Vol. 1, eds. D.W. Orme-Johnson and J.T. Farrow. New York: M.E.R.U. Press, 1977: 140-141.

Ball, O.E. "The Effect of TM and the TM-Sidhi Program on Verbal and Figural Creativity (TTCT), Auditory Creativity (S and I), and Hemispheric Dominance (SOLAT)." unpublished doctoral dissertation, University of Georgia, 1980.

Ballou, D. "TM Research: Minnesota State Prison." *The Psychobiology of TM*, eds. D.P. Kanellakos and P.C. Ferguson. Los Angeles: MIV Press, 1973.

Ballou, D. "The Transcendental Meditation Program at Stillwater Prison." In *Scientific Research on the Transcendental Meditation Program: Collected Papers.* Vol. 1, eds. D.W. Orme-Johnson and J.T. Farrow. New York: M.E.R.U. Press, 1977: 569-576.

Banquet, J.P. "EEG and Meditation." *Electroencephalography and Clinical Neurophysiology* 33 (1972): 454.

Banquet, J.P. "Spectral Analysis of the EEG in Meditation." *Electroencephalography and Clinical Neurophysiology* 35 (1973): 143-151.

Banquet, J.P., and M. Sailhan. "EEG Analysis of Spontaneous and Induced States of Consciousness." *Revue d'Electroencephalographie et de Neurophysiologie Clinique* 4 (1974): 445-453.

Banquet, J.P., and M. Sailhan. "Quantified EEG Spectral Analysis of Sleep and Transcendental Meditation." In *Scientific Research on the Transcendental Meditation Program: Collected Papers.* Vol. I, eds. D.W. Orme-Johnson and J.T. Farrow. New York: M.E.R.U. Press, 1977: 182-186.

Banquet, J.P., C. Haynes, H. Russel, et al. "Analysis of Sleep in Altered States of Consciousness by Classical Electroencephalogram and Coherence Spectra." *Electroencephalography and Clinical Neurophysiology* 43 (1977): 503.

Barbieri, P. "Using Meditation and RT/CT to Help Students with Cognitive Challenges Be 'Creative' in Reorganizing More Effective Behaviors." *Journal of Reality Therapy* 14, no. 1 (1994): 18-25.

Barmark, S.M., and S.C.B. Gaunitz. "Transcendental Meditation and Heterohypnosis as Altered States of Consciousness." *International Journal of Clinical and Experimental Hypnosis* 27, no. 3 (1979): 227-239.

Barnes, R.M. "A Study of the Psychological Structures of Transcendental, Yoga, and Ignatian Meditation as Allied Phenomena." *Dissertation Abstracts International* 41, no. 11-B (1981): 4243.

Barr, Basil P., and H. Benson. "The Relaxation Response and Cardiovascular Disorders." *Behavioral Medicine Update* 6, no. 4, (1984): 28-30.

Barr, W.H. "College Student Development and TM: An Analysis and Comparison." *Dissertation Abstracts International* 35 (1975): 5840A.

Barron, F. "The Outer Limits of Educability: A Challenge for Creative Education." *Journal of Creative Behavior* 23, no. 2 (1989): 85-92.

Bartels, W.J. "The Effects of a Western Meditation on a Measure of Self-actualization." *Dissertation Abstracts International* 34, no. 9-A (1976): 5840.

Barwood, T.J., J.A.C. Empson, S.G. Lister, et al. "Auditory Evoked Potentials and Transcendental Meditation." *Electroencephalography and Clinical Neurophysiology* 45, no. 5, (1978): 671-673.

Bassford, R.D. "TM and Stress (Physiological and Subjective), Internal vs. External Locus of Control and Self-concept" unpublished doctoral dissertation, University of Western Ontario, London, ON, 1973.

Bauhofer, V. "Physiological Cardiovascular Effects of the Transcendental Meditation Technique." Unpublished doctoral dissertation, Julius-Maximilian University, Wurzburg, West Germany, 1978.

Beary, J.F., and H. Benson. "A Simple Physiologic Technique Which Elicits the Hypometabolic Changes of the Relaxation Response." *Psychosomatic Medicine* 36 (1974): 115-120.

Beauchamp-Turner, D.L., and D.M. Levinson. "Effects of Meditation on Stress, Health, and Affect." *Medical Psychotherapy: An International Journal* 5 (1992): 123-131.

Becker, D.E., and D. Shapiro. "Physiological Responses to Clicks during Zen, Yoga and Transcendental Meditation." *Psychophysiology* 18, no. 6 (1981): 694-699.

Becker, E. "The Central Psychologic Role of the Trance of Zen Therapy." *American Journal of Psychotherapy* 15, no. 4 (1961): 645-651.

Beery, R.C. "The Psychology of Spiritual Evolution: The Nature and Experience of, and Characteristics Leading to Attainment of, Higher States of Consciousness." *Dissertation Abstracts International* 51, no. 6-B (1990): 3111.

Behanan, Kovoor. *Yoga as Scientific Study.* New Haven, CT: Yale University Press, 1937.

Beiman, I.H., S.A. Johnson, A.E. Puente, et al. "The Relationship of Client Characteristics to Outcome for Transcendental Meditation, Behavior Therapy, and Self-relaxation." In *Meditation: Classic and Contemporary Perspectives*, eds. D.H. Shapiro and R.N. Walsh. New York: Aldine, 1984: 565-571.

Bennett, J.E., and J. Trinder. "Hemispheric Laterality and Cognitive Style Associated with Transcendental Meditation." *Psychophysiology* 14, no. 3 (1977): 293-294.

Benson, H. "Yoga for Drug Abuse." *New England Journal of Medicine* 281, no. 20, (1969): 1133.

Benson, H. "Transcendental Meditation—Science or Cult?" *JAMA* 227 (1974a): 807.

Benson, H. "Decreased Alcohol Intake Associated with the Practice of Meditation: A Retrospective Investigation." *Annals of the New York Academy of Science* 233 (1974b): 174-177.

Benson, H. *The Relaxation Response.* New York: William Morrow, 1975.

Benson, H. "The Relaxation Response and Cardiovascular Diseases." *Chest, Heart, Stroke Journal* 1 (1976): 28-31.

Benson, H. "Reply to Muchlman." *New England Journal of Medicine* 297, no. 9 (1977a): 513.

Benson, H. "Systemic Hypertension and the Relaxation Response." *New England Journal of Medicine* 296 (1977b): 1152-1156.

Benson, H. "Your Innate Asset for Combatting Stress." *Harvard Business Review* 58 (1980): 86-92.

Benson, H. "The Relaxation Response: History, Physiologic Basis, and Clinical Usefulness." *Acta Medica Scandinavica* 660, supplementum (1982a): 231-237.

Benson, H. "Body Temperature Changes during the Practice of gTum-mo Yoga (Matters Arising)." *Nature* (1982b): 298-402.

Benson, H. "The Relaxation Response and Norepinephrine." *Integrative Psychiatry* 1 (May-June 1983a): 15-19.

Benson, H. "The Relaxation Response: Its Subjective and Objective Historical Precedents and Physiology." *Trends in Neurosciences* 6, no. 7 (1983b): 281-284.

Benson, H. "The Relaxation Response: Physiologic Basis and Clinical Applicability." In *Biobehavioral Bases of Coronary Heart Disease*, eds. T. Dembroski, T. Schmidt, and G. Blumchen. Basel: Karger, 1983c: 439-449.

Benson, H. *Beyond the Relaxation Response*. New York: Times Books, 1984a.

Benson, H. "The Relaxation Response and the Treatment of Anxiety." In *Psychiatric Update*. ed. L. Grinspoon. *The American Psychiatric Association Annual Review*. Vol. III, American Psychiatric Press, 1984b: 440-448, 530-531.

Benson, H. "The Use of Relaxation Techniques in the Management of Hypertension." *Primary Cardiology* 10 (1984c): 137-144.

Benson, H. "Stress, Anxiety and the Relaxation Response." *Behavioral Biology in Medicine* A Monograph Series, No. 3. *Meducation* (1985a): 1-28.

Benson, H. "Stress, Health and the Relaxation Response." *Behavioral Medicine: Work, Stress and Health*, eds. W.D. Gentry, H. Benson, and C.J. deWolbb. NATO ASI Series D, No. 19 (1985b): 15-32.

Benson, H. "The Relaxation Response. How to Lower Blood Pressure, Cope with Pain and Reduce Anxiety in 20 Minutes a Day." *Harvard Medical Alumni Bulletin* 60 (1986): 33-35.

Benson, H. "The Relaxation Response and Norepinephrine: A New Study Illuminates Mechanisms." *Australian Journal of Clinical Hypnotherapy and Hypnosis* 10, no. 2 (1989): 91-96.

Benson H. "Mind over Maladies: Can Yoga, Prayer and Meditation be Adapted for Managed Care?" [interview by Jim Montague] *Hospital Health Network* Apr 20 1996, 70 (8) p 26-7.

Benson, H., and R.L. Allen. "How Much Stress Is Too Much?" *Harvard Business Review* 58 (1980): 86-92.

Benson, H., and M. Caudill. "The Use of Relaxation Techniques in the Management of Hypertension." *Primary Cardiology* 10 (1984): 137-144.

Benson, H., and R. Friedman. "A Rebuttal to the Conclusions of David S. Holmes' Article: 'Meditation and Somatic Arousal Reduction.'" *American Psychologist* 40, no. 6 (1985): 725-728.

Benson, H., and I. Goodale. "The Relaxation Response: Your Inborn Capacity to Counteract the Harmful Effects of Stress." *Journal of Florida Medical Association* 68 (1981): 265-267.

Benson, H., and W. Proctor. *Your Maximum Mind*. New York: Avon Books, 1987.

Benson, H., and M. Stark, *Timeless Healing: The Power and Biology of Belief*. New York: Scribner, 1996.

Benson, H., and R. Wallace. "Decreased Blood Pressure in Hypertensive Subjects Who Practiced Meditation." *Circulation* 46, no. 1, supplement 11 (1972a): 130.

Benson, H., and R. Wallace. "Decreased Drug Abuse with Transcendental Meditation: A Study of 1862 Subjects." In *Drug Abuse. Proceedings of the International Conference*, ed. J.D. Zarafonetis. Philadelphia: Lea and Febiger, (1972b): 369-376.

Benson, H., B. Malvea, and J. Graham. "Physiologic Correlates of Meditation and their Clinical Effects in Headache: An Ongoing Investigation." *Headache* 13, no. 1 (1973a): 23-24.

Benson, H., B. Rosner, and B. Marzetta. "Decreased Systolic Blood Pressure in Hypertensive Subjects Who Practiced Meditation." *Journal of Clinical Investigation* 52 (1973b): 8a.

Benson, H., J.F. Beary, and M.P. Carol. "The Relaxation Response." *Psychiatry* 37 (1974a): 37-46.

Benson, H., H.P. Klemchuk, and J.R. Graham. "The Usefulness of the Relaxation Response in the Therapy of Headache." *Headache* 14 (1974b): 49-52.

Benson, H., B.R. Marzetta, and B.A. Rosner. "Decreased Blood Pressure Associated With Regular Elicitation of the Relaxation Response: A Study of

Hypertensive Subjects." In *Contemporary Problems in Cardiology Series: Stress and the Heart.*, ed. R.S. Eliot. New York: Futura, 1974c.

Benson, H., B. Rosner, and B. Marzetta. "Decreased Blood Pressure in Untreated Borderline Hypertensive Subjects Who Regularly Elicited the Relaxation Response." *Clinical Research* 22 (1974d): 262.

Benson, H., B. Rosner, B. Marzetta, et al. "Decreased Blood Pressure in Borderline Hypertensive Subjects Who Practiced Meditation." *Journal of Chronic Disease* 27 (1974e): 163-169.

Benson, H., B. Rosner, B. Marzetta, et al. "Decreased Blood Pressure in Pharmacologically Treated Hypertensive Patients Who Regularly Elicited the Relaxation Response." *Lancet* (February 1974f): 289-291.

Benson, H., S. Alexander, and C.L. Feldman. "Decreased Premature Ventricular Contractions Through the Use of the Relaxation Response in Patients with Stable Ischemic Heart Disease." *Lancet* 2 (1975a): 380-382.

Benson, H., M. Greenwood, and H. Klemchuk. "The Relaxation Response: Psychophysiological Aspects and Clinical Applications." *International Journal of Psychiatry in Medicine* 6 (1975b): 87-98.

Benson, H., R. Steinert, M. Greenwood, et al. "Continuous Measurement of O_2 Consumption and CO_2 Elimination during a Wakeful Hypometabolic State." *Journal of Human Stress* 1 (1975c): 37-44.

Benson, H., J.B. Kotch, and K.D. Crassweller. "The Usefulness of the Relaxation Reponse in the Treatment of Stress-related Cardiovascular Diseases." *J S C Medical Associates* 72 (1976): 50-56.

Benson, H., T. Dryer, and L. Hartley. "Decreased Oxygen Consumption at a Fixed Work Intensity with Simultaneous Elicitation of the Relaxation Response." *Clinical Research* 25 (1977a): 453A.

Benson, H., J.B. Kotch, and K.D. Crassweller. "The Relaxation Response: A Bridge between Psychiatry and Medicine." *Medical Clinic of North America* 61 (1977b): 929-938.

Benson, H., J.B. Kotch, K.D. Crassweller, and M.M. Greenwood. "Historical and Clinical Considerations of the Relaxation Response." *American Science* 65 (1977c): 441-445.

Benson, H., T. Dryer, and L. Hartley. "Decreased CO_2 Consumption during Exercise with Elicitation of the Relaxation Response." *Journal of Human Stress* 4, no. 2 (1978a): 38-42.

Benson, H., F.H. Frankel, R. Apfel, et al. "Treatment of Anxiety: A Comparison of the Usefulness of Self-hypnosis and a Meditational Relaxation Technique." *Psychotherapy and Psychosomatics* 30 (1978b): 229-242.

Benson, H., P. Arns, and J. Hoffman. "The Relaxation Response and Hypnosis." *International Journal of Clinical and Experimental Hypnosis* 29 (1981): 259-270.

Benson, H., J.W. Lehmann, M.S. Malhotra, et al. "Body Temperature Changes during the Practice of gTum-mo (Heat) Yoga." *Nature* 295 (1982a): 234-236.

Benson, H., B. Pomeranz, I. Kutz, et al. "Discriminating Groups of Hypnotized and Meditating Subjects from Normal Subject with the Altered States of Consciousness Inventory." *Dissertation Abstracts International* 43, no. 5-B (1982b): 1594.

Benson, H., B. Pomeranz, and I. Kutz. "Pain and the Relaxation Response." In *Textbook of Pain*, eds. P.D. Wall and R. Melzack. Churchill Livingstone, 1984: 817-822.

Benson, H., M.S. Malhotra, R.F. Goldman, G.D. Jacobs, et al. "Three Case Reports of the Metabolic and Electroencephalographic Changes during Advanced Buddhist Meditation Techniques." *Behavioral Medicine* 16, no. 2 (1990): 90-95.

Benson, H., A. Kornhaber, C. Kornhaber, M.N. LeChanu, P.C. Zuttermeister, P. Myers, and R. Friedman. "Increases in Positive Psychological Characteristics with the New Relaxation Response Curriculum in High School Students." *Journal for Research and Development in Education* 27 (1994): 226-231.

Berger, B.G., E. Friedmann, and M. Eaton. "Comparison of Jogging, the Relaxation Response, and Group Interaction for Stress Reduction." *Journal of Sport and Exercise Psychology* 10, no. 4 (December 1988): 431-447.

Berkowitz, A.H. "The Effect of Transcendental Meditation on Trait Anxiety and Self-esteem." *Dissertation Abstracts International* 38, no. 5-B (1977): 2353.

Bernhard, J., J. Kristeller, and J. Kabat-Zinn. "Effectiveness of Relaxation and Visualization Techniques as an Adjunct to Phototherapy and Photochemotherapy of Psoriasis." *Journal of the American Academy of Dermatology* 19 (1988) 572-573.

Berwick, P., and L.J. Oziel. "The Use of Meditation as Behavioral Technique." *Behavior Therapy* 4, no. 5 (1973): 743-745.

Bevan, A.J. "Endocrine Changes in Transcendental Meditation." *Clinical and Experimental Pharmacology and Physiology* 7, no. 1, (1980): 75-76.

Bevan, A.J., P.M. Young, M.L. Wellby, et al. "Endocrine Changes in Relaxation Procedures." *Proceedings of the Endocrine Society of Australia* 19 (1976): 59.

Bevan, A.J., R.G. Symons, G.G. Beng, et al. "Short-term Endocrine Changes in Transcendental Meditation." *Proceedings of the Endocrine Society of Australia* 22 (1979): 56.

Bhalla, V.K. "Neuroendocrinal, Cardiovascular, and Musculoskeletal Analysis of the Holistic Approach to Stress Reduction." *Dissertation Abstracts International* 42, no. 2-B, (1981): 556.

Bindler, P. "Meditative Prayer and Rabbinic Perspectives on the Psychology of Consciousness: Environmental, Physiological, and Attentional Variables." *Journal of Psychology and Judaism* 4, no. 4 (1980): 228-248.

Bitting, A.L. "Meditation and Biofeedback: A Comparison of Effects on Anxiety, Self-actualization, Openness and Self-esteem." unpublished doctoral dissertation, California School of Professional Psychology, Berkeley, 1976.

Black, H.R. "Nonpharmacologic Therapy for Hypertension." *American Journal of Medicine* 66 (1979): 837-842.

Blackburn, P.W.R. "'Minding Steps' and Other Matters." *Dissertation Abstracts International* 51, no. 3-A (1989): 672.

Blackwell, B., I.B. Hanenson, S.S. Bloomfield, et al. "Effects of Transcendental Meditation on Blood Pressure: A Controlled Pilot Experiment." *Psychosomatic Medicine* 37 (1975): 86.

Blackwell, B., S. Bloomfield, P. Gartside, et al. "Transcendental Meditation in Hypertension: Individual Response Patterns." *Lancet* 1, no. 7953 (1976): 223-226.

Blair, M. "Meditation in the San Francisco Bay Area: An Introductory Survey." *Journal of Transpersonal Psychology* 2, no. 1 (1970): 61-70.

Blanchard, E.B., K.A. Applebaum, C.L. Radnitz, B. Morrill, et al. "A Controlled Evaluation of Thermal Biofeedback and Thermal Biofeedback Combined with Cognitive Therapy in the Treatment of Vascular Headache." *Journal of Consulting and Clinical Psychology* 58, no. 2 (1990): 216-224.

Blanz, L.T. "Personality Changes as a Function of Two Different Meditative Techniques." *Dissertation Abstracts International* 34, no. 11-A (1974): 7035-7036.

Blasdell, K.A. "The Effects of the Transcendental Meditation Technique upon a Complex Perceptual-motor Task." In *Scientific Research on the Transcendental Meditation Program: Collected Papers.* Vol. I, eds. D.W. Orme-Johnson and J.T. Farrow. New York: M.E.R.U. Press, 1977: 322-325.

Blasdell, K.S. "Acute Immunoreactivity Modified by Psychosocial Factors: Type A/B Behavior, Transcendental Meditation and Lymphocyte Transformation." *Dissertation Abstracts International* 50, no. 10-B (1990): 4806.

Bleick, C.R. "Case Histories: Using the Transcendental Meditation Program with Alcoholics and Addicts." *Alcoholism Treatment Quarterly* 11, no. 3-4 (1994): 243-269.

Bleick, C.R., and A.I. Abrams. "The Transcendental Meditation Program and Criminal Recidivism in California." *Journal of Criminal Justice* 15, (1987): 211-230.

Blevens, B.K. "The Effect of Relaxation Training on Anxiety for the Poetry Recitation Tasks among Elementary School Children." *Dissertation Abstracts International* 45, no. 5-A (1985): 1200.

Bligh, D. "Dealing with the Effect of Schismatic Experiences in Childhood: A Hypnotherapeutic Approach." *Australian Journal of Clinical Hypnotherapy and Hypnosis* 15, no. 1 (1994): 39-48.

Block, B. "Transcendental Meditation as a Reciprocal Inhibitor in Psychotherapy." *Journal of Contemporary Psychology* 9, no. 1 (1977): 78-82.

Bloomfield, H.H. "Some Observations on the Uses of the Transcendental Meditation Program in Psychiatry." In *Scientific Research on the Transcendental Meditation Program: Collected Papers.* Vol 1, eds. D.W. Orme-Johnson and J.T. Farrow. New York: M.E.R.U. Press, 1977: 605-622.

Bloomfield, H.H. *Transcendental Meditation: Discovering Inner Energy and Overcoming Stress.* London: Unwin Paperbacks, 1978.

Bloomfield, H.H., M. Cain, and R. Jaffe. *Transcendental Meditation: Discovering Inner Energy and Overcoming Stress.* New York: Dell, 1975.

Boals, G.F. "Toward a Cognitive Reconceptualization of Meditation." *Journal of Transpersonal Psychology* 10, no. 2 (1978): 143-182.

Bodin, A.V. "Stress Management Rituals for Daily Work Transitions of Mental Health Professionals." *Dissertation Abstracts International* 50, no. 12-A (1989): 3891.

Boerstler, R.W. "Meditation and the Dying Process." *Journal of Humanistic Psychology* 26, no. 2 (1986): 104-124.

Boerstler, R.W., and H.S. Kornfeld. "Meditation as a Clinical Intervention." *Journal of Psychosocial Nursing and Mental Health Services* 26, no. 6 (June 1987): 29-32.

Bogart, G. "The Use of Meditation in Psychotherapy: A Review of the Literature." *American Journal of Psychotherapy* 45, no. 3 (1991): 383-412.

Boisset, M., and M.A. Fitzcharles. "Alternative Medicine Use by Rheumatology Patients in a Universal Health Care Setting." *Journal of Rheumatology* 21, no. 1 (1994): 148-152.

Bole, D.N. "The Effect of the Relaxation Response on the Positive Personality Characteristics of Paraprofessional Counselors." *Dissertation Abstracts International* 39, no. 4-A (1978): 2136.

Bolen, J.S. "Meditation and Psychotherapy in the Treatment of Cancer." *Psychic* 4, no. 6 (1973): 19-22.

Bono, J. "Psychological Assessment of Transcendental Meditation." In *Meditation: Classic and Contemporary Perspectives*, eds. D.H. Shapiro and R.N. Walsh. New York: Aldine, 1984: 209-217.

Boorstein, S. "The Use of Bibliotherapy and Mindfulness Meditation in a Psychiatric Setting." *The Journal of Transpersonal Psychology* 15, no. 2 (1983): 173-179.

Borelli, M.D. "The Effect of the Practice of Meditation by Eight to Eleven Year Old Children on their Trait Anxiety and Self-esteem." *Dissertation Abstracts International* 43, no. 4-B (1982): 1040.

Borkovec, T.D. "Physiological and Cognitive Processes in the Regulation of Anxiety." In *Consciousness and Self-regulation: Advances in Research*, eds. G.E. Schwartz and D. Shapiro. New York: Plenum Press, 1976.

Borkovec, T.D., and B.L. Hennings. "The Role of Physiological Attention Focusing in the Relaxation Treatment of Sleep Disturbance, General Tension, and Specific Stress Reaction." *Behavior Research and Therapy* 16 (1978): 7-19.

Borland, C., and G. Landrith. "Improved Quality of City Life through the Transcendental Meditation Program: Decreased Crime Rate." In *Scientific Research on the Transcendental Meditation Program: Collected Papers*. Vol I, eds. D.W. Orme-Johnson and J.T. Farrow. New York: M.E.R.U. Press, 1977: 639-648.

Boswell, P.C., and A.J. Murray. "Effects of Meditation on Psychological and Physiological Measures of Anxiety." *Journal of Consulting and Clinical Psychology* 47, no. 3 (1979): 606-607.

Boudreau, L. "Transcendental Meditation and Yoga as Reciprocal Inhibitors." *Journal of Behavior Therapy and Experimental Psychology* 3, no. 2 (1972): 97-98.

Bourguignon, E. "Trance and Meditation." In *Psychological Anthropology*., ed. P.K. Bock. Westport, CT: Praeger, 1994: 297-313.

Bourne, P.G. "Non-pharmacological Approaches to the Treatment of Drug Abuse." *American Journal of Chinese Medicine* 3, no. 3 (1975): 235-244.

Bowman, P.L. "A Phenomenological Comparison of Vipassana Meditation and Existential Psychotherapy." *Dissertation Abstracts International* 48, no. 2-B (1987): 558.

Bradley, B.W., and T.R. McCanne. "Autonomic Responses to Stress: The Effects of Progressive Relaxation, the Relaxation Response, and Expectancy of Relief." *Biofeedback and Self-Regulation* 6, no. 2 (1981): 235-251.

Brach, A.V. "Clinical Applications of Meditation: A Treatment Outcome Evaluation Study of an Intervention for Binge Eating Among the Obese that Combines Formal Meditation and Contingent Formal and Informal Meditation." *Dissertation Abstracts International* 52 no. 7-B (1992): 3898.

Branca, B. "The Effects of Two Cognitively Based Interventions on High, Medium, and Low Levels of Test Anxious College Students." *Dissertation Abstracts International* 49, no. 8-B (1989): 3430.

Brandi, J.F. "A Theory of Moral Development and Competitive Sports." *Dissertation Abstracts International* 50, no. 4-A (1989): 894.

Brandon, J.E. "A Comparative Evaluation of Three Relaxation Training Procedures." *Dissertation Abstracts International* 43, no. 7-A (1983): 2279.

Brannigan, E.J. "Relaxation Techniques for Adults: A Guide." *Masters Abstracts* 28, no. 4 (1990): 479.

Braud, W.G. "Meditation and Psychokinesis." *Parapsychology Review* 21, no. 1 (1990): 9-11.

Brautigam, E. "Effects of the Transcendental Meditation Program on Drug Abusers: A Prospective Study." In *Scientific Research on the Transcendental Meditation Program: Collected Papers.* Vol I, eds. D.W. Orme-Johnson and J.T. Farrow. New York: M.E.R.U. Press, 1977: 506-514.

Bray, J.D. "The Relationship of Creativity, Time Experience and Mystical Experience." *Dissertation Abstracts International* 50, no. 8-B (1989): 3,394.

Bridgewater, M.J. "The Relative Efficacy of Meditation in Reducing an Induced Anxiety Reaction." *Dissertation Abstracts International* 40, no. 2-B (1979): 903-904.

Bright, D., V.A. Buccola, W.J. Stone, et al. "What School Physicians, Nurses and Health Educators Should Know about Transcendental Meditation." *Journal of School Health (U.S.A.)* 43, no. 3 (1973): 192-194.

British Medical Journal. "Meditation and Bodily Changes." 1, no. 6010 (13 March 1976): 610.

British Medical Journal. "Meditation or Methyldopa?" (editorial). 1, no. 6023 (1976): 1421-1422.

British Medical Journal. "Transcendental Meditation" (letter) 1, no. 6157 (1979): 201.

Brooke, Avery. *Learning and Teaching Christian Meditation.* Revised Edition. Cambridge, MA: Crowley Publ. 1990. (Original work published 1977).

Brooks, J. "The Application of Maharishi Ayur-Veda to Mental Health and Substance Abuse Treatment." *Alcoholism Treatment Quarterly* 11, no. 3-4 (1994): 395-411.

Brooks, J.S. "Transcendental Meditation in the Treatment of Post-Vietnam Adjustment. Special Issue: Paradigm Shifts: Considerations for Practice." *Journal of Counseling and Development* 64, no. 3 (1985): 121-215.

Brosse, T. "A Psychophysiological Study." *Main Currents in Modern Thought* 4 (1946): 77-84.

Brown, C., R. Fischer, A. Wagman, et al. "The EEG in Meditation and Therapeutic Touch Healing." *Journal of Altered States of Consciousness* 3 (1977-78): 169-180.

Brown, D., and J. Engler. "The Stages of Mindfulness Meditation: A Validation Study." *Journal of Transpersonal Psychology* 12, no. 2 (1980): 143-192.

Brown, D., and J. Engler. "A Rorschach Study of the Stages of Mindfulness Meditation." In *Meditation: Classic and Contemporary Perspectives*, eds. D. Shapiro and R.N. Walsh. New York: Aldine, 1984: 232-262.

Brown, D., M. Forte, P. Rich, et al. "Phenomenological Differences among Self-hypnosis, Mindfulness Meditation, and Imaging." *Imagination, Cognition and Personality* 2, no. 4 (1982-83): 291-309.

Brown, D., M. Forte, and M. Dysart. "Differences in Visual Sensitivity among Mindfulness Meditators and Non-meditators." *Perceptual and Motor Skills* 58, no. 3 (1984a): 727-733.

Brown, D., M. Forte, and M. Dysart. "Visual Sensitivity and Mindfulness Meditation." *Perceptual and Motor Skills* 58 (1984b): 775-784.

Brown, D.A. "A Model for the Levels of Concentrative Meditation." *International Journal of Clinical and Experimental Hypnosis* 25, no. 4 (1977): 236-273.

Brown, L.L., and S.E. Robinson. "The Relationship Between Meditation and/or Exercise and Three Measures of Self-actualization." *Journal of Mental Health Counseling* 15, no. 1 (1993): 85-93.

Brown, S.W., and J. Blodgett. "EEG Kappa Rhythms during Transcendental Meditation and Possible Perceptual Threshold Changes Following." In *The Psychobiology of Transcendental Meditation: A Literature Review*, ed. D. Kanellakos. Menlo Park, CA: W.A. Benjamin, 1974.

Bruner, R. "The Reduction of Anxiety and Tension States through Learning the Relaxation Response: A Theoretical Study with Clinical Applications." *Dissertation Abstracts International* 39 (1978): 370-371.

Bruning, N.S., and D.R. Frew. "Effects of Exercise, Relaxation, and Management Skills Training on Physiological Stress Indicators: A Field Experiment." *Journal of Applied Psychology* 72, no. 4 (November 1987): 515-521.

Buckler, W. "Transcendental Meditation" (letter). *Canadian Medical Association Journal* 115, no. 7 (1976): 607.

Bucknell, R.S. *The Twilight Language: Explanations in Buddhist Meditation and Symbolism*. New York: St. Martin, 1986.

Bujatti, M., and P. Riederer. "Serotonin, Noradrenaline, Dopamine Metabolites in Transcendental Meditation." *Journal of Neural Transmission* 39, no. 3 (1976): 257-267.

Bunk, B.E. "Effects of Hatha Yoga and Mantra Meditation on the Psychological Health and Behavior of Incarcerated Males." *Dissertation Abstracts International* 40, no. 2-B (1979): 904.

Burnard, P. "Meditation: Uses and Methods in Psychiatric Nurse Education." *Nurse Education Today* 7, no. 4 (1987): 187-191.

Burnes, J.E. "TM in the Boardroom." *Industrial Management* 17, no. 4 (1975): 13-15.

Burns, D., and R.J. Ohayv. "Psychological Changes in Meditating Western Monks in Thailand." *Journal of Transpersonal Psychology* 12, no. 1 (1980): 11-24.

Burrows, C.H. "The Effects of Meditation on Counselor Candidates' Self-actualization." *Dissertation Abstracts International* 45, no. 3-A (1984): 749.

Busby, K., and J. DeKoninck. "Short-term Effects of Strategies for Self-regulation on Personality Dimensions and Dream Content." *Perceptual and Motor Skills* 50 (1980): 751-765.

Bynum, J.L. "Christian Meditation and Biofeedback Training as Psychotherapeutic Agents in the Treatment of Essential Hypertension." *Dissertation Abstracts International* 41, no. 6-A (1980): 2506-2507.

Cadarette, B.S., J.W. Hoffman, M. Caudill, I. Kutz, L. Levine, H. Benson, and R.F. Goldman. "Effect of the Relaxation Response on Selected Cardiorespiratory Response During Physical Exercise." *Medical Science in Sports* 14 (1982): 117.

Callahan, R. "The Use of Christian Meditation in Moncrief Army Hospital with Persons Suffering with Distress." *Dissertation Abstracts International* 47, no. 10-A (1986): 3786.

Campbell, C. "The Facts of Transcendental Meditation: Transcendence is as American as Ralph Waldo Emerson." *Psychology Today* 7 (April 1974): 37-38.

Cancrini, M.G., F.R. De Gregorio, and F. Cardella. "Therapeutic Communities." *Journal of Drug Issues* 24, no. 4 (1994): 639-656.

Candelent, T., and G. Candelent. "Teaching Transcendental Meditation in a Psychiatric Setting." *Hospital and Community Psychiatry* 26, no. 3 (1976): 156-159.

Cangelosi, A. "The Differential Effects of Three Relaxation Techniques: A Physiological Comparison." *Dissertation Abstracts International* 42, no. 1-B (1981): 418.

Cara, A.J. "Transcendental Meditation: An Analysis of the Rhetoric of a Social Movement as Innovation." *Dissertation Abstracts International* 41, no. 8-A (1981): 3318.

Carlson, C.R., P.E. Bacaseta, and D.A. Simanton. "A Controlled Evaluation of Devotional Meditation and Progressive Relaxation." *Journal of Psychology and Theology* 16, no. 4 (Winter 1988): 362-368.

Carpenter, J.T. "Meditation, Esoteric Traditions: Contributions to Psychotherapy." *American Journal of Psychotherapy* 31, no. 3 (1977): 394-404.

Carrington, P. *Freedom in Meditation.* Garden City, NY: Anchor Press/ Doubleday, 1977.

Carrington, P., and H.S. Ephron. "Clinical Use of Meditation." *Current Psychiatric Theories* 15 (1975a): 101-108.

Carrington, P., and H.S. Ephron. "Meditation and Psychoanalysis." *Journal of American Academy of Psychoanalysis* 3 (1975b): 43-57.

Carrington, P., and H.S. Ephron. "Meditation as an Adjunct of Psychotherapy." In *The World Biennial of Psychotherapy and Psychiatry (III)*, eds. S. Arieti and G. Chrzanowski. New York: John Wiley and Sons, 1975c.

Carrington, P., G. Collings, H. Benson, et al. "The Use of Meditation-Relaxation Techniques for the Management of Stress in a Working Population." *Journal of Occupational Medicine* 22, no. 4 (1980): 221-231.

Carruthers, M.E. "Voluntary Control of the Involuntary Nervous System: Comparison of Autogenic Training and Siddha Meditation." *Experimental and Clinical Psychology* 6 (1981): 171-181.

Carsello, C.J., and J.W. Creaser. "Does Transcendental Meditation Training Affect Grades?" *Journal of Applied Psychology* 63, no. 5 (1978): 644-645.

Carson, L.G. "Zen Meditation in the Elderly." *Dissertation Abstracts International* 36, no. 2-B (1975): 903-904.

Carson, V.B. "Prayer, Meditation, Exercise, and Special Diets: Behaviors of the Hardy Person with HIV/AIDS." *J Assoc Nurses AIDS Care* 4, no. 3 (1993): 18-28.

Casper, M. "Space Therapy and the Maitri Project." *Journal of Transpersonal Psychology* 6, no. 1 (1974): 57-67.

Cassel, R.N. "Basic Fundamentals of Mind Control and Transcendental Meditation." *Psychology* 11, no. 2 (1974): 26-33.

Cassel, R.N. "Fostering Transcendental Meditation Using Biofeedback Eliminates Hoax and Restores Credibility to Art." *Psychology* 13, no. 2 (1976a): 58-64.

Cassel, R.N. "Fundamentals Involved in the Scientific Process of Transcendental Meditation." *Journal of Instructional Psychology* 3, no. 3 (1976b): 2-11.

Castillo, R.J. "Depersonalization and Meditation." *Psychiatry* 53, no. 2 (1990): 158-168.

Cataldi, O.B. *Psychophysiology and Its Therapeutic Effects on Stress: An Annotated Bibliography.* Dayton, OH: Wright State University, 1982.

Caudill, Margaret. "Decreased Clinic Utilization by Chronic Pain Patients after Behavioral Medicine Intervention." *Pain* 45 (1991): 334-335.

Caudill, M., E. Stuart, R. Friedman, C. Dorrington, J. Leserman, and H. Benson. "A Nonpharmacologic Program for Multiple Risk Factor Reduction in Hypertensive Patients." *Circulation* 70 (1984a).

Caudill, M., E. Stuart, R. Friedman, J. Leserman, and H. Benson. "The Nonpharmacologic Treatment of Hypertension." *Psychosomatic Medicine* 46 (1984b): 84-85

Caudill, M., R. Friedman, and H. Benson. "Relaxation Therapy in the Control of Blood Pressure." *Bibliotheca Cardiologica* 41 (1987): 106-119.

Cauthen, N., and C. Prymak. "Meditation versus Relaxation: An Examination of the Physiological Effects of Relaxation Training and of Different Levels of

Experience with Transcendental Meditation." *Journal of Consulting and Clinical Psychology* 45, no. 3 (1977): 496-497.

Cavanaugh, K.L., and K.D. King. "Simultaneous Transfer Function Analysis of Okun's Misery Index: Improvements in the Economic Quality of Life Through Maharishi's Vedic Science and Technology of Consciousness." Paper presented at the Annual Meeting of the American Statistical Association, New Orleans, Louisiana, August 22–25, 1988. An abridged version of this paper appeared in *Proceedings of the American Statistical Association, Business and Economics Statistics Section*, 1988: 491–496.

Cavanaugh, K.L., K.D. King, and C. Ertuna. "A Multiple-Input Transfer Function Model of Okun's Misery Index: An Empirical Test of the Maharishi Effect." Paper presented at the Annual Meeting of the American Statistical Association, Washington, DC, August 6–10, 1989. An abridged version of this paper appears in *Proceedings of the American Statistical Association, Business and Economics Statistics Section*. Alexandria, VA: American Statistical Association, 1989a: 565-570.

Cavanaugh, K.L., K.D. King, and B.D. Titus. "Consciousness and the Quality of Economic Life: Empirical Research on the Macroeconomic Effects of the Collective Practice of Maharishi's Transcendental Meditation and TM-Sidhi Program." in R.G. Greenwood, ed. *Proceedings of the Midwest Management Society*. Chicago: Midwest Management Society, 1989b: 183–190. This is a revised version of a paper presented at the Annual Meeting of the Midwest Management Society, Chicago, Illinois, March 1989.

Cerpa, H. "The Effects of Clinically Standardized Meditation on Type II Diabetics." *Dissertation Abstracts International* 49, no. 8-B (1989): 3432.

Chalmers, R.A., L.J. Davis, and B.P. Rigby. "Can We Still Recommend Meditation?" (response letter). *British Medical Journal* 288 (1984): 795.

Chalmers, R.A., G. Clements, H. Schenkluhn, and H. Weinless, eds. *Scientific Research on the Transcendental Meditation Program: Collected Papers*. Vol. 2. Seelisberg, Switzerland: Maharishi European Research University Press, 1989a.

Chalmers, R.A., G. Clements, H. Schenkluhn, and H. Weinless, eds. *Scientific Research on the Transcendental Meditation Program: Collected Papers*. Vol. 3. Vlodrop, The Netherlands: MVU Press, 1989b.

Chalmers, R.A., G. Clements, H. Schenkluhn, and H. Weinless, eds. *Scientific Research on the Transcendental Meditation Program: Collected Papers*. Vol. 4. Vlodrop, The Netherlands: MVU Press, 1989c.

Chan, D.W. "Introducing the Chinese Hexiangzhuang (Flying Crane) Gigong Therapy." *International Journal of Psychosomatics* 34, no. 4 (1987): 28-34.

Chandler, H.M. "Transcendental Meditation and Awakening Wisdom: A 10-Year Longitudinal Study of Self-development." *Dissertation Abstracts International* 51, no. 10-B (1991): 5048.

Chang, S.C. "Morita Therapy." *American Journal of Psychotherapy* 28, no. 2 (1974): 208-221.

Chen, M.E. "A Comparative Study of Dimensions of Healthy Functioning between Families Practicing the TM Program for Five Years or for Less than a Year." *Dissertation Abstracts International* 45, no. 10-B (1985): 3206.

Chihara, T. "Psychological Studies on Zen Meditation and Time Experience." In *Psychological Studies on Zen*, ed. Y. Akishige. Tokyo: Zen Institute of Komazawa University, 1977.

Chihara, T. "Zen Meditation and Time Experience." *Psychologia* 32, no. 4 (1989): 211-220.

Childs, J. "The Use of the Transcendental Meditation Program as a Therapy with Juvenile Offenders." *Dissertation Abstracts International* 34, no. 8-A, pt. 1 (1974): 4732-4733.

Choudhary, K. "Meditation and Tantra—a Psychiatric Perspective." *Dynamic Psychiatry* 18, nos. 3-4 (1985): 276-282.

Chriss, G.M. "Effects of Biofeedback and Relaxation Training among Children Diagnosed as Having Attentional Deficit Disorders." *Dissertation Abstracts International* 44, no. 8-B (1984): 2539.

Clark, H.M. "The Effects of Meditation Training on Vigilance Performance." *Masters Abstracts* 27, no. 1 (1988): 154.

Clark, V.L. "Absorption as a Mediator of the Effect of Meditation on Attention and Anxiety." *Dissertation Abstracts International* 44, no. 8-B (1984): 2549.

Clark, M., and S. Monroe. "Meditation Therapy: Treatment of High Blood Pressure." *Newsweek* 85 (1975): 51.

Claxton, G. "Meditation as Self-destruction." *Bulletin of the British Psychological Society* 37 (1984): 106.

Clements, G., and S.L. Milstein. "Auditory Thresholds in Advanced Participants in the Transcendental Meditation Program." In *Scientific Research on the Transcendental Meditation Program: Collected Papers.* Vol. 1, eds. D.W. Orme-Johnson and J.T. Farrow. New York: M.E.R.U. Press, 1977: 719-722.

Clements, G., L. Krenner, and W. Molk. "The Use of the Transcendental Meditation Program in the Prevention of Drug Abuse and in the Treatment of Drug-addicted Persons." *Bulletin on Narcotics* 40, no. 1 (1988): 51-56.

Coffelt, R.L. "The Effects of Guided Imagery Exercises upon Self-image, Inner-directedness, and Self-control in First and Second Grade Students (Meditation, Imagery)." *Dissertation Abstracts International* 47, no. 7-A (1986): 2449.

Cohen, Bernard B. "A Combined Approach Using Meditation-Hypnosis and Behavioral Techniques in the Treatment of Smoking Behavior: Case Studies of Five Stressed Patients." *International Journal of Psychosomatics* 31, no. 1 (1984): 33-39.

Colby, F. "The Effects of Three Procedures Designed to Produce Alternate States of Consciousness upon Self-reports of Memory and Current Awareness (Hypnosis, Relaxation, Meditation)." *Dissertation Abstracts International* 47, no. 8-B (1986): 3513.

Colby, F. "An Analogue Study of the Initial Carryover Effects of Meditation, Hypnosis, and Relaxation Using Naive College Students." *Biofeedback and Self-Regulation* 16, no. 2 (1991): 157-165.

Coleman, S.R. "Effects of Progressive Muscle Relaxation and Meditation on State Anxiety in Disturbed Children and Adolescents." *Dissertation Abstracts International* 51, no. 6-B (1990): 3125.

Collier, R.W. "The Effect of the Transcendental Meditation Program upon University Academic Attainment." In *Scientific Research on the Transcendental Meditation Program: Collected Papers*. Vol. 1, eds. D.W. Orme-Johnson and J.T. Farrow. New York: M.E.R.U. Press, 1977: 393-395.

Collings, G.H. "Stress Containment through Meditation." *Prevention in Human Services* 6, no. 2 (1989): 141-150.

Comer, J.F. "Meditation and Progressive Relaxation in the Treatment of Test Anxiety." *Dissertation Abstracts International* 38, no. 12-B (1978): 6142-6143.

Compton, W.C. "Meditation and Self-actualization: A Cautionary Note on the Sallis Article." *Psychologia* 27, no. 2 (1984): 125-127.

Compton, W.C. "Self-Report of Attainment in Experienced Zen Meditators: A Cautionary Note on Objective Measurement." *Psychologia* 34 (1991): 15-17.

Compton, W.C., and G.M. Becker. "Self-actualizations and Experience with Zen Meditation: Is a Learning Period Necessary for Meditation?" *Journal of Clinical Psychology* 39, no. 6 (1983): 925-926.

Cooper, M.J., and M.M. Aygen. "Effect of Meditation on Serum Cholesterol and Blood Pressure." *Journal of the Israel Medical Association* 95, no. 1 (1978): 1-2.

Cooper, M.J., and M.M. Aygen. "A Relaxation Technique in the Management of Hypercholesterolemia." *Journal of Human Stress* 5, no. 4 (1979): 24-27.

Cooper, R., B. Joffe, A. Lamprey, et al. "Hormonal and Biochemical Responses to Transcendental Meditation." *Postgraduate Medical Journal* 61 (1985): 301-304.

Corby, J.C., W.T. Roth, V.P. Zarcone, et al. "Psychophysiological Correlates of the Practice of Tantric Yoga Meditation." *Archives of General Psychiatry* 35, no. 5 (1978): 571-577.

Corcoran, K.J. "Experiential Empathy: A Theory of a Felt-level Experience." *Journal of Humanistic Psychology* 21 (1981): 29-38.

Coren, B. "A Qualitative and Quantitative Study of the Effects of Trance and Meditation." *Masters Abstracts* 28, no. 4 (1990): 636.

Corey, P.W. "Airway Conductance and Oxygen Consumption Changes Associated with Practice of the Transcendental Meditation Technique." In *Scientific Research on the Transcendental Meditation Program: Collected Papers.* Vol. I, eds. D.W. Orme-Johnson and J.T. Farrow. New York: M.E.R.U. Press, 1977: 94-107.

Cort, D.A. "A Comparison of Compliance to Group Meditation, Individual Meditation and Didactic Group Training in a Program to Help Lower Blood Pressure in Black Adults." *Dissertation Abstracts International* 50, no. 6-B (1989): 2617.

Couture, R.T., M. Singh, W. Lee, et al. "The Effect of Mental Training on the Performance of Military Endurance Tasks in the Canadian Infantry." *International Journal of Sport Psychology* 25, no. 2 (1994): 144-157.

Cowger, E.L. "The Effects of Meditation (Zazen) upon Selected Dimensions of Personality Development." *Dissertation Abstracts International* 34, no. 8-A, pt. 1 (1974a): 4734.

Cowger, E.L. "Personality Changes as a Function of Two Different Meditative Techniques." *Dissertation Abstracts International* 34, no. 11-A (1974b): 7035-7036.

Cowger, E.L., and E.P. Torrance. "Further Examination of the Quality of Changes in Creative Functioning Resulting from Meditation (Zazen) Training." *The Creative Child and Adult Quarterly* 7, no. 4 (1982): 211-217.

Cox, D.J., A. Freundlich, and R.G. Meyer. "Differential Effectiveness of Feedback, Verbal Relaxation Instructions and Meditation Placebo for Tension Headaches." *Journal of Consulting and Clinical Psychology* 43 (1975): 892-898.

Cox, S.B. "TM and the Criminal Justice System." *Kentucky Law Journal* 60 (1971-72): 2.

Cranson, R.W. "Intelligence and the Growth of Intelligence in Maharishi's Vedic Psychology and Twentieth Century Psychology." *Dissertation Abstracts International* 50, no. 8-A (1989): 2,427.

Cranson, R.W., D.W. Orme-Johnson, J. Gackenbach, et al. "Transcendental Meditation and Improved Performance on Intelligence-Related Measures: A Longitudinal Study." *Personality and Individual Differences* 12, no. 10 (1991): 1105-1116.

Craven, J.L. "Meditation and Psychotherapy." *Canadian Journal of Psychiatry* 34, no. 7 (1989): 648-653.

Credidio, S.G. "Comparative Effectiveness of Patterned Biofeedback vs. Meditation Training on EMG and Skin Temperature Changes." *Behavior Research and Therapy* 20, no. 3 (1982): 233-241.

Crowe, R.L. "Time Perception and Hassles Appraisal in Beginning Meditators and Non-meditators." *Dissertation Abstracts International* 50, no. 9-B (1989): 3916.

Cummings, V.T. "The Effects of Endurance Training and Progressive Relaxation-meditation on the Physiological Response to Stress." *Dissertation Abstracts International* 45, no. 2-A (1984): 451.

Cunningham, M., and W. Koch. "The Transcendental Meditation Program and Rehabilitation: A Pilot Project at the Federal Correctional Institution at Lompoc, California." In *Scientific Research on the Transcendental Meditation Program: Collected Papers.* Vol. I, eds. D.W. Orme-Johnson and J.T. Farrow. New York: M.E.R.U. Press, 1977:562-568.

Curtin, T.G. "The Relationship between Transcendental Meditation and Adaptive Regression." *Dissertation Abstracts International* 34, no. 4-A (1973): 1969.

Curtis, M.J. "The Relationship between Bimodal Consciousness, Meditation and Two Levels of Death Anxiety." *Dissertation Abstracts International* 41, no. 6-B (1980): 2314.

Curtis, W.D., and H.W. Wessberg. "A Comparison of Heart Rate, Respiration and Galvanic Skin Response among Meditators, Relaxers and Controls." *Journal of Altered States of Consciousness* 2 (1975-76): 319-324.

Cuthbert, B. "Voluntary Slowing of Heart Rate: A Comparison of Various Techniques." *Dissertation Abstracts International* 37 (1976): 3067.

Cuthbert, B., J. Kristeller, R. Simons, et al. "Strategies of Arousal Control: Biofeedback, Meditation and Motivation." *Journal of Experimental Psychology General* 110, no. 4 (1981): 518-546.

Czaharyn, A.G. "A Simple Form of Meditation for Use in Clinical Practice" (letter). *American Family Physician* June 1996, 53 (8), 2440-2.

Daniels, D. "Comparison of the Transcendental Meditation Technique to Various Relaxation Procedures." Doctoral diss., University of Exeter, England, 1976.

Daniels, F.S., and B. Fernhall. "Continuous EEG Measurement to Determine the Onset of a Relaxation Response during a Prolonged Run." *Medicine and Science in Sports and Exercise* 16, no. 2 (1984): 182.

Daniels, L.K. "The Treatment of Psychophysiological Disorders and Severe Anxiety by Behavior Therapy, Hypnosis and Transcendental Meditation." *American Journal of Clinical Hypnosis* 17, no. 4 (1975): 267-270.

Dardes, J.A. "Psychological Changes Associated with the Practice of TM and Personality Characteristics of Self-selected Meditators." unpublished doctoral dissertation, Bucknell University, 1974.

Das, J. "Yoga and Hypnosis." *International Journal of Clinical and Experimental Hypnosis* 11 (1963): 31-37.

Das, N., and H. Gastaut. "Variations in the Electrical Activity of the Brain, Heart, and Skeletal Muscles during Yogic Meditation and Trance." *Electroencephalography and Clinical Neurophysiology*, supplement no. 6 (1955): 211-219.

Dash, P., and C.N. Alexander. "Electrophysiological Characteristics during Transcendental Meditation and Napping." Doctoral dissertation, University of California at Santa Cruz, 1977.

Datey, K.K., S.N. Deshmukh, C.P. Dalvi, et al. "Shavasan: A Yogic Exercise in the Management of Hypertension." *Angiology* 20 (1969): 325-333.

Datta, G.P., and R.K. Upadhyay. "Transcendental Meditation." *Indian Journal of Psychiatric Social Work* 6 (1977): 18-27.

Davidson, G.C. "Systematic Desensitization as a Counter-conditioning Process." *Journal of Abnormal Psychology* 73 (1968): 91-99.

Davidson, J.M. "The Physiology of Meditation and Mystical States of Consciousness." *Perspectives in Biology and Medicine* 19, no. 3 (1976): 345-380.

Davidson, R.J., and D.J. Goleman. "The Role of Attention in Meditation and

Hypnosis: A Psychobiological Perspective on Transformations of Conscious-ness." *The International Journal of Clinical and Experimental Hypnosis* 25, no. 4 (1977): 291-308.

Davidson, R.J., and G.E. Schwartz. "The Psychobiology of Relaxation and Related States: A Multiprocess Theory." In *Behavior Control and Modification of Physiological Activity*, ed. D.I. Mostofsky. Englewood Cliffs, NJ: Prentice-Hall, 1976.

Davidson, R.J., and G.E. Schwartz. "Matching Relaxation Therapies to Types of Anxiety: A Patterning Approach." In *Meditation: Classic and Contemporary Perspectives*, eds. D.H. Shapiro and R.N. Walsh. New York: Aldine, 1984.

Davidson, R.J., D.J. Goleman, and G.E. Schwartz. "Attentional and Affective Concomitants of Meditation: A Cross-sectional Study." *Journal of Abnormal Psychology* 85, no. 2 (1976a): 235-238.

Davidson, R.J., D. Schwartz, and L. Rothman. "Attentional Style under Self-regulation of Mode Specific Attention: An Electroencephalographic Study." *Journal of Abnormal Psychology* 85 (1976b): 611-621.

Davies, J. "The Transcendental Meditation Program and Progressive Relaxation: Comparative Effects on Trait Anxiety and Self-actualization." In *Scientific Research on the Transcendental Meditation Program: Collected Papers*. Vol. 1, eds. D.W. Orme-Johnson and J.T. Farrow. New York: M.E.R.U. Press, 1977: 449-452.

Davies, J.L., and C.N. Alexander. "Alleviating Political Violence through Enhanc-ing Coherence in Collective Consciousness: Impact Assessment Analyses of the Lebanon War." Paper presented to the 85th Annual Meeting of the American Political Science Association, Atlanta, September 1989.

Davis, J. "Ego Development of Buddhist Meditators: A Qualitative Study." *Dissertation Abstracts International* 48, no. 5-B (November 1987): 1527-1528.

Davis, L. "Hormonal and Biochemical Responses to Transcendental Medita-tion" (letter). *Postgraduate Medical Journal* 62, no. 723 (1986): 69.

Day, R., and S. Sadek. "The Effect of Benson's Relaxation Response on the Anxiety Levels of Lebanese Children under Stress." *Journal of Experimental Child Psychology* 34 (1982): 350-356.

Dayton, T., and D.B. Boles. "No Difference in Cerebral Hemispheric Asymme-try of Meditators as Opposed to Nonmeditators." *Bulletin of the Psychonomic Society* 28, no. 3 (1990): 211-214.

Deabler, H.L., E. Fidel, R.L. Dillenkoffer, et al. "The Use of Relaxation and Hypnosis in Lowering High Blood Pressure." *American Journal of Clinical Hypnosis* 16, no. 2 (1973): 75-83.

Dean, S. "Metapsychiatry: The Interface between Psychiatry and Mysticism." *American Journal of Psychiatry* 130 (1973): 1036-1038.

Deathridge, G. "The Clinical Use of 'Mindfulness' Meditation Techniques in Short-term Psychotherapy." *Journal of Transpersonal Psychology* 7, no. 2 (1975): 133-143.

DeBerry, S. "The Effects of Meditation-relaxation on Anxiety and Depression in Geriatric Population." *Psychotherapy Theory, Research and Practice* 19, no. 4 (1982): 512-521.

DeBerry, S., S. Davis, and K.E. Reinhard. "A Comparison of Meditation-relaxation and Cognitive/Behavioral Techniques for Reducing Anxiety and Depression in a Geriatric Population." *Journal of Geriatric Psychiatry*. 22, no. 2 (1989): 231-247.

DeBlassie, P.A. "Christian Meditation: A Clinical Investigation." *Dissertation Abstracts International* 42, no. 3-B (1981): 1167.

DeBont, H.G. "Transcendental Meditation: A Critical View." *Tijdschrift voor Psychotherapie* 6, no. 1 (1980): 1-11.

Deepak, K.K., S.K. Manchanda, and M.C. Maheshwari. "Meditation Improves Clinicoelectroencephalographic Measures in Drug-Resistant Epileptics." *Biofeedback and Self Regulation* 19, no. 1, (1994): 25-40.

de Grace, G. "Effects of Meditation on Personality and Values." *Journal of Clinical Psychology* 32, no. 4 (1976): 809-813.

Deikman, A.J. "Experimental Meditation." *Journal of Nervous and Mental Disease* 136 (1963): 329-343.

Deikman, A.J. "De-automatization of the Mystic Experience." *Psychiatry* 29 (1966a): 324-338.

Deikman, A.J. "Implications of Experimentally Produced Contemplative Meditation." *Journal of Nervous and Mental Disease* 142, no. 2 (1966b): 101-116.

Deikman, A.J. "Bimodal Consciousness." *Archives of General Psychiatry* 25 (1971): 481-489.

Deikman, A.J. "The State-of-the-Art of Meditation." In *Meditation: Classic and Contemporary Perspectives*, eds. D.H. Shapiro and R.N. Walsh. New York: Aldine, 1984: 679-680.

Deikman, A.J. Review of *Freedom from the Self—Sufism, Meditation and Psychotherapy* by M. Shafii. *Journal of Nervous and Mental Disease* 174, no. 8 (1986): 503-504.

Deikman, A.J., and M. Braidwood. "Treatment of Retarded Ejaculation with Psychotherapy and Meditative Relaxation: A Case Report." *Psychological Reports* 47 (1980): 8-10.

Del Gaudio, D.J. "The Effects of Meditation Based Coping Skills Training in the Treatment of Dental Phobia under Exposure and Non-exposure Conditions." *Dissertation Abstracts International* 48, no. 12-B (1987): 3676.

DeLiz, A.J. "Meditation, Protein, Diet, and Megavitamins in the Treatment of a Progressive, Iatrogenic Cardiac Psychotic Condition." *Journal of Orthomolecular Psychiatry* 6, no. 1 (1977): 44-49.

Delmonte, M.M. "Pilot Study on Conditional Relaxation during Simulation Meditation." *Psychological Reports* 45, no. 1 (1979): 44-49.

Delmonte, M.M. "Personality Characteristics and Regularity of Meditation." *Psychological Reports* 46 (no. 3, pt. 1) (1980): 703-712.

Delmonte, M.M. "Expectation and Meditation." *Psychological Reports* 49, no. 3 (1981a): 699-709.

Delmonte, M.M. "Suggestibility and Meditation." *Psychological Reports* 48, no. 3 (1981b): 727-737.

Delmonte, M.M. "Mantras and Meditation: A Literature Review." *Perceptual and Motor Skills* 57 (1983a): 64-66.

Delmonte, M.M. "Some Cognitive Aspects of Meditation Practice." *Perceptual and Motor Skills* 57, no. 1 (1983b): 160-162.

Delmonte, M.M. "Case Reports on the Use of Meditative Relaxation as an Intervention Strategy with Retarded Ejaculation." *Biofeedback and Self-Regulation* 9, no. 2 (1984a): 209-214.

Delmonte, M.M. "Electrocortical Activity and Related Phenomena Associated with Meditation Practice: A Literature Review." *International Journal of Neuroscience* 24 (1984b): 217-231.

Delmonte, M.M. "Factors Influencing the Regularity of Meditation Practice in a Clinical Population." *British Journal of Medical Psychology* 57 (1984c): 275-278.

Delmonte, M.M. "Meditation Practice as Related to Occupational Stress, Health and Productivity." *Perceptual and Motor Skills* 59 (1984d): 581-582.

Delmonte, M.M. "Meditation: Similarities with Hypnoidal States and Hypnosis." *International Journal of Psychosomatics* 31, no. 3 (1984e): 24.

Delmonte, M.M. "Physiological Responses during Meditation and Rest." *Biofeedback and Self-Regulation* 9, no. 2 (1984f): 181-200.

Delmonte, M.M. "Psychometric Scores and Meditation Practice: A Literature Review." *Personality and Individual Differences* 5, no. 5 (1984g): 559-563.

Delmonte, M.M. "Anxiety, Defensiveness and Physiological Responsivity in Novice and Experienced Meditators." *International Journal of Eclectic Psychotherapy* 4, no. 1-2 (1985a): 1-13.

Delmonte, M.M. "Biochemical Indices Associated with Meditation Practice: A Literature Review." *Neuroscience Behavioral Reviews* 9, no. 4 (1985b): 557-561.

Delmonte, M.M. "Effects of Expectancy on Physiological Responsivity in Novice Meditators." *Biological Psychology* 21, no. 2 (1985c): 107-121.

Delmonte, M.M. "Meditation and Anxiety Reduction: A Literature Review." *Clinical Psychology Review* 5 (1985d): 91-102.

Delmonte, M.M. "Physiological Concomitants of Meditation Practice." *International Journal of Psychosomatics* 31, no. 4 (1985e): 23-26.

Delmonte, M.M. "Response to Meditation in Terms of Physiological, Behavioral, and Self-report Measures: A Brief Summary." *Psychological Reports* 56, no. 1 (1985f): 9-10.

Delmonte, M.M. "The Effects of Meditation on Drug Usage: A Literature Review." *Gedrag: Tijdschrift voor Psychologie* 13, no. 2 (1985g): 36-48.

Delmonte, M.M. "Expectancy and Response to Meditation." *International Journal of Psychosomatics* 33, no. 2 (1986a): 28-34.

Delmonte, M.M. "Meditation as a Clinical Intervention Strategy: A Brief Review." *Internal Journal of Psychosomatics* 33, no.3 (1986b): 9-12.

Delmonte, M.M. "Constructivist View of Meditation." *American Journal of Psychotherapy* 41, no. 2 (1987): 286-298.

Delmonte, M.M. "Personality Correlates of Meditation Practice Frequency and Dropout in an Outpatient Population." *Journal of Behavioral Medicine* 11, no. 6 (December 1988): 593-597.

Delmonte, M.M. "Meditation, the Unconscious, and Psychosomatic Disorders. Special Issue: Biofeedback and Diagnostic Techniques." *International Journal of Psychosomatics* 36, nos. 1-4 (1989): 45-52.

Delmonte, M.M. "Meditation and Change: Mindfulness Versus Repression. 22nd International Congress of Applied Psychology" *Australian Journal of Clinical Hypnotherapy and Hypnosis* 11, no. 2 (1990a): 57-63.

Delmonte, M.M. "The Relevance of Meditation to Clinical Practice: An Overview." *Applied Psychology: An International Review* 39, no. 3 (1990b): 331-354.

Delmonte, M.M. "Repression and Somatization: A Case History of Hemodynamic Activation." *International Journal of Psychosomatics* 37, no. 1-4 (1990c): 37-39.

Delmonte, M.M., and V. Kenny. "An Overview of the Therapeutic Effects of Meditation." *Psychologia* 28, no. 4 (1985): 189-202.

Delmonte, M.M., and V. Kenny. "Conceptual Models and Functions of Meditation in Psychotherapy." *Journal of Contemporary Psychotherapy* 17, no. 1 (1987): 38-59.

DeLone, Susan T. "The Psychological Effect of Movement Meditation as a Self-control Strategy for Stress Management." *Dissertation Abstracts International* 47, no. 3-B (1986): 1311.

Denmark, T.H. "Approaches to Self-realization in Adult Education through Meditation." *Dissertation Abstracts International* 37, no. 1-A (1976), 96.

Denny, M.C. "Self-hypnotic Absorption and Affective Change in a Program of Spiritual Exercises." *Dissertation Abstracts International* 41, no. 10-B (1981): 3917.

de Santis, J. "Effects of the Intensive Zen Buddhist Meditation Retreat on Rogerian Congruence as Real-self/Ideal-self Disparity on the California Q-Sort." *Dissertation Abstracts International* 46, no. 10-B (1986): 2801.

de Silva, P. "Early Buddhist and Modern Behavioral Strategies for the Control of Unwanted Intrusive Cognitions." *Psychological Record* 35, no. 4 (1985): 437-443.

de Silva, P. Review of *The Psychology of Meditation*, by M.A. West. In *Behavior Research and Therapy* 27, no. 4 (1989): 483.

de Vol, T.I. "Ecstatic Pentecostal Prayer and Meditation." *Journal of Religion and Health* 13, no. 4 (1974): 285-288.

Dhanaraj, V., and M. Singh. "Reduction in Metabolic Rate during the Practice of the Transcendental Meditation Technique." In *Scientific Research on the Transcendental Meditation Program: Collected Papers*. Vol. 1, D.W. Orme-Johnson and J.T. Farrow,, ed. New York: M.E.R.U. Press, 1977: 137-139.

Dhume, R.R., and R.A. Dhume. "A Comparative Study of the Driving Effects of Dextroamphetamine and Yogic Meditation on Muscle Control for the Performance of Balance on Balance Board." *Indian Journal of Physiological Pharmacology* 35, no. 3 (1991): 191-194.

Dice, M.L. "The Effectiveness of Meditation on Selected Measures of Self-actualization." *Dissertation Abstracts International* 40, no. 5-A (1979): 2534.

Dick, L.D. "A Study of Meditation in the Service of Counseling." *Dissertation Astracts International* 34, no. 8-B (1974): 4037.

Dillbeck, M.C. "The Effect of the Transcendental Meditation Technique on Anxiety Level." *Journal of Clinical Psychology* 33, no. 4 (1977a): 1076-1078.

Dillbeck, M.C. "The Effects of the TM Technique on Visual Perception and Verbal Problem Solving." *Dissertation Abstracts International* 37, no. 10-B (1977b): 5319-5320.

Dillbeck, M.C. "Meditation and Flexibility of Visual Perception and Verbal Problem Solving." *Memory and Cognition* 10, no. 3 (1982): 207-215.

Dillbeck, M.C. "Testing the Vedic Psychology of the Bhagavad-Gita." *Psychologia* 26 (1983): 232–240.

Dillbeck, M.C. "The Concept of Self in the Bhagavad-Gita and in the Vedic Psychology of Maharishi Mahesh Yogi: A Further Note on Testability." *Psychologia: An International Journal of Psychology in the Orient.* 33, no. 1 (1990): 50-56.

Dillbeck, M.C. "Test of a Field Theory of Consciousness and Social Change: Time Series Analysis of Participation in the TM-Sidhi Program and Reduction of Violent Death in the U.S." *Social Indicators Research* 22, no. 4 (1990): 399-418.

Dillbeck, M.C., and A.I. Abrams. "The Application of the Transcendental Meditation Program to Corrections." *International Journal of Comparative and Applied Criminal Justice* 11, no. 1 (Spring 1987): 111-132.

Dillbeck, M.C., and C.N. Alexander. "Higher States of Consciousness: Maharishi Mahesh Yogi's Vedic Psychology of Human Development." *The Journal of Mind and Behavior* 10, no. 4 (1989): 307-334.

Dillbeck, M.C., and E.C. Bronson. "Short-term Longitudinal Effects of the Transcendental Meditation Technique on EEG Power and Coherence." *International Journal of Neuroscience* 14 (1981): 147-151.

Dillbeck, M.C., and D.W. Orme-Johnson. "Physiological Differences Between Transcendental Meditation and Rest." *American Psychologist* 42 (1987): 879–881.

Dillbeck, M.C., and S.A. Vesely. "Participation in the Transcendental Meditation Program and Frontal EEG Coherence during Concept-learning." *International Journal of Neuroscience* 29, nos. 1-2 (1986): 45-55.

Dillbeck, M.C., A.P. Aron, and S.L. Dillbeck. "The TM Program as an Educational Technology: Research and Applications." *Educational Technology* 19, no. 11 (1979): 7-13.

Dillbeck, M.C., D.W. Orme-Johnson, and R.K. Wallace. "Frontal EEG Coherence, H-Reflex Recovery, Concept Learning, and the TM-Sidhi Program." *International Journal of Neuroscience* 15 (1981a): 151–157.

Dillbeck, M.C., G. Landrith III, and D.W. Orme-Johnson. "The Transcendental Meditation Program and Crime Rate Change in a Sample of Forty-eight Cities." Findings previously published in *Journal of Crime and Justice* 4 (1981b): 25–45.

Dillbeck, M.C., P.D. Assimakis, and D. Raimondi. "Longitudinal Effects of the Transcendental Meditation and TM-Sidhi Program on Cognitive Ability and Cognitive Style." *Perceptual Motor Skills* 62, no. 3 (1986): 731-738.

Dillbeck, M.C., K.L. Cavanaugh, T. Glenn, D.W. Orme-Johnson, and V. Mittlefehldt. "Consciousness as a Field—the Transcendental Meditation and TM-Sidhi Program and Changes in Social-Indicators." *Journal of Mind and Behavior* 8, no. 1 (1987): 67-103.

Dillbeck, M.C., C.B. Banus, C. Polanzi, and G.S. Landrith. "Test of a Field Model of Consciousness and Social Change: The Transcendental Meditation and TM-Sidhi Program and Decreased Urban Crime." *Journal of Mind and Behavior* 9, no. 4 (1988): 457-485.

Di Nardo, P.A., and J.B. Raymond. "Locus of Control and Attention during Meditation." *Journal of Consulting and Clinical Psychology* 47 no. 6 (1979): 1136-1137.

Diner, M.D. "The Differential Effects of Meditation and Systematic Desensitization on Specific and General Anxiety." *Dissertation Abstracts International* 39, no. 4-B (1978): 1950.

Dinklage, H.A. "Personal Prevention: Meditation May Be the Answer." *Journal of the American Society for Preventive Dentistry* 5 (1975): 23.

Dixon, C.A. "Consciousness and Cognitive Development: A Six-Month Longitudinal Study of Four-Year-Olds Practicing the Children's TM Technique." *Dissertation Abstracts International* 51, no. 3-B (1990): 1518.

Doi, M. "Psychological Study of the Relation between Respiratory Function and Mental Self-control." In *Psychological Studies of Zen*, ed. Y. Akishige. Tokyo: Zen Institute of Komazawa University, 1977.

Domaingue, R.C. "Learning for Discovery: Exploring Theoretical Foundations for Anticipatory Learning." *Dissertation Abstracts International* 51, no. 4-A (1990): 1081.

Domar, Alice D. "The Preoperative Use of the Relaxation Response with Ambulatory Surgery Patients." *Journal of Human Stress* 13(3) (1987); 101-107.

Domar, A.D., P.C. Zuttermeister, M. Seibel, and H. Benson "Psychological Improvement in Infertile Women After Behavioral Treatment: A Replication." *Fertility and Sterility* 58 (1992): 144-147.

Domash, L.H. "The Transcendental Meditation Technique and Quantum Physics: Is Pure Consciousness a Macroscopic Quantum State in the Brain?" In *Scientific Research on the Transcendental Meditation Program: Collected Papers.* Vol. 1, eds. D.W. Orme-Johnson and J.T. Farrow. New York: M.E.R.U. Press, 1977: 652-670.

Domino, G. "Transcendental Meditation and Creativity: An Empirical Investigation." *Journal of Applied Psychology* 62, no. 3 (1977): 358-362.

Domitor, P.J. "Zen Meditation, Expectancy and Their Relative Contributions to Changes in Perceptual Flexibility." *Dissertation Abstracts International* 38, no. 12-B (1978): 6145.

Don, N.S. "The Transformation of Conscious Experience and Its EEG Correlates." *Journal of Altered States of Consciousness* 3, (1977-78): 147-168.

Doner, D.W., Jr. "The TM Program: A New Dimension in Living for Dialysis/Transplant Clients." *Journal of the American Association of Nephrology Nurses and Technicians* 3 (1976): 119-125.

Dostalek, C., E. Roldan, and V. Lepicovska. "EEG Changes in the Course of Hatha-Yogic Exercises Intended for Meditation." *Activitas Nervos Superior* 22, no. 2 (1980): 123-124.

Dostalek, C., J. Faber, E. Krasa, et al. "Yoga Meditation Effect on the EEG and EMG Activity." *Activitas Nervos Superior (Praha)* 21, no. 1 (1979): 41.

Doyle, R.B., D.F. O'Rourke, C. Conger, and G.R. Smith. "Intentional Modulation of Peripheral Skin Temperature: A Comparison Between Experienced Meditators and Controls." *Biofeedback and Self-Regulation* 14, no. 2 (1989): 138.

Dreifuss, A. "A Phenomenological Inquiry of Six Psychotherapists Who Practice Buddhist Meditation." *Dissertation Abstracts International.* 51, no. 5-B (1990): 2617.

Drennen, W., and B. Chermol. "Relaxation and Placebo-suggestion as Uncontrolled Variables in TM Research." *Journal of Humanistic Psychology* 18 (1978): 89-93.

Driscoll, F. "TM as a Secondary School Subject." *Phi Delta Kappa* 54, no. 4 (1982): 236-237.

Driskill, J.D. "Meditation as a Therapeutic Technique." *Pastoral Psychology* 38, no. 2 (1989): 83-103.

Dua, J.K., and M.L. Swinden. "Effectiveness of Negative-thought-reduction, Meditation, and Placebo Training Treatment in Reducing Anger." *Scandinavian Journal of Psychology* 33 (1992): 135-146.

Dubin, W. "The Use of Meditative Techniques in Psychotherapy Supervision." *Journal of Transpersonal Psychology* 45, no. 3 (1991): 65-80.

Dubin, W. "The Use of Meditative Techniques for Teaching Dynamic Psychology." *Journal of Transpersonal Psychology* 26, no. 1 (1994): 19-36.

Dubs, G. "Acquisition of a Novel View of Reality: A Study of Psycho-spiritual Development in Zen Buddhism." *Dissertation Abstracts International* 48, no. 3-B (September 1987a): 873-874.

Dubs, G. "Psycho-spiritual Development in Zen Buddhism—A Study of Resistance in Meditation." *Journal of Transpersonal Psychology* 19, no. 1 (1987b): 19-86.

Dwivedi, K.N., V.M. Gupta, and K.N. Udupa. "A Preliminary Report on Some Physiological Changes Due to Vipashyana Meditation." *Indian Journal of Medical Science* 31, no. 3 (1977): 51-54.

Earle, J.B. "Cerebral Laterality and Meditation: A Review of the Literature." *Journal of Transpersonal Psychology* 13, no. 2 (1981): 155-173.

Easterlin, B. *Buddhist Vipassana Meditation and Daily Living.* unpublished doctoral dissertation. California Institute of Integral Studies, 1992.

Easterlin, B., and E. Cardena. "Cognitive and Emotional Differences Between Short- and Long-term Vipassana Meditators." Paper presented at the 101st Annual Convention of the American Psychological Association, 1993.

Echenhofer, F.G., and M.M. Coombs. "A Brief Review of Research and Controversies in EEG Biofeedback and Meditation." *The Journal of Transpersonal Psychology* 19, no. 2 (1987): 161-171.

Eckholm, E. "Value of Meditation against Stress Now Questioned." *The New York Times*, 24 July 1984.

Edwards, D.L. "A Meta-analysis of the Effects of Meditation and Hypnosis on Measures of Anxiety." *Dissertation Abstracts International* 52, no. 2-B (1991): 1039.

Edwards, L.R. "Psychological Change and Spiritual Growth through the Practice of Siddha Yoga." *Dissertation Abstracts International* 48, no. 2-A (1987): 340.

Ehrlich, M.P. "Family Meditation." *Journal of Family Counseling* 4, no. 2 (1976): 40-45.

Eisen, A.R., R.M. Rapee, and D.H. Barlow. "The Effects of Breathing Rate and CO_2 Levels on Relaxation and Anxiety in a Non-clinical Population." *Journal of Anxiety Disorders* 4, no. 3 (1990): 183-190.

Ellis, A. "The Place of Meditation in Cognitive Behavior Therapy and Rational Emotive Therapy." In *Meditation: Classic and Contemporary Perspectives*, eds. D.H. Shapiro and R.N. Walsh. New York: Aldine Books, 1984: 671-673.

Ellis, G.A. "Removing the Motivator: A Holistic Solution to Substance Abuse." *Alcoholism Treatment Quarterly* 11, no. 3-4 (1994): 271-296.

Ellis, S. "Meditation and Psychotherapy." *Dissertation Abstracts International* 46, no. 10-B (1986): 3591.

Elson, B.D. "Ananda-Marga Meditation." *Archives of General Psychiatry* 36, no. 5 (1979): 605-606.

Elson, B.D., P. Hauri, and D. Cunis. "Physiological Changes in Yoga Meditation." *Psychophysiology* 14, no. 1 (1977): 55-57.

Emerson, V. "Can Belief Systems Influence Neurophysiology: Some Implications of Research on Meditation." *R.N. Bucke Memorial Society Newsletter Review* 5, no. 1-2 (1972).

Emerson, V. "Research on Meditation." In *What is Meditation?*, ed. J. Shite. New York: Anchor Books, 1974.

Engle, B. "Comments on Herbert Benson's Article" (letter). *Integrative Psychiatry* (May-June 1983): 20.

Engler, J. "Therapeutic Aims in Psychotherapy and Meditation: Developmental Stages in the Representation of Self." *Journal of Transpersonal Psychology* 16, no. 1 (1984): 25-61.

English, E.H. "Relaxation Training and Blood Pressure Responses to Experimental Stress." *Dissertation Abstracts International* 42, no. 5-B (1981): 2052.

Eppley, K.R., A.I. Abrams, and J. Shear. "Differential Effects of Relaxation Techniques on Trait Anxiety: A Meta-Analysis." *Journal of Clinical Psychology* 45, no. 6 (1989): 957-974.

Epstein, M. "The Deconstruction of the Self: Ego and 'Egolessness' in Buddhist Insight Meditation." *Journal of Transpersonal Psychology* 20, no. 1 (1988): 61-69.

Epstein, M. "Forms of Emptiness: Psychodynamic, Meditative and Clinical Perspectives." *Journal of Transpersonal Psychology* 21, no. 1 (1989): 61-71.

Epstein, M. "Beyond the Oceanic Feeling: Psychoanalytic Study of Buddhist Meditation." *International Review of Psycho-Analysis* 17, no. 2 (1990a): 159-166.

Epstein, M. "Psychodynamics of Meditation: Pitfalls on the Spiritual Path." *Journal of Transpersonal Psychology* 22, no. 1 (1990b): 17-34.

Epstein, M. *Thoughts Without a Thinker.* New York: Basic Books, 1995.

Epstein, M.D., and J.D. Lieff. "Psychiatric Complications of Meditation Practice." *Journal of Transpersonal Psychology* 13, no. 2 (1981): 137-147.

Evans, G.S. "A Comparative Statistical Analysis of Three Therapeutic Approaches to Stress." *Dissertation Abstracts International* 51, no. 1-B (1989): 464.

Everly, George S. "Disorders of Arousal and the Relaxation Response: Speculations on the Nature and Treatment of Stress-related Diseases. Special Issue: Biofeedback and Diagnostic Techniques." *International Journal of Psychosomatics,* 36(1-4) (1989): 15-21

Eyerman, J. "TM and Mental Retardation." *Journal of Clinical Psychiatry* 42, no. 1 (1981): 35-36.

Faber, P.A., G.S. Suayman, and S.W. Touyz. "Meditation and Archetypal Content on Nocturnal Dreams." *Journal of Analytical Psychology* 23, no. 1 (1978): 1-22.

Fabick, S.D. "The Relative Effectiveness of Systematic Desensitization, Cognitive Modification, and Mantra Meditation in the Reduction of Test Anxiety." *Dissertation Abstracts International* 37, no. 8-A (1976): 4862.

Farge, E.J., G.H. Hartung, and C.M. Borland. "Runners and Meditators: A Comparison on Personality Profiles." *Journal of Personality Assessment* 43, no. 5 (1979): 501-503.

Farrow, J.T. "Physiological Changes Associated with Transcendental Consciousness, the State of Least Excitation of Consciousness." In *Scientific Research on the Transcendental Meditation Program: Collected Papers.* Vol. I, eds. D.W. Orme-Johnson and J.T. Farrow. New York: M.E.R.U. Press, 1977: 108-133.

Farrow, J.T., and J.R. Hebert. "Breath Suspension during the Transcendental Meditation Technique." *Psychosomatic Medicine* 44, no. 2 (1982): 133-153.

Febick, S.D. "The Relative Effectiveness of Systematic Desensitization, Cognitive Modification, and Mantra Meditation in the Reduction of Test Anxiety." *Dissertation Abstracts International* 37, no. 8-A (1977): 4862.

Fee, R.A., and D.A. Girdano. "The Relative Effectiveness of Three Techniques to Induce the Trophotropic Response." *Biofeedback and Self-Regulation* 3, no. 2 (1978): 145-157.

Fehr, T. "A Longitudinal Study of the Effect of the Transcendental Meditation Program on Changes in Personality." In *Scientific Research on the Transcendental Meditation Program: Collected Papers.* Vol. I, eds. D.W. Orme-Johnson and J.T. Farrow. New York: M.E.R.U. Press, 1977: 476-483.

Fehr, T., U. Nerstheimer, and S. Tober. "Study of Personality Changes Resulting from the Transcendental Meditation Program: Freiburger Personality Inventory." In *Scientific Research on The Transcendental Meditation Program: Collected Papers.* Vol. I, eds. D.W. Orme-Johnson and J.T. Farrow. New York: M.E.R.U. Press, 1977: 420-424.

Fentress, D.W., B.J. Masek, J.E. Mehegan, and H. Benson. "Biofeedback and Relaxation-response Training in the Treatment of Pediatric Migraine." *Dev Med Child Neurol* 28 (1986): 139-46.

Fenwick, P. "Can We Still Recommend Meditation?" *British Medical Journal* 287 (1983): 1401.

Fenwick, P. "Can We Still Recommend Meditation?" (reply). *British Medical Journal* 288, no. 6419 (1984): 796.

Fenwick, P., S. Donaldson, L. Gillis, et al. "Metabolic and EEG Changes during Transcendental Meditation: An Explanation." *Biological Psychology* 5, no. 2 (1977): 101-118.

Fenz, W.D., and J.M. Plapp. "Voluntary Control of Heart Rate in a Practitioner of Yoga: Negative Findings." *Perceptual and Motor Skills* 30 (1970): 493-494.

Ferguson, P.C. "The Psychobiology of Transcendental Meditation: A Review." *Journal of Altered States of Consciousness* 2, no. 1 (1975): 15-36.

Ferguson, P.C. "Transcendental Meditation and Its Potential Application in the Field of Special Education." *Journal of Special Education* 10, no. 2 (1976): 211-220.

Ferguson, P.C. "The Integrative Meta-analysis of Psychological Studies Investigating the Treatment Outcomes of Meditation Techniques." *Dissertation Abstracts International* 42, no. 4-A (1981): 1547.

Ferguson, P.C., and J. Gowan. "Transcendental Meditation: Some Preliminary Psychological Findings." *Journal of Humanistic Psychology* 16, no. 3 (1976): 51-60.

Fergusson, L.C. "Field Independence and Art Achievement in Meditating and Nonmeditating College Students." *Perceptual and Motor Skills* 75 (1992): 1171-1175.

Fergusson, L.C. "Field Independence, Transcendental Meditation, and Achievement in College Art: A Reexamination" *Perceptual and Motor Skills* 77, (1993): 1104-1106.

Fernhall, B., and F.S. Daniels. "Electoencephalographic Changes after a Prolonged Running Period—Evidence for a Relaxation Response." *Medicine and Science in Sports and Exercise* 16, no. 2 (1984): 181.

Fertig, B.L. "A Workshop in Meditation and Visualization as Applied to Therapy with Functional Voice Disorders: A Case Study." *Folia Phoniatrica* 35, no. 3-4 (1983): 122.

Fiebert, M.S. "Responsiveness to an Introductory Meditation Method." *Perceptual and Motor Skills* 45, no. 3, pt. 1 (1977): 849-850.

Fiebert, M.S., and T.M. Mead. "Meditation and Academic Performance." *Perceptual and Motor Skills* 53, no. 2 (1981): 447-450.

Finney, J.R. "Contemplative Prayer as an Adjunct to Pychotherapy." *Dissertation Abstracts International* 46, no. 4-8 (1984): 1334.

Finney, J.R., and H.N. Malony. "Contemplative Prayer and Its Use in Psychotherapy: A Theoretical Model." *Journal of Psychology and Theology* 13, no. 3 (1985): 172-181.

Fischer, R.A. "A Cartography of the Ecstatic and Meditative States." *Science* 174 (1971): 897-904.

Fischer, R.A. "Transformations of Consciousness: A Cartography. II: The Perception-meditation Continuum." *Confina Psychiatrica* 19, no. 1 (1976): 1-23.

Fling, S., A. Thomas, and M. Gallaher. "Participant Characteristics and the Effects of Two Types of Meditation vs. Quiet Sitting." *Journal of Clinical Psychology* 37, no. 4 (1981): 784-790.

Forte, M., D. Brown, and M. Dysart. "Through the Looking Glass: Phenomenological Reports of Advanced Meditators at Visual Threshold." *Imagination, Cognition and Personality* 4, no. 4 (1984-85): 323-328.

Forte, M., D. Brown, and M. Dysart. "Differences in Experience among Mindfulness Meditators." *Imagination, Cognition and Personality* 7, no. 1 (1987-88): 47-60.

Fox, D. *Meditation and Reality: A Critical Review.* Atlanta, GA: John Knox, 1986.

Francis, T. "Meditation as an Alternative to Substance Misuse: A Current Review." *Therapeutic Recreation Journal* 25, no. 4 (1991): 50-60.

Frank, M.R. "Transactional Analysis and Meditation Training as Interventions in Teacher Education: An Exploratory Study." *Dissertation Abstracts International* 39, no. 2-A (1978): 823-824.

Frank, N.L. "Study of Meditation and Blood Pressure" (letter). *The New England Journal of Medicine* 294, no. 14 (1976): 786.

Frankel, B.L. "TM and Hypertension." *Lancet* 1, no. 7959 (1976): 589.

Frankel, B.L., D. Patel, D. Horwitz, et al. "Treatment of Hypertension with Biofeedback and Relaxation Techniques." *Psychosomatic Medicine* 40 (1978): 276-293.

Freed, S. "Induced Specific Immunological Unresponsiveness and Conditioned Behavioral Reflexes in Functional Isomorphism-meditation and Conditioned Specific Unresponsiveness." *International Journal of Neuroscience* 44, no. 3-4 (1989): 275-281.

French, A.P., and J. Tupin. "Therapeutic Application of a Simple Relaxation Method." *American Journal of Psychotherapy* 28, no. 2 (1974): 282-287.

French, A.P., A.C. Smid, and E. Ingalls. "Transcendental Meditation, Altered Reality Testing and Behavioral Change: A Case Report." *Journal of Nervous and Mental Disease* 161, no. 1 (1975): 55-58.

Frew, D.R. "Transcendental Meditation and Productivity." *Academy of Management Journal* 17, no. 2 (1974): 362-368.

Friedman, M., S.O. Byers, R.H. Rosenman, et al. "Coronary-prone Individuals (Type A Behavior Pattern): Some Bio-chemical Characteristics." *Journal of the American Medical Association* 212 (1970): 1030-1037.

Friend, K.E. "Effects of the Transcendental Meditation Program on Work Attitudes and Behavior." In *Scientific Research on the Transcendental Meditation Program: Collected Papers.* Vol. 1, eds. D.W. Orme-Johnson and J.T. Farrow. New York: M.E.R.U. Press, 1977: 630-638.

Friskey, L.M. "Effects of a Combined Relaxation and Meditation Training Program on Hypertensive Patients." *Dissertation Abstracts International* 46, no. 1-B (1985): 300.

Fritz, G. "The Effects of Meditation upon Peer Counselor Effectiveness." *Dissertation Abstracts International* 40, no. 11-A (1980): 5730-5731.

Fromm, E. "Psychoanalysis and Zen Buddhism." *Psychologia* 2 (1959): 79-99.

Fromm, E., D.T. Suzuki, and R. de Martino. *Zen Buddhism and Psychoanalysis.* London: George Allen and Unwin, 1960.

Fromm, G.H., "Neurophysiological Speculations on Zen Enlightenment." *Journal of Mind and Behavior* 13, no. 2 (1992): 163-169.

Frumkin, L.R., and R.R. Pagano. "Effect of TM on Iconic Memory." *Biofeedback and Self-Regulation* 4, no. 4 (1979): 313-322.

Fulton, M.A. "The Effects of Relaxation Training and Meditation on Stress, Anxiety, and Subjective Experience in College Students." *Dissertation Abstracts International* 51, no. 2-A (1990): 414.

Fulton, P.R. "The Ethnography of Anatta: Self and Selves in American Vipassana Buddhism." *Dissertation Abstracts International* 47, no. 6-A (1986): 2213.

Funderburk, J. *Science Studies Yoga: A Review of Physiological Data.* Glenview, IL: Himalayan International Institute of Yoga Science and Philosophy, 1977.

Fuson, J.W. "The Effects of Transcendental Meditation on Sleeping and Dreaming Patterns." MD dissertation, Yale Medical School, New Haven, CN, 1976.

Galanter, M., and P. Buckley. "Evangelical Religion and Meditation: Psychotherapeutic Effects." *Journal of Nervous and Mental Disease* 166, no. 10 (1978): 685-691.

Ganguli, H.C. "Meditation Subculture and Drug Use." *Human Relations* 38, no. 10 (1985): 953-962.

Ganguli, H.C. "Meditation Subculture and Social Skills." *Indian Journal of Social Work* 49, no. 2 (1988): 141-153.

Garfield, E. "Meditation, Learning, and Creativity 1: The Practice and Physiologic Effects of Meditation." *Current Contents* 29 (1985a): 3-11.

Garfield, E. "Meditation, Learning, and Creativity 2: Can Meditation Increase Learning Power and Creativity?" *Current Contents* 30 (1985b): 3-11.

Garrett, J.C. "The Prayer of Francis of Assisi: A Counselor's Prayer." *Counseling and Values* 39, no. 1 (1994): 73-76.

Gash, A., and J.S. Karliner. "No Effect of Transcendental Meditation on Left Ventricular Function." *Annals of Internal Medicine* 88, no. 2 (1978): 215-216.

Gaston, L., J.C. Crombez, and G. Dupuis. "An Imagery and Meditation Technique in the Treatment of Psoriasis: A Case Study Using an A-B-A Design." *Journal of Mental Imagery* 13, no. 1 (Spring 1989): 31-38.

Gaston, L., J.C. Crombez, J. Joly, S. Hodgins, et al. "Efficacy of Imagery and Meditation Techniques in Treating Psoriasis." *Imagination, Cognition and Personality* 8, no. 1 (1988-89): 25-38.

Gattozzi, A.A., and G. Luce. "Physiological Effects of a Meditation Technique and a Suggestion for Curbing Drug Abuse." In *Mental Health Program Reports,* ed. J. Sigal. 5 DHEW Pub. No. HSM 72-9042. Washington, DC: US Government Printing Office, 1971.

Gaughan, A.M. "Pain Perception Following Regular Practice of Meditation, Progressive Muscle Relaxation and Sitting." *Dissertation Abstracts International* 52, no. 4-B (1991): 2295.

Gaylord, C., D. Orme-Johnson, and F. Travis. "The Effects of the Transcendental Meditation Technique and Progressive Muscle Relaxation on EEG Coherence,

Stress Reactivity, and Mental Health in Black Adults." *International Journal of Neuroscience* 46 (1989): 77-86.

Gayten, W. "An Investigation of Physiological Changes during the Practice of Tai Chi Ch'uan: A Moving Meditation." *Dissertation Abstracts International* 39, no. 12-B (1978): 6177.

Gelderloos, P., and Z. Beto. "The Transcendental Meditation and TM-Sidhi Program and Reported Experiences of Transcendental Consciousness." *Psychologia* 32, no. 2 (1989): 91-103.

Gelderloos, P., P.H. Goddard, H.H. Ahlstrom, and R. Jacoby. "Cognitive Orientation toward Positive Values in Advanced Participants of the TM and TM-Sidhi Program." *Perceptual and Motor Skills* 64 (1987a): 1003-1012.

Gelderloos, P., R.J. Lockie, and S. Chuttoorgoon. "Field Independence of Students at Maharishi School of the Age of Enlightenment and a Montessori School." *Perceptual and Motor Skills* 65, no. 2 (1987b): 613-614.

Gelderloos, P., K.L. Cavanaugh, and J.L. Davies. "The Dynamics of US-Soviet Relations, 1979–1986: Effects of Reducing Social Stress Through the Transcendental Meditation and TM-Sidhi Program." *Proceedings of the American Statistical Association, Social Statistics Section.* Alexandria, VA, 1990a.

Gelderloos, P., H.J. Hermans, H.H. Ahlscrom, and R. Jacoby. "Transcendence and Psychological Health: Studies with Long-term Participants of the Transcendental Meditation and TM-Sidhi Program." *Journal of Psychology* 124, no. 2 (1990b): 177-197.

Gelderloos, P., K. Walton, D. Orme-Johnson, and C. Alexander. "Effectiveness of the Transcendental Meditation Program in Preventing and Treating Substance Misuse: A Review." *International Journal of the Addictions* 26, no. 3 (1991): 293-325.

Gellhorn, E., and W.F. Kiely. "Mystical States of Consciousness: Neurophysiological and Clinical Aspects." *The Journal of Nervous and Mental Disease* 154, no. 8 (1972): 399-405.

George, L. Review of *Meditation—Classic and Contemporary Perspectives*, eds. D.H. Shapiro and R.N. Walsh. In *Journal of Parapsychology* 50, no. 3 (1986): 280-284.

Germaine, L.M. "Behavioral Treatment of Menopausal Hot Flashes: Evaluation by Objective Methods." *Dissertation Abstracts International* 45, no. 3-B (1984): 1054.

Gersten, D.J. "Meditation as an Adjunct to Medical and Psychiatric Treatment." *American Psychiatric Association Journal* 135, no. 5 (1978): 598-599.

Ghista, D.N., A. Mukherji, D. Nandagopal, et al. "Physiological Characteristics of the 'Meditative State' during Intuitional Practice (the Ananda Marga System of Meditation) and Its Therapeutic Value." *Medical and Biological Engineering* 14, no. 2 (1976): 209-213.

Gilbert, G.S., J.C. Parker, and C.D. Claiborn. "Differential Mood Changes in Alcoholics as a Function of Anxiety Management Strategies." *Journal of Clinical Psychology* 34, no. 1 (1978): 229-232.

Gill, G.V., S. Redmond, F. Garratt, et al. "Diabetes and Alternative Medicine: Cause for Concern." *Diabetic Medicine* 11, no. 2 (1994): 210-213.

Gilmore, J.V. "Relative Effectiveness of Meditation and Autogenic Training for the Self-regulation of Anxiety." *Dissertation Abstracts International* 45, no. 8-B (1985): 2686.

Girodo, M. "Yoga Meditation and Flooding in the Treatment of Anxiety Neurosis." *Journal of Behavior Therapy and Experimental Psychiatry* 5, no. 2 (1974): 157-160.

Gitiban, K. "Anxiety Reduction through Muscular Relaxation and Meditation." *Dissertation Abstracts International* 44, no. 2-B (1983): 607.

Glanz, R.S. "The Effect of the Relaxation Response on Complex Cognitive Processes." *Dissertation Abstracts International* 53 no. 4-B (1992): 2088.

Glaser, J.L. "Clinical Applications of Maharishi Ayur-Veda in Chemical Dependency Disorders." *Alcoholism Treatment Quarterly* 11, no. 3-4 (1994): 367-394.

Glaser, J., J. Brind, M. Eisner, J. Vogelman, M. Dillbeck, D. Chopra, and K. Wallace. "Elevated Serum Dehydroepiandrosterone Sulfate Levels in Older Practitioners of the Transcendental Meditation and TM-Sidhi Programs." *Age* 10, no. 4 (1987): 160.

Glaser, J., J. Brind, J. Vogelman, et al. "Elevated Serum Dehydroepiandrosterone Sulfate Levels in Practitioners of the Transcendental Meditation (TM) and TM-Sidhi Programs." *Journal of Behavioral Medicine* 15, no. 4 (1992): 327-341.

Globus, G.G. "Potential Contributions of Meditation to Neuroscience." In *Meditation: Classic and Contemporary Perspectives*, eds. D.H. Shapiro and R.N. Walsh. New York: Aldine, 1984: 681-685.

Glueck, B.C., and C.F. Stroebel. "Biofeedback as Meditation in the Treatment of Psychiatric Illnesses." *Comprehensive Psychiatry* 16, no. 4 (1975): 303-321.

Glueck, B.C., and C.F. Stroebel. "Meditation in the Treatment of Psychiatric Illness." In *Expanding Dimensions of Consciousness*, eds. A. Sugurman and R. Tarter. New York: Springer, 1978.

Glueck, B.C., and C.F. Stroebel. "Psychophysiological Correlates of Meditation: EEG Changes during Meditation." In *Meditation: Classic and Contemporary Perspectives*, eds. D.H. Shapiro and R.N. Walsh. New York: Aldine, 1984: 519-524.

Goddard, P.H. "Transcendental Meditation as an Intervention in the Aging of Neurocognitive Function: Reduced Age-related Declines of P300 Latencies in Elderly Practitioners." *Dissertation Abstracts International* 53, no. 6-B (1992): 3189.

Goldberg, D.L., K.H. Kaplan, M.G. Nadeau, C. Brodeur, S. Smith, and C.H. Schmid "A Controlled Study of a Stress-reduction, Cognitive-behavioral Treatment Program in Fibromyalgia." *Journal of Musculoskeletal Pain.* 2 (1994): 53-66.

Goldberg, L.S., and C. Meltzer. "Arrow-dot Scores of Drug Addicts Selecting General or Yoga Therapy." *Perceptual and Motor Skills* 40, no. 3 (1975): 726.

Goldberg, R.J. "Anxiety Reduction by Self-regulation: Theory, Practice and Evaluation." *Annals of Internal Medicine* 96 (1982): 483-487.

Goldman, B.L. "The Efficacy of Meditation in the Reduction of Reported Anxiety with Controls for Expectancy." *Dissertation Abstracts International* 38, no. 12-B (1978): 6152-6153.

Goldman, B.L., B.J. Domitor, and E.J. Murray. "Effects of Zen Meditation on Anxiety Reduction and Perceptual Functioning." *Journal of Consulting and Clinical Psychology* 47, no. 3 (1979): 551-556.

Goldstein, J. *The Experience of Insight.* Boulder, CO: Shambhala, 1982.

Goldstein, J., and J. Kornfield. *Seeking the Heart of Wisdom: The Path of Insight Meditation.* Boulder, CO: Shambhala, 1987.

Goldstein, J., and M. Soares. *The Joy Within: A Step-by-Step Guide to Meditation.* New York: Prentice-Hall Press, 1990.

Goleman, D. "Meditation as Meta-therapy: Hypotheses towards a Proposed Fifth State of Consciousness." *Journal of Transpersonal Psychology* 3, no. 1 (1971): 1-25.

Goleman, D. "The Buddha on Meditation and States of Consciousness. Part I: The Teaching; Part II: A Typology of Meditation Techniques." *Journal of Transpersonal Psychology* 4, no. 1-2 (1972): 1-44, 151-210.

Goleman, D. "Meditation and Stress Reactivity." PhD thesis, Harvard University, 1974.

Goleman, D. "Mental Health in Classical Buddhist Psychology." *Journal of Transpersonal Psychology* 7, no. 2 (1975): 176-181.

Goleman, D. "Meditation and Consciousness: An Asian Approach to Mental Health." *American Journal of Psychotherapy* 30, no. 1 (1976a): 41-54.

Goleman, D. "Meditation Helps Break the Stress Spiral." *Psychology Today*, no. 9 (February 1976b): 82-84, 86, 93.

Goleman, D. *The Varieties of the Meditative Experience.* New York: E.P. Dutton, 1977.

Goleman, D. "A Taxonomy of Meditation-specific Altered States." *Journal of Altered States of Consciousness* 4, no. 2 (1978-79): 203-213.

Goleman, D. "Buddhist and Western Psychology: Some Commonalities and Differences." *Journal of Transpersonal Psychology* 13, no. 2 (1981): 125-136.

Goleman, D. *The Meditative Mind.* Los Angeles: J.P. Tarcher, 1988.

Goleman, D., and M. Epstein. "Meditation and Well-being." *Revision* 3, no. 2 (1980).

Goleman, D.J., and G.E. Schwartz. "Meditation as an Intervention in Stress Reactivity." *Journal of Consulting and Clinical Psychology* 44, no. 3 (1976): 456-466.

Gong, B., Q.Z. Mo, X.W. Kuang, X.P. Qian, H.M. Mao, J.M. Wang, B.X. Wang, Y.Y. Lu, H.F. Wang, L.Q. Yu, et al. "Biochemical and Immunological Studies on Treatment of Asthmatic Children Means of Propagated Sensation along Channels Elicited by Meditation." *Journal of Traditional Chinese Medicine* 6, no. 4 (1986): 257-62.

Good, M. "Complementary Modalities/Part 2: Relaxation Techniques for Surgical Patients." *American Journal of Nursing* 95, no. 5 (1995): 38-43.

Goodale, I.L., A. D. Domar, and H. Benson, "Alleviation of Premenstrual Symptoms with the Relaxation Response." *Obstetrics and Gynecology* 75, no. 4 (1990): 649-655.

Goodpaster, J.R. "Theravada Buddhism and Jungian Psychology: A Comparative Study." *Dissertation Abstracts International* 4509-B (1984): 3056.

Goodman, S.B. "A Buddhist Proof for Omniscience: The 'Sarvajnasiddhi' of Ratnakirti." *Dissertation Abstracts International* 50, no. 6-A (1989): 1699.

Gordon, J. "The Inner Life (Use of Meditation in Therapy)." *Atlantic* 267, no 5 (May 1991): 115.

Gordon, R.L. "The Effects of Transcendental Meditation upon Ego Permissiveness, Anxiety and Neuroticism." *Dissertation Abstracts International* 40, no. 8-A (1980): 4488.

Goswell, M. "Motivational Factors in the Life of a Religious Community, and Related Changes in the Experience of Self." Vols. I and II (England, Monks, Buddhist). *Dissertation Abstracts International* 50, no. 2-A (1988): 465.

Gowan, J.C. "The Facilitation of Creativity through Meditational Procedures." *Journal of Creative Behavior* 12, no. 3 (1978): 156-160.

Goyeche, J., T. Chihara, and H. Shimizu. "Two Concentration Methods: A Preliminary Comparison." *Psychologia* 15 (1972): 110-111.

Goyeche, J., Y. Abo, and Y. Ikemi. "Asthma: The Yoga Perspective, Part II: Yoga Therapy in the Treatment of Asthma." *Journal of Asthma* 19, no. 3 (1982): 189-201.

Grace, G.D. "Effects of Meditation on Personality and Values." *Journal of Clinical Psychology* 32, no. 4 (1976): 809-813.

Graham, J. "Effects of Transcendental Meditation upon Auditory Thresholds." In *Scientific Research on the Transcendental Meditation Program.* Vol. I, eds. D. Johnson, L. Domash, and J. Farrow. Switzerland: MIU Press, p. 175.

Green, D.B. "The Relationship of a Counselor-guided Meditation to Counselor Presence as Defined in Psychosynthesis." *Dissertation Abstracts International* 41, no. 6-A (1980): 2450.

Green, E.E., and A.M. Green. *Beyond Biofeedback.* New York: Delacorte Press, 1977.

Green, E.E., A.M. Green, and E.D. Walters. "Voluntary Control of Internal States: Psychological and Physiological." *Journal of Transpersonal Psychology* 2, no. 1 (1970): 1-26.

Greene, Y.N., and B. Hiebert. "A Comparison of Mindfulness Meditation and Cognitive Self-observation." *Canadian Journal of Counselling* 22, no. 1 (January 1988): 25-34.

Greenfield, T.K. "Individual Differences and Mystical Experience in Response to Three Forms of Meditation." *Dissertation Abstracts International* 38, no. 11-B (1978): 5569-5570.

Greenspan, M. "Therapeutic Touch and Healing Meditation: A Threesome with Education." *Early Child Development and Care* 98, March (1994): 121-129.

Greenwood, M., and H. Benson. "The Efficacy of Progressive Relaxation in Systematic Desensitization and a Proposal for an Alternative Competitive Response: The Relaxation Response." *Behavior Research and Therapy* 15 (1977): 337-343.

Gregoire, J. "Therapy with the Person Who Meditates: Diagnosis and Treatment Stategies." *Transactional Analysis Journal* 20, no 1 (1990): 60-76.

Griffith, F. "Meditation Research: Its Personal and Social Implications." In *Frontiers of Consciousness*, ed. J. White. New York: Julian Press, 1974.

Griffiths, P. *On Being Mindless: Buddhist Meditation and the Mind-Body Problem.* Peru, IL: Open Court, 1986.

Griffiths, T.J., D.H. Steel, P. Vaccaro, et al. "The Effects of Relaxation Techniques on Anxiety and Underwater Performance." *International Journal of Sport Psychology* 12, no. 3 (1981): 176-182.

Griggs, S.T. "A Preliminary Study into the Effect of TM on Empathy." Doctoral diss., United States International University, 1976.

Griggs, S.T. "Clairvoyance and the Transcendental Meditation Sidhi Program." *Dissertation Abstracts International* 43, no. 6-B (1982): 1980.

Grim, P.F. "Relaxation, Meditation, and Insight." *Psychologia* 18, no. 3 (1975): 125-133.

Grub, P.H.W. "Healing through Meditation." *London Quarterly and Holborn Review* 181 (1956): 186-190.

Guam, E.A. "Moksha and the Transcendental Meditation of Maharishi Mahesh Yogi—A Science of Religion Research." *Dissertation Abstracts International* 50, no. 7-A (1988): 2112.

Gunda, R.H., N. Krishnaswamy, R.L. Narasimbaiya, et al. "Some Experiments on a Yogi in Controlled States." *Pratibha, Journal of the All India Institute for Mental Health* 1 (1958): 99-106.

Gupta, N.C. "Effects of TM on Anxiety and Self-concept." Doctoral diss., Ball State University, Indiana, 1976.

Gussner, R.E., and S.D. Berkowitz. "Scholars, Sects and Sanghas. 1. Recruitment to Asian-based Meditation Groups in North America." *Sociological Analysis* 49, no. 2 (1988): 136-170.

Haartman, K. "Beyond the Nirvana Principle: Buddhist Themes in the Psychoanalytic Writings of M.D. Faber and Jacques Lacan." *Melanie Klein and Object Relations* 12, no. 2 (1994): 41-63.

Hack, S.N. "Collective Identity and Sacred Space: A Study of Seven Zen Communities in Northern California." *Masters Abstracts* 28, no. 3 (1989): 353.

Hafner, R.J. "Psychological Treatment of Essential Hypertension: A Controlled Comparison of Meditation and Meditation plus Biofeedback." *Biofeedback and Self-Regulation* 7, no. 3 (1982): 305-316.

Hager, J.L., and R.S. Surwit. "Hypertension Self-control with a Portable Feedback Unit or Meditation-Relaxation." *Biofeedback and Self-Regulation* 3, no. 3 (1978): 269-276.

Hahn, H.R., and T.E. Whalen. "The Effects of the TM Program on Levels of Hostility, Anxiety and Depression." Doctoral dissertation, California State University, Hayward, 1974.

Haimes, N. "Zen Buddhism and Psychoanalysis." *Psychologia* 15 (1972): 22-30.

Hall, E.G., and C.J. Hardy. "Ready, Aim, Fire...Relaxation Strategies for Enhancing Pistol Marksmanship." *Perceptual and Motor Skills* 72 (1991): 775-786.

Handmacher, B.H. "Time in Meditation and Sex Differences Related to Intrapersonal and Interpersonal Orientation." *Dissertation Abstracts International* 39, no. 2-A (1978): 676-677.

Hanley, C.P., and J.I. Spates. "Transcendental Meditation and Psychological Attitudes." *Journal of Psychology* 99, no. 2 (1978): 121-127.

Hanson, C.M. "State-of-Consciousness Psychotechnology and Instructional Technology: An Investigation of the Theories and Practices of Systems for a Deliberate Change in Consciousness." *Dissertation Abstracts International* 50, no. 3-A (1988): 671.

Haratani, T., and T. Henmi. "Effects of Transcendental Meditation on Health Behavior of Industrial Workers." *Japanese Journal of Public Health* 37, no. 10 (1990a): 729.

Haratani, T., and T. Henmi. "Effects of Transcendental Meditation on Mental Health of Industrial Workers." *Japanese Journal of Industrial Health* 32, no. 7 (1990b): 177.

Hardt, J.V., et al. "Studying Power: Zen Meditation." *Biofeedback and Self-Regulation* 1 (1976): 362-363.

Harris, T.G. "Why Pros Meditate." *Psychology Today* 9, no. 5 (1975): 4.

Harrison, S.D., R. Pagano, and S. Warrenburg. "Meditation and Right Hemispheric Functioning—Spatial Localization." In *Proceedings of the Biofeedback Research Society, 7th Annual Meeting.* Colorado Springs, Colorado, 27 February 1976.

Hart, D.E., and J.R. Means. "Effects of Meditation vs. Professional Reading on Students' Perceptions of Para-professional Counselors' Effectiveness." *Psychological Reports* 51 (1982): 479-482.

Harung, H.S., D.P. Heaton, W.W. Graff, and C.N. Alexander. "Heightened Awareness and Peak Performance." *Journal of Managerial Psychology* 11, no. 4 (1996): 3-23.

Harvey, J.R. "The Effect of Yogic Breathing Exercises on Mood." *Journal of the American Society of Psychosomatic Dentistry and Medicine* 30, no. 2 (1983): 39-48.

Hassett, J. "Meditation Can Hurt." *Psychology Today* 12, no. 6 (1978): 125-126.

Hatchard, G.D., A.J. Deans, K.L. Cavanaugh, and D.W. Orme-Johnson. "The Maharishi Effect: A Model for Social Improvement: Time Series Analysis of a Phase Transition to Reduced Crime in Merseyside Metropolitan Area." *Psychology, Crime, and Law* 2, no. 3 (1996): 165-174.

Hattauer, E.A. "Clinically Standardized Meditation (CSM) and Counselor Behavior." *Dissertation Abstracts International* 41, no. 10-B (1981): 3892.

Haynes, C.T., J.R. Hebert, W. Reber, et al. "The Psychophysiology of Advanced Participants in the Transcendental Meditation Program: Correlation of EEG Coherence, Creativity, H-reflex Recovery, and Experience of Transcendental Consciousness." In *Scientific Research on the Transcendental Meditation Program: Collected Papers. Vol. I,* eds. D.W. Orme-Johnson and J.T. Farrow. New York: M.E.R.U Press 1977: 208-212.

Haynes, S., D. Mosley, and W. McGowan. "Relaxation Training and Biofeedback in the Reduction of Frontalis Muscle Tension." *Psychophysiology* 12 (1975): 547-552.

Heaton, D.P., and D.W. Orme-Johnson. "The Transcendental Meditation Program and Academic Achievement." In *Scientific Research on the Transcendental Meditation Program: Collected Papers. Vol. I,* eds. D.W. Orme-Johnson and J.T. Farrow. New York: M.E.R.U. Press, 1977: 396-399.

Hebert, J.R. "Periodic Suspension of Respiration during the Transcendental Meditation Technique." In *Scientific Research on the Transcendental Meditation Program: Collected Papers. Vol. I,* eds. D.W. Orme-Johnson and J.T. Farrow. New York: M.E.R.U. Press, 1977: 134-136.

Hebert, J., and D. Lehmann. "Theta Bursts: An EEG Pattern in Normal Subjects Practicing the Transcendental Meditation Technique." *Electroencephalography and Clinical Neurophysiology* 42, no. 3 (1977): 397-405.

Heide, F.J. "Habituation of Alpha Blocking during Meditation." *Psychophysiology* 16, no. 2 (1979): 198.

Heide, F.J. "Psychophysiological Responsiveness to Auditory Stimulation during Transcendental Meditation." *Psychophysiology* 23, no. 1 (1986): 71-75.

Heide, F.J., and T.D. Borkovec. "Relaxation-induced Anxiety: Paradoxical Anxiety Enhancement due to Relaxation Training." *Journal of Consulting and Clinical Psychology* 51, no. 2 (1983): 171-182.

Heide, F.J., W.L. Wadlington, and R.M. Lundy. "Hypnotic Responsivity as a Predictor of Outcome in Meditation." *International Journal of Clinical and Experimental Hypnosis* 28, no. 4 (1980): 358-366.

Heider, John. "The Enhancement of Perceptual Acuity as a Result of Meditation." Major Area Paper, Duke University, 1965.

Heider, John. "The Flexibility and Rigidity of Perceptual/cognitive Constructs: A Study of Creative States of Awareness." Doctoral dissertation, Duke University, 1968.

Heikkinen, C.A. "Reorientation from Altered States: Please, More Carefully." *Journal of Counseling and Development* 67, no. 9 (May 1989): 520-521.

Heil, J.D. "Visual Imagery Change during Relaxation Meditation Training." *Dissertation Abstracts International* 43, no. 7 (1983): 2338.

Hellman, C.J., M. Budd, J. Borysenko, D.C. McClelland, and H. Benson. "A Study of the Effectiveness of Two Group Behavioral Medicine Interventions for Patients with Psychosomatic Complaints." *Behavioral Medicine*, 16 (1990): 165-73.

Helminiak, D.A. "Meditation: Psychologically and Theologically Considered." *Pastoral Psychology* 30, no. 1 (1981): 6-20.

Helminiak, D.A. "How is Meditation Prayer?" *Review for Religious*, 41 (1982): 774-782.

Hendricks, C.G. "Meditation as Discrimination Training: A Theoretical Note." *Journal of Transpersonal Psychology* 7, no. 2 (1975): 144-146.

Hendricksen, N.E. "The Effects of Progressive Relaxation and Meditation on Mood Stability and State Anxiety in Alcoholic Patients." *Dissertation Abstracts International* 39, no. 2-B (1978): 981.

Henry, J.P. "Relaxation Methods and the Control of Blood Pressure." *Psychosomatic Medicine* 40, no. 4 (1978): 273-275.

Herbert, R., and D. Lehmann. "Theta Bursts: An EGG Pattern in Normal Subjects Practicing the Transcendental Meditation Technique." *Electroenphalography and Clinical Neurophysiology* 42 (1977): 387-405.

Hernandez, R.S. "The Effects of Task Condition on the Relationship of EEG Coherence and Full-scale IQ in Children." *Dissertation Abstracts International* 49, no. 8-B (1988): 3032.

Herron, R.E., S.L. Hillis, J.V. Mandarino, D.W. Orme-Johnson, and K.G. Walton. "Reducing Medical Costs: The Impact of Transcendental Meditation on Government Payments to Physicians in Quebec." *American Journal of Health Promotion* 1996a Vol. 10, No. 3, p. 208-216.

Herron, R.E., S.L. Hillis, J.V. Mandarino, et al. "Stress Reduction in Decreasing Health Care Costs: Does Transcendental Meditation Have An Effect?" *American Journal of Health Promotion* 10, no. 3 (1996b): 208-16.

Herron, R.E., R.H. Schneider, J.V. Mandarino, et al. "Cost-Effective Management of Hypertension Using an Alternative Approach: A Comparison of Conventional Drug Therapies and Transcendental Meditation." *American Journal of Managed Care* 2, no. 4 (1996c): 455-465.

Hershfield, N.B., W. Kubryn, and L.R. Sutherland. "Meditation Training as Adjunct Therapy in the Management of Crohn's Disease: A Pilot Study." *Canadian Journal of Gastoenterology* 7, no. 8 (1993): 613-615.

Herzberger, H.G. "Voice Quality and Maharishi's Transcendental Meditation and TM-Sidhi Program: Vocal Acoustics in Health and Higher States of Awareness." *Dissertation Abstracts International* 53, no. 6-B (1992): 3190.

Herzog, H., V.R. Lele, T. Kuwert, K. Langen, E.R. Kops, and L.E. Feinendegen. "Changed Pattern of Regional Glucose Metabolism during Yoga Meditative Relaxation." *Neuropsychobiology* 23, no. 4 (1990-91): 182-187.

Hewitt, J., and R. Miller. "Relative Effects of Meditation vs. Other Activities on Ratings of Relaxation and Enjoyment of Others." *Psychological Reports* 48, no. 2 (1981): 395-398.

Hickman, J.L., M. Murphy, and M. Spino. "Psychophysical Transformations through Meditation and Sport." *Simulation and Games* 8, no. 1 (1977): 49-60.

Hill, D.A. "Beta-Adrenergic Receptor Sensitivity, Autonomic Balance and Serotonergic Activity in Practitioners of Transcendental Meditation." *Dissertation Abstracts International* 50, no. 8-B (1990): 3330.

Hirai, T. "Electroencephalographic Study on the Zen Meditation (Zazen): EEG Changes during the Concentrated Relaxation." *Psychiatrica et Neurologia Japanica* 62 (1960): 76-105.

Hirai, T. *The Psychophysiology of Zen.* Tokyo: Igaku Shoin, 1974.

Hirai, T. *Zen Meditation Therapy.* Tokyo: Japan Publications, 1975.

Hirai, T. *Zen Meditation and Psychotherapy.* Tokyo: Japan Publications, 1986.

Hirai, T., S. Izawa, and E. Koga. "EEG and Zen Buddhism: EEG Changes in the Course of Meditation." *Electroencephalography and Clinical Neurophysiology,* supplement no. 18 (1959): 52-53.

Hirai, T., Y. Ikeda, and S. Watanabe. "Biofeedback and Electrodermal Self-regulation in Zen Meditator." *Psychophysiology* 14, no. 1 (1977): 103.

Hirss, J.R. "A Comparison of Two Types of Meditation to Reduce Stress in a Teaching Population." *Dissertation Abstracts International* 43, no. 12 (1983): 3847.

Hjelle, L.A. "TM and Psychological Health." *Perceptual and Motor Skills* 39 (1974): 623-628.

Hoenig, J. "Medical Research on Yoga." *Confina Psychiatrica* 11 (1968): 69-89.

Hoffman, J.W., P.A. Arns, G.L. Stainbrook, L. Lansberg, J.B. Young, A. Gill, F.H. Frankel, and H. Benson. "Altered Sympathetic Nervous System Reactivity with the Relaxation Response." *Clinical Research* 29 (1981a): 207.

Hoffman, J.W., P.A. Arns, G.L. Stainbrook, A. Gill, F.H. Frankel, L.H. Hartley, and H. Benson. "Effect of the Relaxation Response on Oxygen Consumption during Exercise." *Clinical Research* 29 (1981b): 207.

Hoffman, J.W., H. Benson, P.A. Arns, G.L. Stainbrook, G.L. Landsberg, J.B. Young, and A. Gill. "Reduced Sympathetic Nervous System Responsivity Associated with the Relaxation Response." *Science* 215 (1982): 190-92.

Holeman, R., and G. Seiler. "Effects of Sensitivity Training and Transcendental Meditation on Perception of Others." *Perceptual and Motor Skills* 49, no. 1 (1979): 270.

Holmes, D.S. "Meditation and Somatic Arousal Reduction: A Review of the Experimental Evidence." *American Psychologist* 39, no. 1 (1984): 1-10.

Holmes, D.S. "To Meditate or Rest? The Answer is Rest." *American Psychologist* 40, no. 6 (1985a): 728.

Holmes, D.S. "To Meditate or to Simply Rest, That is the Question: Response to the Comments of Shapiro." *American Psychologist* 40, no. 6 (1985b): 722.

Holmes, D.S. "Self-control of Somatic Arousal." *American Behavioral Scientist* 28, no. 4 (1985c): 486-496.

Holmes, D.S., S. Solomon, B.M. Cappo, et al. "Effects of Transcendental Meditation versus Resting on Physiological and Subjective Arousal." *Journal of Personality and Social Psychology* 44, no. 6 (1983): 1245-1252.

Holt, J.C. "Theravada Meditation: The Buddhist Transformation of Yoga." *Journal Asian Studies* 41, no. 2 (1982): 420-421.

Holt, W.R., J.L. Caruso, and J.B. Riley. "Transcendental Meditation versus Pseudo-meditation on Visual Choice Reaction Time." *Perceptual and Motor Skills* 46, no. 3, pt. 1 (1978): 726.

Honsberger, R.W., and A.F. Wilson. "The Effect of TM upon Bronchial Asthma." *Clinical Research* 21 (1973a): 278.

Honsberger, R.W., and A.F. Wilson. "Transcendental Meditation in Treating Asthma." *Respiratory Therapy. Journal of Inhalation Technology* 3 (1973b): 79-81.

Honsberger, R.W., J.T. Chiu, and H.S. Novey. "Transcendental Meditation and Asthma." *Respiration* 32 (1975): 74-80.

Howell, S.L. "Natural/Alternative Health Care Practices Used by Women with Chronic Pain: Findings from a Grounded Theory Research Study." *Nurse Practitioner Forum* 5, no. 2 (1994): 98-105.

Hu, S.Q., and J.R. Ma. "Selection of Indices of Meditation in the Practice of Relaxation Exercise." *Chung Hsi I Chieh Ho Tsa Chih* 6, no. 6 (1986): 348-50.

Huang, Guozhi. "Physiological Effects During Relaxation Qigong Exercise." *Psychosomatic Medicine* 53 (1991): 228.

Humphreys, A. "Neutral Hypnosis, Progressive Muscular Relaxation and the Relaxation Response: A Reply to Edmonston's Comment." *British Journal of Experimental and Clinical Hypnosis* 2, no. 1 (1985): 30.

Hungerman, P.W. "The Effectiveness of the Relaxation Response in Reducing Anxiety and Promoting Self-actualization in Counselor Trainees." *Dissertation Abstracts International* 46, no. 4-B (1985): 1324.

Hussey, H.H., ed. "Meditation May Find Use in Medical Practice." *Journal of the American Medical Association* 219 (1972): 295-299.

Hustad, P., and J. Carnes. "The Effectiveness of Walking Meditation on EMG Readings in Chronic Pain Patients." *Biofeedback and Self-Regulation* 13, no. 1 (1988): 69.

Ikegami, R. "Psychological Study of Zen Posture." *Bulletin of the Faculty of Literature of Kyushu University* 5 (1974): 105-135.

Ikemi, A. "Psychophysiological Effects of Self-regulation Method: EEG Frequency Analysis and Contingent Negative Variations." *Psychotherapy and Psychosomatics* 49, nos. 3-4 (1988): 230-239.

Ishii, M. "Attending Zen Meditation Sessions: Monologue of a Head Nurse." *Kangogaku Zasshi* 48, no. 4 (1984): 445.

Jackson, Y. "Learning Disorders and the Transcendental Meditation Program: Retrospects and Prospects (A Preliminary Study with Economically Deprived Adolescents)." *Dissertation Abstracts International* 38, no. 6-A (1977): 3351-3352.

Jacobs, G.D., and J.F. Luber. "Spectral Analysis of the Central Nervous System Effects of the Relaxation Response Elicited by Autogenic Training." *Behavioral Medicine* 15 (1989): 125-132.

Jacobs, G.D., H. Benson, and R. Friedman. "Home-Based Central Nervous System Assessment of a Multifactor Behavioral Intervention for Chronic Sleep-Onset Insomnia." *Behavior Therapy* 24 (1993a) 159-74.

Jacobs, G.D., P.A. Rosenberg, R. Friedman, et al. "Multifactor Behavioral Treatment of Chronic Sleep-Onset Insomnia Using Stimulus Control and the Relaxation Response." *Behavior Modification* 17, no. 4 (1993b): 498-509.

Janby, J. "Immediate Effects of the Transcendental Meditation Technique: Increased Skin Resistance during First Meditation after Instruction." In *Scientific Research on the Transcendental Meditation Program: Collected Papers.* Vol. 1, eds. D.W. Orme-Johnson and J.T. Farrow. New York: M.E.R.U. Press, 1977.

Jangid, R.K., J.N. Vays, and T.R. Shukla. "Effect of Transcendental Meditation in Cases of Anxiety Neurosis." *Indian Journal of Clinical Psychology* 15, no. 2 (Sept-1988a): 77-79.

Jangid, R.K., J.N. Vays, and T.R. Shukla. "The Effect of the Transcendental Meditation Programme on the Normal Individuals." *Journal of Personality and Clinical Studies* 4, no. 2 (Sept-1988b): 145-149.

Janowiak, J.J., and R. Hackman. "Meditation and College Students' Self-actualization and Rated Stress." *Psychological Reports* 75, no. 2 (1994): 1007-1010.

Jarrell, H.R. *International Meditation Bibliography: 1950-1982.* Metuchen, NJ: Scarecrow, 1985.

Jedrczak, A., and G. Clements. "The TM-Sidhi Program and Field Independence." *Perceptual and Motor Skills* 59, no. 3 (1984): 999-1000.

Jedrczak, A., M. Beresford, and G. Clements. "The TM-Sidhi Program, Pure Consciousness, Creativity and Intelligence." *Journal of Creative Behavior* 19, no. 4 (1985): 270-275.

Jedrczak, A., M. Toomey, and G. Clements. "The TM-Sidhi Program, Age, and Brief Tests of Perceptual-motor Speed and Nonverbal Intelligence." *Journal of Clinical Psychology* 42, no. 1 (1986): 161-164.

Jevning, R. "Major Change in Intermediary Metabolism by Behavioral Rest States." *Psychophysiology* 19 (1982): 327.

Jevning, R., and J.P. O'Halloran. "Metabolic Effects of Transcendental Meditation: Toward a New Paradigm of Neurobiology." In *Meditation: Classic and Contemporary Perspectives*, eds. D.H. Shapiro and R.N. Walsh. New York: Aldine, 1984: 465-472.

Jevning, R., and A.F. Wilson. "Altered Red Cell Metabolism in TM." *Psychophysiology* 14, no. 1 (1977): 94.

Jevning, R., and A.F. Wilson. "Behavioral Increase of Cerebral Blood Flow." *The Physiologist* (1978): 21.

Jevning, R., A.F. Wilson, E. Vanderlaan, et al. "Plasma Prolactin and Cortisol during Transcendental Meditation." *The Endocrine Society Program, 57th Annual Meeting.* New York City (June 18-20, 1975): 257.

Jevning, R., W.R. Smith, A.F. Wilson, et al. "Alterations in Blood Flow during Transcendental Meditation." *Psychophysiology* 13, no. 1 (1976): 168.

Jevning, R., H.C. Pirkle, and A.F. Wilson. "Behavioral Alteration of Plasma Phenylalanine Concentration." *Physiology and Behavior* 19, no. 5 (1977a): 611-614.

Jevning, R., A.F. Wilson, and W.R. Smith. "Plasma Amino Acids during the Transcendental Meditation Technique: Comparison to Sleep." In *Scientific Research on the Transcendental Meditation Program: Collected Papers.* Vol. 1, eds. D.W. Orme-Johnson and J.T. Farrow. New York: M.E.R.U. Press, 1977b: 145-147.

Jevning, R., A.F. Wilson, and J.M. Davidson. "Adrenocortical Activity during Meditation." *Hormones and Behavior* 10, no. 1 (1978a): 54-60.

Jevning, R., A.F. Wilson, and E. Vanderlaan. "Plasma Prolactin and Growth Hormone during Meditation." *Psychosomatic Medicine* 40, no. 4 (1978b): 329-333.

Jevning, R., A.F. Wilson, W.R. Smith, et al. "Redistribution of Blood Flow in Acute Hypometabolic Behavior." *American Journal of Physiology* 235, no. 1 (1978c): 89-92.

Jevning, R., A.F. Wilson, and W.R. Smith. "The Transcendental Meditation Technique, Adrenocortical Activity and Implications for Stress." *Experientia* 34, no. 5 (1978d): 618-619.

Jevning, R., A.F. Wilson, and J.P. O'Halloran. "Muscle and Skin Blood Flow and Metabolism during States of Decreased Activation." *Physiology and Behavior* 29 (1982): 343-348.

Jevning, R., A.F. Wilson, H. Pirkle, et al. "Metabolic Control in a State of Decreased Activation: Modulation of Red Blood Cell Metabolism." *American Journal of Physiology* 245, no. 5 (1983): 457-461.

Jevning, R., H. Pirkle, R.N. Walsh, and A.F. Wilson. "Hormonal Control of Metabolism in States of Decreased Activation." *Federal Proceedings* 44, no. 3 (1985a): 1312.

Jevning, R., A.F. Wilson, and H. Pirkle. "Modulation of Red Cell Metabolism by States of Decreased Activation: Comparison between States." *Physiology and Behavior* 35, no. 5 (1985b): 679-682.

Jevning, R., I. Wells, A.F. Wilson, and S. Guich. "Plasma Thyroid Hormones, Thyroid Stimulating Hormone, and Insulin during Acute Hypometabolic States in Man." *Physiology and Behavior* 40, no. 5 (1987): 603-606.

Jevning, R., R.K. Wallace, and M. Beiderbach. "The Physiology of Meditation: A Review. A Wakeful Hypometabolic Integrated Response." *Neuroscience and Biobehavioral Reviews* 16 (1992): 415-424.

Jewell, H.A. "The Effects of Meditation and Progressive Relaxation upon Heroin Addicts during Methadone-aided Detoxification." *Dissertation Abstracts International* 45, no. 1-B (1984): 354

Jhunijhunwala, L.N., R.J. Iyer, and P.K. Srivastava. "Indian Psycho-philosophy and Human Response in Organizations." *Hindustan Electro-Graphites* 12, no. 1 (January-March 1987): 33-42.

Jichaku, P., G. Fujita, and S.I. Shapiro. "The Double Bind and Koan Zen." *The Journal of Mind and Behavior* 5, no. 2 (Spring 1984): 211-222.

Jin, P. "Changes in Heart Rate, Noradrenaline, Cortisol and Mood during Tai Chi." *Journal of Psychosomatic Research* 33, no. 2 (1989): 197-206.

Joffe, B.I., and H.C. Seftel. "Hormonal and Biochemical Responses to Transcendental Meditation." *Postgraduate Medical Journal* 62, no. 723 (1986): 69.

Johnson, J. "Maximizing Musicianship through Biofeedback and Somatic Studies (A Written Contextual Piece of Inquiry and a Videotape Production)." *Dissertation Abstracts International* 49, no. 6-A (1987): 1307.

Johnson, L.M.H. "Psychotherapy and Spirituality: Techniques, Interventions and Inner Attitudes." *Dissertation Abstracts International* 50, no. 12-A (1989): 3897.

Johnson, W. *Riding the Ox Home: A History of Meditation from Shamanism to Science.* Boston: Beacon, 1986 (reprint).

Jones, R.C. "A Comparison of Aerobic Exercise, Anaerobic Exercise and Meditation on Multidimensional Stress Measures." *Dissertation Abstracts International* 43, no. 6-B (1981): 2504-2505.

Joscelyn, L.A. "The Effects of the Transcendental Meditation Technique on a Measure of Self-actualization." *Dissertation Abstracts International* 39, no. 8-B (1979): 4104.

Joseph, A.B. "The Influence of One Form of Zen Meditation on Levels of Anxiety and Self-actualization." *Dissertation Abstracts International* 40, no. 3-B (1979): 1335-1336.

Jourdan, J. "Near-death and Transcendental Experiences: Neurophysiological Correlates of Mystical Traditions." *Journal of Near-death Studies* 12, no. 3 (1994): 177-200.

Journal of the American Medical Association, "Meditation May Find Use in Medical Practice." 219, no. 3 (1972): 295.

Jovanovic, U.J., L. Hahn, and W. Dogs. "EEG in Hypnosis and Transcendental Meditation." *Electroencephalography and Clinical Neurophysiology* 69, no. 1 (1988): 13.

Juhl, Al, and S. Strandgaard. "Treatment of Hypertension with Relaxation and Biofeedback." *Scandinavian Journal of Clinical and Laboratory Investigation* 45, no. 176 (1985): 70-80.

Kabat-Zinn, J. "An Outpatient Program in Behavioral Medicine for Chronic Pain Patients Based on the Practice of Mindfulness Meditation: Theoretical Considerations and Preliminary Results." *General Hospital Psychiatry* 4 (1982): 33-47.

Kabat-Zinn, J. *Full-Catastrophe Living: Using the Wisdom of Your Body and Mind to Face Stress, Pain, and Illness.* New York: Delacorte Press, 1990.

Kabat-Zinn, J. "Meditation." In B. Moyers, ed. *Healing and the Mind.* New York: Doubleday, 1993a, 115-143.

Kabat-Zinn, J. "Mindfulness Meditation: Health Benefits of an Ancient Buddhist Practice." In D. Goleman and J. Gurin, eds. *Mind/Body Medicine.* Yonkers, NY: Consumer Reports Books, 1993b

Kabat-Zinn, J. "Psychosocial Factors in Coronary Heart Disease: Their Importance and Management." In I.S. Ockene and J. Ockene, eds. *Prevention of Coronary Heart Disease.* Boston: Little Brown, 1993c, 299-333.

Kabat-Zinn, J. *Wherever You Go, There You Are: Mindfulness Meditation in Everyday Life.* New York: Hyperion, 1994.

Kabat-Zinn, J., and B. Beall. "A Systematic Mental Training Program Based on Mindfulness Meditation to Optimize Performance in Collegiate and Olympic Rowers." Paper Presented to Department of Athletics, M.I.T., Cambridge, 1987.

Kabat-Zinn, J., and R. Burney. "The Clinical Use of Awareness Meditation in the Self-regulation of Chronic Pain" (abstract). *Pain Supplement* (1981): 273.

Kabat-Zinn, J., and A. Chapman-Waldrop. "Compliance with an Out-patient Stress Reduction Program: Rates and Predictors of Program Completion." *Journal of Behavioral Medicine* 11 (1988): 333-352.

Kabat-Zinn, J., B. Beall, and J. Rippe. "A Systematic Mental Training Program Based on Mindfulness Meditation to Optimize Performance in Collegiate and Olympic Rowers." Paper Presented at *Proceedings of the VI World Congress in Sport Psychology*, Copenhagen, 1984a.

Kabat-Zinn, J., L. Lipworth, W. Sellers, et al. "Reproducibility and Four-year Follow-up of a Training Program in Mindfulness Meditation for the Self-regulation of Chronic Pain" (abstract). *Pain Supplement* 2 (1984b): 303.

Kabat-Zinn, J., L. Lipworth, and R. Burney. "The Clinical Use of Mindfulness Meditation for the Self-regulation of Chronic Pain." *Journal of Behavioral Medicine* 8, no. 2 (1985): 163-190.

Kabat-Zinn, J., L. Lipworth, R. Burney, and W. Sellers. "Four-Year Follow-up of a Meditation-based Program for the Self-regulation of Chronic Pain: Treatment Outcomes and Compliance." *Clinical Journal of Pain* 2 (1986): 159-173.

Kabat-Zinn, J., A. Massion, J. Kristeller, et al. "Effectiveness of a Meditation-based Stress Reduction Program in the Treatment of Anxiety Disorders." *American Journal of Psychiatry* 149, no. 7 (1992): 936-943.

Kabat-Zinn, J., A. Massion, J.R. Hebert, and E. Rosenbaum. "Meditation." In J. Holland, ed. *Textbook of Psycho-oncology*. Oxford: Oxford University Press, 1997.

Kahn, Michael. "Vipassana Meditation and the Psychobiology of Wilheim Reich." *Journal of Humanistic Psychology* 25, no. 3 (1985): 117-128.

Kaivalyadhama Shreeman Madhava Yoga Mandira Samiti. "Experiments on Pranayama: Bhastrika Pranayama. Effect on Urinary Acid Excretion and pH." *Yoga-Mimamsa* 6 (1956): 9-18.

Kaivalyadhama Shreeman Madhava Yoga Mandira Samiti. "Studies in Alveolar Air I: Carbon Dioxide Concentration in Different Parts of the Alveolar Air Samples." *Yoga-Mimamsa* 7 (1957a).

Kaivalyadhama Shreeman Madhava Yoga Mandira Samiti. "Studies in Alveolar Air II: Variation in Composition of Different Parts Resting Alveolar Air." *Yoga-Mimamsa* 7 (1957b): 9-17.

Kaivalyadhama Shreeman Madhava Yoga Mandira Samiti. "Studies in Alveolar Air III: Carbon Dioxide Concentration on Resting Alveolar Air." *Yoga-Mimamsa* 7 (1957c): 79-86.

Kaivalyadhama Shreeman Madhava Yoga Mandira Samiti. "Studies in Alveolar Air at the End of Two Minutes Kapalabhati." *Yoga-Mimamsa* 7 (1957d): 18-25.

Kaivalyadhama Shreeman Madhava Yoga Mandira Samiti. "Studies in Alveolar Air in Kapalabhati II: Alveolar Air at the End of Five Minutes Kapalabhati." *Yoga-Mimamsa* 7 (1957e): 87-94.

Kalayil, J.A. "A Controlled Comparison of Progressive Relaxation and Yoga Meditation as Methods to Relieve Stress in Middle Grade School Children." *Dissertation Abstracts International* 49, no. 12-A, pt. 1 (June 1989): 3626.

Kambe, T., J. Sato, and K. Naggua. "Medical and Psychological Studies on Zen." *Proceedings of 25th Convention of J.P.A.* (1961): 287.

Kamiya, J. "Conscious Control of Brain Waves." *Psychology Today* 1, no. 1 (1968): 57-60.

Kamiya, J. "Operant Control of the EEG Alpha Rhythm … Consciousness." In C. Tart, ed. *Altered States of Consciousness.* New York: Julian, 1969a.

Kamiya, J. "A Fourth Dimension of Consciousness." *Experimental Medicine and Surgery* 27 (1969b): 13-18.

Kamiya, J. "Autoregulation of the EEG Alpha Rhythm: A Program for the Study of Consciousness." In M.H. Chase, ed. *Operant Control of Brain Activity.* Brain Information Service, Brain Research Institute, U.C.L.A., 1974.

Kanas, N., and M.J. Horowitz. "Reactions of Transcendental Meditators and Nonmeditators to Stressful Films: A Cognitive Study." *Archives of General Psychiatry* 34, no. 12 (1977): 1431-1436.

Kanellakos, D.P. "Transcendental Consciousness: Expanded Awareness as a Means of Preventing and Eliminating the Effects of Stress." In *Stress and Anxiety* (Clinical Psychology Series). Vol. 1, C.D. Spielberger and I.G. Sarason, eds. New York: Halsted Press, 1977.

Kanellakos, D.P., and J. Lukas. *The Psychobiology of Transcendental Meditation: A Literature Review.* Menlo Park, CA: W.A. Benjamin, 1974.

Kaplan, K.H., D.L. Goldberg, and M. Galvin-Nadeau. "The Impact of a Meditation-Based Stress Reduction Program on Fibromyalgia." *General Hospital Psychiatry* 15, no. 5 (1993): 284-289.

Kaplan, S. "Appraisal of a Psychological Approach to Meditation." *Zygon* 13 (1978): 83-101.

Karambelkar, P.V., S.L. Vinekar, and M.V. Phole. "Studies on Human Subjects Staying in an Airtight Pit." *Indian Journal of Medical Research* 56 (1968): 1282-1288.

Karambelkar, P., M. Bhole, and M. Gharotte. "Effect of Yogic Asanas on Uropepsin Excretion." *Indian Journal of Medical Research* 57 (1969a): 944-947.

Karambelkar, P., M. Bhole, and M. Gharotte. "Muscle Activity in Some Asanas." *Yoga-Mimamsa* 12 (1969b): 1-13(b).

Kasamatsu, A., and T. Hirai. "Science of Zazen." *Psychologia* 6 (1963): 86-91.

Kasamatsu, A., and T. Hirai. "An EEG Study on the Zen Meditation (Zazen)". *Folia Psychiatrica et Neurologia Japonica* 20, no. 4 (1966): 315-336.

Kasamatsu, A., and T. Hirai. "An EEG Study on the Zen Meditation (Zazen)." *Psychologia* 12, nos. 3-4 (1969a): 205-225.

Kasamatsu, A., and T. Hirai. "An Electroencephalographic Study of Zen Meditation." In C. Tart, ed. *Altered States of Consciousness*. New York: John Wiley and Sons, 1969b.

Kasamatsu, A., and T. Hirai. "An Electroencephalographic Study of the Zen Meditation (Zazen)." *Journal of American Institute of Hypnosis* 14, no. 3 (1973): 107-114.

Kasamatsu, A., T. Okuma, and S. Takenaka. "The EEG of 'Zen' and 'Yoga' Practitioners." *EEG Clinical Neurophysiology*, supplement 9 (1957): 51-52.

Kasamatsu, A., T. Hirai, and N. Ando. "EEG Responses to Click Stimulation in Zen Meditation." *Proceedings of the Japanese EEG Society* (1962a): 77-78.

Kasamatsu, A., T. Hirai, and H. Izawa. "Medical and Psychological Studies on Zen." *Proceedings of the 26th Convention of J.P.A.* 1962b.

Katcher, A., H. Segal, and A. Beck. "Comparison of Contemplation and Hypnosis for the Reduction of Anxiety and Discomfort during Dental Surgery." *American Journal of Clinical Hypnosis* 27, no. 1 (1984): 14-21.

Katz, D. "Decreased Drug Use and Prevention of Drug Use through the Transcendental Meditation Program." In *Scientific Research on the Transcendental Meditation Program: Collected Papers*. Vol. 1, eds. D.W. Orme-Johnson and J.T.

Farrow. New York: M.E.R.U. Press, 1977: 536-543.

Katz, S.B. "East Meets West: An Integrative Psychology (Meditation)." *Dissertation Abstracts International* 50, no. 8-A (1989): 2433.

Kaye, M.E. "The Effects of Brief Flotation Rest on Physiological, Cognitive, and Mood Measures." *Dissertation Abstracts International* 49, no. 4-B (1987): 1390.

Keefe, T. "Meditation and the Psychotherapist." *American Journal of Orthopsychiatry* 45, no. 3 (1975): 484-489.

Keene, G. "Meditation and Transcendence." *Australian Psychologist* 16, no. 2 (1981): 285.

Keithler, M.A. "The Influence of the Transcendental Meditation Program and Personality Variables on Auditory Thresholds and Cardiorespiratory Responding." *Dissertation Abstracts International* 42, no. 4-B (1981): 1662-1663.

Kelton, J.J. "Perceptual and Cognitive Processes in Meditation." *Dissertation Abstracts International* 38, no. 8-B (1978): 3931.

Kember, P. "The Transcendental Meditation Technique and Postgraduate Academic Performance." *British Journal of Educational Psychology* 55, no. 2 (1985): 164-166.

Kemmerling, T. "Effect of Transcendental Meditation on Muscular Tone." *Psychopathometric* 44 (1978): 437-440.

Keniston-Dubocq, L. "The Family Practitioner and the Treatment of Alcoholism through Marharishi Ayur-Veda: A Case Report." *Alcoholism Treatment Quarterly* 11, no. 3-4 (1994): 413-428.

Kennett, J. "On Meditation." *Journal of Transpersonal Psychology* 6, no. 2 (1974): 111-123.

Kenny, V., and M. Delmonte. "Meditation as Viewed through Personal Construct Theory." *Journal of Contemporary Psychotherapy* 16, no. 1 (1986): 4-22.

Kesterson, J.B. "Changes in Respiratory Patterns and Control during the Practice of the Transcendental Meditation Technique." *Dissertation Abstracts International* 47, no. 10-B (1986): 4337.

Kesterson, J., and N.F. Clinch. "Metabolic-rate, Respiratory Exchange Ratio, and Apneas during Meditation." *American Journal of Physiology* 256, no. 3 (1989): 632-638.

Khalsa, S. "Effects of Two Types of Meditation on Self-esteem of Introverts and Extraverts." *Dissertation Abstacts International* 51, no. 9-A (1991): 3018.

Kielly, W.F. "Critique of Mystical States: A Reply." *Journal of Nervous and Mental Diseases* 159, no. 3 (1974): 196-197.

Kim, Y.M. "Meditation and Behavioral Therapy." *Interciencia* 5, no. 3 (1980): 157-158.

Kindler, H.S. "The Influence of a Meditation-relaxation Technique on Group Problem-solving Effectiveness." *Dissertation Abstracts International* 39, no. 7-A (1979): 4370-4371.

Kindlon, D.J. "The Relationship between Meditation Practice and Components of Anxiety and Creativity." *Dissertation Abstracts International* 42, no. 8-A (1982): 3511.

Kindlon, D.J. "Comparison of Use of Meditation and Rest in Treatment of Test Anxiety." *Psychological Reports* 53 (1983): 931-938.

King, J.W. "Meditation and the Enhancement of Focusing Ability." *Dissertation Abstracts International* 40, no. 6-B (1979): 2844.

Kinoshita, K. "A Study on Response of EEG during Zen Meditation: Alphablocking to Name Calling." *Psychiatria et Neurologia Japonica* 77, no. 9 (1975): 623-629.

Kirkland, K., and J. Hollandsworth. "Effective Test Taking: Skills-acquisition versus Anxiety-reduction Techniques." *Journal of Consulting and Clinical Psychology* 48 (1980): 431-439.

Kirsch, I., and D. Henry. "Self-desensitization and Meditation in the Reduction of Public Speaking Anxiety." *Journal of Consulting and Clinical Psychology* 47, no. 3 (1979): 536-541.

Kirschner, S. "Zen Meditators: A Clinical Study." *Dissertation Abstracts International* 36, no. 7-B (1976): 3613-3614.

Klajner, F., L. Hartman, and M. Sobell. "Treatment of Substance Abuse by Relaxation Training: A Review of Its Rationale, Efficacy and Mechanisms." *Addictive Behaviors* 9 (1984): 41-55.

Klemons, I.M. "Changes in Inflammation in Persons Practicing the Transcendental Meditation Technique." In *Scientific Research on the Transcendental Meditation Program: Collected Papers.* Vol. I, eds. D.W. Orme-Johnson and J.T. Farrow. New York: M.E.R.U. Press, 1977.

Kliger, R. "Somatization: Social Control and Illness Production in a Religious Cult." *Culture, Medicine and Psychiatry* 18, no. 2 (1994): 215-245.

Kline, K.S. "Effects of a Transcendental Meditation Program on Personality and Arousal." *Dissertation Abstracts International* 36, no. 12-B, pt.1 (1976): 6386-6387.

Kline, K.S., E.M. Docherty, and F.H. Farley. "TM, Self-actualization and Global Personality." *Journal of General Psychology* 106, no. 1 (1982): 3-8.

Knewitz, J.M. "The Explication of Zen Buddhism as a Foundation for Counseling." *Dissertation Abstracts International* 50, no. 6-A (1988): 1564.

Knight, S. "Use of Transcendental Meditation to Relieve Stress and Promote Health." *British Journal of Nursing* 4, no. 6 (1995): 315-318.

Koar, W.H. "Meditation, T-cells, Anxiety, Depression and HIV Infection." *Subtle Energies* 6, no. 1, (1995): 89-97.

Kobal, G., A. Wandohoefer, and K.H. Plattig. "EEG Power Spectra and Auditory Evoked Potentials in Transcendental Meditation." *Pflueger's Archives* 359 (1975).

Kobayashi, K. "The Effect of Zen Meditation on the Valence of Intrusive Thoughts." *Dissertation Abstracts International* 43, no. 1-B (1982): 280.

Kohn, L., ed. *Taoist Meditation and Longevity Techniques.* University of Michigan Center for Chinese Studies, 1989.

Kohr, R.L. "Dimensionality in Meditative Experience: A Replication." *Journal of Transpersonal Psychology* 9, no. 2 (1977a): 193-203.

Kohr, R.L. "Changes in Subjective Meditation Experience during a Short-term Project." *Journal of Altered States of Consciousness* 3, no. 3 (1977b): 221-234.

Kokoszka, A. "Limitations of a Psychobiological Concept of the Integration of Psychotherapy and Meditation." *American Journal of Psychiatry* 143, no. 10 (1986): 1315.

Kokoszka, A. "Axiological Aspects of Comparing Psychotherapy and Meditation. Special Issue: Between Life and Death: Aging." *International Journal of Psychosomatics*, 37, no. 1-4 (1990): 78-81.

Kokoszka, A. "A Rationale for a Multilevel Model of Relaxation." *International Journal of Psychosomatics* 41, no. 1-4 (1994): 4-10.

Kolanczyk, A. "How to Study Creative Intuition?" *Polish Psychological Bulletin* 20, no. 1 (1989): 57-68.

Kondo, A. "Zen in Psychotherapy." *Chicago Review* 12 (1958): 57-64.

Kongtawng, T. "Effects of Meditation on Self-concept." *Dissertation Abstracts International* 38, no. 3-A (1977): 1230.

Kormendy, E. "Autogenic Training and Meditation." *Off Gesundheitswes* 48, no. 7 (1986): 354-7.

Kornfield, J. "Meditation: Aspects of Research and Practice." *Journal of Transpersonal Psychology* 2 (1978): 122-124.

Kornfield, J. "Intensive Insight Meditation: A Phenomenological Study." *Journal of Transpersonal Psychology* 11, no. 1 (1979): 41-58.

Kornfield, J. "The Psychology of Mindfulness Meditation." *Dissertation Abstracts International* 44, no. 2-B (1983): 610.

Kory, R. "TM: An Investment with Positive Returns." *Management World* 5, no. 11 (1978): 8-11.

Kory, R., and P. Hufnagel. "The Effect of the Science of Creative Intelligence Course on High School Students: A Preliminary Report." In *Scientific Research on the Transcendental Meditation Program: Collected Papers.* Vol. 1, eds. D.W. Orme-Johnson and J.T. Farrow. New York: M.E.R.U. Press, 1977: 400-402.

Korzak, G.G. "The Influence of Hatha Yoga on Nasal Laterality among Yoga Practitioners." *Dissertation Abstracts International* 50, no. 3-A (1988): 650.

Kothari, L.K., A. Bordia, and O.P. Gupta. "The Yogic Claim of Voluntary Control over the Heart Beat: An Unusual Demonstration." *American Heart Journal* 86 (1973): 282-284.

Krahne, W., and G. Tenoli. "EEG and Transcendental Meditation." *Pfleuger's Archives* 359 (1975).

Kras, D.J. "The Transcendental Meditation Technique and EEG Alpha Activity." In *Scientific Research on the Transcendental Meditation Program: Collected Papers.* Vol. 1, D.W. Orme-Johnson and J.T. Farrow, eds. New York: M.E.R.U. Press, 1977: 173-181.

Kretschmer, W. "Meditative Techniques in Psychotherapy." In C.T. Tart, ed. *Altered States of Consciousness.* New York: Anchor, 1969.

Krippner, S., and B. Colodzin. "Multi-cultural Methods of Treating Vietnam Veterans with Post-traumatic Stress Disorder. Special Issue: Biofeedback and Diagnostic Techniques." *International Journal of Psychosomatics* 36, no. 1-4 (1989): 79-85.

Krippner, S., and M. Maliszewski. "Meditation and the Creative Process." *Journal of Indian Psychology* 1, no. 1 (1978): 40-58.

Krishna, G. "Meditation: Is It Always Beneficial? Some Positive and Negative Views." *Journal of Altered States of Consciousness* 2, no. 1 (1975): 37-47.

Kristeller, J.L. "Heart Rate Slowing: Biofeedback vs. Meditation." In D. Osborne, ed. *Research in Psychology and Medicine*. London Academic Press, 1 (1979): 486.

Kroll, U. *The Healing Potential of Transcendental Meditation*. Atlanta, GA: John Knox Press, 1974.

Krueger, R.C. "The Comparative Effects of Zen Focusing and Muscle Relaxation Training on Selected Experimental Variables." *Dissertation Abstracts International* 40, no. 4-A (1980): 1405.

Krynicki, V.E. "The Double Orientation of the Ego in the Practice of Zen." *American Journal of Psychoanalysis* 40, no. 3 (1980): 239-248.

Krystal, S., and J.E. Zweben. "The Use of Visualization as a Means of Integrating the Spiritual Dimension into Treatment: A Practical Guide." *Journal of Substance Abuse Treatment* 5, no. 4 (1988): 229-238.

Kubose, S.K. "An Experimental Investigation of Psychological Aspects of Meditation." *Psychologia* 19, no. 1 (1976): 1-10.

Kubose, S.K., and T. Umemoto. "Creativity and the Zen Koan." *Psychologia* 23, no. 1 (1980): 1-9.

Kuchera, M.M. "The Effectiveness of Meditation Techniques to Reduce Blood Pressure Levels: A Meta-analysis." *Dissertation Abstracts International* 47, no. 11-B (1987): 4639.

Kuna, D.J. "Meditation and Work." *Vocational Guidance Quarterly* 23, no. 4 (1975): 342-346.

Kutz, I., M. Caudill, and H. Benson. "The Role of Relaxation in Behavioral Therapies of Chronic Pain." In *Pain Management*, eds. J. Stein and C. Winfield. Boston: Little, Brown, 1983: 193-200.

Kutz, I., J. Borysenko, and H. Benson. "Meditation and Psychotherapy: A Rationale for the Integration of Dynamic Psychotherapy, the Relaxation Response, and Mindfulness Meditation." *The American Journal of Psychiatry* 142, no. 1 (1985a): 1-8.

Kutz, I., J. Leserman, C. Dorrington, et al. "Meditation as an Adjunct to Psychotherapy: An Outcome Study." *Psychotherapy and Psychosomatics* 43 (1985b): 209-218.

Lahr, J.J. "Relationship between Experience in TM and Adaption to Life Events and Related Stress." Doctoral diss., Ohio State University, Columbus, Ohio, 1974.

Lang, P.J. "The Varieties of Emotional Experience: A Meditation on James-Lange Theory." *Psychological Review* 101, no. 2 (1994): 211-221.

Lang, R. "Effect of Meditation Procedures on Essential Hypertension." *Therapiewoche* 34, no. 16 (1984): 2466-2480.

Lang, R., K. Dehob, K. Meurer, et al. "Sympathetic Activity and TM." *Journal of Neural Transmission* 44, no. 1-2 (1979): 117-135.

Larsson, G. "Routinization of Mental Training in Organizations: Effects on Performance and Well-being." *Journal of Applied Psychology* 72, no. 1 (February 1987): 88-96.

Laubry, C., and T. Brosse. "Data Gathered in India on a Yogi with Simultaneous Registration of the Pulse, Respiration, and Electrocardiogram." *Presse Medicale* 44 (1963): 1601-1604.

Laughlin, C.D., J. McManus, and E.G. Daquili. "Mature Contemplation." *Zygon* 28, no. 2 (1993): 133-176.

Laurie, G. "An Investigation into the Changes in Skin Resistance during the Transcendental Meditation Technique. In *Scientific Research on the Transcendental Meditation Program: Collected Papers*. Vol. I, eds. D.W. Orme-Johnson and J.T. Farrow. New York: M.E.R.U. Press, 1977: 216-223.

Lazar, Z., L. Farwell, and J.T. Farrow. "The Effects of the Transcendental Meditation Program on Anxiety, Drug Abuse, Cigarette Smoking, and Alcohol Consumption." In *Scientific Research on the Transcendental Meditation Program: Collected Papers*. Vol. I, eds. D.W. Orme-Johnson and J.T. Farrow. New York: M.E.R.U. Press, 1977: 524-535.

Lazarus, A. "Psychiatric Problems Precipitated by Transcendental Meditation." *Psychological Reports* 39, no. 2 (1976): 601-602.

Lazarus, A. "Meditation: The Problems of Any Unimodal Technique." In *Meditation: Classic and Contemporary Perspectives*, eds. D.H. Shapiro and R.N. Walsh. New York: Aldine, 1984: 691.

Legrand, P., M. Toubol, J. Barrabino, et al. "Contingent Negative Variation in Meditation." *Electroencephalography and Clinical Neurophysiology* 43, no. 4 (1977): 532-533.

Lehmann, J.W. "Reduced Pupillary Sensitivity to Topical Phenylephrine Associated with the Relaxation Response." *Journal of Human Stress* 12(3) (1986): 101-104.

Lehmann, J.W., and H. Benson. "Nonpharmacologic Therapy of Blood Pressure." *General Hospital Psychiatry* 4 (1982): 27-32.

Lehmann, J.W., and H. Benson. "The Behavioral Treatment of Hypertension." In *Hypertension: Physiopathology and Treatment*, eds. J. Genest, et al. New York: McGraw-Hill, 1983.

Lehmann, J.W., I. Goodale, and H. Benson. "Effect of Meditation Procedures on Essential Hypertension." *Journal of Human Stress* 12 (1986): 101-104.

Lehrer, P.M., and R.L. Woolfolk. "Respiratory System Involvement in Western Relaxation and Self-regulation." In *Behavioral and Psychological Approaches to Breathing Disorders,* eds. B.H. Timmons and R. Ley. New York: Plenum, 1994: 191-203.

Lehrer, P.M., S. Schoicket, P. Carrington, et al. "Psychophysiological and Cognitive Responses to Stressful Stimuli in Subjects Practicing Progressive Relaxation and Clinically Standardized Meditation." *Behavior Research and Therapy* 18, no. 4 (1980): 293-303.

Lehrer, P.M., R.L. Woolfolk, A.J. Rooney, et al. "Progressive Relaxation and Meditation." *Behavior Research Therapy* 21, no. 6 (1983): 651-662.

Lemond, E.K. "Treatment of Chronic Pain: Effects of a Multidisciplinary Pain Clinic." *Dissertation Abstracts International* 50, no. 6-B (1988): 2662.

Leoshko, J. Review of *The Twilight Language—Explorations in Buddhist Meditation and Symbolism,* by R.S. Buchnell and M. Stuartfox. In *Journal of Asian Studies* 47, no. 2 (1988): 397-399.

Leserman, J., E. Stuart, M.E. Mamish, and H. Benson "The Efficacy of the Relaxation Response in Preparing for Cardiac Surgery." *Behavioral Medicine* 15 (1989a): 111-17.

Leserman, J., E. Stuart, M.E. Mamish, J. Deckro, R.J. Beckam, R. Freidman, and H. Benson "Nonpharmacologic Intervention for Hypertension: Long-term Follow-up." *Journal of Cardiopulmonary Rehabilitation* 9 (1989b): 316-24.

Lesh, T.V. "The Relationship between Zen Meditation and the Development of Accurate Empathy." *Dissertation Abstracts International* 30, no. 11-A (1970a): 4778-4779.

Lesh, T.V. "Zen and Psychotherapy: A Partially Annotated Bibliography." *Journal of Humanistic Psychology* 10, no. 1 (1970b): 75-83.

Lesh, T.V. "Zen Meditation and the Development of Empathy in Counselors." *Journal of Humanistic Psychology* 10, no. 1 (1970c): 39-74.

LeShan, L. *How to Meditate: A Guide to Self-Discovery.* Boston: Little, Brown, 1974.

LeShan, L. "The Case for Meditation." *Saturday Review* 2 (1975): 26-27.

LeShan, L. *Cancer as a Turning Point.* New York: NAL-Dutton, 1989.

Lester, D. "Transcendental Meditation in Correctional Settings: A Review and Discussion." *Corrective and Social Psychiatry* 28, no. 2 (1982): 63-64.

Leung, P. "Comparative Effects of Training in External and Internal Concentration on Two Counseling Behaviors." *Journal of Counseling Psychology* 20 (1973): 227-234.

Levander, V.L., H. Benson, R.C. Wheeler, et al. "Increased Forearm Blood Flow during a Wakeful Hypometabolic State." *Federation Proceedings* 31 (1972): 405.

Levin, S. "The Transcendental Meditation Technique in Secondary Education." *Dissertation Abstracts International* 38, no. 2-A (1977): 706-707.

Levine, P.H. "Analysis of the EEG by COSPAR: Application to TM." In J.I. Martin, ed. *Proceedings of the San Diego Biomedical Symposium.* 15 (1976): 237-247.

Levine, P.H., J.R. Hebert, C.T. Haynes, et al. "EEG Coherence during the Transcendental Meditation Technique." In *Scientific Research on the Transcendental Meditation Program: Collected Papers.* Vol. I, eds. D.W. Orme-Johnson and J.T. Farrow. New York: M.E.R.U. Press, 1977: 187-207.

Levine, S. *A Gradual Awakening.* Garden City, NY: Anchor, 1979.

Levy, A.S. "An Exploration into the Psychoanalytic Treatment of the Meditating Patient." *Dissertation Abstracts International* 46, no. 10-B (1986): 3623.

Lewis, J. "The Effects of a Group Meditation Technique upon Degree of Test Anxiety and Level of Digit-letter Retention in High School Students." *Dissertation Abstracts International* 38, no. 10-A (1978a): 6015-6016.

Lewis, J. "Jungian Depth Psychology and Transcendental Meditation: Complementary Practices for the Realization of the Self." *Dissertation Abstracts International* 39, no. 2-B (1978b): 986-987.

Liberman, R.P. "Treatment and Rehabilitation of the Seriously Mentally Ill in China: Impressions of a Society in Transition." *American Journal of Orthopsychiatry* 64, no. 1 (1994): 68-77.

Linden, W. "Practicing of Meditation by School Children and Their Levels of Field Dependence-independence, Test Anxiety, and Reading Achievement." *Journal of Consulting and Clinical Psychology* 41, no. 1 (1973): 139-143.

Linden, W., and L. Chambers. "Clinical Effectiveness of Non-drug Treatment for Hypertension" A Meta-analysis." *Annals of Behavioral Medicine* 16 (1994): 35-45.

Ling, P.K. "The Intensive Buddhist Meditation Retreat and the Self: Psychological and Theravadin Considerations." *Dissertation Abstracts International* 42, no. 7-B (1982): 2992-2993.

Lintel, A.G. "Physiological Anxiety Responses in Transcendental Meditators and Nonmeditators." *Perceptual and Motor Skills* 50 (1980): 295-300.

Lionel, N.D. "Meditation and Medicine." *Ceylon Medical Journal* 21, no. 1 (1976): 1-2.

Loliger, S. "Relationship between Subjective Bliss, 5-Hydroxy-3-Indoleacetic Acid and the Collective Practice of Maharishi's Transcendental Meditation and TM-Sidhi Program." *Dissertation Abstracts International* 52, no. 1-B (1991): 551.

Lourdes, P.B. "Implications of the Transcendental Meditation Program for Counseling: The Possibility of a Paradigm Shift." *Dissertation Abstracts International* 39, no. 3-A (1978): 1343-1344.

Lovell-Smith, H.D. "Transcendental Meditation and Infertility." *New Zealand Medical Journal* 28, no. 789 (1985a): 922.

Lovell-Smith, H.D. "Transcendental Meditation and Three Cases of Migraine." *New Zealand Medical Journal* 98, no. 80 (1985b): 443-445.

Lowenthal, R.M. "Can Cancer be Cured by Meditation and Natural Therapy—Review of *You Can Conquer Cancer* by Ian Gawler." *Medical Journal of Australia* 151, (1989): 710-715.

Lowrison, M. "Transcendental Meditation vs. Relaxation Therapy." *Bulletin of the British Psychological Society*, 32 (1979): 39.

Luks, A. "Exercise, Meditation and Drinking Reduction—'The 20/20 Method'." *Proceedings of the 35th International Congress on Alcoholism and Drug Dependence.* International Council on Alcohol and Addictions (ICAA). Oslo, Norway, 1988.

Lyne, B.A., and P.R. Waller. "The Denver Nursing Project in Human Caring: A Model for AIDS Nursing Care and Professional Education. Special Issue: AIDS: Clinical Perspective." *Family and Community Health* 13, no. 2 (1990): 78-84.

Lyubimov, N.N. "Mobilization of the Hidden Reserves of the Brain." *Program Abstracts of the 2nd Russian-Swedish Symposium "New Research in Neurobiology,"* Brain Research Institute, Russian Academy of Medical Sciences, Moscow, May 19–21, 1992.

MacCallum, M.J. "The Transcendental Meditation Program and Creativity." *Scientific Research on the Transcendental Meditation Program: Collected Papers.* Vol. 1, eds. D.W. Orme-Johnson and J.T. Farrow. New York: M.E.R.U. Press, 1977: 410-414.

MacLean, C.R., K.G. Walton, S.R. Wenneberg, et al. "Altered Responses of Cortisol, GH, TSH and Testosterone to Acute Stress After Four Months' Practice of Transcendental Meditation." *Annals of the New York Academy of Science* 746, (November 1994): 381-384.

MacMuehlman, B.A. "Transcendental Meditation." *New England Journal of Medicine* 297, no. 9 (1977): 513.

MacRae, J.A. "A Comparison between Meditating Subjects and Non-meditating Subjects on Time Experience and Human Field Motion." *Dissertation Abstracts International* 43, no. 11-B (1983): 3537.

Magarey, C. "Anxiety, Fear, and Meditation." *Medical Journal of Australia* 1, no. 7 (1981a): 375.

Magarey, C. "Healing and Meditation in Medical Practice." *Medical Journal of Australia* 1, no. 7 (1981b): 338-341.

Magarey, C. "Holistic Cancer Therapy." *Journal of Psychosomatic Research* 27, no. 3 (1983): 181-184.

Maher, M.F. "Movement Exploration and Zazen Meditation: A Comparison of Two Methods of Personal-Growth-Group Approaches on the Self-actualization Potential of Counsel Candidates." *Dissertation Abstracts International* 39, no. 9-A (1979): 5329.

Malec, J., and C.N. Sipprelle. "Physiological and Subjective Effects of Zen Meditation and Demand Characteristics." *Journal of Consulting and Clinical Psychology* 45, no. 2 (1977): 339-340.

Malhotra, J.C. "Yoga and Psychiatry." *Journal of Neuropsychiatry* 4 (1962): 375-385.

Maliszewski, M. "Need for Stimulation: Its Relationship to Interest in and the Practice of Transcendental Meditation Technique." *Dissertation Abstracts International* 38, no. 8-B (1978): 3932-3933.

Maliszewski, M. "Medical Healing and Spiritual Components of Asian Martial Arts: A Preliminary Field Study Exploration." *Journal of Asian Martial Arts* 1(2)(1992a): 24-55.

Maliszewski, M. "Meditative-Religious Traditions of Fighting Arts and Martial Ways." *Journal of Asian Martial Arts* 1(3) (1992b): 1-104.

Maliszewski, M., S.W. Twemlow, D.P. Brown, et al. "A Phenomenological Typology of Intensive Meditation: A Suggested Methodology using the Questionnaire Approach." *ReVision* 4, no. 2 (1981): 3-27.

Mandle, C.L., A.D. Domar, D.P. Harrington, et al. "Relaxation Response in Femoral Angiography." *Radiology* 174 (1990): 737-739.

Maquet, J. "Expressive Space and Theravada Values: A Meditation Monastery in Sri Lanka." *Ethos* 3, no. 1 (1975a): 1-21.

Maquet, J. "Meditation in Contemporary Sri Lanka: Idea and Practice." *Journal of Transpersonal Psychology* 7, no. 2 (1975b): 182-196.

Maras, M.L., C.R. Stephens, W.J. Rinke, et al. "Effect of Meditation on Insulin Dependent Diabetes Mellitus." *The Diabetes Educator* (Spring 1984): 22-25.

Marcus, J.B. "Transcendental Meditation: A New Method of Reducing Drug Abuse." *Drug Forum* 3, no. 2 (1974): 113-136.

Marcus, J.B. "Transcendental Meditation: Consciousness Expansion as a Rehabilitation Technique." *Journal of Psychedelic Drugs* 7, no. 2 (1975): 169-179.

Marcus, J.B. "What the Supervisor Should Know about TM (Part I)." *Supervisory Management* 23, no. 6 (1978): 31-41.

Marcus, S.J. "The Influence of Transcendental Meditation on the Marital Dyad." *Dissertation Abstracts International* 38, no. 8-B (1978): 3895.

Margid, S. "Meditation, Creativity, and the Composing Process of Student Writers." *Dissertation Abstracts International* 46, no. 9-A (1986): 2603.

Maris, L., and M. Maris. "Mechanics of Stress Release: The TM Program and Occupational Stress." *Police Stress* 1, no. 2 (1979): 29-36.

Marlatt, G., and J. Margues. "Meditation, Self-control and Alcohol Use." In R.B. Stuart, ed. *Behavioral Self-Management Strategies, Techniques and Outcomes.* New York: Brunner Mazel, 1977.

Marlatt, G., R. Pagano, R. Rose, et al. "Effects of Meditation and Relaxation Training upon Alcohol Use in Male Social Drinkers." In *Meditation: Classic and Contemporary Perspectives*, D. Shapiro and R.N. Walsh, eds. New York: Aldine, 1984.

Marron, J.P. "Transcendental Meditation: A Clinical Evaluation." *Dissertation Abstracts International* 34, no. 8-B (1974): 4051.

Marteau, L. Review of *The Psychology of Meditation*, by M.A. West. In *British Journal of Psychiatry* 152 (April 1988): 585.

Martinetti, P. "Influence of Transcendental Meditation on Perceptual Illusion." *Perceptual and Motor Skills* 43 (1976): 822.

Martinsen, E.W. "The Role of Aerobic Exercise in the Treatment of Depression." *Stress Medicine* 3, no. 2 (April-June 1987): 93-100.

Masarsky, C.S. "Structural Implications of Meditation: A Review of Principles and Speculation of Chiropractic Applications." *Journal of Manipulative and Physiological Therapeutics* 6, no. 3 (September 1983): 143-145.

Mason, L.I. "Electrophysiological Correlates of Higher States of Consciousness During Sleep." *Dissertation Abstracts International* 56, no. 10B (1995): 5338.

Mason, L.I., C.N. Alexander, and F. Travis. "The Psychophysiology of Growth of Higher States of Consciousness: EEG Correlates of Consciousness During Sleep." *Lucidity Letter* 9, no. 2 (1991): 85-87.

Mason, L.I., C.N. Alexander, F. Travis, et al. "EEG Correlates of Higher States of Consciousness During Sleep." *Sleep Research.* 24, 1995: 152.

Massion, A.O., J. Teas, J.R. Hebert, et al. "Meditation, Melatonin and Breast/Prostate Cancer: Hypothesis and Preliminary Data." *Medical Hypotheses* 44, no. 1 (1995): 39-46.

Matheson, C.M. "Exercise and Meditation as a Lifestyle Intervention for Addictive Behaviors." *Dissertation Abstracts International* 42, no. 12-B (1982): 4935.

Maupin, E.W. "Zen Buddhism: A Psychological Review." *Journal of Consulting Psychology* 26 (1962a): 362-378.

Maupin, E.W. "An Exploratory Study of Individual Differences in Response to a Zen Meditation Exercise." Doctoral diss., University of Michigan, Ann Arbor, Michigan, 1962b.

Maupin, E.W. "Individual Differences in Response to a Zen Meditation Exercise." *Journal of Consulting Psychology* 29 (1965): 139-145.

Maupin, E.W. "Meditation." In *Ways of Growth*, eds. H. Otto and J. Mann. New York: Viking, 1968.

Maupin, E.W. "On Meditation." In C.T. Tart, ed. *Altered States of Consciousness: A Book of Readings.* New York: John Wiley and Sons, 1969.

Mayer, E.L. "On the Psychological Nature of Resistances to Meditation Which Arise during the Meditation Process: A Study of a Form of Alternative Education." *Dissertation Abstracts International* 35, no. 9-A (1975): 5929-5930.

McCuaig, L.W. "Salivary Electrolytes, Protein and pH during TM." *Experientia* 30, no. 9 (1974): 988-989.

McDonagh, J.M., and T. Egenes. "The Transcendental Meditation Technique and Temperature Homeostasis." In *Scientific Research on the Transcendental Meditation Program: Collected Papers.* Vol. I, eds. D.W. Orme-Johnson and J.T. Farrow. New York: M.E.R.U. Press, 1977: 261-263.

McEvoy, T.M., L.R. Frumkin, and S.W. Harkins. "Effects of Meditation on Brainstem Auditory Evoked Potentials." *International Journal of Neuroscience* 10 (1980): 165-170.

McIntyre, M.E., F.H. Silverman, and W.D. Trotter. "Transcendental Meditation and Stuttering: A Preliminary Report." *Perceptual and Motor Skills* 39, no. 1 (1974): 294.

McKinnon, P. *In Stillness Conquer Fear: Overcoming Anxiety Through Meditation.* Introduction by A. Meares. New York: Meyer Stone Books, 1989.

McLean, J. "The Use of Relaxation Techniques in General Practice." *Practitioner* 230 (1986): 1442.

McLeod, J. "The Social Psychology of Meditation." *Bulletin of the British Psychological Society* 32 (1979): 219.

McRae, J.R. Review of *Dogen Manuals of Zen Meditation,* by C. Bielefeldt. In *Journal of Asian Studies* 48, no. 4 (1989): 853-854.

Meares, A. "Regression of Cancer after Intensive Meditation." *Medical Journal of Australia* 2, no. 5 (1976a): 184.

Meares, A. "The Relief of Anxiety through Relaxing Meditation." *Australian Family Physician* 5, no. 7 (1976b): 906-910.

Meares, A. "Atavistic Regression as a Factor in the Remission of Cancer." *Medical Journal of Australia* 2, no. 4 (1977): 132-133.

Meares, A. "The Quality of Meditation Effective in the Regression of Cancer." *Journal of the American Society of Psychosomatic Dentistry and Medicine* 25, no. 4 (1978a): 129-132.

Meares, A. "Regression of Osteogenic Sarcoma Metastases Associated with Intensive Meditation." *Medical Journal of Australia* 2, no. 9 (1978b): 433.

Meares, A. "Vivid Visualization and Dim Visual Awareness in the Regression of Cancer in Meditation." *Journal of the American Society of Psychosomatic Dentistry and Medicine* 25, no. 3 (1978c): 85-88.

Meares, A. "Regression of Cancer of the Rectum after Intensive Meditation." *Medical Journal of Australia* 17 (1979a): 539-540.

Meares, A. "Meditation: A Psychological Approach to Cancer Treatment." *Practitioner* 222, no. 1327 (1979b): 119-122.

Meares, A. "What Can the Cancer Patient Expect from Intensive Meditation?" *Australian Family Physician* 9 (1980a): 322-325.

Meares, A. "Remission of Massive Metastasis from Undifferentiated Carcinoma of the Lung Associated with Intensive Meditation." *Journal of the American Society of Psychosomatic Dentistry and Medicine* 27, no. 2 (1980b): 40-41.

Meares, A. "Regression of Recurrence of Carcinoma of the Breast at Mastectomy Site Associated with Intensive Meditation." *Australian Family Physician* 10 (1981): 218-219.

Meares, A. "A Form of Intensive Meditation Associated with the Regression of Cancer." *American Journal of Clinical Hypnosis* 25, no. 2-3 (1982a): 114-121.

Meares, A. "Stress, Meditation, and the Regression of Cancer." *The Practitioner* (Australia) 226 (1982b): 1607-1609.

Meares, A. "Psychological Mechanisms in the Regression of Cancer." *Medical Journal of Australia* 1(12) (1983:583-584.

Meissner, J., and M. Pirot. "Unbiasing the Brain: The Effects of Meditation upon the Cerebral Hemispheres." *Social Behavior and Personality* 11, no. 11 (1983): 65-76.

Mengel, G.S.E. "The Effects of TM on the Reading Achievement of Learning-disabled Youngsters." *Dissertation Abstracts International* 39, no. 11-A (1978): 6,699.

Meserve, H.C. "Meditation and Health." *Journal of Religion and Health* 19, no. 1 (1980): 3-6.

Meuhlman, M. "Transcendental Meditation." *New England Journal of Medicine* 297, no. 9 (1977): 513.

Michaels, R.R., M.J. Huber, and D.S. McCann. "Evaluation of Transcendental Meditation as a Method of Reducing Stress." *Science* 192, no. 4245 (1976): 1242-1244.

Michaels, R.R., J. Parra, D.S. McCann, et al. "Renin, Cortisol and Aldosterone during Transcendental Meditation." *Psychosomatic Medicine* 41, no. 1 (1979): 50-54.

Mikulas, W.L. "Buddhism and Behavior Modification." *Psychological Record* 31, no. 3 (1981): 331-342.

Miles, W.R. "Oxygen Consumption during Three Yoga-type Breathing Patterns." *Journal of Applied Physiology* 19 (1964): 75-82.

Miller, J. "The Unveiling of Traumatic Memories and Emotions Through Mindfulness and Concentration Meditation: Clinical Implications and Three Case Reports." *The Journal of Transpersonal Psychology* 25, no. 2 (1993): 169-180.

Miller, J., K. Fletcher, and J. Kabat-Zinn. "Three-year Follow-up and Clinical Implications of a Mindfulness-based Intervention in the Treatment of Anxiety Disorders." *General Hospital Psychiatry* 17 (1995): 192-200.

Miller, K., and P. Perry. "Relaxation Technique and Postoperative Pain in Patients Undergoing Cardiac Surgery." *Heart and Lung* 19, no. 2 (1990): 136.

Miller, M.P., P.J. Murphy, and J.P. Miller. "Comparison of EMG Feedback and Progressive Relaxation Training in Treating Circumscribed Anxiety Stress Reactions." *Journal of Consulting and Clinical Psychology* 46 (1978): 1291-1298.

Mills, G.K., and K. Campbell. "A Critique of Gellhorn and Kiely's Mystical States of Consciousness." *Journal of Nervous and Mental Disease* 159 (1974): 191.

Mills, P.J. "Cardiovascular and Adrenergic Reactivity and Beta-Adrenergic Receptor Sensitivity in Practitioners of the Transcendental Meditation Program and Type A Behavior." *Dissertation Abstracts International* 58, no. 6-B (1987): 1,612.

Mills, P.J., R.H. Schneider, D. Hill, K.G. Walton, et al. "Beta-Adrenergic Receptor Sensitivity in Subjects Practicing Transcendental Meditation." *Journal of Psychosomatic Research* 34, no. 1 (1990): 29-33.

Mills, W.W., and J. Farrow. "The TM Technique and Acute Experimental Pain." *Psychosomatic Medicine* 43, no. 2 (1981): 157-164.

Miskiman, D.E. "The Effect of the Transcendental Meditation Program on Compensatory Paradoxical Sleep." In *Scientific Research on the Transcendental Meditation Program: Collected Papers.* Vol. 1, eds. D.W. Orme-Johnson and J.T. Farrow. New York: M.E.R.U. Press, 1977a: 292-295.

Miskiman, D.E. "Long-term Effects of the Transcendental Meditation Program in the Treatment of Insomnia." In *Scientific Research on the Transcendental Meditation Program: Collected Papers.* Vol. 1, eds. D.W. Orme-Johnson and J.T. Farrow. New York: M.E.R.U. Press, 1977b: 299.

Miskiman, D.E. "Performance on a Learning Task by Subjects Who Practice the Transcendental Meditation Technique." In *Scientific Research on the Transcendental Meditation Program: Collected Papers.* Vol. 1, eds. D.W. Orme-Johnson and J.T. Farrow. New York: M.E.R.U. Press, 1977c: 382-384.

Miskiman, D.E. "The Treatment of Insomnia by the Transcendental Meditation Program." In *Scientific Research on the Transcendental Meditation Program: Collected Papers.* Vol. 1, eds. D.W. Orme-Johnson and J.T. Farrow. New York: M.E.R.U. Press, 1977d: 296-298.

Miskiman, D.E. "Effects of the Transcendental Meditation Program on the Organization of Thinking and Recall." In *Scientific Research on the Transcendental Meditation Program: Collected Papers.* Vol. 1, eds. D.W. Orme-Johnson and J.T. Farrow. New York: M.E.R.U. Press, 1977e: 385-392.

Moles, E.A. "Zen Meditation: A Study of Regression in Service of the Ego." *Dissertation Abstracts International* 38, no. 6-B (1977): 2,871-2,872.

Monahan, R.J. "Secondary Prevention of Drug Dependence through the Transcendental Meditation Program in Metropolitan Philadelphia." *International Journal of the Addictions* 12, no. 6 (1977): 729-754.

Monro, R., A.K. Ghosh, D. Kalish. *Yoga Research Bibliography: Scientific Studies on Yoga and Meditation.* Cambridge: Yoga Biomedical Trust, 1989.

Moore, C.W. *The Meditation Process: Practical Strategies for Resolving Conflicts.* San Francisco: Jossey-Bass, 1986.

Morales, A., and E. Edgardo. "The Way of Everyday Life: A Qualitative Study of the Experience of Mindfulness Meditation in Daily Life." *Dissertation Abstracts International* 47, no. 7-A (1986): 2515.

Moretti-Altuna, G.E. "The Effects of Meditation Versus Medication in the Treatment of Attention Deficit Disorder with Hyperactivity." *Dissertation Abstracts International* 47, no. 11-B (1987): 4658.

Morgan, W.D. "Change in Meditation: A Phenomenological Study of Vipassana Meditators' Views of Progress." *Dissertation Abstracts International* 51, no. 7-B (1991): 3575.

Morrell, E. "The Effect of a Regularly Practiced Relaxation Procedure on Stressed and Resting Plasma Catecholamine Levels, Heart Rate, and Blood Pressure." *Dissertation Abstracts International* 46, no. 6-B (1985): 2115.

Morrell, E. "Meditation and Somatic Arousal." *American Psychologist* 41, no. 6 (1986): 712-713.

Morrell, E.M., and J. Hollandsworth. "Norepinephrine Alterations under Stress Conditions following the Regular Practice of Meditation." *Psychosomatic Medicine* 48, nos. 3-4 (1986): 270-277.

Morrissey, B. "The Race is on Towards the Fully Automated Accelerated Learning Classroom." *Journal of Instructional Psychology* 21, no. 3 (1994): 258-259.

Morse, D.R. "Meditation in Dentistry." *General Dentistry* 24, no. 5 (1976a): 57-59.

Morse, D.R. "Use of a Meditative State for Hypnotic Induction in the Practice of Endodontics." *Oral Surgery, Oral Medicine, Oral Pathology* 41 (1976b): 664-672.

Morse, D.R. "An Exploratory Study of the Use of Meditation Alone and in Combination with Hypnosis in Clinical Dentistry." *Journal of the American Society of Psychosomatic Dentistry and Medicine* 24, no. 4 (1977a): 113-120.

Morse, D.R. "Overcoming Practice Stress via Meditation and Hypnosis." *Dental Survey* 53, no. 7 (1977b): 32-36.

Morse, D.R. "Variety, Exercise, and Meditation Can Relieve Practice Stress." *Dental Studies* 56, no. 3 (1977c): 26-29.

Morse, D.R. "Who Benefits from Meditation?" *International Journal of Psychosomatics* 31, no. 2 (1984): 2.

Morse, D.R., and B.B. Cohen. "Desensitization Using Meditation-Hypnosis to Control Needle Phobia in Two Dental Patients." *Anesthesia Progress*, (May/June 1983): 83-85.

Morse, D.R., and C. Hilderbrand. "Case Report: Use of TM in Periodontal Therapy." *Dental Survey* 52 (1976): 36-39.

Morse, D.R., and J.M. Wilcko. "Nonsurgical Endodontic Therapy for a Vital Tooth with Meditation-Hypnosis as the Sole Anesthetic: A Case Report." *American Journal of Clinical Hypnosis* 21, no. 4 (1979): 258-262.

Morse, D.R., J.S. Martin, M.L. Furst, et al. "A Physiological and Subjective Evaluation of Meditation, Hypnosis and Relaxation." *Psychosomatic Medicine* 39, no. 5 (1977): 304-324.

Morse, D.R., J.S. Martin, M.L. Furst, et al. "A Physiological and Subjective Evaluation of Neutral and Emotionally-charged Words for Meditation, Part 1." *Journal of the American Society of Psychosomatic Dentistry and Medicine* 26, no. 1 (1979a): 31-38.

Morse, D.R., J.S. Martin, M.L. Furst, et al. "A Physiological and Subjective Evaluation of Neutral and Emotionally-charged Words for Meditation, Part 2." *Journal of the American Society of Psychosomatic Dentistry and Medicine* 26, no. 2 (1979b): 56-62.

Morse, D.R., J.S. Martin, M.L. Furst, et al. "A Physiological and Subjective Evaluation of Neutral and Emotionally-charged Words for Meditation, Part 3." *Journal of the American Society of Psychosomatic Dentistry and Medicine* 26, no. 3 (1979c): 106-112.

Morse, D.R., G.R. Schacterle, M.L. Furst, et al. "Stress, Relaxation, and Saliva: A Pilot Study Involving Endodontic Patients." *Oral Surgery* (September 1981): 308-313.

Morse, D.R., G.R. Schacterle, M.L. Furst, et al. "The Effect of Stress and Meditation on Salivary Protein and Bacteria: A Review and Pilot Study." *Journal of Human Stress* 8, no. 4 (1982): 31-39.

Morse, D.R., G.R. Shacterle, J.V. Esposito, et al. "Stress, Meditation and Saliva: A Study of Separate Salivary Gland Secretions in Endodontic Patients." *Journal of Oral Medicine*, 1983, 38, no. 4 (1983): 150-160.

Morse, D.R., R.R. Hancock, and B.B. Cohen. "In Vivo Desensitization using Meditation-hypnosis in the Treatment of Tactile-induced Gagging in a Dental Patient." *International Journal of Psychosomatics* 31, no. 3 (1984a): 20-23.

Morse, D.R., L. Cohen, M.L. Furst, and J.S. Martin. "A Physiological Evaluation of the Yoga Concept of Respiratory Control of Autonomic Nervous System Activity." *International Journal of Psychosomatics* 31, no. 1 (1984b): 3-19.

Morse, D.R., R.S. Schoor, and B.B. Cohen. "Surgical and Non-surgical Dental Treatments for a Multi-allergic Patient with Meditation—Hypnosis as the Sole Anesthetic: Case Report." *International Journal of Psychosomatics* 31, no. 2 (1984c): 27-33.

Muchlman, M. "Transcendental Meditation." *New England Journal of Medicine* 297, no. 9 (1977): 513.

Murase, T., and Johnson. "Naikan, Morita, and Western Psychotherapy: A Comparison." *Archives of General Psychiatry* 31, no. 1 (1974): 121-128.

Murdock, M.H. "Meditation with Young Children." *Journal of Transpersonal Psychology* 10, no. 1 (1978): 29-44.

Murphy, M. *Jacob Atabet: A Speculative Fiction.* Millbrae, CA: Celestial Arts, 1977.

Murphy, M. *The Future of the Body: Explorations into the Evolution of Human Nature.* Los Angeles: J.P. Tarcher, 1992.

Murphy, M., and S. Donovan. "A Bibliography of Meditation Theory and Research: 1931-1983." *The Journal of Transpersonal Psychology* 15, no. 2 (1988): 181-228.

Murphy, M.J. "Explorations in the Use of Group Meditation with Persons in Psychotherapy." *Dissertation Abstracts International* 33, no. 12-B (1973): 6089.

Murphy, T.J., R.R. Pagano, and G.A. Marlatt. "Lifestyle Modification with Heavy Alcohol Drinkers: Effects of Aerobic Exercise and Meditation." *Addictive Behavior* 11, no. 2 (1986): 175-186.

Murray, J. Review of *Meditation—A Sensible Guide to a Timeless Discipline*, by J.C. Smith. In *American Journal of Clinical Hypnosis* 30, no. 3 (1988): 216-217.

Murray, J.B. "What is Meditation? Does It Help?" *Genetic Psychology Monographs* 106, no. 1 (1982): 85-115.

Murthy, C.V., and T.R. Rao. "A Study on the Effect of Japayoga on Reactions to Frustration and Personality Dimensions." *Indian Journal of Behaviour* 11, no. 1 (January 1987): 24-28.

Muskatel, N., R.L. Woolfold, P. Carrington, et al. "Effect of Meditation Training on Aspects of Coronary-prone Behavior." *Perceptual and Motor Skills* 58, no. 2 (1984): 515-518.

Muzika, E.G. "Evolution, Emptiness and the Fantasy Self." *Journal of Humanistic Psychology*. 30, no. 2 (1990): 89-108.

Myers, M. "Psychological and other Scientific Perspectives of the New Paradigm Providing a Rationale for Meditation Techniques in Consciousness Development." *Dissertation Abstracts International* 46, no. 6-A (1985): 1,553.

Naifeh, K., and J. Kamiya. "Changes in Alveolar Carbon Dioxide Tension during Meditation." *Biofeedback and Self-Regulation* 5 (1980): 378-379.

Naranjo, C., and R.E. Ornstein. *On the Psychology of Meditation*. New York: Viking, 1971.

Narita, T., S. Morozumi, and T. Yagi. "Psychophysiological Analysis during Autogenic Training." *Advances in Biological Psychiatry* 16 (1987): 72-89.

Nash, C.B. "Hypnosis and Transcendental Meditation as Inducers of ESP." *Parapsychology* 13, no. 1 (1982): 19-20.

Neki, J. "Guru-Chela: The Possibility of a Therapeutic Paradigm." *American Journal of Orthopsychiatry* 43 (1973): 5.

Neptune, C. "An Investigation of the Effect of Meditation Training in a Cigarette Smoking Extinguishment Program." *Dissertation Abstracts International* 39, no. 1-B (1978): 416.

Nespor, K. "The Combination of Psychiatric Treatment and Yoga." *International Journal of Psychosomatics* 32, no. 2 (1985): 24-27.

Neurnberger, E.P. "The Use of Meditation in the Treatment of Alcoholism." *Dissertation Abstracts International* 38, no. 3-B (1977): 1413.

New England Journal of Medicine. "Study of Meditation and Blood Pressure" (letter). 14 (1976): 294.

Nidich, S.I. "A Study of the Relationship of Transcendental Meditation to Kohlberg's Stages of Moral Reasoning." *Dissertation Abstracts International* 36, no. 7-A (1976): 4361-4362.

Nidich, S.I., W. Seeman, and T. Dreskin. "Influence of Transcendental Meditation on a Measure of Self-actualization: A Replication." *Journal of Counseling Psychology* 20, no. 6 (1973): 565-566.

Nidich, S.I., W. Seeman, and M. Seibert. "Influence of TM on State Anxiety." In *Scientific Research on the Transcendental Meditation Program: Collected Papers*. Vol. I, eds. D.W. Orme-Johnson and J.T. Farrow. New York: M.E.R.U. Press, 1977: 434-438.

Nidich, S.I., R.J. Nidich, and M. Rainforth. "School Effectiveness: Achievement Gains at the Maharishi School of the Age of Enlightenment." *Education* 107, no. 1 (Fall 1986): 49-54.

Nixon, P.G. "Meditation or Methyldopa." *British Medical Journal* 2, no. 6034 (1976): 525.

Nolly, G.A. "The Immediate After-effects of Meditation on Perceptual Awareness." *Dissertation Abstracts International* 36, no. 2-B (1975): 919.

Nordberg, R.B. "Meditation: Future Vehicle for Career Exploration." *Vocational Guidance Quarterly* 22, no. 4 (1974): 267-271.

Norman, W.H. "Asceticism in Mysticism: Transcendental Meditation." *Sociological Spectrum* 2 (1982): 315-331.

Norton, G.R., L. Rhodes, J. Hauch, E.A. Kaprowy. "Characteristics of Subjects Experiencing Relaxation and Relaxation-induced Anxiety." *Journal of Behavioral Therapy and Experimental Psychiatry* 16, no. 3 (1985): 211-216.

Norwood, J.E. "An Investigation of a Zen Meditation Procedure and Its Effect on Selected Personality and Psychotherapeutic Variables." *Dissertation Abstracts International* 43, no. 11-B (1983): 3721.

Novak, P. "The Dynamics of Attention in Spiritual Discipline." In J. Duerlinger, ed. *Ultimate Reality and Spiritual Discipline.*, 83-100, 1984a.

Novak, P. "The Dynamics of Attention: Core of the Contemplative Way." *Studies in Formative Spirituality* 5, no. 1 (1984b): 65-80.

Novak, P. "The Buddha and the Computer—Meditation in an Age of Information." *Journal of Religion and Health* 25, no. 3 (1986): 188-192.

Nugent, P. Review of *Traditions of Meditation in Chinese Buddhism*, by P.N. Gregory. In *Pacific Affairs* 60, no. 4 (1988): 668-669.

Nurnberg, H. "Meditation and Psychotherapy." *World Journal of Psychosynthesis* 10, no. 1 (1978): 37-40.

Nystul, M.S., and M. Garde. "Comparison of Self-concepts of Transcendental Meditators and Non-meditators." *Psychological Reports*, 41(1) (1977): 303-306.

Nystul, M.S., and M. Garde. "The Self-concepts of Regular Transcendental Meditators, Dropout Meditators, and Nonmeditators." *Journal of Psychology* 103, no. 1 (1979): 15-18.

Ockene, J., G. Sorenson, J. Kabat-Zinn, I.S. Ockene, and G. Donneley. "Benefits and Costs of Lifestyle Change to Reduce Risk of Chronic Disease." *Preventive Medicine* 17 (1988): 224-234.

O'Connell, D. "The Use of Transcendental Meditation in Relapse Prevention Counseling." *Alcoholism Treatment Quarterly* 8, no. 1 (1991): 53-68.

O'Connell, D. "Possessing the Self: Maharishi Ayur-Veda and the Process of Recovery from Addictive Diseases." *Alcoholism Treatment Quarterly* 11, no. 3-4 (1994): 459-495.

O'Connell, D., and C.N. Alexander "Introduction: Recovery from Addictions Using Transcendental Meditation and Maharishi Ayur-Veda." *Alcoholism Treatment Quarterly* 11, no. 1-2 (1994a): 1-10.

O'Connell, D., and C.N. Alexander, eds. *Self Recovery: Treating Addictions Using Transcendental Meditation and Maharishi Ayur-Veda.* Binghamton, NY: Haworth Press, 1994b.

O'Connell, W.E. "Letting Go and Hanging On: Confessions of a Zen Adlerian." *Individual Psychology: Journal of Adlerian Theory, Research and Practice* 40, no. 1 (1984): 71-82.

Odanjnyk, V.W. "Gathering the Light: A Jungian Exploration of the Psychology of Meditation." *Quadrant* 21, no. 1 (1988): 35-51.

Odier, D. *Nirvana-Tao: The Secret Meditation Techniques of the Taoist and Buddhist Masters.* Rochester, VT: Inner Traditions, 1986.

O'Haire, T.D., and J.E. Marcia. "Some Personality Characteristics Associated with Ananda Marga Meditators: A Pilot Study." *Perceptual and Motor Skills* 51, no. 2 (1980): 447-452.

O'Halloran, J.P., et al. "Hormonal Control in a State of Decreased Activation: Potentiation of Arginine Vasopressin Secretion." *Physiology and Behavior* 35, no. 4 (1985): 591-595.

O'Kane, T.A. "Transpersonal Dimensions of Transformation: A Study of the Contributions Drawn from the Sufi Order Teachings and Training to the Emerging Field of Transpersonal Psychology." *Dissertation Abstracts International* 49, no. 11-B (1987): 5047.

Oldfield, R.R. "The Effects of Meditation on Selected Measures of Human Potential." *Dissertation Abstracts International* 42, no. 11-A (1982): 4717.

Oliveros, J.C., A.M. Selman, T. Ortiz, et al. [Silva's Method of Mental Control and Changes in the EEG Alpha Rhythm.] (Spanish). *Actas Luso-Espanolas de Neurologia, Psiquiatria y Ciencias Afines* 22, no. 6 (1994): 290-291.

O'Murchu, D. "Spirituality, Recovery, and Transcendental Meditation." *Alcoholism Treatment Quarterly* 11, no. 1-2 (1994): 169-184.

Onda, A. "Zen, Autogenic Training and Hypnotism." *Psychologia* 10 (1967): 133-136.

Onda, A. "Zen, Hypnosis and Creativity." *Interpersonal Development* 5, no. 3 (1974-75): 156-163.

O'Regan, B. "Mind/Body Effects: The Physiological Consequence of Tibetan Meditation." *Newsletter of the Institute of Noetic Sciences* 10, no. 2 (1982).

Orme-Johnson, D.W. "Autonomic Stability and Transcendental Meditation." *Psychosomatic Medicine* 35, no. 4 (1973): 341-349.

Orme-Johnson, D.W. "Coherence during Transcendental Consciousness." *Electroencephalography and Clinical Neurophysiology* 43, no. 4 (1977a): 581.

Orme-Johnson, D.W. "The Dawn of the Age of Enlightenment: Experimental Evidence that the Transcendental Meditation Technique Produces a Fourth and Fifth State of Consciousness in the Individual and a Profound Influence of Orderliness in Society." In *Scientific Research on the Transcendental Meditation Program: Collected Papers.* Vol. I, eds. D.W. Orme-Johnson and J.T. Farrow. New York: M.E.R.U. Press, 1977b: 671-691.

Orme-Johnson, D.W. "Prison Rehabilitation and Crime Prevention through the TM and TM-Sidhi Program." In L.J. Hippchen, ed. *Holistic Approaches to Offender Rehabilitation.* Springfield, IL: Charles C. Thompson, 1980.

Orme-Johnson, D.W. "Medical-Care Utilization and the Transcendental Meditation Program." *Psychosomatic Medicine* 49, no. 5 (1987): 493-507.

Orme-Johnson, D.W. "Transcendental Meditation as an Epidemiological Approach to Drug and Alcohol Abuse: Theory, Research, and Financial Impact Evaluation. *Alcoholism Treatment Quarterly* 11, no. 1-2 (1994): 119-168.

Orme-Johnson, D.W., and B. Duck. "Psychological Testing of MIU Students: First Report." In *Scientific Research on the Transcendental Meditation Program: Collected Papers.* Vol. I, eds. D.W. Orme-Johnson and J.T. Farrow. New York: M.E.R.U. Press, 1977: 470-475.

Orme-Johnson, D.W., and J.T. Farrow, eds. *Scientific Research on the Transcendental Meditation Program: Collected Papers.* Vol. I. New York: M.E.R.U. Press, 1977.

Orme-Johnson, D.W., and P. Gelderloos. "Topographic EEG Brain Mapping during Yogic Flying." *International Journal of Neuroscience* 35 (1987).

Orme-Johnson, D.W., and B. Granieri. "The Effects of the Age of Enlightenment

Governor Training Courses on Field Independence, Creativity, Intelligence, and Behavioral Flexibility." In *Scientific Research on the Transcendental Meditation Program: Collected Papers.* Vol. I, eds. D.W. Orme-Johnson and J.T. Farrow. New York: M.E.R.U. Press, 1977: 713-718.

Orme-Johnson, D.W., and C.T. Haynes. "EEG Phase Coherence, Pure Consciousness, Creativity, and TM-Sidhi Experiences." *International Journal of Neuroscience* 13 (1981): 211-217.

Orme-Johnson, D.W., G. Clements, C.T. Haynes, et al. "Autonomic Stability and Transcendental Meditation." *Psychosomatic Medicine* 35, no. 4 (1973): 341-349.

Orme-Johnson, D.W., D. Kolb, and J.R. Hebert. "An Experimental Analysis of the Effects of the Transcendental Meditation Technique on Reaction Time." In *Scientific Research on the Transcendental Meditation Program: Collected Papers.* Vol. I, eds. D.W. Orme-Johnson and J.T. Farrow. New York: M.E.R.U. Press, 1977a: 316-321.

Orme-Johnson, D.W., G. Clements, C.T. Haynes, et al. "Higher States of Consciousness: EEG Coherence, Creativity and Experiences of the Sidhis." In *Scientific Research on the Transcendental Meditation Program: Collected Papers.* Vol. I, eds. D.W. Orme-Johnson and J.T. Farrow. New York: M.E.R.U. Press, 1977b: 705-712.

Orme-Johnson, D.W., J. Kiehlbauch, R. Moore, et al. "Personality and Autonomic Changes in Prisoners Practicing the Transcendental Meditation Technique." In *Scientific Research on the Transcendental Meditation Program: Collected Papers.* Vol. I, eds. D.W. Orme-Johnson and J.T. Farrow. New York: M.E.R.U. Press, 1977c: 556-561.

Orme-Johnson, D.W., G.K. Arthur, L. Franklin, et al. "The Transcendental Meditation Technique and Drug Abuse Counselors." In *Scientific Research on the Transcendental Meditation Program: Collected Papers.* Vol. I, eds. D.W. Orme-Johnson and J.T. Farrow. New York: M.E.R.U. Press, 1977d: 597-599.

Orme-Johnson, D.W., M.C. Dillbeck, and R.K. Wallace. "Intersubject EEG Coherence: Is Consciousness a Field?" *International Journal of Neuroscience* 160 (1982): 203-209.

Orme-Johnson, D.W., C.N. Alexander, J.L. Davies, H.M. Chandler, et al. "International Peace Project in the Middle East: The Effects of the Maharishi Technology of the Unified Field." *Journal of Conflict Resolution* 32, no. 4 (December 1988): 776-812,

Orme-Johnson, D.W., C.N. Alexander, and J.L. Davies. "The Effects of the Maharishi Technology of the Unified Field: Reply to a Methodological Critique." *Journal of Conflict Resolution* 34, no 4 (1990): 756-768.

Orme-Johnson, D.W., C.N. Alexander, and M.C. Dillbeck. *The Vedic Psychology of Maharishi Mahesh Yogi.* Fairfield, IA: Maharishi University of Management Press, 1996.

Osis, K., and E. Bokert. "ESP and Changed States of Consciousness Induced by Meditation." *Journal of the American Society of Psychical Research* 65, no. 1 (1971): 17-65.

Osis, K., E. Bokert, and M.L. Carlson. "Dimensions of the Meditative Experience." *Journal of Transpersonal Psychology* 5, no. 2 (1973): 109-135.

Otis, L.S. "Meditation or Simulated Meditation by Nonpredisposed Volunteers." In E. Taub, ed. *The Psychobiology of Meditation.* Symposium presented at American Psychology Association, Montreal, August 1973.

Otis, L.S. "The Facts on Transcendental Meditation: III. If Well-integrated but Anxious, Try TM." *Psychology Today* 7, no. 11 (1974): 45-46.

Otis, L.S. "Adverse Effects of Transcendental Meditation." In *Meditation: Contemporary and Classical Perspectives,* eds. D.H. Shapiro and R.N. Walsh. New York: Aldine, 1984: 201-208.

Otis, L.S., D.P. Kanellakos, J.S. Lukas, et al. "The Psychophysiology of Transcendental Meditation: A Pilot Study." In *The Psychobiology of Transcendental Meditation: A Literature Review,* eds. D.S. Kanellakos and J.S. Lukas. Menlo Park, CA: W.A. Benjamin, 1974.

Ottens, A.J. "The Effect of Transcendental Meditation upon Modifying the Cigarette Smoking Habit." *The Journal of School Health* 45, no. 10 (1975): 577-583.

Oudshoorn, M., and P. Ransijn. "Transcendental Meditation and Dianetics, Two Ways of Confronting Comments." *Sedrag Tijdschrift Voor Psychologie* 7, no. 4 (1979): 255-259.

Overbeck, K.D. "Effects of the Transcendental Meditation Technique on the Psychological and Psychosomatic State" (abstract). *Psychotherapie, Psychosomatik, Medizinische, Psychologie* 32 (1982): 188-192.

Pagano, R.R., and L.R. Frumkin. "The Effect of Transcendental Meditation on Right Hemispheric Functioning." *Biofeedback and Self-Regulation* 2, no. 4 (1977): 407-415.

Pagano, R.R., R.M. Rose, R.M. Stivers, et al. "Sleep during Transcendental Meditation." *Science* 191 (1976): 308-309.

Pahnos, M.L. "Effects of Relaxation Training on Public School Teachers." *Dissertation Abstracts International* 45, no. 11-A (1985): 3285.

Palmer, D.K. "Inspired Analgesia through TM." *New Zealand Dentistry Journal* 76 (1980): 61-63.

Palmer, J., K. Khamashta, and K. Israelson. "An ESP Ganzfeld Experiment with Transcendental Meditators." *Journal of American Society of Psychical Research* 73, no. 4 (1979): 333-348.

Pan, W., L. Zhang, and Y. Xia. "The Difference in EEG Theta Waves between Concentrative and Non-Concentrative Qigong States—A Power Spectrum and Topographic Mapping Study." *Journal of Traditional Chinese Medicine* 14, no. 3 (1994): 212-218.

Parker, J.C. "The Effects of Progressive Relaxation Training and Meditation on Autonomic Arousal in Alcoholics." *Dissertation Abstracts International* 37, no. 9-B (1977): 4697-4698.

Parker, J.C., and G.S. Gilbert. "Anxiety Management in Alcoholics: A Study of Generalized Effects of Relaxation Techniques." *Addictive Behavior* 3, no. 2 (1978): 123-127.

Parker, J.C., G.S. Gilbert, and R. Thoreson. "Reduction of Autonomic Arousal in Alcoholics: A Comparison of Relaxation and Meditation Techniques." *Journal of Consulting and Clinical Psychology* 46, no. 5 (1978): 879-886.

Parulkar, V.G., S.L. Prabhavalker, and J.V. Bhall. "Observations on Some Physiological Effects of Transcendental Meditation." *Indian Journal of Medical Science* 28, no. 3 (1974): 156-158.

Paskewitz, D.A. "EEG Alpha Activity and Its Relationship to Altered States of Consciousness." *Annals of the New York Academy of Science* 296 (1977): 154-161.

Patel, C.H. "Yoga and Biofeedback in the Management of Hypertension." *Lancet* 2 (1973): 1053-1055.

Patel, C.H. "Yoga and Biofeedback in the Management of 'Stress' in Hypertensive Patients." *Clinical Science and Molecular Medicine* 48 (1975a): 171-174.

Patel, C.H. "Yoga and Biofeedback in the Management of Hypertension." *Journal of Psychosomatic Research* 19 (1975b): 355-360.

Patel, C.H. "Twelve-month Follow-up of Yoga and Biofeedback in the Management of Hypertension." *Lancet* 2 (1975c): 62-64.

Patel, C.H. "TM and Hypertension." *Lancet* 1, no. 7958 (1976): 539.

Patel, C.H. "Biofeedback-aided Relaxation and Meditation in the Management of Hypertension." *Biofeedback and Self-Regulation* 2, no. 1 (1977): 1-41.

Patel, C.H. "Meditation in General Practice." *British Medical Journal* 282 (1981): 528-529.

Patel, C.H. "A Holistic Approach to Cardiovascular Diseases." *British Journal of Holistic Medicine* 1 (1984): 30-40.

Patel, C.H., and M. Carruthers. "Coronary Risk Factor Reduction through Biofeedback-aided Relaxation and Meditation." *Journal of the Royal College of General Practitioners* 27, no. 180 (1977): 401-405.

Patel, C.H., and W.R. North. "Randomized Controlled Trial of Yoga and Biofeedback in Management of Hypertension." *Lancet* 2 (1975): 93-95.

Patel, C.H., M.M. Marmot, D.J. Terry, et al. "Coronary Risk Factor Reduction through Biofeedback-aided Relaxation and Meditation." *Circulation* 60, abstract 882 (1979): 211-226.

Patel, C.H., M.M. Marmot, and D.J. Terry. "Controlled Trial of Biofeedback-aided Behavioral Methods in Reducing Mild Hypertension." *British Medical Journal* 282 (1981): 2005-2008.

Patel, C.H., M.M. Marmot, D.J. Terry, et al. "Trial of Relaxation in Reducing Coronary Risk: Four Year Follow-up." *British Medical Journal* 290, no. 6475, (1985): 1103-1106.

Patey, J., J.D. Vincent, and J.M.A. Faure. "CNV Studies during Meditation." *Electroencephalography and Clinical Neurophysiology* 43 (1977): 540.

Patrik, L.E. "Phenomenological Method and Meditation." *Journal of Transpersonal Psychology* 26, no. 1 (1994): 37-54.

Paul, G.L. "Physiological Effects of Relaxation Training and Hypnotic Suggestion." *Journal of Abnormal Psychology* 74 (1969): 425-437.

Peerbolte, M. "Meditation for School Children." *Main Currents in Modern Thought* 24 (1967): 19-21.

Pelletier, K.R. "Altered Attention Deployment in Meditation." In *The Psychobiology of Transcendental Meditation*, eds. D. Kanellakos and J. Lukas. Reading, MA: W.A. Benjamin, 1974a.

Pelletier, K.R. "Influence of Transcendental Meditation upon Autokinetic Perception." *Perceptual and Motor Skills* 39, no. 3 (1974b): 1031-1034.

Pelletier, K.R. "Neurological, Psychophysiological, and Clinical Differentiation of the Alpha and Theta Altered States of Consciousness." *Dissertation Abstracts International* 35 (1974c): 806.

Pelletier, K.R. "Psychophysiological Parameters of the Voluntary Control of Blood Flow and Pain." In *The Psychobiology of Transcendental Meditation*, eds. D. Kanellakos and J. Lukas. Reading, MA: W.A. Benjamin, 1974d.

Pelletier, K.R. "Applications of Meditative Exercises in Enhancing Clinical Biofeedback Outcome." *Proceedings of the Biofeedback Research Society.* Denver: Biofeedback Research Society, 1976a.

Pelletier, K.R. "Increased Perceptual Acuity following Transcendental Meditation." In *Scientific Research on Transcendental Meditation: Collected Papers*, eds. L. Domash, J. Farrow, and D. Orme-Johnson. Los Angeles: Maharishi International University Press, 1976b.

Pelletier, K.R. "Developing a Biofeedback Model: Alpha EEG Feedback as a Means for Pain Control." *International Journal of Clinical and Experimental Hypnosis* 25, no. 4 (1977a): 361-371.

Pelletier, K.R. "The Effects of the Transcendental Meditation Program on Perceptual Style: Increased Field Independence." In *Scientific Research on the Transcendental Meditation Program: Collected Papers.* Vol. I, D.W. Orme-Johnson and J.T. Farrow, eds. New York: M.E.R.U. Press, 1977b: 337-345.

Pelletier, K.R. *Mind as Healer: Mind as Slayer.* New York: Delacorte, 1977c.

Pelletier, K.R. *Toward a Science of Consciousness.* New York: Delacorte, 1978.

Pelletier, K.R. "Adjunctive Biofeedback with Cancer Patients: A Case Presentation." In C. Garfield, ed. *Stress and Survival: The Emotional Realities of Life-threatening Illness.* St. Louis: C.V. Mosby, 1979: 86-91.

Pelletier, K.R. "Influence of Transcendental Meditation upon Autokinetic Perception." In D.H. Shapiro and R.N. Walsh, eds. *Meditation: Classic and Contemporary Perspectives.* Hawthorne, NY: Aldine Publishing, 1984: 223-226.

Pelletier, K.R., and C. Garfield. *Consciousness: East and West.* New York: Harper and Row, 1976.

Pelletier, K.R., and C. Garfield. "Meditative States of Consciousness." In *Psychology for Our Times*, eds. P. Zimbardo and C. Maslach. New York: Scott, Foresman, 1977.

Pelletier, K.R., and E. Peper. "The Chutzpah Factor in Altered States of Consciousness." *Journal of Humanistic Psychology* 17, no. 1 (1977a): 63-73.

Pelletier, K.R., and E. Peper. "Alpha EEG Feedback as a Means for Pain Control." *Journal of Clinical and Experimental Hypnosis* 25, no. 41 (1977b): 361-371.

Penner, W.J., H.W. Zingle, R. Dyke, and S. Truch. "Does an In-depth Transcendental Meditation Course Effect Change in the Personalities of the Participants?" *Western Psychology* 4, no. 4 (1974): 104-111.

Peper, E., and S. Ancoli. "The Two End Points of an EEG Continuum of Meditation: Alpha/Theta and Fast Beta." In *Mind/Body Integrations: Essential Readings in Biofeedback*, eds. E. Peper, S. Ancoli, and M. Quinn. New York: Plenum, 1979.

Persinger, M.A. "Striking EEG Profiles from Single Episodes of Glossolalia and Transcendental Meditation." *Perceptual and Motor Skills* 58 (1984): 127-133.

Persinger, M.A. "Enhanced Incidence of 'The Sensed Presence' in People Who Have Learned to Meditate: Support for the Right Hemisphere Intrusion Hypothesis." *Perceptual and Motor Skills* 75 (1992): 1308-1310.

Persinger, M.A. "Transcendental Meditation and General Meditation are Associated with Enhanced Complex Partial Epileptic-like Signs: Evidence for 'Cognitive' Kindling?" *Perceptual and Motor Skills* 76 (1993): 80-82.

Peters, D., and D. Morgan. "Perceptual Phenomena Resulting from Steady Visual Fixation and Repeated Auditory Input under Experimental Conditions and in Meditation." *Journal of Altered States of Consciousness* 3, no. 3 (1977-78): 197-203.

Peters, R.K., and H. Benson. "Time Out from Tension." *Harvard Business Review* 56 (1978): 120-124.

Peters, R.K., H. Benson, and D. Porter. "Daily Relaxation Response Breaks in a Working Population: 1. Health, Performance and Well-being." *American Journal of Public Health* 67 (1977a): 946-953.

Peters, R.K., H. Benson, and J.M. Peters. "Daily Relaxation Response Breaks in a Working Population: 2. Blood Pressure." *American Journal of Public Health* 67 (1977b): 954-959.

Pickersgill, M.J., and W. White. "Subjective States during Transcendental Meditation." *International Journal of Psychophysiology* 23 (1984a): 229-230.

Pickersgill, M.J., and W. White. "The Physiological and Psychological States of Subjects Practicing Transcendental Meditation." *Bulletin Europeen de Physiopathologie Respiratoire-Clinical Respiratory Physiology* 20, no. 1 (1984b): 94-95.

Pietromonaco, J. "A Phenomenological Study of Mindfulness Meditation." *Dissertation Abstracts International* 47, no. 9-B (1987): 3968.

Piggins, D., and D. Morgan. "Note upon Steady Visual Fixation and Repeated Auditory Stimulation in Meditation and the Laboratory." *Perceptual and Motor Skills* 44, no. 2 (1977): 357-358.

Piggins, D., and D. Morgan. "Perceptual Phenomena Resulting from Steady Visual Fixation and Repeated Auditory Input under Experimental Conditions and in Meditation." *Journal of Altered States of Consciousness* 3, no. 3 (1977-78): 197-203.

Pirot, M. "The Effects of the Transcendental Meditation Technique upon Auditory Discrimination." In *Scientific Research on the Transcendental Meditation Program: Collected Papers*. Vol. I, eds. D.W. Orme-Johnson and J.T. Farrow. New York: M.E.R.U. Press, 1977: 331-334.

Plummer, C.M. "Developing a Model for Motivating Spiritual Growth through Prayer and Meditation in Welch Memorial United Methodist Church." *Dissertation Abstracts International* 48, no. 5-A (1987): 1228.

Pollack, A.A., M.A. Weber, D.B. Case, et al. "Limitations of Transcendental Meditation in the Treatment of Essential Hypertension." *Lancet* 1, no. 8002 (1977): 71-73.

Pollard, G., and R. Ashton. "Heart Rate Decrease: A Comparison of Feedback Modalities and Biofeedback with Other Procedures." *Biological Psychology* 14 (1982): 245-257.

Polowniak, W.A. "The Meditation-Encounter-Growth Group." *Dissertation Abstracts International* 34, no. 4-B (1973): 1732.

Preston, D.L. "Meditative Ritual Practice and Spiritual Conversion-Commitment: Theoretical Implications Based on the Case of Zen." *Sociological Analysis* 43, no. 3 (1982): 257-270.

Pribram, K., and D. McGuiness. "Arousal, Activation, and Effort in the Control of Attention." *Psychological Review* 82 (1975): 116-149.

Prince, R. "Meditation: Some Psychological Speculations." *Psychiatric Journal of the University of Ottawa* 3, no. 3 (1978): 202-209.

Progoff, I. *The Practice of Process Meditation: The Intensive Journal Way to Spiritual Experience.* New York: Dialogue House Library, 1980.

Puente, A.E. "Psychophysiological Investigations on Transcendental Meditation." *Biofeedback and Self-Regulation* 6, no. 3 (1981): 327-342.

Puente, A.E. and I. Beiman. "The Effects of Behavior Therapy, Self-relaxation, and Transcendental Meditation on Cardiovascular Stress Response." *Journal of Clinical Psychology* 36, no. 1 (1980): 291-295.

Puryear, H.B., C.T. Cayce, and M.A. Thurston. "Anxiety Reduction Associated with Meditation: Home Study." *Perceptual and Motor Skills* 43, no. 2 (1976): 527-531.

Quinn, A.A. "Commentary on Complementary Self-care Strategies for Healthy Aging." *AWHONN'S Women's Health Nursing Scan* 8, no. 2 (1994): 6.

Rachman, A.W. "Clinical Meditation in Groups." *Psychotherapy: Theory, Research and Practice* 18, no. 2 (1981): 252-258.

Radford, J. "What We Can Learn from Zen? Review of Some Speculations." *Journal of Psychology of the Orient* 19, no. 2 (1976): 57-66.

Rahav, G. "Transcendental Meditation Program in Prison. TM and Rehabilitation: Another View." *Criminal Justice and Behavior* 7, no. 1 (1980): 11-17.

Rama, Swami, et al., eds. *Meditation in Christianity*. Honesdale, PA: Himalayan International Institute of Yoga Science and Philosophy of the USA, 1983.

Ramakrishna, R. "Anomalies of Consciousness: Indian Perspectives and Research." *Journal of Parapsychology* 58, no. 2 (1994): 149-187.

Ramsey, M.K. "A Comparative Study of the Effectiveness of the Relaxation Response and Personalized Relaxation Tapes in Medical Technology Students." *Dissertation Abstracts International* 45, no. 11-A (1985): 3285.

Randolph, G.L., and J.L. Price. "Stress: Meditation vs. the Rat Race." *Nursing Management* 16, no. 2 (1985).

Rao, K.R., and I. Puri. "Subsensory Perception (SSP), Extrasensory Perception (ESP) and Transcendental Meditation (TM)." *Journal of Indian Psychology* 1, no. 1 (1978): 69-74.

Rao, K.R., H. Dukhan, and P.V. Krishna. "Yogic Meditation and PSI Scoring in Forced-choice and Free-response Tests." *Journal of Indian Psychology* 1, no. 2 (1978): 160-175.

Rao, S. "Metabolic Cost of Head-stand Posture." *Journal of Applied Physiology* 17 (1962): 117-118.

Rao, S. "Yoga and Autohypnotism." *British Journal of Medical Hypnotism* 17 (1965): 38-40.

Rao, S. "Oxygen Consumption during Yoga-type Breathing at Altitudes of 520M and 3800M." *Indian Journal of Medical Research* 56 (1968): 701-705.

Raskin, M., L.R. Bali, and H.V. Peeke. "Muscle Biofeedback and Transcendental Meditation: A Controlled Evaluation of Efficacy in the Treatment of Chronic Anxiety." *Archives of General Psychiatry* 37, no. 1 (1980): 93-97.

Ray, J.T. "Concentrative Meditation: Some Psychological Effects with Children." *Dissertation Abstracts International* 46, no. 4-B (1984): 1358.

Reddy, M.K., A.J. Lakshmi, and V.R. Rao. "The Effects of the Transcendental Meditation Program on Athletic Performance." In *Scientific Research on the Transcendental Meditation Program: Collected Papers*. Vol. 1, eds. D.W. Orme-Johnson and J.T. Farrow. New York: M.E.R.U. Press, 1977: 346-358.

Redfering, D.L., and M.J. Bowman. "Effects of a Meditative-relaxation Exercise on Non-attending Behaviors of Behaviorally Disturbed Children." *Journal of Clinical Child Psychology* 10, no. 2 (1981): 126-127.

Redmond, D.P. "Meditation and Medicine: Combined Strategies for Treating Hypertension." *Behavioral Medicine* 7, no. 6 (1980): 14-18.

Reed, H. "Improved Dream Recall Association with Meditation." *Journal of Clinical Psychology* 34, no. 1 (1978): 150-156.

Reed, J.I. "The Impact of Transcendental Meditation on Cognitive Flexibility, Field Dependence, and Directional Priorities in Attention Deployment." *Dissertation Abstracts International* 37, no. 1-B (1976): 475-476.

Reiman, J.W. "The Impact of Meditative Attentional Training on Measures of Select Attentional Parameters and on Measures of Client Perceived Counselor Empathy." *Dissertation Abstracts International* 46, no. 6-A (1985): 1569.

Reynolds, D.K. "Naikan Therapy: An Experimental View." *Journal of Social Psychology* 23, no. 4 (1977): 252-263.

Rhead, J.C., and G.G. May. "Meditation in a Specialized Correctional Setting: A Controlled Study." *Corrective and Social Psychiatry* 29, no. 4 (1983): 105-111.

Rhyner, B. Review of *Naikan Psychotherapy—Meditation for Self-development* by D.K. Reynolds. *Psychologia* 28, no. 2 (1985): 128-129.

Rice, V.H. "Relaxation Training and Response to Cardiac Catheterization: A Pilot Study." *Nursing Research* 35, no. 1 (1986): 39-43.

Riddle, A.G. "Effects of Selected Elements of Meditation on Self-actualization, Locus of Control, and Trait Anxiety." *Dissertation Abstracts International* 40, no. 7-B (1980): 3,419.

Riechert, H. "Plethysmographic Studies in Concentration and Meditation Exercises." *Aerztliche Forschung* 21 (1976): 61-65.

Riedesel, B. "Meditation and Empathic Behavior: A Study of Clinically Standardized Meditation and Effective Sensitivity." *Dissertation Abstracts International* 43 (1983): 3274.

Riley, T.G. "A Study of the Attentional Characteristics of Long-term Zen Meditators." *Dissertation Abstracts International* 51, no. 4-B (1990): 2049.

Rimol, A.G. "The Transcendental Meditation Technique and Its Effects on Sensory-motor Performance." In *Scientific Research on the Transcendental Meditation Program: Collected Papers.* Vol. I, eds. D.W. Orme-Johnson and J.T. Farrow. New York: M.E.R.U. Press, 1977: 326-330.

Rios, R.J. "The Effect of Hypnosis and Meditation on State and Trait Anxiety and Locus of Control." *Dissertation Abstracts International* 40, no. 12-A, pt. 1 (1980): 6209-6210.

Rivers, S.M., and N.P. Spanos. "Personal Variables Predicting Voluntary Participation in and Attrition from a Meditation Program." *Psychological Reports* 49, no. 3 (1981): 795-801.

Robertson, D.W. "The Short and Long Range Effects of the Transcendental Meditation Technique on Fractionated Reaction Time." *Journal of Sports Medicine* 23 (1983): 113-120.

Roche, L.A. "Structures in the Language of Meditative Experience: Taxonomic and Multidimensional Representations." *Dissertation Abstracts International* 48, no. 12-A (1987): 3057.

Rogers, C.A., and D.D. Livingston. "Accumulative Effects of Periodic Relaxation." *Perceptual and Motor Skills* 44 (1977): 690.

Roll, W.G., and P.V.K. Rao. "PSI and Meditation: A Further Investigation." *Journal of Parapsychology* 48, no. 3 (1984): 241.

Roll, W.G., G.F. Solfvin, and J. Krieger. "Meditation and ESP: An Overview of Four Studies." *Journal of Parapsychology* 43, no. 1 (1979): 44-45.

Roll, W.G., G.F. Solfvin, J. Krieger, et al. "Group ESP Scores, Mood, and Meditation." *Journal of Parapsychology* 44, no. 1 (1980): 74-75.

Ronis, D.J. "Bridging the Gap to Peace: From a New Way of Thinking into Action (New Age, Spiritual Awareness)." *Dissertation Abstracts International* 49, no. 1-A (1987): 102.

Rosenbluh, E.S. "The Relaxation Response as Prescription in Crisis Intervention." *Emotional First Aid: A Journal of Crisis Intervention* 1, no. 1 (1984): 23-26.

Ross, J. "The Effects of Transcendental Meditation Program on Anxiety, Neuroticism, and Psychoticism." In *Scientific Research on the Transcendental Meditation Program: Collected Papers*. Vol. 1, eds. D.W. Orme-Johnson and J.T. Farrow. New York: M.E.R.U. Press, 1977: 594-598.

Roth, B., and T.T. Creaser. "A Bilingual Mindfulness Meditation-Based Stress Reduction Program for the Inner City: Preliminary Research Findings." *Nurse Practitioner: American Journal of Primary Health Care*, May 1997.

Routt, T.J. "Low Normal Heart and Respiration Rates in Individuals Practicing the Transcendental Meditation Technique." In *Scientific Research on the Transcendental Meditation Program: Collected Papers*. Vol. 1, eds. D.W. Orme-Johnson and J.T. Farrow. New York: M.E.R.U. Press, 1977: 256-260.

Royer, A. "The Role of the Transcendental Meditation Technique in Promoting Smoking Cessation: A Longitudinal Study." *Alcoholism Treatment Quarterly* 11, no. 1-2 (1994): 221-239.

Royer-Bounouar, P.A. "The Transcendental Meditation Technique: A New Direction for Smoking Cessation Programs." *Dissertation Abstracts International* 50, no. 8-B (1989): 3428.

Rubin, J.B. "Meditation and Psychoanalytic Listening." *Psychoanalytic Review* 72, no. 4 (1985): 599-613.

Rubin, J.B. "Pathways to Transformation: An Integrative Study of Psychoanalysis and Buddhism." *Dissertation Abstracts International* 49, no. 3-B (1987): 906.

Rubottom, A.E. "TM." *Yale Alumni Magazine*, February 1972a.

Rubottom, A.E. "TM and Its Potential Use in Schools." *Social Education* 36, no. 4 (1972b): 851-857.

Russel, N.M. "The Effects of Biofeedback and Relaxation Response Training on Submaximal Exercise." *Dissertation Abstracts International* 42 (1981): 601.

Russell, P.J. "Transcendental Meditation." *Lancet* 1, no. 7760 (1972): 1125.

Russell, P.J. *The TM Technique: An Introduction to Transcendental Meditation and the Teachings of Maharishi Mahesh Yogi.* London: Routledge and Kegan, 1976.

Russell, W.R. "Yoga and the Vertebral Arteries." *British Medical Journal* 1 (1972): 685.

Russie, R.E. "The Influence of Transcendental Meditation on Positive Mental Health and Self-actualization and the Role of Expectation, Rigidity and Self-control in the Achievement of These Benefits." *Dissertation Abstracts International* 36, no. 11-B (1976): 5816.

Sabel, B.A. "Transcendental Meditation in Psychology, Psychiatry and Psychotherapy." *Medizinische Klinik* 74, no. 47 (1979): 1779-1784.

Sabel, B.A. "TM and Concentration Ability." *Perceptual and Motor Skills* 50, no. 3, pt. 1 (1980): 799-802.

Sacerdote, P. "Application of Hypnotically Elicited Mystical States of the Treatment of Physical and Emotional Pain." *International Journal of Clinical and Experimental Hypnosis* 25 (1977): 309-324.

Sacks, H.L. "The Effect of Spiritual Exercises on the Integration of Self-system." *Journal for the Scientific Study of Religion* 18, no. 1 (1979): 46-50.

Sacks, S., J. Avorn, and H. Benson. "Plasma 17— Hydroxycorticosteroid Levels in Healthy Subjects Practicing Meditation." *Clinical Research* 21 (1973): 959.

Sagert, J.M. "The Influence of Attentional Self-regulation and Personality-based Hardiness." *Dissertation Abstracts International* 46, nos. 4-8 (1984): 1370.

Saletu, B. "Brain Functions during Hypnosis, Acupuncture and Transcendental Meditation: Quantitative EEG Studies." *Advances in Biological Psychiatry* 16 (1987): 18-40.

Sallis, J.F. "Meditation and Self-actualization: A Theoretical Comparison." *Psychologia: International Journal of Psychology in the Orient* 25, no. 1 (1982): 59-64.

Salmon, P., S. Santorelli, and J. Kabat-Zinn. "Intervention Elements Promoting Adherence to Mindfulness-based Stress Reduction Programs in the Clinical Behavioral Meditation Setting." In Shumaker, Schron, Ockene, and McBee, eds. *Handbook for Health Behavior Change*, 2nd edition. Springer, 1997.

Salsbury, J.C. "Relaxation Response: An Evaluation of a Technique for Anxiety Reduction among College Graduate Students." *Dissertation Abstracts International* 40 (1979): 2415.

Sanderlin, M.A. "The Effects of Open Focus Meditation Versus Progressive Muscle Relaxation on Blood Pressure, Heart Rate, and Peripheral Skin Temperature." *Dissertation Abstracts International* 52 no. 3-A (1991): 807.

Sands, D. "Introducing Maharishi Ayur-Veda into Clinical Practice." *Alcoholism Treatment Quarterly* 11, no. 3-4 (1994): 335-365.

Sanford, D.E. "Inspiration in the Creative Process and Meditation." *Dissertation Abstracts International* 39, no. 5-B (1978): 2481.

Santorelli, S.F. "A Qualitative Case Analysis of Mindfulness Meditation Training in an Out-patient Stress-reduction Clinic and its Implications for the Development of Self Knowledge. Doctoral Dissertation, University of Massachusetts, 1992.

Saraydarian, T. *The Science of Meditation*. Reseda, CA: Aquarian Educational Group, 1971.

Sargant, W. *The Mind Possessed*. New York: Lippincott, 1974.

Sato, K. "Psychotherapeutic Implications of Zen." *Psychologia* 1 (1958): 213-218.

Sawada, Y., and A. Steptoe. "The Effects of Brief Meditation Training on Cardiovascular Stress Responses." *Journal of Psychophysiology* 2, no. 4 (1988): 249-257.

Saxena, R.P. *Transcendental Meditation: A Scientific Approach*. London, Essex: International Society for Prevention of Stress, 1978.

Scardapane, J.R. "A Developmental Study of the Effects of Progressive Muscle Relaxation and Meditation on State Anxiety in Children and Adolescents." *Dissertation Abstracts International* 46, no. 3-B (1985): 969.

Scharfetter, C., and G. Benedetti. "Meditation as a Conceptual Field, the Sifting of Findings, and Application in Psychotherapy." *Psychotherapie Medizinische Psychologie* 29, no. 3 (1979): 78-95.

Schechter, H. "The Transcendental Meditation Program in the Classroom: A Psychological Evaluation." In *Scientific Research on the Transcendental Meditation Program, Collected Papers.* Vol. I, eds. D. Orme-Johnson, L. Domash, and J. Farrow. Switzerland: MIU Press, 1975: 403-409.

Schenkluhn, H., and M. Geisler. "A Longitudinal Study of the Influence of the Transcendental Meditation Program on Drug Abuse." In *Scientific Research on the Transcendental Meditation Program: Collected Papers.* Vol. I, eds. D.W. Orme-Johnson and J.T. Farrow. New York: M.E.R.U. Press, 1977: 544-555.

Schildkraut, J.J., J.J. Mooney, S.C. Jacobs, R. Friedman, et al. "Enhanced Transduction by Adenylate Cyclase Following Elicitation of the Relaxation Response: Preliminary Findings." *Journal of Psychiatric Research* 24, sup. I (1990): 55-56.

Schilling, P.B. "The Effect of the Regular Practice of the Transcendental Meditation Technique on Behavior and Personality." In *Scientific Research on the Transcendental Meditation Program: Collected Papers.* Vol. I, eds. D.W. Orme-Johnson and J.T. Farrow. New York: M.E.R.U. Press, 1977: 453-461.

Schindler, D. "An Examination of Alpha Learning as a Viable Instructional Approach to Teach People to Learn (Biofeedback, Hypnosis)." *Dissertation Abstracts International* 48, no. 4-A (1987): 823.

Schmeidler, G.R. "High ESP Scores after a Swami's Brief Instruction in Meditation and Breathing." *Journal of American Society of Psychical Research* 64, no. I (1970): 100-103.

Schmidt, K.E. "Transcendental Meditation." *British Medical Journal* I, no. 6007 (1976): 459.

Schmidt-Wilk, J., C.N. Alexander, and G. Swanson. "Developing Consciousness in Organizations: The Transcendental Meditation Program in Business." *Journal of Business and Psychology* 10, no. 4 (1996).

Schneider, R.H., P.J. Mills, W. Schramm, and R.K. Wallace. "Luteinizing-Hormone—a Marker for Type A Behavior and Its Modification by the Transcendental Meditation Program." *Psychosomatic Medicine* 49, no. 2 (1987): 212-213.

Schneider, R.H., P.J. Mills, W. Schramm, K.G. Walton, M.C. Dillbeck, and R.K. Wallace. "Dehydroepiandrosterone Sulfate (DHEAS) Levels in Type A Behavior and the Transcendental Meditation Program." *Psychosomatic Medicine* 51, no. 2 (1989): 256.

Schneider, R.H., C.N. Alexander, and R.K. Wallace. "In Search of an Optimal Behavioral Treatment for Hypertension: A Review and Focus on Transcendental Meditation." In *Personality, Elevated Blood Pressure, and Essential Hypertension,* eds. E.H. Johnson, W.D. Gentry, and S. Julius. Washington, DC: Hemisphere, 1992: 291-312.

Schneider, R.H., F. Staggers, C.N. Alexander, et al. "Stress Reduction for the Treatment of Hypertension in Older African-Americans: A Controlled Clinical Trial of Transcendental Meditation and Progressive Muscle Relaxation." *Hypertension* 26 (1995): 820-827.

Schoicket, S.L. "Meditation Training and Stimulus Control as Treatments for Sleep-Maintenance Insomnia." *Dissertation Abstracts International* 47, no. 11-B: 4664.

Schoicket, S.L., A.D. Bertelson, and P. Lacks. "Is Sleep Hygiene a Sufficient Treatment for Sleep-maintenance Insomnia?" *Behavior Therapy* 19, no. 2 (Spring 1988): 183-190.

Schrodt, P.A. "A Methodological Critique of a Test of the Effects of the Maharishi Technology of the Unified Field." *Journal of Conflict Resolution* 34, no. 4 (1990): 745-755.

Schultz, T. "What Science is Discovering about the Potential Benefits of Meditation: Transcendental Meditation." *Today's Health* (1972): 34-37, 64-67.

Schuster, L. "The Effects of Brief Relaxation Techniques and Sedative Music on Levels of Tension." *Dissertation Abstracts International* 43, no. 6-B (1982): 2002.

Schuster, R. "Meditation: Philosophy and Practice in a Drug Rehabilitation Setting." *Drug Forum* 5, no. 2 (1975-76): 163-170.

Schwartz, G. "The Facts on Transcendental Meditation: TM Relaxes Some People and Makes Them Feel Better." *Psychology Today* 7, no. 11 (1974): 39-44.

Schwartz, G. "Biofeedback, Self-regulation, and the Patterning of Physiological Processes." *American Scientist* 63, no. 3 (1975): 314-324.

Schwartz, G.E., R.J. Davidson, and D.J. Goleman. "Patterning of Cognitive and Somatic Processes in Self-regulation of Anxiety." *Psychosomatic Medicine* 40, no. 4 (1978): 321-328.

Scott, L.J. "Transcendental Meditation: Effect of Pre-treatment Personality and Prognostic Expectancy upon Degree of Reported Personality Change." *Dissertation Abstracts International* 38, no. 5-B (1977): 2383.

Scuderi, R.J. "The Effects of Meditation on General Anxiety, Test Anxiety, and Non-verbal Intelligence." *Dissertation Abstracts International* 38, no. 10-A (1978): 5930-5931.

Seeman, W., D. Nidich, and T. Banta. "Influence of Transcendental Meditation on a Measure of Self-actualization." *Journal of Counseling Psychology* 19, no. 3 (1972): 184-187.

Seer, P. "Psychological Control of Essential Hypertension: Review of the Literature and Methodological Critique." *Psychological Bulletin* 86 (1979): 1015-1043.

Seer, P. "Concentrative Meditation and Cognitive Behavior Therapy." *Psychother. Psychosom. Med. Psychol. (West Germany)* 36, nos. 9-10 (1986): 301-306.

Seer, P., and J.M. Raeburn. "Meditation Training and Essential Hypertension: A Methodological Study." *Journal of Behavioral Medicine* 3, no. 1 (1980): 59-70.

Seiler, G., and V. Seiler. "The Effects of Transcendental Meditation on Periodontal Tissue." *Journal of the American Society of Psychosomatic Dentistry and Medicine* 26, no. 1 (1979): 8-12.

Sekida, K. *Zen Training: Methods and Philosophy.* Tokyo: John Weatherhill, 1975.

Sereda, L. "Some Effects of Relaxative and Meditative States on Learning, Memory and Other Cognitive Processes." *Dissertation Abstracts International* 38, no. 8-A (1978): 4697-4698.

Sethi, A.S. "Meditation as an Intervention in Stress Reactivity." *Stress in Modern Society Series.* no. 12. AMS Press, 1987.

Seithi, A.S., and A. Daya. "Management and Meditation." *Dimensions in Health Services* 55, no. 7 (1978): 32-33.

Severtsen, B., and M.A. Bruya. "Effects of Meditation and Aerobic Exercise on EEG Patterns." *J Neurosci. Nurs.* 18, no. 4 (1986): 206-10.

Shafii, M. "Adaptive and Therapeutic Aspects of Meditation." *International Journal of Psychoanalytic Psychotherapy* 2, no. 3 (1973a): 364-382.

Shafii, M. "Silence in the Service of Ego: Psychoanalytic Study of Meditation." *International Journal of Psychoanalysis* 54, no. 4 (1973b): 431-443.

Shafii, M. *Freedom for the Self: Sufism, Meditation, and Psychotherapy.* Human Sciences Press, 1985.

Shafii, M., R. Lavely, and R. Jaffe. "Meditation and Marijuana." *American Journal of Psychiatry* 131 (1974): 60-63.

Shafii, M., R. Lavely, and R. Jaffe. "Meditation and the Prevention of Alcohol Abuse." *American Journal of Psychiatry* 132, no. 9 (1975): 924-945.

Shapiro, D.H. "The Effects of a 'Zen Meditation-Behavioral Self-management' Training Package in Treating Methadone Addiction: A Formative Study." *Dissertation Abstracts International* 34, no. 6-B (1973): 2952-2953.

Shapiro, D.H. "A Combined Personal Self-management and Environmental Consultation Strategy." In *Counseling Methods*, eds. J.P. Krumboltz and C.E. Thoreson. New York: Holt, Rinehart and Winston, 1976a.

Shapiro, D.H. "Zen Meditation and Behavioral Self-management Applied to a Case of Generalized Anxiety." *Psychologia* 19, no. 3 (1976b): 134-138.

Shapiro, D.H. "Behavioral and Attitudinal Changes Resulting from a Zen Experience Workshop in Zen Meditation." *Journal of Humanistic Psychology* 18, no. 3 (1978a): 21-29.

Shapiro, D.H. "Instructions for a Training Package Combining Formal and Informal Zen Meditation with Behavioral Self-control Strategies." *Psychologia: International Journal of Psychology in the Orient* 21, no. 2 (1978b): 70-76.

Shapiro, D.H. "Meditation and the East: The Zen Master. In D.H. Shapiro, ed. *Precision Nirvana*. Englewood Cliffs, NJ: Prentice-Hall, 1978c.

Shapiro, D.H. *Precision Nirvana*. Englewood Cliffs, NJ: Prentice-Hall, 1978d.

Shapiro, D.H. "Meditation and Holistic Medicine." In *Holistic Medicine*, eds. A. Hastings, J. Fadiman, and J. Gordon. Rockville, MD: NIMH, 1980a.

Shapiro, D.H. *Meditation: Self-regulation Strategy and Altered State of Consciousness: A Scientific/Personal Exploration*. New York: Aldine, 1980b.

Shapiro, D.H. "Meditation: Clinical and Health-related Applications." *The Western Journal of Medicine* 134, no. 2 (1981): 141-142.

Shapiro, D.H. "Overview: Clinical and Physiological Comparison of Meditation and Other Self-control Strategies." *American Journal of Psychiatry* 139, no. 3 (1982): 267-274.

Shapiro, D.H. "A Content Analysis of Views of Self-control: Relation to Positive and Negative Values and Implications for a Working Definition." *Biofeedback and Self-Regulation* 8, no. 1 (1983a): 73-86.

Shapiro, D.H. "Meditation as an Altered State of Consciousness: Empirical Contributions of Western Behavioral Science." *Journal of Transpersonal Psychology* (1983b).

Shapiro, D.H. "Classic Perspectives of Meditation: Toward an Empirical Understanding of Meditation as an Altered State of Consciousness." In *Meditation: Classic and Contemporary Perspectives*, eds. D.H. Shapiro and R.N. Walsh. New York: Aldine, 1984a: 13-23.

Shapiro, D.H. "Meditation and Behavioral Medicine: Application of a Self-regulation Strategy to the Clinical Management of Stress." In S. Burchfield, ed. *Physiological and Psychological Interactions in the Response to Stress.* New York: Hemisphere, 1984b.

Shapiro, D.H. "A Systems Approach to Meditation Research: Guidelines and Suggestions." In *Meditation: Classic and Contemporary Perspectives*, eds. D.H. Shapiro and R.N. Walsh. New York: Aldine, 1984c.

Shapiro, D.H. "Clinical Use of Meditation as a Self-regulation Strategy: Comments on Holmes's Conclusions and Implications." *American Psychologist* 40, no. 6 (1985): 719.

Shapiro, D.H. "A Preliminary Study of Long-term Meditators: Goals, Effects, Religious Orientation, Cognitions." *Journal of Transpersonal Psychology* 24, no. 1 (1992a): 23-38.

Shapiro, D.H. "Adverse Effects of Meditation: A Preliminary Investigation of Long-term Meditators" *International Journal of Psychosomatics* 39, no. 1-4 (1992b): 62-67.

Shapiro, D.H. "Examining the Content and Context of Meditation: A Challenge for Psychology in the Areas of Stress Management, Psychotherapy, and Religion/Values." *Journal of Humanistic Psychology* 34, no. 4 (1994): 101-135.

Shapiro, D.H., and D. Giber. "Meditation and Psychotherapeutic Effects: Self-regulation Strategy and Altered State of Consciousness." *Archives of General Psychiatry* 35, no. 3 (1978): 294-302.

Shapiro, D.H., and R.N. Walsh. *Meditation: Classic and Contemporary Perspectives.* New York: Aldine, 1984.

Shapiro, D.H., and S.M. Zifferblatt. "An Applied Clinical Combination of Zen Meditation and Behavioral Self-management Techniques: Reducing Methadone Dosage in Drug Addiction." *Behavior Therapy* 7 (1976a): 694-695.

Shapiro, D.H., and S.M. Zifferblatt. "Zen Meditation and Behavioral Self-control: Similarities, Differences and Clinical Applications." *American Psychologist* 31, no. 7 (1976b): 519-532.

Shapiro, D.H., B. Tursky, and G. Schwartz. "Differentiation of Heart Rate and Systolic Blood Pressure in Man by Operant Conditioning." *Psychosomatic Medicine* 32, no. 4 (1970): 417-423.

Shapiro, D.H., B. Tursky, G. Schwartz, et al. "Smoking on Cue: A Behavioral Approach to Smoking Reduction." *Journal of Health and Social Behavior* 12 (1971): 108-113.

Shapiro, D.H., T. Barber, L. DiCara, et al. *Biofeedback and Self-control: An Aldine Annual on the Regulation of Body Processes and Consciousness.* Chicago: Aldine, 1973.

Shapiro, D.H., T. Barber, L. DiCara, et al. "Meditation and Psychotherapeutic Effects: Self-regulation Strategy and Altered States of Consciousness." *Archives of General Psychiatry* 35, no. 3 (1978): 294-302.

Shapiro, D.H., J. Shapiro, R. Walsh, et al. "Effects of Intensive Meditation on Sex Role Identification: Implications for a Control Model of Psychological Health." *Psychological Reports* 51, no. 1 (1982): 44-46.

Shapiro, E.H. "Behavioral Treatment of Anticipatory Nausea Associated with Cancer Chemotherapy." *Dissertation Abstracts International* 49, no. 3-B (1987): 920.

Shapiro, J. "The Relationship of Selected Characteristics of TM to Measures of Self-actualization, Negative Personality Characteristics and Anxiety." *Dissertation Abstracts International* 36, no. 1-A (1975): 137.

Shapiro, J. "The Relationship of the Transcendental Meditation Program to Self-actualization and Negative Personality Characteristics." In *Scientific Research on the Transcendental Meditation Program: Collected Papers,* Vol. 1, eds. D.W. Orme-Johnson and J.T. Farrow. New York: M.E.R.U. Press, 1977.

Sharma, H., and C.N. Alexander. (1996). "Maharishi Ayur-Veda—A Comprehensive System of Natural Medicine and Preventive Health Care: A Research Review (Part I): Herbal Preparations and Clinical Studies." *Alternative Medicine Journal* 3, no. 1 (1996a): 21-28.

Sharma, H., and C.N. Alexander. (1996). "Maharishi Ayur-Veda—A Comprehensive System of Natural Medicine and Preventive Health Care: A Research Review (Part II): Herbal Preparations and Clinical Studies." *Alternative Medicine Journal* 3, no. 2 (1996b): 17-28.

Sharma, H.M., et al. "Physiological Response to Transcendental Meditation (TM) and TM-Sidhi Program." *Federation Proceedings* 45, no. 3 (1986): 173.

Sharma, H.M., R.E. Stephens, N.P. Singh, G. Tejwani, K.K. Vaswani, and H.A.I. Newman. "Physiological Response to Transcendental Meditation (TM) and TM-Sidhi Program." *Proceedings of the 70th Annual Meeting of the Federation of American Societies for Experimental Biology (FASEB) in St. Louis, Missouri, April 13-18, 1986,* Federation of American Societies for Experimental Biology.

Sharma, M., V. Kumaraiah, H. Mishra, and J. Balodhi. "Therapeutic Effects of Vipassana Meditation in Tension Headache." *Journal of Personality and Clinical Studies* 6 no. 2 (1990): 201-206.

Sharma, H.M., M.C. Dillbeck, and S.L. Dillbeck. "Implementation of the Transcendental Meditation Program and Maharishi Ayur-Veda to Prevent Alcohol and Drug Abuse Among Juveniles at Risk." *Alcoholism Treatment Quarterly* 11, no. 3-4 (1994): 429-457.

Shaw, P.H. "Relaxation Training in Anxiety and Stress Management: Differential Effects of an Audible vs. Imaginal Meditation Focus." *Dissertation Abstracts International* 47, no. 11-B (1986): 4,664.

Shaw, R., and D. Kolb. "Reaction Time following the Transcendental Meditation Technique." In *Scientific Research on the Transcendental Meditation Program: Collected Papers*, Vol. 1, eds. D.W. Orme-Johnson and J.T. Farrow. New York: M.E.R.U. Press, 1977.

Shecter, H.E. "The Transcendental Meditation Program in the Classroom: A Psychological Evaluation." In *Scientific Research on the Transcendental Meditation Program: Collected Papers*, Vol. 1, eds. D.W. Orme-Johnson and J.T. Farrow. New York: M.E.R.U. Press, 1977.

Shecter, H.E. "A Psychological Investigation into the Source of the Effect of the Transcendental Meditation Technique." *Dissertation Abstracts International* 38, no. 7-B (1978): 3,372-373.

Sherman, B.Z. "Attentional Style in Undergraduates as a Function of Experience with Transcendental Meditation." *Dissertation Abstracts International* 40, no. 3-B (1979): 1,342.

Shimano, E.T., and D.B. Douglas. "On Research in Zen." *American Journal of Psychiatry* 132, no. 12 (1975): 1,300-1,302.

Shimizu, H. "Two Concentration Methods." *Psychologia* 15 (1972): 110-111.

Shipp, J.A. "A Study of Metaphysical Techniques and Principles as used by Selected Musicians (Imagery, Visualization, Meditation)." *Dissertation Abstracts International* 47, no. 6-A (1986): 1,923.

Shoicket, S., A. Bertelson, and P. Lacks. "Is Sleep Hygiene a Sufficient Treatment for Sleep-maintenance Insomnia?" *Behavior Therapy* 19 (1988): 183-190.

Short, D. "Meditation or Methyldopa." *British Medical Journal* 1, no. 6025 (1976): 1,592.

Shultz, J.V. "Stages on the Spiritual Path: A Buddhist Perspective." *Journal of Transpersonal Psychology* 7, no. 1 (1975): 14-28.

Shuster, R. "Meditation: Philosophy and Practice in a Drug Rehabilitation Setting." *Drug Forum* 5, no. 2 (1975-76): 163-170.

Silver, J. "The Effects of Transcendental Meditation and Masker Uncertainty on the Detection of a Masked Psychoacoustic Signal: A Selective Attention Theoretical Approach." *Dissertation Abstracts International* 37, no. 8-B (1977): 4,167.

Sim, M.K., and W.F. Tsoi, "The Effects of Centrally Acting Drugs on the EEG Correlates of Meditation." *Biofeedback and Self-Regulation* 17, no. 3 (1992): 215-220.

Simon, D.B., S. Oparil, and C.P. Kimball. "The Transcendental Meditation Program and Essential Hypertension." In *Scientific Research on the Transcendental Meditation Program: Collected Papers,* Vol. I, eds. D.W. Orme-Johnson and J.T. Farrow. New York: M.E.R.U. Press, 1977.

Simon, J. "Creativity and Altered States of Consciousness." *American Journal of Psychoanalysis* 37 (1977): 3-12.

Simon, J. Review of *Naikan Psychotherapy—Meditation for Self-development,* by D.K. Reynolds. *Journal of Nervous and Mental Disease* 173, no. 5 (1985): 319-320.

Sinclair, T.G. "Transcendental Meditation." *New England Journal of Medicine* 292, no. 2 (1978): 114.

Singh, B.S. "Ventilatory Response to CO_2 II. Studies in Neurotic Psychiatric Patients and Practitioners of Transcendental Meditation." *Psychosomatic Medicine* 46, no. 4 (1984): 347-362.

Sinha, S.N., S.C. Prasad, and K.N. Sharma. "An Experimental Study of Cognitive Control and Arousal Processes during Meditation." *Psychologia* 21, no. 4 (1978): 227-230.

Sisley, D. "Transcendental Meditation and TM-Sidhi Program: Ongoing Psychometric Evaluation." *New Zealand Psychologist* 8 (1979): 49.

Slaughter, E. "Hypertension: A Comparative Study of Self-regulation Strategies." *Dissertation Abstracts International* 45, no. 2-B (1984): 687.

Smail, K.H. "Runners, Meditators, Weightlifters and Skydivers: A Comparison of Psychological Characteristics." *Dissertation Abstracts International* 41, no. 4-B (1980): 1,527-1,528.

Smith, D.E., J.L. Glaser, R.H. Schneider, and M.C. Dillbeck. "Erythrocyte Sedimentation Rate (ESR) and the Transcendental Meditation (TM) Program." *Psychosomatic Medicine* 51, no. 2 (1989): 259.

Smith, G.R., C. Conger, D.F. O'Rourke, R.W. Steele, R. Charlton, and S.S. Smith. "Modulation of Cellular Immunity by Meditation." *Psychosomatic Medicine* 51, no. 2 (1989): 246.

Smith, J.C. "Meditation as Psychotherapy." *Dissertation Abstracts International* 36, no. 6-B (1975a): 3,073.

Smith, J.C. "Meditation as Psychotherapy: A Review of the Literature." *Psychological Bulletin* 32, no. 4 (1975b): 553-564.

Smith, J.C. "Psychotherapeutic Effects of Transcendental Meditation with Controls for Expectation of Relief and Daily Sitting." *Journal of Consulting and Clinical Psychology* 44, no. 4 (1975c): 630-637.

Smith, J.C. "Personality Correlates of Continuation and Outcome in Meditation and Erect Sitting Control Treatments." *Journal of Consulting and Clinical Psychology* 46, no. 2 (1978): 272-279.

Smith, J.C. "Meditation Research: Three Observations of the State-of-the-art." In *Meditation: Classic and Contemporary Perspectives*, eds. D.H. Shapiro and R.N. Walsh. New York: Aldine, 1984a.

Smith, J.C. "Self-reported Physical Stress Reactions: First- and Second-order Factors." *Biofeedback and Self-Regulation* Jun 1984b Vol 9(2) 215-227.

Smith, J.C. *Relaxation Dynamics: Nine World Approaches to Self-relaxation.* Champaign, IL: Research Press, 1985.

Smith, J.C. "Meditation, Biofeedback, and the Relaxation Controversy: A Cognitive-behavioral Perspective." *American Psychologist* 41, nc. 9 (1986): 1,007-1,009.

Smith, J.C. *Meditation: A Sensible Guide to a Timeless Discipline.* Champaign, IL: Research Press, 1986.

Smith, J.C. "Meditation as Psychotherapy: A New Look at the Evidence." In Michael A. West, ed. *The Psychology of Meditation.* pp. 136-149, Oxford: Clarendon Press/Oxford University Press, 1987.

Smith, J.C. "Steps Toward a Cognitive-behavioral Model of Relaxation." *Biofeedback and Self-Regulation*, 1988 Dec Vol 13(4) 307-329.

Smith, J.C. *Cognitive-behavioral Relaxation Training: A New System of Strategies for Treatment and Assessment.* New York: Springer Publishing Co, 1990.

Smith, J.C. *Stress Scripting: A Guide to Stress Management.* New York: Praeger, 1991.

Smith, J.C. *Understanding Stress and Coping.* New York: Macmillan, 1993.

Smith, J.C. A. Amutio, J.P. Anderson, and L.A. Aria "Relaxation: Mapping an Uncharted World." *Biofeedback and Self-Regulation,* 21(1996): 63-90.

Smith, M.S., and W.M. Womack. "Stress Management—Techniques in Childhood and Adolescence—Relaxation Training, Meditation, Hypnosis, and Biofeedback—Appropriate Clinical Applications." *Clinical Pediatrics* 26, no. 11 (1987): 581-585.

Smith, T.R. "The Transcendental Meditation Technique and Skin Resistence Response to Loud Tones." In *Scientific Research on the Transcendental Meditation Program: Collected Papers,* Vol. I, eds. D.W. Orme-Johnson and J.T. Farrow. New York: M.E.R.U. Press, 1977.

Snaith, R.P., D. Owens, and E. Kennedy. "An Outcome Study of a Brief Anxiety Management Programme: Anxiety Control Training." *Irish Journal of Psychological Medicine* 9, no. 2 (1992): 111-114.

Sollod, R.N. Review of *Freedom from the Self—Sufism, Meditation and Psychotherapy,* by M. Shafii. In *Contemporary Psychology* 31, no. 9 (1986): 656-657.

Solomon, E.G., and A.K. Bumpus. "The Running Meditation Responses: An Adjunct to Psychotherapy." *American Journal of Psychotherapy* 32, no. 4 (1978): 583-592.

Solvin, G., W.G. Roll, and J. Krieger. "Meditation and ESP: Remote Viewing." *Journal of Parapsychology* 41 (1977): 261-263.

Soskis, D.A. "Teaching Meditation to Medical Students." *Journal of Religion and Health* 17, no. 2 (1978): 136-143.

Soskis, D.A., E.C. Orne, M.T. Orne, and D.F. Dinges. "Self-hypnosis and Meditation for Stress: A Six-month Follow-up." *International Journal of Clinical and Experimental Hypnosis* 34, no. 3 (1986): 272.

Soskis, D.A., E.C. Orne, M.T. Orne, and D.F. Dinges. "Self-hypnosis and Meditation for Stress Management—A Brief Communication." *International Journal of Clinical and Experimental Hypnosis* 37, no. 4 (1989): 285-289.

Sothers, K., and K.N. Anchor. "Prevention and Treatment of Essential Hypertension with Meditation-relaxation Methods." *Medical Psychotherapy: An International Journal* 2 (1989): 137-156.

Spanos, N.P., S.M. Rivers, and J. Gottlieb. "Hypnotic Responsivity, Meditation and Laterality of Eye Movements." *Journal of Abnormal Psychology* 87, no. 5 (1978): 566-569.

Spanos, N.P., S. Steggles, H.L. Radtke, et al. "Nonanalytic Attending, Hypnotic Susceptibility and Psychological Well-being in Trained Meditators and Nonmeditators." *Journal of Abnormal Psychology* 88, no. 1 (1979): 85-87.

Spanos, N.P., J. Gottlieb, and S.M. Rivers. "The Effects of Short-term Meditation Practice on Hypnotic Responsivity." *Psychological Record* 30, no. 3 (1980a): 343-348.

Spanos, N.P., H.J. Stam, S.M. Rivers, et al. "Meditation Expectation and Performance on Indices of Nonanalytic Attending." *International Journal of Clinical and Experimental Hypnosis* 28, no. 2 (1980b): 244-251.

Staggers, F., C.N. Alexander, and K.G. Walton. "Importance of Reducing Stress and Strengthening the Host in Drug Detoxification: The Potential Offered by Transcendental Meditation." *Alcoholism Treatment Quarterly* 11, no. 3-4 (1994): 297-331.

Stainbrook, G.L., J.W. Hoffman, and H. Benson. "Behavioral Therapies of Hypertension: Psychotherapy, Biofeedback and Relaxation/Meditation." *International Review of Applied Psychology* 32 (1983): 119-135.

Stamatelos, T., and D.W. Mott. "Creative Potential among Persons Labeled Developmentally Delayed, 2: Meditation as a Technique to Release Creativity." *Arts in Psychotherapy* 13, no. 3 (1986): 229-234.

Steinmiller, G.A. "The Relaxation Response as a Stress Coping Strategy for Student Teachers." *Dissertation Abstracts International* 46, no. 6-A (1985): 1,601.

Stek, R.M., and B.A. Bass. "Personal Adjustment and Perceived Locus of Control among Students Interested in Meditation." *Psychological Reports* 32, no. 3, pt. 1 (1973): 1,019-1,022.

Steptoe, A., and H. Fidler. "Stage Fright in Orchestral Musicians: A Study of Cognitive and Behavioural Strategies in Performance Anxiety." *British Journal of Psychology* 78, no. 2 (May 1987): 241-249.

Steptoe, A., and N. Kearsley. "Cognitive and Somatic Anxiety." *Behavior Research and Therapy* 28 (1990): 75-81.

Stern, M. "The Effects of the Transcendental Meditation Program on Trait Anxiety." In *Scientific Research on the Transcendental Meditation Program: Collected Papers*, Vol. 1, eds. D.W. Orme-Johnson and J.T. Farrow. New York: M.E.R.U. Press, 1977.

Sternberg, M.B. "Man, Mind and Meditation." *Dissertation Abstracts International* 35, no. 5-B (1974): 2,449-2,450.

Stewart, R.A. "Self-realization as the Basis of Psychotherapy: A Look at Two

Eastern-based Practices, Transcendental Meditation and Alpha Brain Wave Biofeedback." *Social Behavior and Personality* 2, no. 2 (1974a): 191-200.

Stewart, R.A. "States of Human Realization: Some Physiological and Psychological Correlates." *Psychologia: An International Journal of Psychology in the Orient* 17 (1974b): 126-134.

Steyn, H.C. "Thomas Merton and Theravada Buddhism—A Comparative Study of Religious Experience." Masters Abstracts 28, no. 1 (1988): 40.

Stigsby, B., J.C. Rodenburg, and H.B. Moth. "Electroencephalographic Findings during Mantra Meditation (Transcendental Meditation): A Controlled, Quantitative Study of Experienced Meditators." *Electroencephalography and Clinical Neurophysiology* 51, no 4 (1981): 434-442.

Stone, J. *Meditation for Healing: Particular Meditations for Particular Results.* San Leandro, CA: Satori Research, 1986 (reprint).

Stone, R., and J. DeLeo. "Psychotherapeutic Control of Hypertension." *New England Journal of Medicine* 2 (1976): 80-84.

Stoyva, J., T. Barber, L. DiCara, et al., eds. *Biofeedback and Self-control: An Aldine Annual on the Regulation of Body Processes and Consciousness.* Chicago: Aldine-Atherton, 1972.

Stroebel, C., and B. Glueck. "Passive Meditation: Subjective and Clinical Comparison with Biofeedback." In *Consciousness and Self-Regulation*, eds. G. Schwartz and D. Shapiro. New York: Plenum, 1977.

Stuart, E., M. Caudill, J. Lesserman, C. Dorrington, R. Friedman, and H. Benson. "Nonpharmacologic Treatment of Hypertension: A Multiple Risk Factor Approach." *Journal of Cardiovascular Nursing* 1 (1987): 1-4.

Suarez, V.W. "The Relationship of the Practice of TM to Subjective Evaluations of Marital Satisfaction and Adjustment." Doctoral diss., University of Southern California, 1976.

Subrahmanyam, S., and K. Porkodi. "Neurohumoral Correlates of TM." *Journal of Biomedicine* 1 (1980): 73-88.

Sudsang, R., V. Chentanez, and K. Veluvan. "Effect of Buddhist Meditation on Serum Cortisol and Total Protein Levels, Blood Pressure, Pulse Rate, Lung Volume and Reaction Time." *Physiology and Behavior* 50, no. 3 (1991): 543-548.

Sugi, Y., and K. Akutsu. "Studies on Respiration and Energy: Metabolism during Sitting in Zazan." *Research Journal of Physiology* 12 (1968): 190-206.

Suinn, R., and F. Richardson. "Anxiety Management Training: A Nonspecific

Behavior Therapy Program for Anxiety Control." *Behavior Therapy* 2, no. 4 (1971): 498-510.

Suler, J.R. "Meditation and Somatic Arousal: A Comment." *American Psychologist* 40, no. 6 (1985): 717.

Suler, J.R. "Images of the Self in Zen Meditation." *Journal of Mental Imagery* 14 no. 3-4 (1990) 197-204.

Sullivan, R.H. "Reading, Anxiety and Behavioral Management as Functions of Attention and Relaxation Training." *Dissertation Abstracts International* 41 (1980): 1,960-1,961A.

Surwillo, W.W., and D.P. Hobson. "Brain Electrical Activity during Prayer." *Psychological Reports* 43, no. 1 (1978): 135-143.

Surwit, R.S., D. Shapiro, and M.I. Good. "Comparison of Cardiovascular Biofeedback, Neuromuscular Biofeedback, and Meditation in the Treatment of Borderline Essential Hypertension." *Journal of Consulting and Clinical Psychology* 46, no. 2 (1978): 252-263.

Sussman, A.R. "Death, Time and Consciousness: A Theoretical Examination of the Psychological Impact of Alterations in Temporal Perspective." *Dissertation Abstracts International* 49, no. 3-B (1987): 922.

Suzuki, T.J. "Psychophysiological Effects of Meditation on Test-anxious Male Youthful Prisoners." *Dissertation Abstracts International* 38, no. 11-B (1978): 5,573.

Swartz, P. "Contributions to the History of Psychology: XLVII. Ignatius Loyola and Behavior Therapy." *Perceptual and Motor Skills* 66, no. 2 (April 1988): 617-618.

Sweet, M.J., and C.G. Johnson. "Enhancing Empathy: The Interpersonal Implications of a Buddhist Meditation Technique. Special Issue: Psychotherapy and Religion." *Psychotherapy* 27, no. 1 (1990): 19-29.

Swinyard, C.A., S. Chaube, and D.B. Sutton. "Neurological and Behavioral Aspects of Transcendental Meditation Relevant to Alcoholism: A Review." *Annals of the New York Academy of Science* 233 (1974): 162-173.

Sykes, D.E. "TM as Applied to Criminal Justice Reform, Drug Rehabilitation, and Society in General." *University of Maryland Law Reform* 3, no. 2 (1973): 37-53.

Taggart, S.R. *Living As If: Belief Systems in Mental Health Practice.* San Francisco: Jossey-Bass, 1994.

Takeda, S. "A Psychological Study on 'Zenjo' and Breath Regulation." In Y. Akishige, ed. *Psychological Studies in Zen.* Tokyo: Zen Institute of the Komazawa University, 1977.

Taneli, B., and W. Krahne. "EEG Changes of Transcendental Meditation Practitioners." *Advances in Biological Psychiatry* 16 (1987): 41-71.

Tart, C.T., ed. *Altered States of Consciousness.* New York: Wiley, 1969.

Tart, C.T. "A Psychologist's Experience with Transcendental Meditation." *Journal of Transpersonal Psychology* 3, no. 2 (1971): 135-140.

Tart, C.T. Review of *The Psychology of Meditation,* by M.A. West. In *Contemporary Psychology* 34, no. 6 (1989): 594-595.

Taub, E., S.S. Steiner, E. Weingarten, et al. "Effectiveness of Broad Spectrum Approaches to Relapse Prevention in Severe Alcoholism: A Long-term, Randomized, Controlled Trial of Transcendental Meditation." *Alcoholism Treatment Quarterly* 11, no. 1-2 (1994): 187-220.

Taylor, E.I. *Psychological Suspended Animation: Heart Rate, Blood Pressure, Time Estimation, and Introspective Reports from an Anechoic Environment.* 1st edition. Privately printed, Dallas, Texas, 1973; 2nd edition. Cambridge, MA: The Essene Press, 1996.

Taylor, E.I., and Schlitz, M. "Meditation." In *The Illustrated Encyclopedia of Body Mind Disciplines.* New York: Rosen Publishing Group, 1997.

Teasdale, J.D., Z. Segal, and J.M. Williams. "How Does Cognitive Therapy Prevent Depressive Relapse and Why Should Attentional Control (Mindfulness) Training Help?" *Behaviour Research and Therapy* 33, no. 1 (1995): 25-39.

Tebecis, A.K. "A Controlled Study of the EEG during Transcendental Meditation: Comparison with Hypnosis." *Folia Psychiatrica et Neurologica Japonica* 29, no. 4 (1975): 305-313.

Tebecis, A.K. "Eye Movements during Transcendental Meditation." *Folia Psychiatrica et Neurologica Japonica* 30, no. 4 (1976): 487-493.

Telles, S., and T. Desiraju. "Autonomic Changes in Brahmakumaris Raja Yoga Meditation." *International Journal of Psychophysiology* 15, no 2 (1993a): 147-152.

Telles, S., and T. Desiraju. "Recording of Auditory Middle Latency Evoked Potentials During the Practice of Meditation with the Syllable Om." *Indian Journal of Medical Research Section B-Biomedical Research Other Than Infectious Diseases* 98, Oct. (1993b): 237-239.

Telles, S., R. Nagarathna, H.R. Nagendra, et al. "Alterations in Auditory Middle Latency Evoked Potential During Meditation on a Meaningful Symbol —OM." *International Journal of Neuroscience* 76, no 1-2 (1994a): 87-93.

Telles, S., B.H. Hanumanthaiah, R. Nagarathna, et al. "Plasticity of Motor Control Systems Demonstrated by Yoga Training." *Indian Journal of Physiology and Pharmacology* 39, no. 2 (1994b): 143-144.

Thomas, B.L. "Self-esteem and Life Satisfaction in Non-institutionalized Elderly Black Females: Effects of Meditation/ Relaxation Training." *Dissertation Abstracts International* 48, no. 4-B (1987): 1,180.

Thomas, D., and K.A. Abbas. "Comparison of TM and Progressive Relaxation in Reducing Anxiety." *British Medical Journal* 2, no. 6,154 (1978): 1,749.

Throll, D.A. "Transcendental Meditation and Progressive Relaxation: Their Psychological Effects." *Journal of Clinical Psychology* 37 (1981): 776-781.

Throll, D.A. "Transcendental Meditation and Progressive Relaxation: Their Physiological Effects." *Journal of Clinical Psychology* 38, no. 3 (1982): 522-530.

Timmons, B., and J. Kamiya. "The Psychology and Physiology of Meditation and Related Phenomena: A Bibliography." *Journal of Transpersonal Psychology* 2, no. 1 (1970): 41-59.

Timmons, B., and D. Kanellakos. "The Psychology and Physiology of Meditation and Related Phenomena: Bibliography II." *Journal of Transpersonal Psychology* 6, no. 1 (1974): 32-38.

Tjoa, A. "Meditation, Neuroticism and Intelligence: A Follow-up." *Gedrag: Tijdschrift voor Psychologie* 3, no. 3 (1975): 167-182.

Tjoa, A. "Increased Intelligence and Reduced Neuroticism through the Transcendental Meditation Program." In *Scientific Research on the Transcendental Meditation Program: Collected Papers*, Vol. 1, eds. D.W. Orme-Johnson and J.T. Farrow. New York: M.E.R.U. Press, 1977a.

Tjoa, A. "Some Evidence that the Transcendental Meditation Program Increases Intelligence and Reduces Neuroticism as Measured by Psychological Tests." In *Scientific Research on the Transcendental Meditation Program: Collected Papers*, Vol. 1, eds. D.W. Orme-Johnson and J.T. Farrow. New York: M.E.R.U. Press, 1977b.

Tloczynski, J. "A Preliminary Study of Opening-Up Meditation College Adjustment and Self-actualization." *Psychological Reports* 75, no. 1 (Part 2) (1994): 449-450.

Toane, E.G. "TM Program." *Canadian Medical Association Journal* 114, no. 12 (1976): 1,095-1,096.

Todd, C. "Meditation, Mystical and Therapeutic." *Bulletin of the British Psychological Society* 34 (1981): 101-102.

Tomassetti, J.T. "An Investigation of the Effects of EMG Biofeedback Training and Relaxation Training on Dimensions of Attention and Learning of Hyperactive Children." *Dissertation Abstracts International* 45, no. 6-B (1985): 2,081.

Torbert, W.R. "Cultivating Postformal Adult Development: Higher Stages and Contrasting Interventions." In *Transcendence and Mature Thought in Adulthood: The Further Reaches of Adult Development,* eds. M.E. Miller and S.R. Cook-Greuter. Lanham, MD: Rowman and Littlefield, 1994: 181-203.

Tornquist, L.M. "The Attitudes of Evangelical Free Church Ministers toward the Use of Meditation as a Technique in Counseling." *Dissertation Abstracts International* 50, no. 3-A (1988): 629.

Towers, D.A. "Cognitive Focusing as an Attentional Self-regulation Strategy in the Treatment of Substance Abuse." *Dissertation Abstracts International* 47, no. 5-B (1986): 2,146.

Trausch, C.P. "PSI Training through Meditation, and Self-actualization as Related to PSI Performance." *Dissertation Abstracts International* 42, no. 4-A (1981): 1,531-1,532.

Traver, M.M. "Efficacy of Short Term Meditation as Therapy for Symptoms of Stress." *Dissertation Abstracts International* 50, no. 12-B (1990): 5897.

Travis, F. "Within Comparison of EEG and Autonomic Patterns during Eyes-closed Rest and TM Practice." *Psychophysiology* S77 (1995).

Travis, F., and S. Miskov. "P300 Latency and Amplitude during Eyes-closed Rest and Transcendental Meditation Practice." *Psychophysiology* 31:S67, (Abstract), 1994.

Travis, F.T. "The TM Technique and Creativity: A Longitudinal Study of Cornell University Undergraduates." *Journal of Creative Behavior* 13, no. 3 (1979): 169-180.

Travis, F.T. "Eyes Open and TM EEG Patterns after One and after Eight Years of TM Practice." *Psychophysiology* 28, no. 3a (1991): 558.

Travis, F.T. "Respiratory, Autonomic, and EEG Correlates of Transcendental Consciousness Experiences during Transcendental Meditation Practice." *Society for Neuroscience Abstracts* 18, no. 1 (1993): 574.15.

Travis, F.T. "The Junction Point Model: A Field Model of Waking, Sleeping, and Dreaming, Relating Dream Witnessing, the Waking/Sleeping Transition, and Transcendental Meditation in Terms of a Common Psychophysiologic State."

Dreaming: Journal of the Association for the Study of Dreams 4, no. 2 (1994): 91-104.

Travis, F.T., and D.W. Orme-Johnson. "Field Model of Consciousness: EEG Coherence Changes as Indicators of Field Effects." *International Journal of Neuroscience* 49 (1989): 203-211.

Travis, F.T., and D.W. Orme-Johnson. "EEG Coherence and Power During Yogic Flying." *International Journal of Neuroscience* 54 (1990): 1-12.

Travis, T., C. Kondo, and J. Knott. "Subjective Aspects of Alpha Enhancement." *British Journal of Psychiatry* 127 (1975): 122-126.

Travis, T., C. Kondo, and J. Knott. "Heart Rate, Muscle Tension, and Alpha Production of Transcendental Meditation and Relaxation Controls." *Biofeedback and Self-Regulation* 1, no. 4 (1976): 387-394.

Traynham, R.N. "The Effects of Experimental Meditation, Relaxation Training, and Electromyographic Feedback on Physiological and Self-report Measures of Relaxation and Altered States of Consciousness." *Dissertation Abstracts International* 38, no. 5-B (1977): 2,386-2,387.

Treichel, M., N. Clinch, and M. Cran. "The Metabolic Effects of Transcendental Meditation." *The Physiologist* 16 (1973): 471.

Trungpa, C. "An Approach to Meditation." *Journal of Transpersonal Psychology* 5, no. 1 (1973): 62-74.

Tsai, S. "The Effects of Relaxation Training, Combining Meditation and Guided Imagery, on Self-perceived Stress Among Chinese Nurses in Large Teaching Hospitals in Taiwan, Republic of China." *Dissertation Abstracts International* 53, no. 8-B (1993): 4037

Tsakonas, F.A. "The Response of Obese and Non-obsese Women to Meditation." *Dissertation Abstracts International* 37, no. 7-B (1977): 3636-3637.

Tsao, Pen-Yen. "Taoist Ritual Music of the Yu-Lan Pen-Hui (Feeding the Hungry Ghost Festival) in a Hong Kong Taoist Temple: A Repertoire Study." *Dissertation Abstracts International* 50, no. 6-A (1989): 1,480.

Tulku, T. "A Review of Mind." *Journal of Transpersonal Psychology* 8, no. 1 (1976): 41-44.

Tulpule, T.H. "Yogic Exercises in the Management of Ischemic Heart Disease." *Indian Heart Journal* 23, no. 4 (1971): 259-264.

Turnbull, M.J., and H. Norris. "Effects of TM on Self-identity Indices and Personality." *British Journal of Psychology* 73, no. 1 (1982): 57-68.

Tyson, P.D. "A General Systems Theory Approach to Consciousness Attention and Meditation." *Psychological Record* 32 (1982): 491-500.

Udupa, K.N. "The Scientific Basis of Yoga." *Journal of the American Medical Association* 220 (1972): 1,365.

Udupa, K.N. "Certain Studies in Psychological and Biochemical Responses to the Practice of Hatha Yoga in Young Normal Volunteers." *Indian Journal of Medical Research* 61, no. 2 (1973): 237-244.

Udupa, K.N., R.H. Singh, K.N. Dwivedi, et al. "Comparative Biochemical Studies on Meditation." *Indian Journal of Medical Research* 63, no. 12 (1975): 1,676-1,679.

Uma, K., H.R. Nagendra, R. Nagarathna, S. Vaidehi, et al. "The Integrated Approach of Yoga: A Therapeutic Tool for Mentally Retarded Children: A One-year Controlled Study." *Journal of Mental Deficiency Research* 33, no. 5 (1989): 415-421.

Unger, K.M. "A Study of Two Systems of Traditional Medicine in India: Ayurveda and Irula Tribal Medicine." *Dissertation Abstracts International* 50, no. 6-B (1989): 2,252.

Vahia, H.S., D.R. Doongaji, D.V. Jeste, et al. "A Deconditioning Therapy Based upon Concepts of Patanjali." *International Journal of Social Psychiatry* 18, no. 1 (1972a): 61-66.

Vahia, H.S., D.R. Doongaji, D.V. Jeste, et al. "Psychophysiologic Therapy Based on the Concepts of Patanjali." *American Journal of Psychotherapy* 27 (1972b): 557-565.

Vahia, H.S., D.R. Doongaji, D.V. Jeste, et al. "Further Experience with the Therapy Based upon Concepts of Patanjali in the Treatment of Psychiatric Disorders." *Indian Journal of Psychiatry* 15 (1973): 32-37.

Vail, L.F. "Renunciation, Love, and Power in Hindu Monastic Life (India)." *Dissertation Abstracts International* 48, no. 4-A (1987): 953.

Vakil, R.J. "Remarkable Feat of Endurance of a Yogi Priest." *Lancet* 2 (1950): 871.

Valois, M.G.L. "The Effects of Transcendental Meditation on the Self Concept as Measured by the Tennessee Self Concept Scale." *Dissertation Abstracts International* 37, no. 1-A (1976): 208.

Van Dalfsen, P.J. "Initial Treatment Response to Relaxation and Meditation Procedures: The Contribution of Individual Differences in Anxiety." *Dissertation Abstracts International* 47, no. 10-B (1986): 4,317.

Van den Berg, W.P., and B. Mulder. "Psychological Research on the Effects of the TM Technique on a Number of Personality Variables." *Gedrag: Tijdschrift voor Psychologie* 4, no. 4 (1976): 206-218.

Van der Lans, J. "Therapeutic Importance of Yoga and Meditation." *Gedrag: Tijdschrift voor Psychologie* 3, no. 2 (1975): 49-62.

Van der Lans, J. "Religious Experience and Meditation." *Psychology* 14 (1979): 154-164.

Van der Lans, J., and M. Jan. "The Value of Sunden's Role-theory Demonstrated and Tested with Respect to Religious Experiences in Meditation." *Journal for the Scientific Study of Religion* 26, no. 3 (Sep 1987): 401-412.

Van Dusen, W. "LSD and the Enlightenment of Zen." *Psychologia* 4 (1961): 11-16.

Van Nuys, D. "A Novel Technique for Studying Attention during Meditation." *Journal of Transpersonal Psychology* 3, no. 2 (1971): 125-133.

Van Nuys, D. "Meditation, Attention and Hypnotic Susceptibility: A Correlational Study." *International Journal of Clinical and Experimental Hypnosis* 21, no. 2 (1973): 59-69.

Vanselow, K. "Meditative Exercises to Eliminate the Effects of Stress." *Hippokrates* 39 (1968): 462-465.

Varni, J. W. "Self-regulation Techniques in the Management of Chronic Arthritic Pain in Hemophilia." *Behavior Therapy* 12, no. 2 (1981): 185-194.

Varvil-Weld, D.C. "Prognostic Expectancies and the Outcome of a Career Treatment." *Dissertation Abstracts International* 42, no. 8-B (1982): 3,448.

Vassallo, J.N. "Psychological Perspectives of Buddhism: Implications for Counseling." *George Washington University School of Education and Human Development Counsel and Values* 28, no. 4 (1984): 179-191.

Vassiliadis, A. "Physiological Effects of Transcendental Meditation: A Longitudinal Study." In *Psychobiology of Transcendental Meditation: A Literature Review*, eds. D.P. Kanellakos and J.S. Lukas. Menlo Park, CA: Stanford Research Institute, 1973.

Vasudevan, A., V. Kumaraiah, H. Mishra, et al. "Yogic Meditation in Tension Headache." *NIMHANS Journal* 12, no. 1 (1994): 69-73.

Vattano, A. "Self Management Procedures for Coping with Stress." *Social Work* 23, no. 2 (1978): 113-119.

Vegors, S. "Transcendental Meditation and Individual Differences in Mental Capacity." *Dissertation Abstracts International* 56, no. 6-B (1995): 3497.

Veith, I. "On the Principles of the Heart and the Psychiatric Insights of Zen." *The New England Journal of Medicine* (1971): 1,458-1,460.

Verma, I.C., B.C. Jayashan, and M. Palani. "Effect of Transcendental Meditation on the Performance of Some Cognitive Psychological Tests." *International Journal of Medical Research* 7 (1982): 136-143.

Volinn, E. "Eastern-meditation Groups: Why Join?" *Sociological Analysis* 46, no. 2 (1985): 147-156.

Vrolijk, A. "Transcendental Meditation and Dianetics." *Gedrag: Tijdschrift voor Psychologie* 6, no. 3-4 (1978): 181-206.

Waalmanning, H.J., and D.A. Jenkins. "Systolic Blood-pressure and Pulse-rate during Transcendental Meditation." *Proceedings of the University of Otago Medical School* 57, no. 3 (1979): 75-76.

Wachsmuth, D. "The EEG during the Technique of Transcendental Meditation and Sleep: A Contribution to the Psychophysiology of Restful Alertness." Doctoral diss., Johann-Wolfgang Goethe University, Frankfurt, West Germany, 1978.

Wachsmuth, D., T. Dolce, and K. Offenloch. "Computerized Analysis of the EEG during Transcendental Meditation and Sleep." *Electroencephalography and Clinical Neurophysiology* 48, no. 3 (1980): 39.

Wada, J.A., and A.E. Hamm. "Electrographic Glimpse of Meditative State: Chronological Observations of Cerebral Evoked Response." *Electroencephalography and Clinical Neurophysiology* 37, no. 2 (1974): 201.

Walder, J.M. "The Effects of a Measure of Self-actualization of adding a Meditation Exercise to a Sensitivity Group/Group Facilitator Training Program." *Dissertation Abstracts International* 36, no. 10-A (1976): 6,533-6,534.

Walker, R. "Contemplative Psychotherapy at the Naropa Institute." *Humanistic Psychologist* 15, no. 2 (Sum 1987): 98-104.

Wallace, R.K. "Physiological Effects of Transcendental Meditation. *Reviste Brasileire de Medicine* 8 (1970): 397-401.

Wallace, R.K. "The Physiological Effects of Transcendental Meditation: A Proposed Fourth Major State of Consciousness." *Dissertation Abstracts International* 31 (1971): 4,303B.

Wallace, R.K. "Neurophysiology of Enlightenment." In *Scientific Research on the Transcendental Meditation Program: Collected Papers,* Vol. 1, eds. D.W. Orme-Johnson and J.T. Farrow. New York: M.E.R.U. Press, 1977a.

Wallace, R.K. "The Physiological Effects of Transcendental Meditation: A Proposed Fourth State of Consciousness." In *Scientific Research on the Transcendental Meditation Program: Collected Papers*, Vol. I, eds. D.W. Orme-Johnson and J.T. Farrow. New York: M.E.R.U. Press, 1977b.

Wallace, R.K. *The Maharishi Technology of the Unified Field: The Neurophysiology of Enlightenment*. Fairfield, IA: Maharishi International University Press, 1986.

Wallace, R.K. *The Physiology of Consciousness*. Fairfield, IA: Maharishi International University Press, 1993.

Wallace, R.K., and H. Benson. "The Physiology of Meditation." *Scientific American* 226, no. 2 (1972): 84-90.

Wallace, R.K., H. Benson, A.F. Wilson, et al. "Decreased Blood Lactate during TM." *Federation Proceedings* 30 (1971a): 376.

Wallace, R.K., H. Benson, and A.F. Wilson. "A Wakeful Hypometabolic Physiologic State." *American Journal of Physiology* 221 (1971b): 795-799.

Wallace, R.K., H. Benson, A.A. Gattozzi, et al. "Physiological Effects of a Meditation Technique and a Suggestion for Curbing Drug Abuse." *Mental Health Program Reports*. National Institute of Mental Health, 1971c.

Wallace, R.K., M. Dillbeck, E. Jacobe, et al. "The Effects of the Transcendental Meditation and TM-Sidhi Program on the Aging Process." *International Journal of Neuroscience* 16 (1982a): 53-58.

Wallace, R.K., P.J. Mills, D.W. Orme-Johnson, et al. "The Paired H Reflex and its Correlation with EEG Coherence and Academic Performance in Normal Subjects Practicing Meditation." *Society for Neuroscience Abstracts* 8: (1982b): 537.

Wallace, R.K., P.J. Mills, D.W. Orme-Johnson, et al. "Modification of the Paired H-Reflex through the Transcendental Meditation and TM-Sidhi Program." *Experimental Neurology* 79 (1983a): 77-86.

Wallace, R.K., J. Silver, P.J. Mills, et al. "Systolic Blood Pressure and Long-term Practice of the Transcendental Meditation and TM-Sidhi Program: Effects of TM on Systolic Blood Pressure." *Psychosomatic Medicine* 45, no. I (1983b): 41-46.

Wallace, R.K., D.W. Orme-Johnson, P.J. Mills, et al. "Academic Achievement and the Paired Hoffman Reflex in Students Practicing Meditation." *International Journal of Neuroscience* 24 (1984): 261-266.

Wallace, R.K., D.W. Orme-Johnson, and M.C. Dillbeck, eds. *Scientific Research on Maharishi's Transcendental Meditation and TM-Sidhi Program: Collected Papers*, Vol. 5. Fairfield, IA: Maharishi International University Press, 1990.

Walrath, L.C., and D.W. Hamilton. "Autonomic Correlates of Meditation and Hypnosis." *American Journal of Clinical Hypnosis* 17, no. 3 (1975): 190-197.

Walsh, R.N. "Initial Meditative Experience: Part I." *Journal of Transpersonal Psychology* 9, no. 2 (1977): 151-192.

Walsh, R.N. "Initial Meditative Experience: Part II." *Journal of Transpersonal Psychology* 10, no. 1 (1978): 1-28.

Walsh, R.N. "Meditation Research: An Introduction and Review." *Journal of Transpersonal Psychology* 11, no. 2 (1979): 161-174.

Walsh, R.N. "The Consciousness Disciplines and the Behavioral Sciences: Questions of Comparison and Assessment." *American Journal of Psychiatry* 137, no. 6 (1980): 663-673.

Walsh, R.N. "The Original Goals of Meditation." *American Journal of Psychiatry* 139, no. 11 (1982a): 1525.

Walsh, R.N. "A Model for Viewing Meditation Research." *Journal of Transpersonal Psychology* 14, no. 1 (1982b): 69-84.

Walsh, R.N. "Meditation Practice and Research." *Journal of Humanistic Psychology* 23, no. 1 (1983): 18-50.

Walsh, R.N. "An Evolutionary Model of Meditation Research." In *Meditation: Contemporary and Classical Perspectives*, eds. D.H. Shapiro and R.N. Walsh. New York: Aldine, 1984: 24-31.

Walsh, R.N., and L. Roche. "Precipitation of Acute Psychotic Episodes by Intensive Meditation in Individuals with a History of Schizophrenia." *American Journal of Psychiatry* 136, no. 8 (1979): 1085-1086.

Walsh, R.N., and D.H. Shapiro, eds. *Beyond Health and Normality: Explorations of Extreme Psychological Well-being*. New York: Van Nostrand, 1983.

Walsh, R.N., D. Goleman, J. Kornfield, et al. "Meditation: Aspects of Research and Practice." *Journal of Transpersonal Psychology* 10, no. 2 (1978): 113-134.

Walter, S. "Does a Systemic Therapist Have Buddha Nature?" *Journal of Systemic Therapies* 13, no. 3 (1994): 42-49.

Walton, K.G., and D. Levitsky. "A Neuroendocrine Mechanism for the Reduction of Drug Use and Addictions by Transcendental Meditation." *Alcoholism Treatment Quarterly* 11, no. 1-2 (1994): 89-117.

Walton, K.G., M. Lerom, J. Salerno, et al. "Practice of the Transcendental Meditation and TM-Sidhi Program May Affect the Circadian Rhythm of Urinary 5-Hydroxyindole Excretion." *Society for Neuroscience Abstracts* 7 (1981): 48.

Walton, K.G., D. Francis, M. Lerom, and C. Tourenne. "Behaviorally Induced Alterations in Human Urinary 5-Hydroxyindoles." *Transactions of the American Society for Neurochemistry* 14: (1983): 199.

Walton, K.G., N.D. Pugh, and G.M. Brown. "Melatonin and Stress: Excretion Rate of 6-Sulfatoxymelatonin Increases with Indicators of Chronic Stress in College Students." *Society for Neuroscience Abstracts* 16 (1990a): 273.

Walton, K.G., G.M. Brown, N. Pugh, et al. "Indole-mediated Adaptation: Does Melatonin Mediate Resistance to Stress in Humans?" *Society for Neuroscience Abstracts* 16: (1990b): 273.

Wampler, L.D. "Transcendental Meditation and Assertive Training in the Treatment of Social Anxiety." *Dissertation Abstracts International* 39, no. 11-B (1978): 5598.

Wandhoefer, A., and K.H. Plattig. "Stimulus-linked DC-shift and Auditory Evoked Potentials in Transcendental Meditation." *Pfleuger's Archives* 343 (1973).

Ward, B. "Holistic Medicine." *Australian Family Physician* 24, no 5 (1995): 761-762, 765.

Warm, J.S., W. Seeman, L. Bean, et al. "Meditation and Sustained Attention." *Bulletin of the Psychonomic Society* 10 (1977): 245.

Warner, T. "Meditation and Developmental Advancement. Meditating Abilities and Conservation Performance." *Dissertation Abstracts International* 47, no. 8-B (1986): 3558.

Warrenburg, S. "Sleep during Transcendental Meditation." *Science* 191 (1976): 308-310.

Warrenburg, S. "Meditation and Hemispheric Specialization." *Dissertation Abstracts International* 40, no. 6-B (1979): 2892-2893.

Warrenburg, S., R. Pagano, M. Woods, et al. "Oxygen Consumption, HR, EMG, and EEG during Progressive Muscle Relaxation (PMR) and Transcendental Meditation (TM)." *Biofeedback and Self-Regulation* 2 (1977): 321.

Warrenburg, S., R. Pagano, M. Woods, et al. "A Comparison of Somatic Relaxation and EEG Activity in Classical Progressive Relaxation and Transcendental Meditation." *Journal of Behavioral Medicine* 3 (1980): 73-93.

Warshal, D. "Effects of the TM Technique on Normal and Jendrassik Reflex Time." *Perceptual and Motor Skills* 50, no. 3, pt. 2 (1980): 1103-1106.

Washburn, M.C. "Observations Relevant to a Unified Theory of Meditation." *Journal of Transpersonal Psychology* 10, no. 1 (1978): 45-65.

Watanabe, T., D. Shapiro, and G.E. Ochwartz. "Meditation as an Anoxic State: A Critical Review and Theory." *Psychophysiologia* 9 (1972): 29.

Watt, P.B. Review of *Traditions of Meditation in Chinese Buddhism*, by P.N. Gregory. In *Journal of Asian Studies* 47, no. 3 (1988): 595-596.

Waxman, J. "A Finite States Model for Meditation Phenomena." *Perceptual and Motor Skills* 49, no. 1 (1979): 123-127.

Weathers, R.S. "Meditation, Altered States, and Unpleasant Experiences: A Structural-Development Analysis." *Dissertation Abstracts International* 46, no. 10-B (1986): 3620-3621.

Webb, W. "Cognitive Behavior Therapy: Application for Employee Assistance Counselors." *Employee Assistance Quarterly* 5, no. 3 (1990): 55-65.

Weiner, A.J. "Attention and Expectations: Their Contribution to the Meditation Effect." *Dissertation Abstracts International* 33, no. 11-B (1973): 5528-5529.

Weiner, D.E. "The Effects of Mantra Meditation and Progressive Relaxation on Self-actualization, State and Trait Anxiety, and Frontalis Muscle Tension." *Dissertation Abstracts International* 37, no. 8-B (1977): 4174.

Weinstein, M., and J.C. Smith. "Isometric Squeeze Relaxation (Progressive Relaxation) vs. Meditation: Absorption and Focusing as Predictors of State Effects." *Perceptual and Motor Skills* 75 (1992): 1263-1271.

Weldon, J.T., and A. Aron. "The Transcendental Meditation Program and Normalization of Weight." In *Scientific Research on the Transcendental Meditation Program: Collected Papers*, Vol. 1, eds. D.W. Orme-Johnson and J.T. Farrow. New York: M.E.R.U. Press, 1977: 301-306.

Welwood, J. "Exploring Mind: Form, Emptiness and Beyond." *Journal of Transpersonal Psychology* 8, no. 2 (1976): 89-99.

Welwood, J. "Meditation and the Unconscious: A New Perspective." *Journal of Transpersonal Psychology* 9, no. 1 (1977): 1-26.

Welwood, J. "Reflections of Psychotherapy, Focusing, and Meditation." *Journal of Transpersonal Psychology* 12, no. 2 (1980): 127-141.

Wenger, M.A., and B.K. Bagchi. "Studies of Autonomic Functions in Practitioners of Yoga in India." *Behavior Science* 6 (1961): 312-323.

Wenger, M.A., B.K. Bagchi, and B.K. Anand. "Experiments in India on Voluntary Control of Heart and Pulse." *Circulation* 24 (1961): 1319-1325.

Wenger, M., B. Bagchi, and B. Anand. "Voluntary Heart and Pulse Control by Yoga Methods." *International Journal of Parapsychology* 5 (1963): 25-41.

Wenneberg, R.S. "The Effects of Transcendental Meditation on Ambulatory Blood Pressure, Cardiovascular Reactivity, Anger, Hostility, and Platelet Aggregation." *Dissertation Abstracts International* 55, no. 6-B (1994): 2120.

Werner, O.R., R.K. Wallace, B. Charles, et al. "Long-term Endocrinologic Changes in Subjects Practicing the Transcendental Meditation and TM-Sidhi Program." *Psychosomatic Medicine* 48, nos. 1-2 (1986): 59-65.

West, L.J. "TM and Other Non-professional Psychotherapies." In *Comprehensive Textbook of Psychiatry*, eds. A. Freedman and H. Kaplan. Baltimore: Williams and Wilkins, 1975.

West, M.A. "Changes in Skin Resistance in Subjects Resting, Reading, Listening to Music, or Practicing the Transcendental Meditation Technique." In *Scientific Research on the Transcendental Meditation Program: Collected Papers*. Vol. I, eds. D.W. Orme-Johnson and J.T. Farrow. New York: M.E.R.U. Press, 1977: 224-229.

West, M.A. "Psychophysiological and Psychological Correlates of Meditation." PhD thesis, University of Wales Institute of Science and Technology, 1978.

West, M.A. "Physiological Effects of Meditation: A Longitudinal Study." *British Journal of Social and Clinical Psychology* 18, no. 2 (1979a): 219-226.

West, M.A. "Meditation." *British Journal of Psychiatry* 135 (1979b): 457-467.

West, M.A. "Transcendental Meditation vs. Relaxation Therapy." *Bulletin of the British Psychological Society* 32 (1979c): 39-40.

West, M.A. "Meditation and the EEG." *Psychological Medicine* 10, no. 2 (1980a): 369-375.

West, M.A. "Meditation, Personality and Arousal." *Personality and Individual Differences* 2 (1980b): 135-142.

West, M.A. "The Psychosomatics of Meditation." *Journal of Psychosomatic Research* 24, no. 5 (1980c): 265-273

West, M.A. "Meditation and Somatic Arousal Reduction." *American Psychologist* 40, no. 6 (1985): 717-719.

West, M.A., ed. *The Psychology of Meditation*. Oxford, England: Clarendon Press, 1987.

Westcott, M. "Hemispheric Symmetry of the EEG during the Transcendental Meditation Technique." In *Scientific Research on the Transcendental Meditation Program: Collected Papers*. Vol. I, eds. D.W. Orme-Johnson and J.T. Farrow. New York: M.E.R.U. Press, 1977: 160-164.

White, J. "Introduction to Meditation." *Fields within Fields* 13 (1974a): 49-53.

White, J. *What Is Meditation?* Garden City, NJ: Anchor, 1974b.

White, K.D. "Salivation: The Significance of Imagery in Its Voluntary Control." *Psychophysiology* 15, no. 3 (1978): 196-203.

Wilber, K., J. Engler, and D. Brown. *Transformations of Consciousness.* Boulder, CO: Shambhala, 1986: ch. 8.

Wilcox, G.G. "Autonomic Functioning in Subjects Practicing the Transcendental Meditation Technique." In *Scientific Research on the Transcendental Meditation Program: Collected Papers.* Vol. I, eds. D.W. Orme-Johnson and J.T. Farrow. New York: M.E.R.U. Press, 1977: 239-242.

Williams, L.R. "Transcendental Meditation and Mirror-tracing Skill." *Perceptual and Motor Skills* 46, no. 2 (1978): 371-378.

Williams, L.R., and P.G. Herbert. "Transcendental Meditation and Fine Perceptual Motor Skill." *Perceptual and Motor Skills* 43, no. 1 (1976): 303-309.

Williams, L.R., and B.L. Vickerman. "Effects of Transcendental Meditation on Fine Motor Skill." *Perceptual and Motor Skills* 43, no. 2 (1976): 607-613.

Williams, L.R., B. Lodge, and P.S. Reddish. "Effects of Transcendental Meditation on Rotary Pursuit Skill." *Research Quarterly* 48, no. 1 (1977): 196-201.

Williams, P., and M. West. "EEG Responses to Photic Stimulation in Persons Experienced at Meditation." *Electroencephalography and Clinical Neurophysiology* 39, no. 5 (1975): 519-522.

Williams, P., A. Francis, and R. Durham. "Personality and Meditation." *Perceptual and Motor Skills* 43 (1976): 787-792.

Williams, R.B., Jr., H. Benson, and M.J. Follick. "Disease as a Reflection of the Psyche." *New England Journal of Medicine* 313 (1985): 1356-1357.

Williams, R.D. "The Effects of Shamatha Meditation on Attentional and Imaginal Variables." *Dissertation Abstracts International* 46, no. 1-B (1985): 319-320.

Willis, C.L.R. "Transcendental Meditation and Its Influence on the Self-concept." *Dissertation Abstracts International* 36, no. 1-A (1975): 139.

Willis, R.J. "Meditation to Fit the Person: Psychology and the Meditative Way." *Journal of Religion and Health* 18, no. 2 (1979): 93-119.

Wilson, A.F., and R. Honsberger. "The Effects of Transcendental Meditation upon Bronchial Asthma." *Clinical Research* 21 (1973): 278.

Wilson, A.F., and R. Jevning. "Rest, Relaxation, Sleep and Transcendental Meditation." *Journal of Chronic Diseases and Therapeutic Research* 1 (1977): 1-4.

Wilson, A.F., R. Honsberger, J.T. Chiu, et al. "Transcendental Meditation and Asthma." *Respiration* 32 (1975): 74-80.

Wilson, A.F., R. Jevning, and S. Guich. "Marked Reduction of Forearm Carbon Dioxide Production during States of Decreased Metabolism. *Physiology and Behavior* 41: (1987): 347–352.

Wilson, J. "Mindfulness." *British Journal of Occupational Therapy* 58, no. 1 (1995): 30.

Winquist, W.T. "TM and Drugs." In E.M. Becker, ed. *Licit and Illicit Drugs.* Boston: Little, Brown, 1972.

Winquist, W.T. "The Transcendental Meditation Program and Drug Abuse: A Retrospective Study." In *Scientific Research on the Transcendental Meditation Program: Collected Papers.* Vol. 1, eds. D.W. Orme-Johnson and J.T. Farrow. New York: M.E.R.U. Press, 1977: 494-497.

Winters, T.H. and J. Kabat-Zinn. "Awareness Meditation for Patients Who Have Anxiety and Chronic Pain in the Primary Care Unit." *Clinical Research* 29, no. 2 (1981): 642.

Wolkove, N., H. Kreisman, D. Darragh, et al. "Effect of Transcendental Meditation on Breathing and Respiratory Control." *Journal of Applied Physiology* 56, no. 3 (1984): 607-612.

Wolman, B.B. "The Protoconscious." *Dynamische Psychiatrie* 22, nos. 1-2 (1989): 22-30.

Wong, M.R., N.B. Brochin, and K.L. Gendron. "Effects of Meditation on Anxiety and Chemical Dependency." *Journal of Drug Education* 11, no. 2 (1981): 91-105.

Wood, C.J. "Meditation and Relaxation and Their Effect upon the Pattern of Physiological Response during Performance of a Fine Motor and Gross Motor Task." *Dissertation Abstracts International* 44, no. 5-A (1983): 1378.

Wood, C.J. "Evaluation of Meditation and Relaxation on Physiological Response during the Performance of Fine Motor and Gross Motor Tasks." *Perceptual and Motor Skills* 62, no. 1 (1986): 91-98.

Wood, D.T. "The Effects of Progressive Relaxation, Heart Rate Feedback, and Content-specific Meditation on Anxiety and Performance in a Class Situation." *Dissertation Abstracts International* 39, no. 6-A (1978): 3458.

Wooley-Hart, A. "Slowing Down the Inevitable." *Nursing Mirror* (October 4, 1979): 36-39.

Woolfolk, R.L. "Psychophysiological Correlates of Meditation." *Archives of General Psychiatry* 32, no. 10 (1975): 1326-1333.

Woolfolk, R.L. "Self-control Meditation and the Treatment of Chronic Anger." In *Meditation: Classic and Contemporary Perspectives*, eds. D.H. Shapiro and R.N. Walsh. New York: Aldine, 1984: 550-554.

Woolfolk, R.L., and C.M. Franks. "Meditation and Behavior Therapy." In *Meditation: Classic and Contemporary Perspectives*, eds. D.H. Shapiro and R.N. Walsh. New York: Aldine, 1984: 674-676.

Woolfolk, R.L., and A.J. Rooney. "The Effect of Explicit Expectations on Initial Meditation Experiences." *Biofeedback and Self-Regulation* 6, no. 4 (1981): 483-491.

Woolfolk, R.L., L. Carr-Kaffashan, and T.F. McNulty. "Meditation Training as a Treatment for Insomnia." *Behavior Therapy* 7, no. 3 (1976): 359-366.

Woolfolk, R.L., P.M. Lehrer, B. McCann, et al. "Effects of Progressive Relaxation and Meditation on Cognitive and Somatic Manifestations of Daily Stress." *Behavior Research Therapy* 20 (1982): 461-467.

Wortz, E. "Application of Awareness Methods in Psychotherapy." *Journal of Transpersonal Psychology* 14, no. 1 (1982): 61-68.

Wu, P. "Zen Meditation, Self-awareness, and Autonomy." *Dissertation Abstracts International* 53, no. 6-B (1992): 3174.

Wuerscher, C. "The Psychological Treatment of Patients with Angina Pectoris." *Dissertation Abstracts International* 45, no. 10-B (1984): 3350.

Xu, S.H. "Psychophysiological Reactions Associated with Qigong Therapy." *Chinese Medical Journal* (English) 107, no. 3 (1994): 230-233.

Yamaoka, T. "Psychological Study of Self-control." In Y. Akishige, ed. *Psychological Studies on Zen.* Tokyo: Komazawa University, 1973.

Yamaoka, T. "Psychological Study of Mental Self-control." *Bulletin of the Faculty of Literature of Kyushu University* 5 (1974): 225-271.

Yoder, N. "Changes in Suggestibility Following Alert Hypnosis and Concentrative Meditation." *Dissertation Abstracts International* 43, no. 6-B (1982): 2013.

Yoon, B.Y. "A Study of an Extended Concept of Human Intrapsychic Capacity as Expressed in D.T. Suzuki's *Zen Buddhism*." *Dissertation Abstracts International* 40, no. 5-B (1979): 2346-2347.

Young, S. "Purpose and Method of Vipassana Meditation." *Humanistic Psychologist* 22, no. 1 (1994): 53-61.

Younger, J., W. Adriance, and R. Berger. "Sleep during Transcendental Meditation." *Perceptual and Motor Skills* 40, no. 3 (1975): 953-954.

Yuille, J.C., and L. Sereda. "Positive Effects of Meditation: A Limited Generalization." *Journal of Applied Psychology* 65, no. 3 (1980): 333-340.

Yung, P.M.B. "Control of Essential Hypertension by Relaxation Training Methods." *Hong Kong Nursing Journal* 64, Dec. (1993): 37-39.

Zaehner, R.C. *Zen, Drugs and Mysticism.* New York: Random House, 1972.

Zaichkowsky, L.D., and R. Kamen. "Biofeedback and Meditation: Effects on Muscle Tension and Locus of Control." *Perceptual and Motor Skills* 45, no. 3, pt. 1 (1978): 955-958.

Zakutney, M.A. "An Investigation of the Transcendental Meditation Technique as a Positive Health Action: Why People Start and Continue the Practice." *Dissertation Abstracts International* 50, no. 7-B (1990): 2852.

Zamarra, G.W.M., I. Besseghini, and S. Wettenberg. "The Effects of the Transcendental Meditation Program on the Exercise Performance of Patients with Angina Pectoris." In *Scientific Research on the Transcendental Meditation Program: Collected Papers.* Vol. 1, eds. D.W. Orme-Johnson and J.T. Farrow. New York: M.E.R.U. Press, 1977: 270-278.

Zamarra, J.W., R.H. Schneider, I. Besseghini, et al. "Usefulness of the Transcendental Meditation Program in the Treatment of Patients with Coronary Artery Disease." *American Journal of Cardiology* 78 (1996): 77-80.

Zastrow, C. "Using Relaxation Techniques with Individuals and with Groups." *Journal of Independent Social Work* 2, no. 1 (Fall 1987): 83-95.

Zastrow, C. "What Really Causes Psychotherapy Change?" *Journal of Independent Social Work* 2, no. 3 (Spring 1988): 5-16.

Zeier, H. "Arousal Reduction and Biofeedback-supported Respiratory Meditation." *Biofeedback and Self-Regulation* 9, no. 4 (1984): 497-508.

Zeier, H. "Relaxation by Biofeedback Controlled Respiratory Meditation and Autogenic Training." *Z Exp Angew Psychol* 32, no. 4 (1985): 682-95.

Zeff, T. "The Psychological and Physiological Effects of Meditation and the Physical Isolation Tank Experience on the Type A Behavior Pattern." *Dissertation Abstracts International* 41, no. 10-B (1981): 3877-3878.

Zika, B. "Meditation and Altered States of Consciousness: A Psychodynamic Interpretation." *Journal of Psychology and Christianity* 3, no. 3 (1985): 65-73.

Zika, B. "The Effects of Hypnosis and Meditation on a Measure of Self-actualization." *Australian Journal of Clinical and Experimental Hypnosis* 15, no. 1 (May 1987): 21-28.

Zimmerman, J.D. "The Influence of Attentional Focus on Mood, Memory, and State Self Consciousness Following Exercise and Meditation." *Dissertation Abstracts International* 47, no. 4-B (1986): 1751.

Zuroff, D.C., and J.C. Schwarz. "Effects of Transcendental Meditation and Muscle Relaxation on Trait Anxiety, Maladjustment, Locus of Control and Drug Use." *Journal of Consulting and Clinical Psychology* 46, no. 2 (1978): 264-271.

Zuroff, D.C., and J.C. Schwarz. "Transcendental Meditation vs. Muscle Relaxation: A Two-year Follow-up of a Controlled Experiment." *American Journal of Psychiatry* 137, no. 10 (1980): 1229-1231.

About the Authors

Michael Murphy is the co-founder and chairman of Esalen Institute and the originator of Esalen's Study of Exceptional Functioning. He is the author of *Golf in the Kingdom; Jacob Atabet; The Psychic Side of Sports* (with Rhea White); *An End to Ordinary History; The Future of the Body;* and *The Life We Are Given* (with George Leonard).

Murphy graduated from Stanford University and lived for more than a year at the Sri Aurobindo Ashram in Pondicherry, India. In 1980, he helped initiate Esalen's Soviet-American Exchange Program which was a premier diplomacy vehicle for citizen-to-citizen Russian-American relations. Citizen exchange groups, which establish contacts outside of normal governmental agencies, played a significant role in breaking down the barriers between the Russian and American peoples. In 1990, Boris Yeltsin's first visit to America was initiated by the Institute.

During his 30-year involvement in the human potential movement, Murphy and his work have been profiled in *The New Yorker* and featured in many magazines and journals worldwide. He speaks at conferences and other events, and consults on organizational change. He recently completed a series of workshops designed to increase worker productivity and job satisfaction for the Arizona Public Service Company, a major power company.

Steven Donovan was inspired to study meditation and other transformative practices in 1977 by Michael Murphy's book, *Jacob Atabet*. As director of Esalen's Study of Exceptional Functioning, and in order to help him understand his meditation experiences, he collected and summarized the scientific literature covered in this book through 1988. From 1985 to 1993 he was president and CEO of Esalen Institute, and he created Esalen's Roundhouse Meditation Center. Since 1989 he has been a student of Zen Buddhism with Richard Baker-roshi in Crestone, Colorado.

Professionally, he is a consultant to governments, corporations, and non-profit institutions. He is a trustee of the California Institute of Integral Studies, which is dedicated to integrating Eastern and Western traditions, and the Gorbachev Foundation/USA, which through its State of the World Forum is giving shape to a holistic and spiritually based worldview. He is a graduate of Hobart College and holds the MBA from Columbia University.

Eugene Taylor is the founder and director of the Cambridge Institute of Psychology and Religion and an archival investigator in the history of American psychology and psychiatry. He is author of *Psychological Suspended Animation: Heart Rate, Blood Pressure, Time Estimation and Introspective Reports from an Anechoic Environment; Cyberphysiology: The Science of Self-regulation; William James on Exceptional Mental States: Reconstruction of the Unpublished 1896 Lowell Lectures; William James on Consciousness Beyond the Margin;* (with Robert Wozniak) (eds); *Pure Experience: The Response to William James;* and *The Epistemological Problem of Consciousness: Essays in the History and Philosophy of Psychology.* He holds the AB and MA in psychology and Asian studies and the PhD in the history and philosophy of psychology. Currently he is an executive faculty member at Saybrook Institute, where he teaches the history of psychology, and lecturer on psychiatry at Harvard Medical School, where he is the historian in the Department of Psychiatry at the Massachusetts General Hospital. He is also Sandan in aikido and chief instructor of the Harvard University Aikido Club.

The Physical and Psychological Effects of Meditation

About Esalen

Esalen Institute is the world's most famous growth center. It was founded by Michael Murphy and Richard Price in 1962 and soon became the most prominent center of the human potential movement. About 10,000 people from many parts of the world participate in approximately 450 seminars each year at Esalen's Big Sur facility. Esalen is a non-profit organization, and has contributing members in 47 states and 27 nations.

Esalen also serves as a ground-breaking research site. Preparatory work for *The Future of the Body* began in 1977 with the building of an archive of more than 10,000 studies of exceptional functioning. The Institute also compiled the most comprehensive bibliography on meditation research in the world. Such major figures within the world of transpersonal psychology as Fritz Perls, the founder of gestalt therapy; Gregory Bateson, the eminent anthropologist; and Stan Grof, the pioneering research psychiatrist, spent many years in residence at Esalen.

About the Institute of Noetic Sciences

Founded in 1973, the Institute of Noetic Sciences is a nonprofit research foundation, educational institution, and membership organization with 53,000 members worldwide. We are comprised of individuals who are committed to the development of human consciousness through scientific inquiry, spiritual understanding, and psychological well-being. We recognize that in this era of globalization and transformative change our most fundamental assumptions about human nature and the nature of reality are being called into question. It is our mission to participate in this change through commitment to rigorous, in-depth exploration of cutting-edge issues, and by a willingness to be transformed by what we learn in this process.

As a research foundation we support leading-edge scientific and scholarly research, conduct in-house research, hold invitational and public conferences to invite intellectual exchange on emerging issues, and publish research-related books, technical reports, and monographs. Our in-house research projects focus on healing, consciousness, and exploring the range of human abilities. The intention of our research program is to support new directions of inquiry and to help important new ideas gain legitimacy.

As an educational institution we organize lectures, sponsor conferences, and publish books, research reports, and other educational materials by leading scientists, philosophers, and scholars. We also publish a quarterly journal, a quarterly newsletter, an annotated guide to relevant books, and program-related books.

As a membership organization we offer opportunities for individuals to integrate scientific and scholarly research into their own life experience, through participation in study groups, travel, conferences, lectures, and meetings, and by participating in field research concerned with members' perceptions and experiences in a changing world.

We define the noetic sciences in a broad sense. *Noetic* is derived from the Greek word *nous,* which means "mind or ways of knowing." Noetic sciences further the explorations of conventional science by rigorous inquiry into aspects of reality—such as mind, consciousness, spirit—that include yet go beyond physical phenomena. Associated with an emerging field, rather than any single institution, some hallmarks of noetic sciences are:

- recognition that consciousness represents a spectrum of experience, ranging from the most bounded to the transcendent;

- rigorous research into the human condition which takes a holistic approach;

- research which attempts to integrate subjective and objective aspects of human experience, and also qualitative and quantitative approaches;

- appreciation for the fact that there are different ways of knowing;

- recognition that the questions we ask are as relevant as their answers, and that the way they are formed reflects an underlying set of assumptions about the nature of reality;

- a systems perspective that acknowledges the importance of interconnectedness and relationships;

- a general orientation that includes the willingness to grapple with difficult and challenging questions—questions which may outstrip the existing modes of inquiry.

The Physical and Psychological Effects of Meditation